New Interpretations in Naval History

U.S. GOVERNMENT
OFFICIAL EDITION NOTICE

Use of ISBN Prefix

This is the Official U.S. Government edition of this publication and is herein identified to certify its authenticity. ISBN 978-1-93-535228-0 is for this U.S. Government Publishing Office Official Edition only. The Superintendent of Documents of the U.S. Government Publishing Office requests that any reprinted edition clearly be labeled as a copy of the authentic work with a new ISBN.

Legal Status and Use of Seals and Logos

The logo of the U.S. Naval War College (NWC), Newport, Rhode Island, authenticates *New Interpretations in Naval History*, edited by Marcus O. Jones, as an official publication of the College. It is prohibited to use NWC's logo on any republication of this book without the express, written permission of the Editor, Naval War College Press, or the editor's designee.

For sale by the Superintendent of Documents, U.S. Government Publishing Office
Internet: bookstore.gpo.gov   Phone: toll free (866) 512-1800;   DC area (202) 512-1800
Fax: (202) 512-2104 Mail: Stop IDCC, Washington, DC 20402-0001

ISBN 978-1-93-535228-0

NAVAL WAR COLLEGE HISTORICAL MONOGRAPH SERIES NO. 23

The historical monographs in this series are book-length studies of the history of naval warfare, edited historical documents, conference proceedings, and bibliographies that are based wholly or in part on source materials in the Historical Collection of the Naval War College.

The editors of the Naval War College Press express their gratitude to the U.S. Naval Academy Foundation, whose generous financial support made possible the publication of this historical monograph.

*New Interpretations in Naval History:
Selected Papers from the Seventeenth
McMullen Naval History Symposium
Held at the United States Naval Academy
15–16 September 2011*

Edited by Marcus O. Jones

NAVAL WAR COLLEGE PRESS
NEWPORT, RHODE ISLAND
2016

The contents of this volume represent the views of the authors. Their opinions are not necessarily endorsed by the Naval War College or by any other agency, organization, or command of the U.S. government.

Printed in the United States of America

Historical Monograph Series

NAVAL WAR COLLEGE PRESS
Code 32
Naval War College
686 Cushing Road
Newport, R.I. 02841-1207

Library of Congress Cataloging-in-Publication Data

Names: United States Naval Academy History Symposium (17th : 2011) | Jones, Marcus O., editor.
Title: New interpretations in naval history : selected papers from the seventeenth McMullen Naval History Symposium held at the United States Naval Academy 15/16 September 2011 / edited by Marcus O. Jones.
Other titles: Selected papers from the seventeenth McMullen Naval History Symposium held at the United States Naval Academy 15/16 September 2011
Description: Newport, Rhode Island : Naval War College Press, [2016] | Series: Naval War College historical monograph series ; no. 23
Identifiers: LCCN 2015049019 | ISBN 9781935352280
Subjects: LCSH: United States—History, Naval—Congresses. | Naval history, Modern—Congresses.
Classification: LCC E182 .U5869 2011 | DDC 359.00973—dc23
LC record available at http://lccn.loc.gov/2015049019

TABLE OF CONTENTS

Foreword, by John. B. Hattendorf. ix
Preface xi
I. Piracy during the First Jewish War. 1
    by Phyllis Culham
II. Sea Power without a Navy? Roman Naval Forces in the Principate 13
    by Jorit Wintjes
III. Toward a Model of Piracy: Lessons from the Seventeenth-Century
    Caribbean. 25
    by Virginia Lunsford
IV. Intervention and Colonial Policy: The Flying Cruiser Squadron of
    the Imperial German Navy as an Instrument of German Foreign Policy
    Overseas, 1886–1893 39
    by Heiko Herold
V. Powering the U.S. Fleet: Propulsion Machinery Design and
    American Naval Engineering Culture, 1890–1945. 51
    by William M. McBride
VI. Theodore Roosevelt, Social Psychology, and Naval Public Relations:
    The 1906 John Paul Jones Reinterment Ceremony 69
    by Lori Lynn Bogle
VII. "The Committee of Four": The "Blue Funk School," the CID,
    and the Myth of the German Peril, 1906–1909. 81
    by Andreas Rose
VIII. Differing Values? The Balance between Speed, Endurance, Firepower,
    and Protection in the Design of British and American Dreadnoughts. 105
    by Angus Ross

IX. Innovation for Its Own Sake: The Type XXI U-boat 145
   by Marcus Jones
X. FREQUENT WIND, Option IV: The 29–30 April 1975
   Helicopter Evacuation of Saigon 159
   by John F. Guilmartin, Jr.
XI. The History of the Twenty-First-Century Chinese Navy 179
   by Bernard D. Cole
   About the Authors 197
   Titles in the Series 201

FOREWORD

The U.S. Naval Academy's naval history symposium, named the McMullen Naval History Symposium since 2006, has been held regularly in Annapolis, Maryland, since its first meeting in 1971. Initially, it was a small event for a limited group of invited speakers, but in 1973 it began to take on its present form. Today, this symposium continues to be one of the most important events for the scholarly and professional exchange of ideas and interpretations in the field of naval history. It serves this purpose not only in the United States, for American naval history, but in the world at large, for global naval history. It has certainly become the largest regular meeting of naval historians in the world. Its meeting location in Annapolis, on the historic grounds of the U.S. Naval Academy, with its large and active history department, fine museum, rich historical collections, and numerous naval memorials, is ideal for bringing together such a large group of highly informed experts, including naval professionals and civilian academics, to exchange research information and ideas on a scholarly level.

More than a dozen published volumes of selected papers have captured the essence and growth of the Naval Academy's symposium over the decades. Like this volume, most have carried the now well-established title of *New Interpretations in Naval History*. Typically, each volume in the series has been a selection from the many papers presented at each symposium and has ranged widely across all periods of naval history and the histories of many navies. Not limited to any particular theme, other than presenting a new interpretation of whatever subject on which the researcher is working, each symposium and its resulting volume present very useful samplings of current thinking, new themes, and new approaches in naval history. Collectively, the series has been a great stimulus to advancing and to encouraging naval history. The volumes that these symposia generate continue to chart the state of naval history as a field of research and inquiry.

This particular volume, from the seventeenth symposium, adds further to the fine tradition established by its predecessors. The eleven excellent papers in this collection range from studies on ancient Rome to China in the twentieth-first century. In between, the subjects vary in focus from seventeenth-century piracy to topics in British, German, and American naval history.

In publishing this volume, the Naval War College, as a graduate-level educational and research institution, and the Naval Academy, at the undergraduate level, join together in the mutual interest of helping to promote a better and deeper understanding of navies and naval history.

JOHN B. HATTENDORF, D.PHIL.
Ernest J. King Professor of Maritime History
Chairman, Maritime History Department

PREFACE

The McMullen Naval History Symposium met at the U.S. Naval Academy (USNA) from 15 to 16 September 2011. More than two hundred scholars and historians from around the world and more than a hundred midshipmen participated in three dozen panels on a broad range of topics in naval and maritime history. The present volume consists of only a small selection from the outstanding contributions of the symposium's participants, as is made necessary by practical and financial constraints. That we have selected so few from so many worthy papers should in no way obscure the great diversity and high standards that characterize the remainder.

The Naval History Symposium could not have taken place without generous financial assistance from the McMullen Seapower Fund, a gift from the late Dr. John J. McMullen, USNA Class of 1940. Dr. McMullen credited his education and development at the Naval Academy for his extraordinarily productive career, which culminated in the establishment of one of the most successful naval architectural and marine engineering companies. In addition to supporting the symposium, the McMullen Seapower Fund underwrote the research for symposium papers by Phyllis Culham, Lori Lyn Bogle, Virginia Lunsford, William McBride, and Marcus Jones—a reminder of how crucial such support is for advancing our knowledge of naval and maritime affairs. Those papers appear in the present volume.

The 2011 symposium followed the general pattern of past meetings, consisting of a two-day event with a call for papers, multiple simultaneous sessions, and the broadest possible representation from the international community of naval and maritime historians. The keynote speaker was Dr. Craig Symonds, the Class of 1957 Distinguished Professor of American Naval Heritage in the History Department of the U.S. Naval Academy for the 2011–12 academic year. After a stimulating reception in the Naval Academy Museum, Dr. Symonds delivered an account of his exciting research on the battle of Midway to an audience of nearly five hundred symposium attendees, officers, and midshipmen in Mahan Auditorium.

Fundamental to the success of the symposium were the tireless efforts of the 2011 Symposium Committee, including Cdr. John Freymann, Capt. Rebecca Bishop, Lt. Barry Cohen, Assistant Professor Sharika Crawford, Professor Robert Love, Assistant Professor Aaron O'Connell, Assistant Professor Richard Ruth, Lt. Keith Skillin, Lt. Cdr. Joseph Slaughter, and Maj. Mark Thompson. Without the dedication of our professional officers and faculty to the academic missions of the Academy and History Department, organizing and hosting the Naval History Symposium would be impossible.

MARCUS O. JONES
Associate Professor, Department of History
U.S. Naval Academy

1 *Piracy during the First Jewish War*

PHYLLIS CULHAM

There is no doubt that the First Jewish War (named, obviously, from the Roman point of view) was primarily a land war in a very Roman genre, relying on the Romans' ability to move massive yet deeply supported forces into any arena. It will not be surprising to readers of naval history that ports were therefore of not only tactical- but strategic-level concern. But one of the oddest consequences, never anticipated by either side at the outset, was an outbreak of Jewish piracy that proved a temporary but strategic-level threat, as was, immediately afterward, waterborne raiding on shipping and on Roman forces in the Black Sea.

It is vital to approach these naval questions with some understanding of how overwhelming Roman force in the Judaean theater both appeared and was. In 67 CE, Vespasian brought two legions and other units into Judaea, meeting his son Titus, with a third legion from Egypt, at Ptolemaïs, a port with an ethnically Greek majority. In Josephus's picture of events, Jewish forces, who had previously been confident in their ability to outnumber the Romans tactically at any point in the theater, lost confidence at the appearance of Roman professionals, with their famously perfect order and unit cohesion, which looked like fearlessness when it was maintained in the face of hostilities. Vespasian began a deliberate campaign of state-directed terror, with the massacre of Gabara.[1] He then attacked Jotapata, where Josephus had taken charge as the Jerusalem-assigned commander of combatants in Galilee. Jotapata fell, and Josephus the captive became translator and adviser to Vespasian and then Titus. His consequent histories are the basis for much of what follows here on the theater in Judaea.[2]

Josephus was not the only ancient author to refer to people whom we might identify as political resisters as robbers, brigands, or—if boats were involved—pirates. Often it was not obvious who was a pirate and who was a politically motivated naval combatant. Judaea was hardly the only theater in which Romans had difficulty telling resistance movements from criminal gangs. Advice on this point would have been something useful Josephus could have supplied his Roman captors; if he had done it badly or deceptively, however, it would have won him no Roman affection, and his later affluent life of leisure in Rome would become harder to explain. Josephus was brutally clear about those participants in the Jewish rebellion whom he consistently calls robbers—that is, that they were bands from among the impoverished and feckless of the countryside and the underclass of the cities following manipulative gang leaders who sought wealth, power, or both. And they were bad Jews. That last opinion is really the only one that distinguishes Josephus from most other elite, affluent, highly educated authors writing in Latin and Greek. It is equally difficult to tell whether the Black Sea raiders simultaneous to the Jewish Revolt were economically desperate pirates without allegiance or political resisters of Roman hegemony. We can deduce less about them since their polyglot, pan-ethnic microsocieties produced no Josephus to testify from the inside; also, as we will see later, it is even less clear what they aimed for.

As the campaigning season of 67 wore down, Vespasian returned to Ptolemaïs and then went on to Caesarea, with its advanced, ocean-engineered breakwaters and superb docking facilities. One deduces that Vespasian wanted to winter on the coast in a friendly, majority-Greek port with outstanding facilities where he could easily be supplied and reinforced. Then Jewish pirates threatened the well-being of his forces, as well as Roman strategic interests. Josephus reports that two groups, one of those expelled from their towns in factional infighting (*stasis,* in the notorious Greek term) and another of refugees (literal *diaphugontes,* the fleeing) who had survived the destruction of their towns, gathered at Joppa (modern Jaffa) and proceeded to rebuild it. (The provincial governor Cestius had sacked and burned the Jewish-majority port and massacred its inhabitants before Vespasian had arrived.)[3] Josephus notes that the refugees who were rebuilding the city turned to piracy because they were surrounded and cut off on the land.[4]

That put pirates between Vespasian and the grain shipments from Egypt, which were also the lifeline of urban Rome and Italy. The late, great E. Mary Smallwood's endnote to the Penguin Josephus on this point states concisely the potential severity of the strategic problem: "At this season Northwest winds prevented direct voyages from Alexandria to Italy, and the Egyptian corn fleet had to sail via the coasts of Palestine, and Asia Minor, and the Aegean."[5] This meant that Jewish insurgents in cheap, small boats could visibly impede one of the biggest bureaucracies in the city of Rome, as well as threaten the emperor himself with political unrest in the capital. If the grain fleet were not visibly delivering plenty of food to Rome, that would be even more politically destabilizing than the delay of American Social Security checks or their arriving with face values lower than expected. Tacitus says with his usual color that "since grain has been imported from [the province of] Africa and from Egypt, the life of the Roman people has been tossed about by ships and disasters."[6] The clearest hint that the new population of Joppa were not merely the desperately displaced, raiding "the Egyptian route" for grain to survive, is that they also sailed the waters off Syria and Phoenicia. That sounds as though they were, as Josephus terms them, pirates, or, as they might have claimed to us in our terms, insurgents. Although they were not prepared later to stand up to Roman legions on land, they were apparently willing to risk conflict with the ships of the great Phoenician naval cities Tyre and Sidon.[7] That is surely a clue regarding the identity of these sailors (or pirates).

A significant percentage of the resettling, new population of Joppa was probably from Galilee, most likely Sepphoris, Tiberias, and Tarichaeae. If we specifically search for displaced groups who had lost factional disputes in their towns, we find the rapidly and repeatedly whipsawing allegiances of Sepphoris, Tiberias, and Tarichaeae in Galilee. For instance, when Vespasian sent one of his legionary commanders with a detached force to Sepphoris, where Josephus had recorded significant support for the revolt, the town opened its gates and advised surrounding villages to join it in cooperation with the Roman government. After this defection of Sepphoris, "the best reputed" city of Galilee, Josephus reports that *stasiodes,* those engaging in *stasis,* and robbers fled to Mount Asamon near Sepphoris to take a stand. "Those engaging in *stasis*" were clearly those who were urging on other Jews in their communities to open attacks against Romans; arrival of Roman legions had rendered them dangerously unpopular with other Jews in some places. Josephus identifies factionalism even among Jews already under arms in the field, where the most determined members of the war party, those unlikely to accept an amnesty, are to Josephus the *stasiastai,* those who had been caught up in *stasis.* In short, there was serious, continuous factionalism among the populations of the major towns on the coast of the Sea of Galilee, and there are no other obvious sites named in Josephus's text from which the alleged drivers/casualties of factionalism might have come.[8]

Others in the second category who turned to piracy in Joppa—that is, refugees who had no cities to which to return to—were not exclusively Galilean; some refugees were created well south of Galilee.[9] It is most likely that both groups who resettled Joppa, "those who had been driven from towns by *stasis*" and "those fleeing the destruction of their homes," were mainly Galilean, since the documented cases that would have created refugees of both types were in Galilee. If most of the new population attempting to rebuild Joppa were Galileans, that would suggest something about the naval capabilities of new squatters from around the Sea of Galilee itself. The other refugees from northern Galilee had economic interests and strategic concerns centered on Phoenician Tyre, not Jerusalem, and would have been well aware of regional trading patterns for valuable merchandise. Meyers has even claimed that "the importance of this fact cannot be overstated; namely, that the heartland of Upper Galilee is trading with and oriented toward the Phoenician coast and not primarily with the Sea of Galilee or Akko-Ptolemais." In fact, Talmudic anecdote paints a later picture of even rural sectors of Upper Galilee as major suppliers of diverse merchandise in regional trade networks. Potters and weavers did not need to be in a city to work. Upper Galilee came to dominate the regional oil markets, as did Galilean potters, and the area was later well known for flaxen fabrics; small farmers made clothing, which was expensive once it reached the affluent Phoenician coast. Coin finds in Galilee are heavily Syrian, supporting Meyers's claim that trade networks in Upper Galilee reached northward.[10]

It may initially seem improbable that rowdy, anti-authoritarian, agrarian factions in northern Galilee would have been quite familiar with Phoenician and regional economic and trade patterns, but that population had become very mixed along the Galilean/Phoenician/Syrian frontier, as political and administrative lines drawn by the Seleucid empire, and after them the Romans, proved very fluid. Nor did these administrative districts ever reflect or affect the inhabitants' senses of their own identity, nor did they have any identified impact on residents' definitions of themselves. In short, they were completely artificial political units imposed for what an ill-informed external power believed to be its convenience. Galilee was the constant center of both religious and agrarian unrest, and the two inevitably intermingled.[11]

Syrians and Phoenicians had taken advantage of Jewish infighting and general chaos before the Roman Pompey's (political and administrative) "settlement" of the region in 63 BCE to move themselves into villages in northern Galilee, where arable land was hard to come by. The triumvir responsible for the area in 42 BCE, Marc Antony, ordered Tyre to return to the Jewish high priest and *ethnarch* Hyrcanus all places taken from Jews by force during the chaos of the recent Mediterranean-wide Roman civil war. A northern Galilean warlord Hezikiah, often identified as a forerunner of both John of Gischala and the Zealots, was executed by Herod for raiding "Syrian" villages along that demographic frontier, this execution a police action much praised by Romans. Nonetheless, Hyrcanus summoned Herod before the Sanhedrin back in Jerusalem for executing Jews without a trial under the "ancestral laws," a harbinger of how one man's commitment to responsible regional peacekeeping under the Roman hegemon was another's disloyal ceding of Jewish-inhabited territory.[12] Nor did the famous "Roman Peace" of the empire end Galilean–Tyrian conflict. Josephus notes in passing that Titus set up a Roman camp at Cydasa, which he labels a heavily fortified, populous town of Tyre always at war with the Galilean people.[13] To integrate the economic history of Galilean flaxen fabrics and oil in Mediterranean-wide trade with local, agrarian, ethnic conflict: Jews of northern Galilee must have known a lot about Phoenicians and Syrians of the coast without having much reason to be influenced by them, or—in the case of Syrians, who kept encroaching on their arable land—to like them. They knew enough about what shipped out of or put into what ports and how it was protected to be pirates.

Another seemingly odd attribute to associate with my posited Galilean refugees is in Josephus's casual statement that the new settlers in Joppa built themselves pirate ships. Actually, there is a little-known history of resistance by Galilean fishermen, as well as other repurposing of shallow-draft boats for combat. Those former residents of Sepphoris, Tiberias, and Tarichaeae on the Sea of Galilee are especially likely suspects for such activity. In the tense months before the initial Roman onslaught, Josephus himself had gathered at Tarichaeae all the *skapha* (usually translated "skiffs") that he could locate quickly to use in intimidating Tiberias, so he must have believed that such *skapha* could plausibly bear combatants who could at least threaten an opposed landing.[14] All dwellers on the Sea of Galiliee would have been familiar with these *skapha*. We can recover some of their capabilities from Vespasian's encounter with them at Tarichaeae in the spring of 68. Since many resisters had gathered into Tarichaeae by that spring, Vespasian began to set up an especially fortified marching camp between the trouble spots of Tiberias and Tarichaeae. The inhabitants had already gathered a large flotilla of *skapha* either to evacuate or to see through a naval battle (quite literally: *dianaumachein*), depending on how things went. Combatants on this flotilla of *skapha* assaulted the Roman camp in time to damage the structure in progress. Josephus claims that they got back on their boats ahead of the Roman counterattack with no casualties and formed up in boats, "just as if arrayed in a phalanx," that kept up arrow fire against the Romans, "conducting a naval battle in a war on land."[15]

Others at Tarichaeae took the unwise decision to emerge from the city to fight the Romans on land, merely because the defenders greatly outnumbered them. Defenders in flight as the city was overrun launched *skapha* onto the sea. Many were killed before they got away from the shore. They may have planned continued resistance from missile-firing formations again, since they were still right there the next day when Vespasian ordered that *schediai* (usually translated "rafts") be put together to end the battle. Oddly, the Romans managed to launch them in such a way as to force the *skapha* in the direction of the shore so they could not escape. The Jewish skiffs went after the Roman rafts rather than the Romans lining the shore. In the ensuing "naval battle," the superiority in numbers of rafts over skiffs was material, as was, Josephus claims, the fact that the skiffs were comparatively weaker in structure than the rafts, since they were "small and built for piracy."[16] Additionally, their small crews were afraid to take on Romans densely packed on rafts, preferring to throw stones and merely scrape up against the rafts. Clearly, they had planned for the likelihood of more "naval" action, or they would not have had rocks on board. They were probably out of arrows, since Romans did fire arrows from the rafts, and that arrow fire was unanswered. As Josephus notes, it was not the rafts that were damaged in these collisions.

We know, therefore, that a number of inhabitants of the cities ringing the Sea of Galilee knew how to equip their boats for hostilities on water and to "fight their boats," many of them preferring to stand against Romans on land from the water, even when there was little hope of tactical victory or even escape. Josephus's initially mysterious remark that these *skapha* were "small and built for piracy" is a clue that matches with two others from, respectively, archaeology and art. In 1985, near Migdal (ancient Tarichaeae), a couple of residents of a local kibbutz discovered what proved to be a small fishing boat probably built around the turning of the first century BCE to the first of the Common Era. The boat had been much repaired and in long use in antiquity, so it had not been wrecked in action in 68. This craft is generally called "the Galilee boat" (or "the Kinneret boat," after the Hebrew name of the sea). It is 8.8 meters long and 2.5 meters wide; it has a very shallow, uniform draft of 1.5 meters and a hull remarkably squarish in cross section. The boat's missing rigging was reconstructed on the basis of a mosaic from ancient Tarichaeae, probably of the first century CE.[17] It did not escape the notice of excavator and curator Shelley Wachsmann that this craft was the right size to have supplied Josephus's fast flotilla under sail out of Tarichaeae and the later combatant vessels used against Vespasian.[18]

I also completely concur with Wachsmann that Josephus's mysterious tagline about pirate craft must actually mean that the ships in the action at Tarichaeae were of a type also commonly used in the piracy always rife along the Syrian and southern coastline—not that there was piracy on the Sea of Galilee itself.[19] The Galilee boat's extremely shallow draft and nearly flat bottom would have been perfect for hiding among rocks on the Judaean coast and for beaching in tiny, hidden coves. Joppa itself was more an anchorage than a port in its all-but-crescent shape. Far from being protective in all conditions, its "horns" had sheer faces and were accompanied by hidden reefs. Josephus stresses that in a north wind staying in the "harbor" was more dangerous than riding it out at sea. In fact, the Greek geographer Strabo identified Joppa as the sheer rocky site to which the mythical Andromeda had been bound, endangering any rescuer.[20]

When Vespasian attacked the Jewish pirates on land at Joppa, he found the city unguarded. Josephus states that the inhabitants were unwilling to face the Romans on land, counting on getting to their boats, on board which they stayed at anchor, just out of reach of Roman arrows.[21] Then they were struck in the night by what Josephus claims was the famous "black norther," although this meteorological phenomenon is not otherwise named in antiquity (see note 5 on prevailing winds). There was no battle for Joppa, since the ships broke up and most of those on board were dashed by waves against sheer rocks. To summarize what we know about these inhabitants of Joppa in action: they built themselves "pirate *skapha*" once they decided they were cut off from the land side; they decided beforehand that when Romans came, they would not oppose land forces; they would ride it out in their boats out of range, just as the Galileans who confronted Vespasian at Taricheae had.

If we ask who could easily and quickly build a fleet of *skapha* to feed themselves, had sufficient experience with small boats to range as far as Syria, could face naval attention from Syrian, Egyptian, Phoenician, and Roman hostile craft, and viewed small craft at sea as safer than encountering Romans on land, refugees from the cities surrounding the Sea of Galilee are excellent candidates. As we have seen above, Upper Galilean refugees would have understood much about Syrian and Phoenician trade and probably about the anchorages of the grain fleet while coasting virtually straight northward at that point from Egypt. They would have known that even some comparatively small vessels carried Roman grain, precisely because they could take advantage of small anchorages in the stormy season.[22] It is very likely, therefore, that the vast majority of the Joppan pirates were Galilean and that they were less determined to survive the war than they were to do strategic-level damage to Roman interests. Running into Judaea rather than, say, the desert to the south, attempting to take refuge with the large Jewish community of Egypt, as other refugees did, was not fleeing trouble.

Josephus's obvious sympathy for the plight of the pirates—he devotes ten times more space in his text to their terrible fate than he does to their depredations—is surprising, given his utter lack of similar sympathy for raiders on land, whom he calls "robbers," "brigands," "gangs," "revolutionaries," and the like. He does not similarly categorize the pirates at Joppa as conducting disguised class warfare or as trying to take over the Jewish state in order to enjoy power. Interestingly, Strabo, writing at about the turn of the first century BCE to the first century CE, reports an earlier history of piracy from Joppa, noting that "the ports of robbers are nothing but robbers' hideouts," so the suitability of the site for hiding small craft might have been well known, even as far as Upper Galilee.[23] So the seaworthy resettlers of Joppa might well have come there fully intending to support themselves in the chaos of revolt by raiding the grain fleet and, if they were fortunate, to take revenge against the invaders by inflicting strategic damage on them at home. It would explain Josephus's uniquely sympathetic view of these particular (waterborne) raiders, if he believed they were fighting for ancestral land rather than private gain.

This episode of Jewish piracy was quickly followed by another outbreak of naval insurgency or piracy in the Black Sea the next year. After Nero's suicide the next summer, in 68, Galba marched on Rome to become emperor. Vitellius successfully followed his example not long after, winning a war with Otho, who had quickly replaced Galba. By the summer of 69, Mucianus, the governor of Syria, and Vespasian planned for Mucianus to campaign in Europe to make Vespasian emperor, while Vespasian ensured that Judaea and perpetually riotous Egypt were under control.

The fact that 69 is called "the year of the four emperors" suggests that there were plenty of reasons for wrongdoers to hope that they might not attract much attention from the usual defenders of peaceable travel and property rights. Mucianus probably provided the immediate, local inspiration for an outbreak of piracy, when he moved the Black Sea squadrons from Trapezos to Byzantium. The obvious reason to do that would be to guard the crossing of legions from Asia Minor and farther south into Europe, but Tacitus assigns him a more offensive intent, claiming that he wanted to be ready in case it seemed like a good idea to blockade the Adriatic or even to harass the coasts of Italy to divide Vitellius's forces well outside Rome.[24]

Unfortunately, back in 64, Nero had already removed from power the client dynasty assigned to Pontus, the Polemonids, who seem to have been pretty well behaved creatures of their Roman masters, supplying forces in regional conflicts; Rome had treated the family as a ready reserve of utility monarchs in the region.[25] When Rome changed Pontus from a client kingdom to a province, it turned the former royal navy into a squadron of the imperial navy based at the free, ethnically Greek city of Trapezos, leaving former units of the royal army, whose members had been given Roman citizenship and Roman weaponry, as the guard of the new imperial squadron. Polemo II made no known fuss when Pontus became a province, and Roman sources claim he agreed to resign.[26]

However, in the chaos of 69, Anicetus, a freed slave of Polemo II who had become admiral of Pontus's royal navy, rejected the new Roman political configuration and started looting. He allied himself with peoples who seemed to Roman authors to epitomize the term "barbarian" and tried to get the destitute of Roman Asia Minor to join him for the loot.[27] He himself, however, directly attacked formerly Pontine forces at Trapezos, in an effort to destroy the main Roman defense on that coast. He claimed to have done this because he was a partisan of Vitellius in the civil war, but Tacitus maintains that he resented the loss of his high position and the turning of the Pontine kingdom into a province. Tacitus refers to Anicetus's forces as a "fleet" (*classis*) of "barbarians," sailing freely over a sea left unpoliced by Mucianus in boats called *camarae,* thrown together with no metal fittings, a type even more strangely constructed than the *skapha* of the Sea of Galilee. Their bows and sterns were identical, and their freeboard was adjusted for water conditions by adding or taking off planks, like leaves of a dining table. In fact, they could be encased by these add-on modules, so that they went bouncing along rough seas like footballs.

Whatever the amusement value of the *camarae,* the problem had strategic significance, since grain and fish from the Black Sea had been important to the Greek-speaking cities of the Aegean for centuries. Vespasian would have viewed hunger in Ephesus or Athens as a problem requiring his personal attention, if not as dangerous as hunger in Rome, and as a usurper he surely did not want to start his regime with the more literate, wealthier, more populated eastern, Greek-speaking

Mediterranean world thinking that he represented a return to the bad old days of the Republic, when Roman hegemony had been famously unable or unwilling to cope with resurgent piracy. Various scholars have suggested other strategic themes, even believing that the creation of a province from a loyal, nontroublesome client kingdom could have been part of an effort in grand strategy to secure Armenia against constant Parthian interest, to keep the Sarmatians from coming farther south, or to deal with other long-term concerns.[28]

Vespasian sent *vexillationes* from his legions under Virdius Geminus to do what he had done himself in Galilee, which was to attack the waterborne looters on land. Having done that successfully, Virdius rapidly built actual *liburnii,* the standard working ship of the Roman navy—a pirate-chasing type, modeled on pirate ships. With them he blockaded Anicetus at the mouth of the River Chobus in Colchis, part of modern Georgia, under the king of the Sedochezi, whom Anicetus had bribed to protect him. Of course, the king kept his money and handed him over to Virdius. Tacitus states that in November 69 Vespasian got the news of the successful outcome in Pontus simultaneously with word of his forces' civil war–winning victory at Cremona in Italy.

There are significant differences between the two nearly contemporaneous instances of waterborne raiding. In Judaea, this raiding was perpetrated by ethnically homogeneous, desperate refugees and hard-core resisters who had already been under arms before they took to the sea. Although Josephus discusses at length (very unfavorably) charismatic leaders of various revolutionary (or brigand) factions in Judaea, he names no leader for the pirates in Joppa, and he was sympathetic to their plight, not accusing them of seizing goods for profit while waving the flag of revolution. In the Black Sea, a single experienced naval commander produced chaos at sea by calling for economically motivated piracy by polyglot peoples of the eastern shore of the sea—peoples whom Romans and Greeks believed to be wild and prone to witchcraft (although Anicetus wanted to attract impoverished Greeks also)—while he attacked Roman military power in Asia Minor.

Nonetheless, there were also meaningful similarities. In both cases, although the pirates worked together purposefully and with initial success at robbing others, they had joined for differing motives, and desperation in times of war motivated some in each case. In both instances, in the absence of regular Roman patrols, sailors without formal naval training were able to do significant damage to Roman strategic-level, not merely tactical- or even theater-level, interests with traditional types of cheap, repurposed craft. In both cases, threats to grain supplies—in one case to Rome itself and in the other to Athens and other significant cities of the Aegean—left an emperor's moral authority vulnerable to injury by peripheral, not generally respectable peoples. The standard Roman practice of isolating the pirate havens on land was a vital part of the solution, forcing the pirates pro tempore to ill-judged actions at sea. In both theaters, pirates were able to profit from confinement of shipping of vital raw materials to narrow sea-lanes.

NOTES I am deeply grateful for the award of a McMullen Seapower Fellowship, which enabled me to explore the complexity of the relationship between insurgency and piracy during the period of insurrection addressed by this paper.

1. Although the town offered little resistance to a consular-rank commander with a force of commensurate size, Vespasian killed outright all but the smallest children and then burned the town itself and all the villages around it. The population of some of these had already fled; where they had not, he enslaved all captured inhabitants. *BJ* 3 [Josephus, *The Jewish War* (Cambridge, Mass.: Harvard Univ. Press, 1927), vols. 1–4, p. 134ff].

2. Josephus's narrative in Greek is the basis for this paper; although many have noted Josephus's highly educated, urbanized, elite bias when he talks about the most dispossessed and anti-authoritarian groups in the region, it is still possible to distinguish differently motivated people among those who drove the revolt. The Greek terms into which Josephus's (probably Aramaic) draft was translated carry much cultural resonance from earlier Greek historians, and Josephus would have understood that. I am going to proceed under the assumption that he means what his text is saying in Greek, which he certainly read and understood, even if he needed help composing in it. I propose one later exception in note 19 and related text in terminology describing a local ship type for which there would have been no standard Hellenistic Greek terminology.

3. Leaving 8,400 dead; *BJ* 2, p. 509.

4. *BJ* 3, pp. 414–31.

5. Josephus, *The Jewish War,* trans. G. A. Williamson, revised, annotated, appendixes by E. Mary Smallwood (New York: Penguin, 1970), p. 440 note 3. Judaea was ordinarily self-sufficient in wheat, and there would have been no necessity for raiding the Roman grain fleet out of Egypt; Ze'ev Safrai, *The Economy of Roman Palestine* (New York: Routledge, 1994), p. 111. Of course, things might have been different in the midst of a war. One may suspect that the grain shipments did not usually literally round the coasts of the Aegean or even cling to the southern coast of Asia Minor, the most notorious lair of "barbarous" pirates in the Mediterranean, but rather engaged in island hopping, Cyprus–Rhodes–Crete, since these were especially well established legs of trading routes even for luxury merchandise; Paul Erdkamp, *The Grain Market in the Roman Empire* (Cambridge, U.K.: Cambridge Univ. Press, 2005), pp. 188–89. Prevailing winds off the coast of Joppa were southwesterly (and still are for modern Jaffa—there is still a tendency for the port to silt with material from the Nile), but winter storms often came from the north; Shlomo Aronson, "Jaffa," in *Jewish Virtual Library*, ed. American-Israeli Cooperative Enterprise, www.jewishvirtuallibrary.org/; Ellsworth Huntington, *Palestine and Its Transformation* (Boston: Houghton Mifflin, 1911), p. 64.

6. *Annales* 12.43.2 [Tacitus, *The Annals, Books IV–VI, XI–XII* (Cambridge, Mass.: Harvard Univ. Press, 1937)]. On the necessity of the Egyptian shipments for feeding the capital, Erdkamp, *Grain Market in the Roman Empire,* pp. 228–35; on how close they often cut it in winter, p. 245.

7. Philip de Souza, *Piracy in the Graeco-Roman World* (Cambridge, U.K.: Cambridge Univ. Press, 1999), p. 210, notes that the proximity of overwhelming land forces to the pirate base meant that "it was unnecessary to employ any naval units in its suppression." De Souza further comments that there is no evidence that any imperial squadron was assigned to control piracy on this rich coastline, along which piracy was common; in fact, there is no attestation of a classis Syriaca, a Syria-based squadron, before Hadrian, whose reign started in 117. De Souza guesses that the classis Alexandrina, the high-priority squadron assigned to protect the grain fleet as it sailed from Alexandria, "was felt sufficient to fulfill any naval duties in the area." The mission of the imperial navy was to control piracy, and it consisted therefore of predominantly lean, pirate-chasing ship types. Small ships manned largely by ethnically Levantine sailors are not well attested in the epigraphic testimony for any era, so absence of evidence is not decisive.

8. Josephus certainly describes brutal factionalism in Jerusalem, but he claims that the more moderate and peaceable people had left and more combative ones flooded in from the countryside. It is surely not likely that the peaceable, frightened groups attempting to escape war in Jerusalem took up piracy. I am assuming that refugees from such earlier events as anti-Jewish rioting in Caesarea in 66, unsettled and uncommented on, would not have been roving along the coast for more than a year.

9. *BJ* 2, p. 513. Cestius had sent forces against some sort of tower at Aphek, where he had heard that forces were gathering. When he got there, it was already abandoned, as were the villages around it, from where I am guessing that armed group of resisters had come; so he burned all the villages in the area. Nonetheless, we are also told, by Josephus, that refugees from these actions were pouring into Jerusalem to make a stand there, so we cannot assume that many of those left homeless by Cestius were still available to resettle Joppa. We have already noted that Vespasian's first target after he arrived in the theater was Galilean Gabara, from which some potential combatants had already fled. Nonetheless, he created more Galilean refugees by destroying towns and villages in that area, many of which had already been abandoned, so populations in hiding could not return to their homes.

10. Ibid., pp. 525, 587–600; Josephus, Vita 13 [Josephus, *The Life; Against Apion* (Cambridge Mass.: Harvard Univ. Press, 1926)]; Eric M. Meyers, "The Cultural Setting of Galilee," in Aufstieg und Niedergang der römischen Welt, ed. Hildegard Temporini and

Wolfgang Haase (Berlin: de Gruyter, 1979) [hereafter ANRW with vol., part, and page numbers and year], vol. II, part 9.1, p. 700. See Safrai, *Economy of Roman Palestine,* pp. 201–202, on the garment industry, well known throughout the Mediterranean world. Donkey caravans wove through the countryside picking up merchandise and taking it mainly to Tyre and Sidon. The donkeys bore Galilean merchandise only into the metropoles—nothing came back on the donkeys; Safrai, Economy of Roman Palestine, pp. 236–37, 264. Maurice Sartre, The Middle East under Rome (Cambridge, Mass.: Belknap, 2005), pp. 260–63, notes that Tyre was probably minting the only high-silver-content universally acceptable coinage in the region. Safrai, Economy of Roman Palestine, p. 402, notes that Galilee was closely tied to Tyre economically by efficient roads, including the Via Maris.

11 Sartre, *Middle East under Rome,* pp. 113–15.

12 Josephus, *Antiquitates Iudaiorum* 14.167 [Josephus, *Jewish Antiquities, Books XII–XIV* (Cambridge, Mass.: Harvard Univ. Press, 1952)]. The decree asserts that this action follows a general policy of forcing everyone to cede territory taken by force in order to restore "justice and piety"; also *BJ* 1, pp. 204–11. Shortly thereafter, one Malichus, an enemy of Herod associated by Josephus with a belief that "other peoples" ought not to be brought among "dwellers of the country" during their periods of purification, faced execution by the Roman governor of Syria as a revolutionary (literally, "among those *eneoterisen,*" "those undertaking a new order"). Subsequently, he tried to slip his son out of Tyre itself, where he was being held hostage for Malichus's continued good conduct—implying insider knowledge of Tyre on the part of Malichus, as well as excellent contacts there; *BJ* 1, pp. 229–32. On the history of conflict in this zone, Shimon Applebaum, "Judaea as a Roman Province," in *ANRW* II.8 (1977), pp. 382–83, 387, noting that this implies a very different, more favorable interpretation of John of Gischala than that offered by Josephus, namely, that local defense against marauders was still necessary and raiding and counterraiding customary. On John's own trading expertise in dealing with Phoenicians as middleman, *BJ* 2, pp. 525, 587–600.

13 *BJ* 4, p. 105.

14 *BJ* 2, pp. 635–41; Josephus, *Vita,* 9.12.

15 *BJ* 3, pp. 466–69.

16 Ibid., pp. 522–31.

17 It matched the Galilee boat in its distinctive high curved stern and especially sharp cutwater, as well as the arrangement of oars and shape of hull, to the extent that that can be seen in the mosaic; Shelley Wachsmann, *The Sea of Galilee Boat* (Cambridge, Mass.: Perseus, 1995), pp. 303–309. Fishing was tremendously important to the Galilean and Judaean diet. Fish were even imported from Egypt. Galilean fishermen were central in meeting regional needs for fish, especially fishermen around Tiberias, so a high percentage of the male population would be very familiar with fishing boats; Safrai, *Economy of Roman Palestine,* pp. 163–64. In addition, the Sea of Galilee was important as a water transportation route per se; ibid., p. 290.

18 Wachsmann has done the math on Josephus's crews of four, with pilot, and his arrested dissidents, and I am simply going to accept all of her work on that; Wachsmann, *Sea of Galilee Boat,* pp. 312–17.

19 Ibid., pp. 318–19. We will have to chalk this up to Josephus's inability to enroll in a course in advanced Greek composition or to his imperfect communication with (or proofreading of the work of) the Greek editors often hypothesized for his literary efforts back in Rome.

20 *BJ* 3, pp. 419–22; Strabo 16.2.28 [Strabo, *Geography, Books XV–XVI* (Cambridge, Mass.: Harvard Univ. Press, 1930)], places Andromeda at Joppa. Huntington, *Palestine and Its Transformation,* p. 64, explains the cliffs and the sharp rocks at widely varying depths in proximity; the shoreline, not geologically old, consists of many kinds of rocks of varying hardness, so that they do not erode at the same rate, making the coastline particularly unpredictable.

21 *BJ* 3, pp. 422–27; de souza, *Piracy in the Graeco-Roman World,* p. 120, claims that the best way to fight pirates in antiquity was from the land, denying them havens. This was certainly the Romans' ordinary procedure.

22 Erdkamp, *Grain Market in the Roman Empire,* p. 178. Incentives were offered to draw larger ships into the trade (p. 245).

23 Strabo 16.2.28 and 16.2.37 states that Moses's descendants were less pious and turned "robbers," preying on Syria and Phoenicia. This is no help in dating the first Jewish pirates at Joppa; perhaps it refers to otherwise unattested events during the chaos of the Roman civil wars. If earlier, it might explain Pompey's decision to take the coast away from the Jewish state.

24 Tac. *Hist.* 2.83, 3.47 [Tacitus, *Histories I–III* (Cambridge, Mass.: Harvard Univ. Press, 1925)].

25 Suet. *Nero* 18 [Suetonius, *The Lives of the Caesars* (Cambridge, Mass.: Harvard Univ. Press: 1914), vol. 2]; E. Olshausen, "Pontos und Rom (63 v.Chr.–64 n.Chr)," *ANRW* II.7.2 (1980), pp. 910–11; R. D. Sullivan, "Dynasts in Pontus," *ANRW* II.7.2 (1980), pp. 926–30. The evidence for the date of the creation of the province is coinage stamped with references to a new "era."

26 Parts of Cilicia had been given him by Claudius, so he might have retired to mountain climes or used his experience to deal with even worse pirates on the notorious Cilician coast.

27 Strabo, a Greek, describes what he claims to be seventy peoples with different languages in what is now Georgia and its environs; he claims that others refer to three hundred distinct peoples. He states that they live separately and do not try to talk to each other, because of their "obstinacy and ferocity"; Strabo 11.2.1.

28 David Magie, *Roman Rule in Asia Minor* (Princeton, N.J.: Princeton Univ. Press, 1975), vol. 1, p. 562, and vol. 2, p. 1418 note 63, entertains various theories for Roman strategic thinking about the political status of Pontus.

II Sea Power without a Navy?
Roman Naval Forces in the Principate

JORIT WINTJES

When one thinks about the Roman military of the Principate, naval forces are likely not to be the first thing that springs to mind. While Rome was, during the time of the Republic, capable of exerting considerable power at sea—as proved, for example, in the Punic Wars—the Rome of the emperors is still primarily seen as a land-based power arranged around a peaceful central lake, the Mediterranean, and Roman naval history as basically coming to a dramatic end in the battle of Actium.[1] To this day the most powerful and iconic symbol of Roman military might is the legion with its eagle, a unit that—at least during the Principate—is supposed to have consisted of hardy professional soldiers drawn from the Roman citizenry and serving as heavily armored infantrymen. In reality, however, Roman legions were anything but pure infantry units, combining instead a number of different combat as well as noncombat capabilities; beside artillery (i.e., catapults and the like), cavalry, and various types of engineering, a certain naval capability was also part of what was at the disposal of a Roman legionary commander. Naval forces did indeed matter to the Romans during the Principate, even though large-scale fleet action was, with very few exceptions, a thing of the past.

Unfortunately, looking closer at the naval forces of imperial Rome can at times be a discouraging experience, as understanding is significantly impaired by three main issues. First of all, the nature of the available sources—and they are few and far between—is unlikely to raise much enthusiasm. Apart from the odd mention of a particularly spectacular feat of arms or navigation (like the—possible—circumnavigation of Jutland under Augustus or the circumnavigation of Britain under Domitian), ancient historiography is decidedly uninterested in Roman naval forces. While some inscriptions and other material of a documentary nature do indeed survive, they pale almost into insignificance compared to the mass of source material available for Roman land forces.[2] Second, combat at sea being the ultimate raison d'être of naval forces, the issue of how these naval forces were actually employed comes up: What did the Romans actually do with their naval forces, and how did they do it? It is probably not too far-fetched to assume that while the Romans seem not to have issued doctrinal publications, some sort of thinking about operational matters certainly must have existed, though almost nothing of it survived.³ And finally, current thinking about Roman naval forces is still deeply influenced by modern, and to a certain extent Western, concepts of how naval forces should be organized. It is thus quite common, particularly in the case of naval units stationed in the provinces, to speak of "fleets," which are supposed to have been organized in "squadrons"—although that assumption is totally unsupported by evidence.⁴

There is very little that can be done about the first issue. Literary references in general are, as was already mentioned, sparse. A considerable amount of specifically military literature both from Greece and from Rome survives, but the same cannot be said of naval matters, apart from a small corpus of Byzantine texts on war at sea.⁵ Epigraphical evidence is—with a few exceptions—fairly rare, too rare for useful statistical evaluation. Archaeological evidence is likewise rather limited; for example, compared to legionary garrisons, which are well attested and consequently well understood, very little is known about naval bases or their layout.⁶ Also, ship finds provide only a very selective picture of Roman military shipbuilding, warships being nearly totally absent from the archaeological record.⁷

The second issue is closely connected to the first. Ancient authors rarely talk about naval forces, and when they do they talk neither directly about doctrine nor even generally about the way naval forces were actually employed. Nor do they give any information about all the appurtenances of large-scale naval operations, ranging from logistics to signaling. As a consequence, operational aspects of Roman naval history have elicited little scholarly interest, which is more than a little bit odd, as the primary purpose of any naval force is obviously combat at sea. Even if there is no fitting Latin equivalent to the clear statement that can be found at the beginning of the U.S. naval doctrine publication on naval warfare that "the success of an organized military force is associated directly with the validity of its doctrine," it cannot be doubted that the Romans (or, for that matter, any other ancient operator of naval forces) saw things in exactly the same way.⁸ For anyone handing out large amounts of money for the construction of ships usable for nothing but combat and for the upkeep of a considerable infrastructure to support these ships, employing them in the most effective way must have been far more important than legal status, naming conventions, etc. Nonetheless, while a closer look at Roman operations could indeed reveal quite a bit about Roman operational procedures, these are not the main purpose of this paper.

Instead, this paper will concentrate on the third issue—the fact that the literature on the Roman navy, which goes back at least to the seventeenth century, is to this day heavily influenced in its thinking about the structure of Roman naval forces by a modern way of categorizing that distinguishes between the army on the one hand and the navy on the other. As a result, the classical historical model of Roman military organization is simple: on the one hand, there was the army, divided into the legions and the auxiliaries, while on the other hand there was the navy, again divided into the "imperial" fleets stationed in Italy and the "provincial" fleets based on the periphery. The most important distinction, in this model, between "imperial" and "provincial" fleets was that the former were manned by citizens, while men serving in the latter had the same legal status as soldiers in auxiliary army units. This parallel construction of an army divided into units of citizen and noncitizen soldiers and an accompanying navy also consisting of citizen and noncitizen crews and soldiers has been the underlying assumption of nearly all research into Roman naval forces ever since Johannes Scheffer wrote his groundbreaking study *De militia navali veterum* in 1654.[9] Yet this assumption is fundamentally flawed.

Dealing with the whole range of Roman naval forces—of which there were more than the "fleets" just mentioned—would be a massive undertaking. Therefore this paper will concentrate on key aspects of the so-called provincial fleets, which the Romans called *classes* and which are usually seen as scaled-down variations of the large imperial fleets, also called *classes*—that is, as naval auxiliary cohorts to the naval legions, to put it pointedly.

Provincial *Classes,* Not Provincial "Fleets"

Perhaps the easiest aspect of Roman *classes* is that of their commanders' social status, if only because quite a reasonable amount of evidence for it survives. It is fairly clear that the commanders of the *classes* stationed in Egypt, on the Danube, and in Syria earned sixty thousand sesterces a year, an entry-level salary for a Roman equestrian intent on making a career in the imperial administration.[10] Although the command positions over the *classes* in Britain and Germany were better paid, they were still seen as low-ranking offices in the course of an equestrian career. Several examples of Roman equestrians are known whose successful careers—after the initial military offices of the *militia equestres*—began with command over provincial *classes*;[11] even a combined command over more than one of these units, a rare occurrence, was not at the top of the career ladder.[12] Commanding one of the imperial *classes* in Italy, however, was quite different—these posts were usually either the final steps of very successful careers or stepping-stones to one of the small number of highly important and eminently prestigious offices, like the prefecture of Egypt.[13]

A comparison between the social status of someone commanding a *classis* in one of the provinces and that of the commander of one of the imperial *classes* may not appear very interesting at first. After all, there was also a considerable social gap between the commander of an auxiliary cohort and a legionary commander. Yet this comparison points precisely to an important characteristic of the *classes* stationed in the provinces. That is, just as an auxiliary cohort had only a fraction of the manpower of a legion, so a *classis* on the Rhine or the Danube or in one of the other border provinces cannot have come even remotely near to the manpower of the *classes* in Italy—otherwise the rank and social status of commanders of provincial *classes* would have been higher. Indeed, if one looks at the commanders of cavalry units, one finds that those of large *alae miliariae,* units of a thousand cavalrymen, were on the same salary level as most men commanding provincial *classes*.[14] This gives a clear indicator for the overall strength of a provincial *classis:* even taking into account the inherent complexity of naval units, which required extensive support services to function properly, it cannot have greatly exceeded the manpower of one of the large *alae*. Allowing for a considerable staff, support services in the home port, etc., a *classis* may have had perhaps around two thousand, certainly no more than three thousand, men on strength. Oared warships being extremely manpower intensive, a *classis* like the classis Britannica, in the English Channel, may have operated fifteen to twenty ships at most.[15] So, as "fleets" come, these *classes* were tiny.

This is important to bear in mind—provincial *classes* cannot have been large units with hundreds of ships and thousands of men, because their commanding officers were far too junior for such responsibilities, and this in turn means they can obviously have had only small numbers of ships at their disposal. In other words, instead of being smaller clones of the Italian *classes,* they were quite unlike the naval units stationed in Ravenna and Misenum. The *classis* in Misenum, perhaps the larger one of the two, must have mustered tens of thousands of men in the early empire. Not only was it possible for Nero in AD 68 to recruit from it a legion, legio I adiutrix (which, even assuming it was understrength, still had several thousand trained soldiers), but even after that the *classis* was still capable of military operations after hiving off so many trained soldiers, strongly suggesting there were considerably more available in the first place.[16] Barely two years later, an Italian *classis* again served as a manpower reserve, when a new legion, legio II adiutrix, was created from personnel from the classis Ravennata.[17] The capability gap, so to speak, between the *classes* stationed in Italy and those stationed in the provinces must have been enormous.

Yet—and this is one of the great mysteries of Roman naval history and its scholarship—Roman naval operations, of which there were many on a large scale throughout the empire, are still very often seen only in the context and within the framework of the provincial *classes:* if there was naval activity going on in a province or on the frontier, then it must have been in the domain of the relevant provincial *classis*. Further, one is tempted to add, that was presumably true because the provincial *classis* was the navy's arm in the affected province; only if the planned operation exceeded the capabilities of the provincial *classis* did detachments of the imperial ones become involved. Even the very brief look at the possible size of the provincial *classes* has shown, however, that such reasoning simply does not fit their actual nature. Instead, a look at large-scale naval operations in the provinces—of which there were many—reveals that although the provincial *classes* did indeed have parts in them, they must have been, numerically speaking, minor. One of the important requirements for any large-scale operation was to have a large number of ships available. For example, the amphibious operations of Germanicus off the German coast in AD 16 involved more than a thousand ships, as did Claudius's invasion of Britain in AD 43; several operations right up to the end of Roman rule in northwestern Europe were on a similar scale.[18] These impressive numbers cannot have been produced by the provincial *classes* alone.

Instead, ships and crews for such undertakings came from three distinctly different sources. First, there were indeed the *classes,* which supplied warships and their crews, as well as—one would assume—key personnel necessary for a major operation, ranging from pilots to logistics specialists. However, in terms of sheer numbers, *classes* can have contributed relatively little, not least because warships formed only a small part of any substantial amphibious force, being probably quite unsuitable in the troop-carrying role.[19]

A much bigger share fell to the army, the second important source for ships and crews, and one that often gets overlooked. There is evidence from Lower Germany of Roman legions having been involved in ship construction;[20] there also survives a list of *immunes*—specialists exempt from certain everyday duties—of the legion, a list composed by the praetorian prefect Tarrutienus Paternus at the end of the second century that includes both *naupegi,* shipwrights, and *gubernatores,* helmsmen.[21] One of the latter, a certain Marcus Minucius Audens, served in the second or third century AD with legio VI in York, as his funerary inscription shows.[22] Thus the legion apparently included personnel experienced in operating ships; indeed, surviving anchors with legionary stamps on them are tangible evidence of these ships.[23] So, just as modern army formations can have boats at their disposal, the Roman legions had some sort of naval capability, which may well have included "proper" warships.[24] Given the considerable resources in terms of both manpower and logistical support at the disposal of a legionary commander, it is perfectly possible that under certain circumstances the naval element, so to speak, of a legion was comparable in size and capability to those of a provincial *classis*.

The third important source for ships and crews was the civilian sector, again something that has seen very little scholarly attention. What is clear from the available sources is that Roman commanders, when necessary, commandeered civilian ships.[25] There is much less certainty about the crews; while some evidence exists for the hiring of civilians to man ships either newly constructed or commandeered, the practical implications are unknown.[26] For many problems, ranging from the legal status of the hired crewmen (what power did a noncommissioned officer have over a civilian?) to the eventual fate of the ships involved in a large-scale operation (did they simply rot away, were they recycled in some way or another, or dumped onto the civilian ship market?), there is insufficient evidence to find answers. Yet it is obvious that the civilian sector must have played a major role in any large-scale naval undertaking.

Large-scale operations are instructive for two reasons. One, their sheer size and the fact that the Romans managed to stage them with surprising frequency point to the limits of what the provincial *classes* could actually provide for such operations. Two, they are reminders of how multifaceted Roman naval operations were in reality. Indeed, there were other units that evidently had naval capabilities but were very different from the *classes*. For example, coastal units of unknown size and function are attested in Spain;[27] river guards, *potamophylaces,* served on the Nile—underscoring that Roman naval operations were anything but confined to a Roman navy.[28]

When the Romans went to sea, they did not call solely on a Roman navy; instead, they tapped very different sources for ships and manpower. Comparing these cases leads to the suspicion that of the three elements involved in getting large-scale operations off the ground—*classes,* legions, and civilian ships and crews—these operations were most likely run by the element with the highest status, the legion. Moreover, in addition to being senior to any nonlegionary unit, the legion had the largest permanent staff organization; the legion—or one of the legions participating in a large-scale campaign—was home to the overall commander, and the highest-ranking officers in any campaign invariably served with the legions. To put it pointedly, one could therefore argue that the history of large-scale naval operations in the Roman Principate is not so much "navy history" as "legionary history"—or "army history."

Roman Provincial *Classes*: What Were They Good For?
Having had a closer look at the nature of Roman provincial *classes*—and in the process having said more about what they were *not* than about what they were—we still face one key question: Given their fairly limited capabilities, what might have been their purpose in everyday life, beyond taking modest parts in large-scale operations? For an answer to this question it is useful to turn to the *classis* stationed in Roman Syria, the classis Syriaca.[29] The general assumption is that this unit was stationed at Seleucia Pieria, the port of Antioch-on-the-Orontes, one of the biggest cities in the East and throughout the Principate the key staging post for any campaign against the Parthians or the Sassanids.[30] All the military supplies and most of the personnel involved in such campaigns went through Seleucia Pieria, which saw extensive building activity right down to late antiquity intended to keep the harbor from silting up.[31] As the most important harbor in Roman Syria, it is more than likely that Seleucia Pieria was indeed the base of the classis Syriaca, though less than a dozen inscriptions of the unit have been found there. Seleucia, which has never been properly excavated, also yields inscriptions of sailors serving with

the *classis* stationed in Misenum.[32] As luck would have it, a papyrus from Egypt, a contract between two sailors about the sale of a slave boy, survives as well;[33] it clearly states that in Seleucia was a base of the *classis* from Misenum.[34] It therefore offers a good starting point for thinking about the function of provincial *classes* in relation to the units stationed in Italy, in the overall context of Roman naval forces.

Obviously, a naval base in or near Seleucia must have existed where the squadron from Misenum was garrisoned, although so far it has not been found. But at the same time—accepting the general assumption that the Syrian *classis* was indeed stationed in Syria's most important port—the classis Syriaca had a base there as well. Why then did the Romans, not known for unnecessarily duplicating military capabilities, station both a detached squadron of the large and powerful Misenate *classis* and also the Syrian *classis* in one and the same port? Merely increasing the overall number of naval personnel stationed in Seleucia cannot have been the reason, as that would have been much easier to achieve by simply increasing the detachment of the Misenate *classis*. The only plausible answer is that the classis Syriaca offered some military capability inherently different from that of the *classis* from Misenum.

What was this military capability? Provincial *classes* seem to have been equipped mainly with ships of the *liburna* type, smaller vessels capable of operating in coastal waters but less well suited to the high seas;[35] that, at least, is what the admittedly poor epigraphical record seems to suggest.[36] This assumption is supported by the fairly small size of the *classes* and the large crew requirements of bigger warships. It is therefore likely that a unit like the classis Syriaca was mainly used for coastal patrols and police duties. Although piracy is generally assumed to have been eliminated by Pompey in his great campaign of 67 BC, low-intensity piracy of the variety best described as petty crime at sea—for example, robbing a fisherman of his catch or capturing a small ferry with two or three passengers—surely continued along the coasts of the Mediterranean, just as highwaymen existed throughout the Roman empire.[37] To keep such activity at a manageable level, units were needed to fulfill the function of something similar to a coastal police or coast guard.

Just as cavalry regiments stationed on the frontiers sent out patrols on a daily basis into neighboring villages to keep contact with the inhabitants of the frontier zone and to act as a border police, units like the classis Syriaca will have sent out ships to coastal communities, showing the flag and dissuading potential troublemakers.[38] This kind of policing work off the coasts of, for example, Roman Syria clearly required a very different set of skills and capabilities than did, for example, controlling the sea-lanes in the Mediterranean or guarding convoys to and from Italy. An in-depth knowledge of both the coast and presumably its immediate hinterland was needed, as was the ability to operate small vessels in both coastal and riverine environments, assets that the *classes* stationed in Italy did not need for their high-seas work. The provincial *classes* thus appear as units composed of specialists whose involvement in large-scale military operations must have been mainly due to their special skills, particularly their intimate knowledge of their coasts.

Provincial *Classes*: A New Model and Its Consequences
So far it has been shown that the commonly accepted picture of what provincial *classes* were is in need of revision. Naval units stationed in the provinces were small, comparable in size to large cavalry regiments and functionally similar to coast guards. This revision has two important consequences regarding the possible existence of naval units currently unattested and the eventual fate of Roman naval forces in late antiquity.

The literature on Roman naval forces has traditionally been careful about assuming into existence provincial *classes* for which there is no epigraphical evidence. Thus, a certain Caius Iulius Libo is attested as a *trierarchus,* a captain, of classis nova Libyca, in an inscription from Constantine in Algeria that happens to be the only evidence for that unit; it has been suggested accordingly that this *classis* was in fact only temporary, possibly consisting of ships detached from either the Italian *classes* or the provincial ones in the eastern Mediterranean.[39] However, given the fairly small size of provincial *classes* and the fact that other units are almost as poorly attested—the classis Syriaca appears on less than a dozen inscriptions, which just as easily might not have survived—it is perfectly possible that other naval units did exist, just as auxiliary units did of which no trace is left. These naval units may have been additional *classes,* like the classis nova Libyca, but they may just as well have been of different types, given that Roman naval forces came in a variety of forms.

As for the eventual fate of the provincial *classes,* it is often assumed that Roman naval forces were run down during the latter half of the third century and that the reforms under Diocletian and Constantine then broke up the older, larger units into smaller squadrons with new names. Units like the classis Anderetianorum and the classis Sambrica, attested in late-fourth-century Gaul, have been interpreted as examples of this development:[40] it has been suggested that these two Gaulish squadrons were the remnants of the old classis Britannica.[41] Such a process—the splitting up of a larger *classis* into smaller squadrons that continue to operate as separate units—rests, however, on the assumption that the provincial *classes* were large enough to allow such a division in the first place. That was not the case, as has been shown above. Even if the classis Britannica was indeed larger than, for example, the classis Syriaca (and the fact that its commander earned more than his Syrian counterpart is a good indicator that it was), it would not, as has been shown above, have exceeded the total manpower of a legion, making a strength of anything much beyond twenty ships highly unlikely. That number, however, is far too small to allow, first, a running-down of the *classis* and then a separation into two units—which, incidentally, must have meant a considerable increase in administrative and other support personnel.

In any case, there is no proper evidence for any downscaling or reorganizing of Roman naval forces in the latter half of the third century. Thus in Roman Syria, a classis Seleucena was stationed in late antiquity at Seleucia Pieria; it was probably simply the classis Syriaca under a new name.[42] Most of the unit names known from the early and high Principate disappear in late antiquity; if one were to draw up two lists of naval units, those of the Principate and of those of the late empire, there would be considerable differences, with a sizable number of new units appearing in the latter.[43] Yet taking these differences at face value is methodologically unsound, as they first and foremost reflect a considerable change in the nature of the available sources. Most unit names from the Principate—not only of naval units but throughout the whole Roman army—are attested on private inscriptions; in the course of the third century, however, the "epigraphical habit" of setting up these private inscriptions changes considerably, and their number rapidly decreases.[44] Thus the lack of epigraphical evidence for naval units in late antiquity must be seen against the background of a general lack of epigraphical evidence for *any* military unit in that period. On the other hand, most of the unit names from late antiquity come from documentary sources like the *notitia dignitatum* or, in the case of the classis Seleucena, the *codex Theodosianus*. Depending on how official one is inclined to consider these sources to be, they could well preserve unit designations that predate late antiquity but do not appear in the epigraphical evidence simply out of personal preference of the sailors; most of the inscriptions did not have an official character, after all.

In conclusion, a closer look at the provincial *classes*—which in the past have often been interpreted as fleets of considerable strength—has shown that they were very different from the *classes* stationed in Italy and were in fact small, highly specialized units fulfilling a very specific function in the overall spectrum of Roman naval warfare. While their contribution to large-scale operations probably was significant in terms of skills and capabilities, provincial *classes* could not run such operations by themselves, nor were they responsible for organizing them; on the frontiers, only the Roman legions had the staff and logistics to support large-scale operations. We have therefore compared the provincial *classes* to coast-guard units; one might also interpret them as army units equipped with boats to gain sufficient mobility for patrolling. One thing they were not—an auxiliary part of a Roman navy that itself was in some way separate from the Roman army.

NOTES 1 To give just one example, William Rodgers pointedly ended his 1937 study on Greek and Roman naval warfare with the following sentence: "After many centuries of naval warfare, the battle of Actium established the economic unity of the Mediterranean basin and thereafter, for over three centuries the peace of Rome prevailed over those waters, during which period the Roman navy shrank to a mere coast guard for the protection of the public against pirates." William Rodgers, *Greek and Roman Naval Warfare*, 2nd ed. (Annapolis, Md.: Naval Institute Press, 1964), p. 538.

2 Vell. 2.106 [William S. Watt, ed.,*Vellei Paterculi Historiarum ad M. Vinicium consulem libri duo*, 2nd ed. (Stuttgart: Teubner, 1998)]; Aug. *hist.* 26 [Hans Volkmann, ed., *Res Gestae Divi Augusti. Das Monumentum Ancyranum*, 3rd ed. (Berlin: De Gruyter, 1969)]; Plin. *NH* 2.167 [Ludwig von Jan and Karl Mayerhoff, *C. Plini Secundi Naturalis historiae libri xxxvii. Vol. i: libri i–vi* (Leipzig: Teubner, 1906)]. Both the dating and the extent of the circumnavigation of Jutland are disputed; see Klaus-Peter Johne, *Die Römer an der Elbe* (Berlin: Akademie-Verlag, 2012), pp. 141–48. For the circumnavigation of Britain, Tac. *Agr.* 10 [Michael Winterbottom and Richard M. Ogilvie, eds., *Cornelii Taciti Opera Minora* (Oxford, U.K.: Oxford Univ. Press, 1975)].

3 Many ancient works on warfare and tactics probably included chapters on naval warfare; for example, the surviving treatise of Aeneas Tacticus breaks off in 40.8 with the words "And inasmuch as these points have been described I shall pass on to naval manoeuvres. Of a naval armament there are two forms of equipment...." Aeneas Tacticus 40.8, in William A. Oldfather et al., trans., *Aeneas Tacticus, Asclepiodotus, and Onasander* (Cambridge, Mass.: Harvard Univ. Press, 1928), p. 199. However, nearly all of these texts must have been lost fairly early, as even at the end of the ninth century the Byzantine emperor Leo VI noted, "We will now set down ordinances for naval warfare.... [W]e found no regulations about it in the older tactical books"; Leo tactica const. 19.1, in George T. Dennis, trans., *The Taktika of Leo VI* (Washington, D.C.: Dumbarton Oaks, 2010), p. 503. The famous fourth-century military handbook by Vegetius includes a small section on naval warfare (Veg. 4.31-46 [Carl Lang, ed., *Flavius Vegetius Renatus: Epitoma Rei Militaris*, 2nd ed. (Leipzig: Teubner, 1885)]), but it concentrates heavily on technological aspects and on the art of navigation and is generally of questionable value. Vegetius weaves together pieces of information that were either badly distorted or not properly understood by him; for an example see Boris Rankov, "Now You See It, Now You Don't: The British Fleet in Vegetius IV.37," in *Limes XVIII: Proceedings of the XVIIIth International Congress of Roman Frontier Studies Held in Amman, Jordan*, ed. Philip Freeman (Oxford, U.K.: Archaeopress, 2002), pp. 921–24.

4 The term used by the Romans for these naval units, *classes*, is usually translated "fleets"; it is used rather indiscriminately by ancient historiographers either for specific units (see, for example, Tac. *hist.* 1.58.1 [Kenneth Wellesley, ed., *P. Cornelius Tacitus. Tomus ii.1: Historiae* (Leipzig: Teubner, 1989), mentioning the classis Germanica] or Tac. *hist.* 4.79.3 [mentioning the classis Britannica]) or as a generic term for a larger naval force (see, for example, Tac. *ann.* 1.70.1 [Kenneth Wellesley, ed., *Cornelii Taciti libri qui supersunt. Tomus i.2: Ab Excessu Divi Augusti libri XI–XVI* (Leipzig: Teubner, 1986)], mentioning the amphibious force employed by Germanicus in AD 15).

5 Alphonse Dain, *Naumachica: Partim adhuc inedicta in unum nunc primum congessit et indice auxit* (Paris: A. Martini, 1943).

6 For the latest collection of the available material see Thomas Schmidts, "Stützpunkte der römischen Flotten in der Kaiserzeit," in *Die Armee der Caesaren: Archäologie und Geschichte*, ed. Thomas Fischer (Regensburg, Ger.: Friedrich Pustet, 2012), pp. 354–65.

7 Outside the Mediterranean, ship finds are extremely rare; out of a total of 1,259 listed by Anthony J. Parker, *Ancient Shipwrecks of the Mediterranean and the Roman Provinces* (Oxford, U.K.: Tempus Reparatum, 1992), only sixty-seven, most of them small vessels used on lakes and rivers, are located outside the Mediterranean. See also the database at *The NAVIS II Project*, www2.rgzm.de/navis2/.

8 U.S. Navy Dept., *Naval Warfare*, Naval Doctrine Publication 1 (Washington, D.C.: Navy Staff, 1994), p. ii.

9 Johannes Scheffer, *De militia navali veterum libri quattuor* (Uppsala, Swed.: Johannes Jansson, 1654). Scheffer's work is the first monographic study on ancient naval warfare published in modern times.

10 Alfred von Domaszewski, *Die Rangordnung des römischen Heeres*, 3rd ed. (Bonn: Marcus und Weber, 1908), pp. 153, 161. See also Chester G. Starr, *The Roman Imperial Navy 31 BC–AD 324* (Ithaca, N.Y.: Cornell Univ. Press, 1941), p. 107; Dietmar Kienast, *Untersuchungen zu den Kriegsflotten der römischen Kaiserzeit* (Bonn: Rudolf Habelt, 1966), pp. 42–43; and Marek Zyromski, *Praefectus Classis: The Commanders of the Roman Imperial Navy during the Principate* (Poznan, Pol.: Adam Mickiewicz Univ. Press, 2001), pp. 32–33.

11 See, for example, the career of Marcus Arruntius Claudianus, who commanded the classis Moesica and eventually went on to become governor of Macedonia early in the second century AD. See Zyromski, *Praefectus Classis*, pp. 73–76, and John Spaul, *Classes Imperii Romani* (Andover (Hants): Nectoreca, 2002), p. 48.

12 Caius Manlius Felix held command of the classis Pannonica and the classis Germanica during Trajan's first Dacian war and continued his procuratorial career afterward; see Zyromski, *Praefectus Classis*, pp. 106–107, and Spaul, *Classes Imperii Romani*, p. 47.

13 See, for example, the career of Quintus Baienus Blassianus, who in the middle of the second century BC first held command of the classis Britannica, then went on to command the classis Ravennatis before eventually holding in succession the three most important equestrian posts: *praefectus vigilum*, *praefectus annonae*, and *praefectus Aegypti*. See Zyromski, *Praefectus Classis*, pp. 78–80, and Spaul, *Classes Imperii Romani*, p. 47.

14 Domaszewski, *Die Rangordnung des römischen Heeres*, p. 141. See also Brian Dobson, "The

Significance of the Centurion and 'Primipilaris' in the Roman Army," in *Aufstieg und Niedergang der römischen Welt,* ed. Hildegard Temporini and Wolfgang Haase (Berlin: de Gruyter, 1974), vol. II, part 1, p. 408.

15 The sizes of warship crews during the Roman Principate are largely unknown, there being very little evidence available. However, a typical crew consisted of a large complement of rowers and a substantial number of trained soldiers, the actual numbers depending on the type of ship; it is generally assumed that Roman triremes were similar in size to Athenian triremes and had around 170 rowers; see John S. Morrison and John F. Coates, The Athenian Trireme (Cambridge, U.K.: Cambridge Univ. Press, 1986), pp. 107–18, and Michel Reddé, *Mare Nostrum: Les infrastructures, le dispositif et l'histoire de la marine militaire sous l'Empire romain* (Rome: École française, 1986), p. 111. The larger penteremes may have been comparable in size to Republican penteremes, which were crewed by three hundred rowers and 120 soldiers; Pol. 1.26.7 [Theodor Büttner-Wobst, *Polybii Historiae. voll. i–v* (Leipzig: Teubner, 1882–1904)]; see also Reddé, Mare Nostrum, p. 113. This view seems to be supported by Pliny, who mentions crew sizes of around four hundred for penteremes, probably giving the overall total (Plin. NH 32.1.4). For *liburna*-type warships, various crew sizes have been suggested, on the basis of the capacity of barrack blocks excavated at the classis Britannica fort at Dover. Brian Philp, *The Roman Forts of the Classis Britannica at Dover 1970–77* (Dover, U.K.: Kent Archaeological Rescue Unit, 1981), p. 102, argues for an overall crew size of sixty-four; however, it has also been suggested that the barracks were used only by the rowers, which pushes the overall crew size closer to a hundred men. See Heinrich C. Konen, *Classis Germanica: Die römische Rheinflotte im 1.–3. Jahrhundert n. Chr.* (St. Katharinen, Ger.: Scripta Mercaturae, 2000), pp. 225–26.

16 Early in AD 69, Othonian naval forces operated off the coast of southern Gaul; Tac. *hist.* 2.12–15; see Kienast, *Untersuchungen zu den Kriegsflotten der römischen Kaiserzeit,* pp. 63–64. That the new legion was not formed from untrained rowers is clear from its combat record during the civil war in the Year of the Four Emperors. Tacitus is quite explicit on its capabilities: *Unicum Othoniani exercitus robur, primanos quartadecumanosque* (Tac. *hist.* 3.13). For legio I adiutrix, Tac. *hist.* 1.6, 2.67; Emil Ritterling, "Legio," in *Paulys Realencyclopädie der classischen Altertumswissenschaft* XII pt. 2 (Stuttgart: Metzler 1925), pp. 1380–404.

17 See Ritterling, "Legio," pp. 1437–56.

18 The naval forces supporting the campaigns of Agricola in the first century and of Septimius Severus in the third must have been considerable; in the second half of the fourth century the later emperor Julian operated in the Rhine estuary with a fleet of six hundred ships, four hundred of which had been specifically constructed for the campaign; Jul. *Ep. ad Ath.* 279d-80a [Friedrich K. Hertlein, ed., *Iuliani imperatoris quae supersunt praeter reliquias apud Cyrillum omnia* (Leipzig: Teubner, 1875)].

19 The clearest example is Caesar's second expedition in AD 54, where he had twenty-eight warships and more than six hundred transports at his disposal; Caes. *Gall.* 5.2 [Wolfgang Hering, ed., *C. Iulii Caesaris commentarii rerum gestarum, Vol. i: Bellum Gallicum* (Leipzig: Teubner, 1987)].

20 In the late second and early third centuries, *optiones navaliorum,* usually understood to be army non-commissioned officers in charge of shipbuilding, are attested in two inscriptions from CIL 13 6712 and 6714 [Otto Hirschfeld and Karl Friedrich Wilhelm Zangemeister, eds., *Inscriptiones Trium Galliarum et Germaniarum latinae. Inscriptiones Germaniae Superioris. Partis secundae fasciculus I* (Berlin: G. Reimer, 1905)]. *Navalia* are further mentioned in CIL 13 11827 [Otto Hirschfeld and Hermann Finke, eds., *Inscriptiones Trium Galliarum et Germaniarum latinae.. consilio et auctoritate Academiae litterarum regiae Borussicae editae. Addenda ad partes prima et secundam* (Berlin: G. Reimer, 1916)]. See Peter Herz, "Zeugnisse römischen Schiffsbaus in Mainz. Die Severer und die expeditio Britannica," *Jahrbuch des Römisch-Germanischen Zentralmuseums* 32 (1985), pp. 425–26. See also Marcus Nenninger, *Die Römer und der Wald* (Stuttgart, Ger.: Franz Steiner, 2001), p. 177.

21 Dig. 50.6.7(6) [Theodor Mommsen and Paul Krüger, *Corpus Iuris Civilis. Vol. I: Institutiones et Digesta* (Berlin: Weidmann, 1911)].

22 RIB 653 [Robin G. Collingwood and Richard P. Wright, eds., *The Roman Inscriptions of Britain. Vol. I: Inscriptions on Stone* (Oxford: Clarendon Press, 1965)]. Mat[ribus] Af[ris] Ita[lis] Ga[llis] / M[arcus] Minu[cius] Aude[n]s / mil[es] leg[ionis] VI Vic[tricis] / guber[nator] leg[ionis] VI / u[otum] s[olvit] l[ibens] l[aetus] m[erito].

23 See, for example, Wilhelm Piepers, "Teile römischer Schiffsanker vom Niederrhein," *Bonner Jahrbücher* 174 (1974), p. 565f, for an anchor with *L V* [= legio V] inscribed on it.

24 Some legions produced tiles stamped with pictures of warships. See, for example, Oliver Höckmann, "Darstellungen von zwei römischen Ziegelstempeln aus Mainz," *Archäologisches Korrespondenzblatt* 14 (1984), p. 321 and tables 39–40.

25 See, for example, Caesar's preparations for his first expedition to England in 55 BC; Caes. *Gall.* 4.22.1–3.

26 For his campaign against the Veneti in 56 BC Caesar apparently hired rowers from southern Gaul. Ibid., 3.9.1.

27 For the enigmatic *cohortes novae tironum orae maritimae* attested on several inscriptions from Spain, see John Spaul, *Cohors 2: The Evidence for and a Short History of the Auxiliary Infantry Units of the Imperial Roman Army* (Oxford, U.K.: Archaeopress, 2000), pp. 137–38.

28 See Raymond H. Lacey, *The Equestrian Officials of Trajan and Hadrian* (Princeton, N.J.: Princeton Univ. Press, 1917), p. 36; Starr, *Roman Imperial Navy,* pp. 112–13; and Reddé, *Mare Nostrum,* pp. 288–90. The relationship of river guards to the classis Alexandrina is not clear; in the second century AD at least one *praefectus* of the *classis,* Lucius Valerius Proculus, also held simultaneously the command over the *potamophylaces;* see Zyromski, *Praefectus Classis,* pp. 121–23, and Spaul, *Classes Imperii Romani,* p. 47. On the *potamophylaces* see

also Kienast, *Untersuchungen zu den Kriegsflotten der römischen Kaiserzeit,* pp. 84–86.

29 On the classis Syriaca, which in the past has not exactly been a focus of scholarly attention, see Starr, *Roman Imperial Navy,* pp. 114–17; Peter Thomsen, "Die römische Flotte in Palästina-Syrien," *Beiträge zur biblischen Landes- und Altertumskunde* 68 (1951), pp. 73–89; Kienast, *Untersuchungen zu den Kriegsflotten der römischen Kaiserzeit,* pp. 87–97; Denis B. Saddington, "The Roman Naval Presence in the East," *Archäologisches Korrespondenzblatt* 31 (2001), pp. 581–86; and Heinrich Konen, "Migration und Mobilität unter den Angehörigen der Alexandrinischen und Syrischen Flotte," *Laverna* 14 (2003), pp. 18–47.

30 On Seleucia in general see Victor Chapot, "Séleucie de Piérie," *Mémoires de la Société Nationale des Antiquaires de France* 66 (1906), pp. 149–226; Ernst Honigmann, "Seleucia (Pieria)," *Realencyclopädie der Klassischen Altertumswissenschaften* 2 A (1923), pp. 1184–2000; Henri Seyrig, "Le Cimetière des marins à Séleucie Piérie," in *Mélanges syriens offerts à R. Dussaud par ses amis et ses élèves* (Paris: Geuthner, 1939), vol. 1, pp. 451–59; Denis van Berchem, "Le port de Séleucie Piérie et l'infrastructure logistique des guerres parthiques," *Bonner Jahrbücher* 185 (1985), pp. 47–87; and Winfried Held, "Die Residenzstädte der Seleukiden," *Jahrbuch des Deutschen Archäologischen Instituts* 117 (2002), pp. 217–49, esp. 240–41. For its importance as a logistics hub for the Roman army in the eastern part of the empire, see van Berchem, "Le port de Séleucie Piérie," pp. 47–50, and Theodor Kissel, *Untersuchungen zur Logistik des römischen Heeres in den Provinzen des griechischen Ostens 27 v. Chr.–235 n. Chr.* (St. Katharinen, Ger.: Scripta Mercaturae, 1995), pp. 72–74.

31 See Oguz Erol and Paolo A. Pirazzoli, "Seleucia Pieria: An Ancient Harbour Submitted to Two Successive Uplifts," *International Journal of Nautical Archaeology* 21 (1992), pp. 317–27, esp. 320–21.

32 In fact, there are around five times as many inscriptions mentioning sailors from the Misenate *classis* as inscriptions mentioning sailors from the classis Syriaca; see Kienast, *Untersuchungen zu den Kriegsflotten der römischen Kaiserzeit,* p. 93; Konen, "Migration und Mobilität," p. 39; and van Berchem, "Le port de Séleucie Piérie," p. 64. The topography of the city is still largely in the dark; apart from some preliminary research during the major excavation campaigns at nearby Antioch—on which see Richard Stillwell, ed., *The Excavations 1937–1939, Antioch-on-the-Orontes III* (Princeton, N.J.: Princeton Univ. Press, 1941), pp. 31–34—little archaeological work has been done on the site.

33 For the British Museum papyrus see Vincenzo Arangio-Ruiz, Giovanni Baviera, and Salvatore Riccobono, eds., *Fontes iuris Romani anteiustiniani,* vol. 3, *Negotia* (Florence, It.: Barbera, 1943), no. 132, and Robert Cavenaile, ed., *Corpus Papyrorum Latinarum* (Wiesbaden, Ger.: Harrassowitz, 1958), no. 120. It is dated to 24 May AD 166 (ll. 29–30).

34 Lines 26–28: *Actum Seleuciae Pieriae, in / castris in hibernis vexillationis / clas[sis] pr[aetoriae] Misenatium.*

35 On *liburnae* see Olaf Höckmann, "The Liburnian: Some Observations and Insights," *International Journal of Nautical Archaeology* 26 (1997), pp. 192–216; John F. Coats, "The Naval Architecture and Oar Systems of Ancient Galleys," in *The Age of the Galley,* ed. Robert Gardiner (London: Conway, 1995), p. 141; and Lionel Casson, *Ships and Seamanship in the Ancient World* (Princeton, N.J.: Princeton Univ. Press, 1971), pp. 141–42.

36 Only two inscriptions belonging to the classis Syriaca mention warships by name, and in both cases these are of the *liburna* type; there is similar, though scanty, evidence from other provincial *classes*. The Italian *classes*, however, consisted mainly of triremes and larger penteremes. See Spaul, *Classes Imperii Romani,* pp. 74–83.

37 For Pompey's campaign of 67 BC see Philip de Souza, *Piracy in the Graeco-Roman World* (Cambridge, U.K.: Cambridge Univ. Press, 1999), pp. 149–78.

38 See Marc Corby, "Cavalry Deployment on the Northern Frontier," in *Polybius to Vegetius: Essays on the Roman Army and Hadrian's Wall Presented to Brian Dobson,* ed. Peter R. Hill (Nottingham, U.K.: Hadrianic Society, 2002), pp. 103–107.

39 Konen, "Migration und Mobilität," pp. 40–42. See, however, Starr, *Roman Imperial Navy,* pp. 117–20. The inscription reads, in part (CIL 8 7030): *"curatoribus et tutoribus dandis / primo constituto curatori Nola / norum fratri Arvali augur[i] sodali Mar / ciano Antoniniano iuridico regionis / Transpadaneae curatori Ariminien / sium curatori civitatum per Aemili / am aedili curuli ab actis senatus se / viro equitum Romanorum quaest[ori] / urbano tribuno leg[ionis] IIII Scythicae / quattuorviro viarum curanda / rum patrono IIII col[oniarum] / C[aius] Iulius Libo triarchus classis no / vae Lybic[a]e patrono d[edit] d[edicavit]. . . ."*

40 For the classis Anderetianorum see ND occ. 42.23 [Otto Seeck, ed., *Notitia dignitatum: accedunt Notitia urbis Constantinopolitanae et Laterculi provinciarum* (Berlin: Weidmann, 1876)], for the classis Sambrica, ND occ. 38.8. See also Robert E. Grosse, *Römische Militärgeschichte von Gallienus bis zum Beginn der byzantinischen Themenverfassung* (Berlin: Weidmann, 1920), pp. 71–72, 76.

41 See, for example, David Mason, *Roman Britain and the Roman Navy* (Stroud, U.K.: Tempus, 2003), pp. 170–71.

42 Cod. Th. 10.23 [Theodor Mommsen and Paul Meyer, eds., *Theodosiani libri xvi cum constitutionibus Sirmondianis et leges novellae ad Theodosianum pertinentes* (Berlin: Weidmann, 1905)]. See Nigel Pollard, *Soldiers, Cities and Civilians in Roman Syria* (Ann Arbor: Univ. of Michigan Press, 2000), p. 281.

43 For a list of naval units of late antiquity see Grosse, *Römische Militärgeschichte,* pp. 70–77; Grosse lists twenty-seven units, including those operating on rivers and lakes, of which only three are attested before AD 300.

44 On this phenomenon see Ramsay MacMullen, "The Epigraphical Habit in the Roman Empire," *American Journal of Philology* 103 (1982), pp. 233–46, and Elizabeth A. Meyer, "Explaining the Epigraphic Habit in the Roman Empire: The Evidence of Epitaphs," *Journal of Roman Studies* 80 (1990), pp. 74–96.

III Toward a Model of Piracy
Lessons from the Seventeenth-Century Caribbean

VIRGINIA LUNSFORD

The spate of attacks by Somali pirates in recent years has taken the world by surprise. Now, Nigerian pirates are making themselves known as well, and they present a growing problem. That piracy exists today—and exists in a form powerful enough to produce hundreds of attacks and captures—surprises many. Indeed, this is not the mythical and romanticized piracy of Hollywood, of ships flying the Jolly Roger and "swashbuckling" captains in search of buried treasure. No, this piracy—like all true piracy—is disturbing, frightening, and costly. It has also been irrepressible. Various naval assets, including a multinational naval task force with U.S. Navy participation (Combined Task Force 151, established in 2009), have been conducting counterpiracy operations in the Gulf of Aden and off Somalia's coast for the last several years, and their presence appears to have resulted in a decrease in piratical activity.[1] Attacks and captures are still occurring, however, and show no sign of ceasing altogether; also, the pirates are becoming more creative in their approach and expanding their reach geographically.[2] Indeed, the United Nations secretary-general, Ban Ki-moon, warns that "while the effectiveness of naval disruption operations has increased and more pirates have been arrested and prosecuted, this has not stopped piracy. The trend of the increased levels of violence employed by the pirates as well as their expanding reach is disconcerting."[3]

The secretary-general's frustrations have long been felt by those charged with suppressing piracy, for as history reveals, the problem of entrenched and flourishing piracy has never been solved by high-seas naval action alone. The "Golden Age of Piracy," from about 1530 to around 1730, was the time in history when seagoing robbery was most prevalent, extensive, profitable, and threatening. Throughout the era and around the globe, a variety of piratical groups practiced their trade. Their depredations challenged the authority of the expanding European empires and the viability of the nascent world economy. As Marcus Rediker has said about piracy vis-à-vis the eighteenth-century British, "pirates created an imperial crisis with their relentless and successful attacks upon merchants' property and international commerce.... Their numbers ... were extraordinary, and their plunderings were exceptional in both volume and value."[4] His comment could be equally applied to the Dutch, the French, the Portuguese, and the party who probably was victimized most severely, the Spanish.

Those who endeavor to combat contemporary piracy would be wise to look back in time, to this Golden Age of Piracy of the sixteenth, seventeenth, and eighteenth centuries. These early-modern episodes provide instructive case studies that reveal how piracy blooms and flourishes over time. In turn, they offer us ways to analyze the pirates of the contemporary world—including those now operating off the coasts of Somalia and Nigeria—so that we can ascertain these modern raiders' viability and learn how to combat them. Although the means, ends, locations, and characters of Golden Age pirate groups often differed noticeably from one to another, pirate communities that achieved lengthy and remunerative existences shared several key qualities. In sum, long-term, intractable, thriving piracy is a complex activity that relies on six integral factors: an available population of potential recruits, access to goods (via vulnerable trade routes or places where wealth is stockpiled), at least one secure base of operations, a sophisticated organization, some degree of outside support, and cultural bonds engendering vibrant group solidarity. Actions that interfere with the smooth workings of any of these factors, especially with more than one, weaken the piracy's sustainability.

Elsewhere, I have analyzed the example of the North African corsairs, whose marauding activities lasted for some three hundred years.[5] The Caribbean buccaneers represent yet another important case study. Who were the buccaneers? The term is typically but erroneously utilized to refer to pirates in general. In actuality, the "Buccaneers" proper (as it will be given hereafter) were a specific group of marauders: a motley yet ferocious brotherhood based in the seventeenth-century Caribbean. While various European countries suffered from their depredations at one time or another, their central operational goals were to assault Spain's American colonies, prey on Spain's lucrative trade in the Americas, and raid Spanish ships bound for Europe. This they did with great savagery and ferocity. The movement expanded over time, ultimately boasting invasion forces numbering in the hundreds and even thousands of men. It captured a number of Spanish ships and, even more strikingly, conquered established and sizable Spanish settlements in the Caribbean, despite the colonies' formidable defensive measures. The wealth the Buccaneers plundered is staggering in its value; the numbers of settlements they attacked and of people they brutally tortured and slew are stunning.

The Buccaneers' piratical endeavors were serious, sensational, and sustained over a lengthy duration of time. Their success can be attributed in large part to the fact that these Caribbean marauders met the six conditions for successful and long-term piracy. That is, they possessed a steady supply of available (and talented) recruits; access to Spanish trade in the Caribbean as well as to Spanish colonial settlements, both coastal and inland; several secure bases of operations; sophisticated organization; financial and political support from several European states; and intense cultural bonds engendering tight group solidarity. The result was a community of fierce, brutal, and seemingly invincible marauders who voraciously raided and terrorized the Caribbean for decades (c. 1600–c. 1700, especially c. 1650–1700).

Our knowledge of Buccaneer exploits and practices comes from a remarkable primary source, Alexander Exquemelin's *Buccaneers of America,* a physician's candid account of his life among the marauders (hereafter, citations to his work, aside from glosses, are given as page numbers in the text).[6] Exquemelin's work, first published in Amsterdam in 1678 as *De Americaensche Zee-Roovers* and thereafter translated into various foreign languages and reprinted a myriad of times, is a rare and revealing window into the history of this long-lost brotherhood. In his remarkably vivid and densely detailed text, Exquemelin recounts his knowledge about the seventeenth-century West Indies, describing its flora and fauna, the customs of its native inhabitants, its climate and weather, the region's natural resources, and the food, occupations, and colorful lifestyles of the colonists. He is no less attentive in presenting information about the Buccaneer community—of which he was a member, serving as a "surgeon" (medical officer) during the era of Henry Morgan—and provides a unique glimpse into this elusive criminal group. Furthermore, what makes Exquemelin's account even more valuable is that it is generally reliable; modern historians judge it to be largely accurate in its descriptions.[7]

These descriptions include revealing accounts of Buccaneer mores, missions, tactics, and means of attack and thus give us greater insight into how this force of outsiders could have been so effective in challenging the organized state power of Spain. The Buccaneers came into existence organically, developing from a concentration of dispossessed hunters and indentured servants on the islands of Hispaniola and Tortuga. Originally French in origin and always retaining a heavy French contingent, their community came to include men of a variety of European ethnic backgrounds, most significantly English and Dutch.

From their first forays around 1602 until the movement ended about a hundred years later, the Buccaneers pressed the Spanish relentlessly. Even more striking, Buccaneer warfare escalated and evolved over the course of the century, transforming itself from mere ship-on-ship attacks by crews of between twenty-five and thirty to sophisticated amphibious landings that involved hundreds, ultimately thousands, of men who raided substantial settlements—sometimes far inland—that they occupied for weeks or even months after victory. One cautious estimate avers that between 1655 and 1671 alone, the Buccaneers sacked eighteen cities, four towns, and thirty-five villages.[8] The monetary results of these raids were impressive; while earlier practitioners, such as the crews of Pierre François of Dunkirk and Bartoloméo Portugues, managed to capture prizes of, respectively, a hundred thousand and seventy thousand pieces of eight, later missions resulted in heists valued conservatively at 250,000–260,000 pieces of eight—and these estimates do not include such ancillary proceeds as slaves, munitions, grain, herds of cattle, and textiles (passim). The Buccaneers sought to capture lucrative goods, ships, property, and people (that is, those who could be ransomed quickly), for their intent was simply to amass as much wealth as possible.

The Spaniards—and later, other European powers who established colonies in the Caribbean—tried to combat the marauders' assaults by sending more soldiers, amassing greater numbers of arms, and building stronger fortifications;[9] nevertheless, colonial settlements often remained quite defenseless.[10] Consequently, beyond the loss of goods and capital, the Buccaneers left death, despoliation, and destruction in their wake. Part and parcel of the Buccaneer style was the constant and often creative use of brutal violence to achieve desired ends. Exquemelin dispassionately reports "the usual manner" of tortures the Buccaneers used.[11] For example, they routinely put their prisoners on the rack, dislocating their arms; in a torture known as "woolding," they twisted cords around their victims' foreheads and wrung so hard that their victims' "eyes bulged out, big as eggs" (p. 200); they hanged prisoners, whipped and bludgeoned them, sliced off noses and ears, singed faces with burning straws, and finally stabbed them to death. Prisoners were strappadoed "so violently that . . . [their] arms were pulled right out of joint."[12] Captives' hair was set on fire, burning fuses were placed between their fingers and toes, and they were crushed by rocks and stones until they were bloody and broken (pp. 147–50, 200). Women were kidnapped, abused, raped, and held for ransom.[13] Children were starved, forced to march long distances, and allowed to perish. Men were hung by their genitals "till the weight of their bodies tore them loose," after which the Buccaneers "would give the wretches three or four stabs through the body with a cutlass. . . . Others they crucified" (p. 151).

Perhaps the barbarous François l'Ollonais stands out for his sheer inventiveness in the infliction of sadistic cruelty:

> The Buccaneers . . . took a number of prisoners, whom they treated most cruelly, inflicting on these poor folk every torment imaginable. When l'Olonnais had a victim on the rack, if the wretch did not instantly answer his questions he would hack the man to pieces with his cutlass and lick the blood from the blade with his tongue. . . . After most of their prisoners had been done to death by the cruelest atrocities, the Buccaneers at last found two . . . men to lead them to their next destination. . . . Then l'Olonnais, being possessed of a devil's fury, ripped open one of the prisoners with his cutlass, tore the living heart out of his body, gnawed at it, and then hurled it in the face of one of the others, saying, "Show me another way, or I will do the same to you."[14]

No less repugnant were the practices of the "maniac" Dutchman Rock Bresiliaan, who, according to Exquemelin, "perpetrated the greatest atrocities possible against the Spaniards. Some of them he tied or spitted on wooden stakes and roasted them alive between two fires, like killing a pig" (p. 80). Other sources relate the gruesome tale of a woman captive who, according to Spanish reports, was "set bare upon a baking stove and roasted, because she did not confess of money" (p. 80). Equally grisly was Montbars of Languedoc, who sliced open the stomachs of his victims, removing one end of the intestines and nailing it to a post, thereafter forcing the prisoners to dance to their deaths by beating their buttocks with burning logs.[15]

In addition to extreme human suffering, this Buccaneer carnage wrought great damage on Spanish colonial trade. The entire Spanish economic system relied on American bullion, primarily Peruvian silver. Spain's claims in the Caribbean and Central American region (incontestably validated, so Spain argued, by God via the pope in the 1494 Treaty of Tordesillas) were organized into a colonial system predicated on the fundamental need to ensure the successful extraction, transport, and delivery of this precious resource.[16] Settlement patterns, military defense, naval operations, and political administration were largely dictated by the supreme need to safeguard the transit of the annual "treasure fleets," each carrying the year's cargo of precious metal, from the West Indies to Seville. The Buccaneers regularly attacked key nodes, pinpointing such "treasure ports" as Vera Cruz, Cartagena, Porto Bello, and Panama for raids and causing Spain to spend money and resources to protect the system's vulnerabilities. Naturally, Buccaneer assaults on intercoastal traffic within the Spanish West Indies dampened local trade as well. As Exquemelin relates, "The Spaniards were compelled to equip . . . frigates to protect their shipping and cruise against the Buccaneers . . . [and] were driven to reduce the number of their [merchant] voyages—but this did them no good" (pp. 69, 83).

The military apparatus guarding Spain's Caribbean colonial system was not inconsequential and, in retrospect, was quite effective against assaults in general. It is easy to focus only on the penetrations of this system, the victories obtained by attackers, and conclude that Spain's defense against outside challengers was flimsy. However, as Paul Hoffman, who has examined the elements of the Spanish defense system in great detail, concludes, the Spanish system was difficult to breach; attackers required both military ingenuity and a concentration of resources if they hoped to achieve their goals.[17] While imperfect and sometimes erratic in its implementation, the defense system consisted of a formidable network of designated nodes (the treasure ports and smaller, ancillary cities) protected by extensive and often well-armed fortifications, several dedicated fleets, local naval patrols, garrisons of Spanish soldiers, and local militias. The Spanish also collected and utilized relevant intelligence and transported the most valuable cargoes under secrecy and heavily armed naval escort.[18] Havana—the jewel in the Caribbean colonial crown, as it were, and the most important of the treasure ports—was so heavily protected that attackers never did it any real damage and indeed were usually hesitant to attack it at all (pp. 128–29). Proof that the defensive system largely worked over several centuries is that the all-important annual treasure fleet was captured only once (1628), despite many attempts to take it.[19]

So how were the Buccaneers able to succeed to the extent they did against this formidable Spanish system? What were the keys to their terrifying effectiveness? One can cite many Buccaneer advantages, including their tactical creativity and flexibility. Paramount, however, was their possession of the six qualities integral to resilient piracy.

First, the Buccaneers had access to a near-limitless pool of potential recruits—alienated, indigent, and dispossessed sailors, soldiers, hunters, and indentured servants who represented the flotsam and jetsam of the harsh colonial systems of France, England, and the Netherlands. Indeed, the Buccaneering movement had its origin in a coterie of French boar and bull hunters on French Hispaniola and Tortuga (a small island off the northwestern coast of Hispaniola), and these hunters continued to support and join the movement as it evolved and expanded (pp. 54–59, 68, 167–68). Sailors and soldiers drifted into the group as well.[20]

According to Exquemelin, however, indentured servants from the French colony of Tortuga/Hispaniola and, after 1655, the English colony of Jamaica represented an especially significant source of men.[21] The rough lives of these men, typically characterized by "atrocious cruelties" and deprivation, noted Exquemelin, toughened and hardened them both physically and psychologically (pp. 55–57, 64–66). Servants who managed to survive their terms of indenture were free but lacked means to support themselves. Thus, they naturally gravitated toward buccaneering, Exquemelin relates, drawing from personal experience. Exquemelin himself had been an indentured servant of the French West India Company on Tortuga. When he completed his period of servitude (which he characterized as very cruel and exploitative, he having fallen "into the hands of the wickedest rogue in the whole island"), he was penniless and, devoid of other opportunities, had no choice, he tells his readers, but to join the Buccaneers (p. 34). Even such celebrated Buccaneer captains as François l'Ollonais and Henry Morgan initially arrived in the Caribbean as indentured servants.[22]

Second, the Buccaneers enjoyed secure and permanent bases of operation, namely, the two islands of Tortuga and Jamaica. The existence of a refuge was hardwired into the movement, in fact, for the brotherhood was born in Tortuga and French Hispaniola in the early years of the seventeenth century, and it was based on Tortuga thereafter. Although early on, Spain tried twice to invade and capture Tortuga to quell the movement and eradicate the growing French presence there, the island's mountainous terrain ultimately made this effort impossible (pp. 31–33). When in 1655 the English invaded and captured Jamaica, buccaneering immediately spread there as well. By the mid-seventeenth-century, then, the movement was firmly entrenched in two key locations, Port Royal (Jamaica) and Tortuga, with Buccaneers from each location freely communicating, supporting, and joining forces with one another (pp. 119–21, 128, 141, 167–68). As a result, the movement quickly intensified, expanding in numbers and evolving in scope and mission (pp. 83–85). Moreover, in addition to these two permanent bases, the Buccaneers utilized an informal network of isolated islands and coastal locations as temporary staging bases and rendezvous points. These spots—such places as Cabo Gracias a Dios, Isla de la Vaca, Bayamo, and islets off the southern coast of Cuba, Bleeckveldt Bay, Cabo Tiburón, and El Golfo Triste—functioned as temporary havens where the Buccaneers could acquire provisions, careen and repair ships, and meet with one another (pp. 72, 79, 80, 168, 171, 215, 219, 224).

Fortunately for the Buccaneers, Tortuga's and Jamaica's strategic locations within the Caribbean gave the marauders a third key advantage—easy access to Spain's colonial settlements and to local and transatlantic shipping routes. The Buccaneers were close to the lively intercoastal traffic of Spanish Hispaniola, Cuba, and the Spanish Main. The treasure ports of Cartagena and Porto Bello were nearby (and Havana too, for that matter, although as noted they opted never to attack seriously this supremely fortified location) (pp. 128–29). Vulnerable settlements, remunerative as targets, abounded. Indeed, as the crow flies, no target was more than a couple of weeks' sail away (p. 69). Occasional impediments, such as uncooperative weather or currents, Spanish naval patrols, hostile or recalcitrant native peoples, or a lack of provisions, sometimes presented problems (for example, see pp. 113–17, 209–18). In general, however, Tortuga and Jamaica offered superb, centrally located staging grounds and sanctuaries. Moreover, these bases were made available by a fourth Buccaneer advantage—the support of the outside parties of France and England, who envied Spanish predominance in the region and aimed to strengthen their own hands at Spanish expense.

Per the Treaty of Tordesillas, the Spanish considered the Caribbean region to be theirs alone; thus all other Europeans were in Spanish eyes invaders and interlopers. Naturally, the French, English, and Dutch were eager to break this Spanish monopoly. All three aided the Buccaneers by providing sporadic legal protection (such as occasional letters of reprisal), donations of materiel, trade opportunities, and injections of capital.[23] Even more important, the French and English eagerly welcomed the quasi-military support that the Buccaneers offered on the colonies of Tortuga and Jamaica. After all, even if the French and English authorities could not directly control the marauders, hosting them in Tortuga and Jamaica delivered formidable advantages. True, the Buccaneers followed no outside party's orders per se, but they represented both a savage attack force that did great damage to the Spanish colonial system and a body of fearless defenders who protected Tortuga and Port

Royal. Additionally, they were the source of periodic economic stimulus, returning from operations with their plunder and spending it in wild orgies and debauchery (pp. 81–82).

Spain, obviously aware of this French and English complicity, repeatedly endeavored to use diplomatic entreaties and pressure at the highest levels to end it. However, taking advantage of the plausible deniability that hosting the Buccaneers conferred, the French and English monarchs ignored the Spanish protestations. Both claimed they had neither knowledge of Buccaneer activities nor control over them. As Exquemelin explains,

> The [Spanish] ambassadors were informed that these men were not subjects of the French and English kings. . . . The King of France excused himself by saying he had no fortifications on Hispaniola [or Tortuga], and received no tribute from the island. The King of England declared he had never commissioned those on Jamaica to conduct hostilities against His Catholic Majesty [of Spain], and to satisfy the Spanish court he recalled the governor of Jamaica and installed another in his place. Meanwhile, the rovers continued their marauding. (p. 67)

Two other factors were central to Buccaneer success, and they were no less instrumental: effective organization and intense cultural solidarity. These qualities both derived from one of the most distinguishing and core qualities of the Buccaneers, their radical and homegrown form of direct democracy. Indeed, this was the fundamental around which their entire society was arranged, the virtue that anchored their special community. The fluid and egalitarian system resulting from their democratic practices and culture produced a potent force of highly organized, passionately committed, cohesive, and adaptable warriors who were impressively successful in their military exploits.

According to Exquemelin, when men joined the Buccaneers they entered a separate culture, a vibrant and rich "manner of living" and "way of life" (pp. 70, 119, 156); it was a society marked by, in the words of pioneering sociologist Émile Durkheim, a distinctive "collective consciousness" that enabled its members to establish deep bonds of solidarity despite their large numbers, their traditional rugged self-reliance, the geographical dislocation between French Tortuga and English Jamaica, and their diverse ethnic backgrounds.[24] Participation in the brotherhood was entirely voluntary; the only requirement was that each member bring "what he needs in the way of weapons, powder and shot."[25] There was no formal hierarchy within the society, no system of operational rank or chain of command. All Buccaneers were equal in status. Together, they resolved "by common vote where they shall cruise" and to that end collectively drew up for each foray a sort of labor agreement —which they called the *"chasse partie"* (literally, the "division of the hunt")—that specified the terms for the mission and the distribution of the profits. Typical *chasse parties* called for equal wages among the men, after the needs of the carpenters, the provisioners, the ship, and the wounded had been met.[26] As Exquemelin explains, "Everything taken—money, jewels, precious stones and goods—must be shared among them all, without any man enjoying a penny more than his fair share" (pp. 71–72).

The functioning of this brotherhood of equals participating in a direct democracy relied on honor, trust, and integrity. The Buccaneers were, as Exquemelin notes, "extremely loyal and ready to help one another." They also were "generous to their comrades: if a man has nothing, the others will come to his help" (pp. 72, 82). Pledging commitment to their fellows and comportment in accordance with group dictates, the Buccaneers swore solemn oaths (on the Bible, no less) to the group and the group code. Before embarking on a military operation, they shook hands and swore oaths "to stand by each other till death" (p. 100). The oath, then, played a vital role in the functioning of the society, in recognition of which the brotherhood declared that "should any man be found to have made a false oath, he would be banished from the rovers, and never more be allowed in their company" (p. 72). They had a justice system—"the duel is their way of settling disputes"—but again, dishonorable conduct in a duel brought severe punishment, execution (pp. 72, 133). During the course of missions—especially those that were large in scope, involving thousands of men—a modicum of "military" order and rank was established, but this stratification was temporary and existed only because the men complied with it. Thus the system of rank was not hierarchical in the classic sense but existed rather for the sake of military efficiency and the sensible division of labor. And always, all major decisions were determined by common vote (pp. 100, 171–73).

There was a mission leader—the captain—but he was chosen by the other Buccaneers (usually because of his courage, experience, access to a ship, or military ingenuity) and thus led only because his men permitted him to do so.[27] Even in cases where a man possessed his own ship and thus considered himself to be a "captain," the other Buccaneers could choose whether they wished to work under his command.[28] If men became dissatisfied with a captain's leadership, they reserved the right to leave (for example, pp. 133, 207–208). Additionally, while a captain always retained the luster of his fame and the influence that renown conferred, once an operation was over his formal leadership power evaporated. The captain's status, then, was mission-specific and temporary; he was only the first among equals, so to speak, and his rank was bestowed on him by his brother Buccaneers, making him the creature of his men. He was the leader, yes, but was considered no better than any other brother and had to rely on the men's goodwill and concurrence in order to lead. While he had the right and responsibility to provide *military* leadership during a mission, his underlying equality in *social* status was manifested in Buccaneer mores. Exquemelin explains, for example, that "the captain is allowed no better fare than the meanest on board. If they notice he has better food, the men bring the dish from their own mess and exchange it for the captain's." Likewise, "when a ship has been captured, the men decide whether the captain should keep it or not" (pp. 70–71). Also, the captain's portion of the profits, which were typically a bit greater in compensation for his leadership, had to be authorized and voted on by the men (p. 172).

Notwithstanding these constraints, Buccaneer captains inspired fervent loyalty from the men. These captains, apparently imbued with special qualities, such as unusual bravery and insight, appear to have enjoyed the distinctive allure of what Max Weber termed "charismatic domination."[29] As a result, a captain was recognized as "singular" and was duly honored by his peers' election of him to the supreme position of power within Buccaneer society. Because of the brotherhood's democratic process, however, each man had a say in the leadership and thus followed because he *wanted* to follow. As Weber said about those who hold charismatic authority, "the leader is personally recognized as the innerly 'called' leader of men. Men do not obey him by virtue of tradition or statute, but because they believe in him."[30]

Buccaneering's democratic ethos and the practices that flowed from it contrasted strikingly with the rigid, hierarchical structure of regular European societies and militaries. During the seventeenth century, Western military culture was in the midst of the profound changes wrought by the early-modern "military revolution," the series of radical transformations that resulted in the creation of the modern, professional, military force. Armies (and navies) were growing in size and complexity, and the tactical role of the infantry and the technological capabilities of artillery were taking center stage. As the state amassed greater power and financial strength, it maintained large, standing military forces rather than disbanding them at the end of conflicts. These standing troops, in turn, were inculcated with both a sense of unity and national identification (manifested in the newly developed uniform) and a deep sense of discipline instilled through incessant drill and the strict, incontestable, and hierarchical leadership of a multitude of junior and middle-grade officers belonging to a new entity, the "professional officers corps."[31] Training was routinized, responsibilities were tied to rank, and as William McNeil avers, "soldiers became replaceable parts in a sort of human machine, and so did their officers."[32] Even England's New Model Army, the militarized arm of Cromwell's Puritan forces in the Civil War, retained a conventional, hierarchical structure and nature, despite the leveling rhetoric of Puritan ideology.[33] It is easy to see, then, how the comparatively liberating and democratic culture of the Buccaneers would be alluring to poor, young men, especially since their options elsewhere were bleak. Indeed, despite all the violence and dangers that the buccaneering life inevitably entailed, its participants remained devoted to their special brotherhood, Exquemelin affirms, "for they are so accustomed to the buccaneering life that it is impossible for them to give it up" (p. 226).

After decades of unbridled success, how did the Buccaneer phenomenon come to an end? Spanish naval intervention and tough defensive measures, while helpful in mitigating the effects of buccaneering, ultimately were not enough to eradicate it. Rather, the demise of buccaneering was primarily due to the weakening of several of the "six factors of piracy," as outlined above. Specifically, the Buccaneers lost the help of outside parties, their permanent bases of operations, and their sources of personnel.

The withdrawal of support from rival European states at the close of the seventeenth century had manifold consequences on the buccaneering movement and it certainly undercut the Buccaneers' strength. Eventually, France and England ceased to provide the levels of financial and legal aid they once had, since they were advancing their interests in the Caribbean in other ways. The Dutch, represented in the Caribbean by the Dutch West India Company, in due course discouraged trade with the marauders as well.[34] Moreover, starting in 1670, when Spain conceded the legality of England's claim to Jamaica, England gradually outlawed its use as a Buccaneer safe haven. At the same time, European states—especially England—were able to co-opt Buccaneers into their official imperial systems by conferring pardons, political and military positions, pecuniary rewards, and prestigious titles. In 1692, a devastating earthquake in Jamaica destroyed much of the infrastructure and personnel the Buccaneers had used to mount their campaigns and sustain their overall way of life. Ten years later, in 1702, when the War of the Spanish Succession erupted, Englishmen in Jamaica were freely given letters of marque to maraud legally as English privateers.[35] Not only did this action serve to bring these surviving Buccaneers under English state control, but it reinforced their English national identity and pitted them against their erstwhile Buccaneer brothers, the French, since France was England's primary adversary in the war. In combination, then, all of these factors eliminated the Buccaneers' safe havens, slashed the pool of possible recruits, lessened the availability of supplies and materiel, and interfered with the unique Buccaneer organization and culture, diluting its beliefs and weakening its bonds of solidarity.

As the world considers what to do about the increasingly problematic phenomenon of contemporary piracy, it would do well to think beyond superficial naval solutions on the high seas and consider also the six factors underlying the long and productive careers of the Caribbean buccaneers. Without a doubt, the key to eradicating Somali (and Nigerian) piracy is disrupting the larger, complex systems that support it. Yes, it is essential to protect maritime commerce in the region and to intercept the pirates in action on the high seas. In the case of Somali piracy, the multinational naval forces now on the scene in the Gulf of Aden should continue to meet this objective. However, Somali piracy is now deeply entrenched, and warships at sea monitoring maritime trade are not enough to quell it definitively. In fact, it is unreasonable to expect that the navies alone, working in isolation, without support, and charged with escort duties and patrols over a vast expanse of open sea, can eliminate Somali piracy. Although hardworking naval personnel may capture a pirate crew here or there or deter them from attacking, there are always more pirates waiting in the wings. And the longer the system supporting the piracy is permitted to stay in place and grow, the more intractable the problem will become. Above all, we must not underestimate contemporary piracy's potential severity simply because we arrogantly assume that pirates in small speedboats (the Somalis' preferred raiding craft) pose no "real" problem. This is the grave mistake that the Spanish of the seventeenth-century Caribbean made vis-à-vis the Buccaneers; such a misfit group with such makeshift means, they thought, was no threat to the power of the Spanish empire and its mighty military (pp. 68, 155–63). How very wrong they were. Indeed, this is one of the vital lessons that the history of the Golden Age of Piracy imparts, and along with our understanding of the six fundamental factors underlying the success of the Buccaneer enterprise, we would be most wise to remember it.

NOTES

1 "U.S. Reports That Piracy off Africa Has Plunged," *New York Times,* 29 August 2012, p. A4.

2 For more information on CTF-151, see *U.S. 5th Fleet: U.S. Naval Forces Central Command,* www.cusnc.navy.mil/. For the most current statistics regarding piracy off the Horn of Africa, see the *ICC Commercial Crime Services: IMB* [International Maritime Bureau] *Piracy Reporting Centre,* www.icc-ccs.org/piracy-reporting-centre.

3 Lauren Ploch et al., *Piracy off the Horn of Africa,* CRS Report for Congress (Washington, D.C.: Congressional Research Service, 27 April 2011), p. 1, available at fpc.state.gov/.

4 Marcus Rediker, *Between the Devil and the Deep Blue Sea: Merchant Seamen, Pirates, and the Anglo-American Maritime World, 1700–1750* (Cambridge, U.K.: Cambridge Univ. Press, 1987), pp. 254–55.

5 See Virginia Lunsford, "What Makes Piracy Work?," *Proceedings: The Independent Forum on National Defense* (December 2008), pp. 28–33.

6 A. O. Exquemelin, *De Americaensche Zee-Roovers . . .* (Amsterdam: Jan ten Hoorn, 1678). An incredibly popular text, *The Buccaneers of America* went through any number of reprintings and translations during the early-modern period. This paper uses the most accurate modern edition in English, one that provides an exact translation from the seventeenth-century Dutch: Alexander O. Exquemelin, *The Buccaneers of America,* trans. Alexis Brown (Mineola, N.Y.: Dover, 2000).

7 See, for example, David Cordingly, who writes of Exquemelin: "Careful comparison of his stories with the events described in Spanish documents of the period has shown that he gets most of the facts right but is often mistaken about place-names and dates. Some of his wilder stories appear to be secondhand accounts which he probably heard in taverns, but it is clear that he took part in a number of buccaneer expeditions. . . . Esquemelin's book . . . has provided the basis for all serious histories of the buccaneers and, in spite of some inaccuracies, remains the standard work on the subject"; David Cordingly, *Under the Black Flag: The Romance & Reality of Life among the Pirates* (New York: Random House, 1995), p. 40. For another balanced appraisal of Exquemelin, see Peter Earle, *The Sack of Panama: Sir Henry Morgan's Adventures on the Spanish Main* (London: Jill Norman & Hobhouse, 1981), pp. 265–66.

8 Jack Beeching, introduction to Exquemelin, *Buccaneers of America,* p. 13.

9 See, for example, the report in the *Ordinaire Leydse Courant,* 29 August 1686, "Nederlanden" section, relating that the French had just sent four frigates to America "to suppress the pirates there."

10 For more on beleaguered Spanish outposts and the Crown's attempts to protect them, see the following documents in the General Archive of the Indies, Seville, Spain: Panama 30, N. 68: *Cartas y Expedientes de Cabildos Seculares: Panamá,* 1616; Mexico 28, N. 28; Panama 95: *Entrada de Piratas en Portobelo, Darien y Mar del Sur,* 1679–1681; Panama 96: *Entrada de Piratas en Portobelo, Darien y Mar del Sur,* 1682–1687; Indiferente 2578: *Piratas en las Costas de Barlovento,* 1681–1684; Santo Domingo 856: *Invasión de Piratas en la Florida,* 1684–1702;

Guatemala 42, N. 77: *Caratas de Cabildos Seculares,* 18 March 1671; Panama 81: *Empréstito de 1000,000 Pesos para Rescutar Portobelo,* 1678; and Panama 99: *Resguardo del Darién y Tierra Firme contra la Piratería,* 1683–1694.

11 For examples, Exquemelin, *Buccaneers of America,* pp. 147, 169, 226.

12 Ibid., p. 150. In this torture, the victim's hands are fastened behind his or her back. The arms are then pulled up by means of a rope attached at one end to the wrists and led through a pulley on the other. The pulley end of the rope is then jerked, causing pain and most likely dislocating both arms. Sometimes weights were added to the victim's body to intensify the pain and physical damage.

13 Ibid., passim. See, for example, p. 201.

14 Ibid., pp. 106–107. It seems fitting that, according to Exquemelin, l'Ollonais met his own horrible end, imprisoned by native American peoples by whom he "was hacked to pieces and roasted limb by limb" (p. 117).

15 Cordingly, *Under the Black Flag,* pp. 127, 129, 131–32.

16 The Treaty of Tordesillas effectively declared that the entire New World belonged to Spain and Portugal.

17 Paul Hoffman, *The Spanish Crown and the Defense of the Caribbean, 1535–1585: Precedent, Patrimonialism, and Royal Parsimony* (Baton Rouge, La.: LSU Press, 1999), p. 224.

18 Ibid., passim.

19 In 1628, a Dutch West India Company fleet led by Piet Heyn captured the treasure fleet in Cuba.

20 For example, see Exquemelin, *Buccaneers of America,* pp. 80, 93. Moreover, the English settlement of Jamaica in 1655 was the result of a failed Cromwellian military invasion of Santo Domingo. Thus there were a plethora of soldiers among the colonial Jamaican population. For more about the character of the English military at this time, see Mark Kishlansky, "The Case of the Army Truly Stated: The Creation of the New Model Army," *Past and Present,* no. 81 (November 1978), pp. 51–74.

21 It was in 1655 that the English invaded and took over the island of Jamaica.

22 Exquemelin, *Buccaneers of America,* pp. 89, 119. Morgan himself disputed this claim and affirmed that he had never been an indentured servant.

23 For example, ibid., pp. 63, 89, 171; J. J. Baud, *Proeve eener Geschiedenis der Strafwetgeving tegen de Zeerooverij* (Utrecht: D. Post Uiterweer, 1854), p. 106; Dionisius van der Sterre, *Zeer aenmerkelijke reysen gedaan door Jan Erasmus Reyning . . .* (Amsterdam: Jan ten Hoorn, 1691), pp. 67–69. Also the following documents in the Dutch West India Company Archive in the Netherlands National Archive (Algemeen Rijksarchief), The Hague, Neth. In WIC #617: "Artijckelen aen Nicolaas van Liebergen," 2 March 1683, *Secrete brieven en papieren van Curaçao, 1680–1689,* fol. 324. In WIC #617: "Interrogatorien van Jan Elkis," 27 February 1683, *Secrete Brieven en Papieren van Curaçao, 1680–1689,* fol. 245–47. In WIC #617: "Interrogatorien van Gerritt Slocker," 1683, *Secrete Brieven en Papieren van Curaçao,* 1680–1689, fol. 249–50. In WIC #617: Article 13, "Pointen ende Articulen bij de Heeren Bewinthebberen vande WIC ter Vergaderinge Vande Thienen," ca. 1683, *Secrete brieven en papieren van Curaçao, 1680–1689,* fol. 349. In WIC #617: Article 1, "Artijckelen van beschuldinge ten laste van de geweesene Director Nicolaes van Liebergen," ca. 1683, *Secrete brieven en papieren van Curaçao, 1680–1689,* fol. 448. In WIC #468: "Brief aan Willem Kerckrink, Directeur van Curaçao," 2 July 1688, *Kopieboeken van brieven naar Amerika, 1684–1689,* fol. 155vs–56. See also the following document in the General Archive of the Indies in Seville, Spain: Escribania 597A: *Comisiones Gobernacion de Cartagena,* 1684.

24 See Émile Durkheim, *The Division of Labor in Society,* trans. W. D. Halls (New York: Free Press, 1984).

25 Exquemelin, *Buccaneers of America,* p. 70. He goes on to explain that the Buccaneers "use good weapons, such as muskets and pistols. . . . They use cartridges, and have a cartouche containing thirty, which they carry with them always, so they are never unprepared" (p. 75). They also carried cutlasses and knives and made use of rudimentary grenades.

26 For a typical *chasse partie,* see ibid., p. 71.

27 For references to the election of the captain, see ibid., pp. 80, 84, 119.

28 See the case of François l'Ollonais, ibid., pp. 89, 93, 105.

29 Weber defines this form of authority in the following manner: "There is the authority of the extraordinary and personal *gift of grace* (charisma), the absolutely personal devotion and personal confidence in revelation, heroism, or other qualities of individual leadership." See Max Weber, "Politics as a Vocation," in *From Max Weber: Essays in Sociology,* ed. and trans. H. H. Gerth and C. Wright Mills (Oxford, U.K.: Oxford Univ. Press, 1946), p. 79.

30 Ibid.

31 See Michael Roberts, "The Military Revolution, 1560–1660," in *The Military Revolution Debate: Readings on the Military Transformation of Early Modern Europe,* ed. Clifford J. Rogers (Oxford, U.K.: Westview, 1995), pp. 13–35; Geoffrey Parker, *The Military Revolution: Military Innovation and the Rise of the West* (Cambridge, U.K.: Cambridge Univ. Press, 1988); and William McNeil, *The Pursuit of Power: Technology, Armed Force, and Society since A.D. 1000* (Chicago: Univ. of Chicago Press, 1982).

32 William McNeil, *The Age of the Gunpowder Empires, 1450–1800* (Washington, D.C.: American Historical Association, 1989), p. 23.

33 Kishlansky, "Case of the Army Truly Stated," pp. 51–74.

34 See the following document in the Dutch West India Company Archive: "Brief aan Willem Kerckrink, Directeur van Curaçao," fol. 155vs–56.

35 See, for example, Daniel Defoe, *A General History of the Pyrates,* ed. Manuel Schonhorn (Mineola, N.Y.: Dover, 1972), p. 71. This text was originally published as Captain Charles Johnson [pseud.], *A General History of the Robberies and Murders of the Most Notorious Pyrates* (London: 1724).

IV Intervention and Colonial Policy
The Flying Cruiser Squadron of the Imperial German Navy as an Instrument of German Foreign Policy Overseas, 1886–1893

HEIKO HEROLD

Although it had always been said in my childhood that the world is already taken, we now call an overseas possession our property that is more than five times bigger than our united motherland, and the history of the acquisition of these wide areas of land will for certain honorably remember, besides the navy in general, the squadron of Admiral Knorr."[1] These lines were written by Vice Adm. Viktor Valois, who served in this squadron himself, in December 1909, exactly twenty-five years after the first German colonial war in Cameroon. But his prophecy was not fulfilled. The missions of that Flying Cruiser Squadron (1886–93), first commanded by Rear Adm. Eduard Knorr, are often mentioned only in passing in contemporary colonial and naval literature. However, the missions of its successor units, the Cruiser Division in East Asia (1894–97) and the East Asian Cruiser Squadron (1897–1914), have found more recognition, especially the occupation of Kiaochow Bay in November 1897 and the naval battles of Coronel and the Falkland Islands in November and December 1914. Until very recently, the Flying Cruiser Squadron has not been historically reviewed.[2]

The Organization of the Imperial German Navy's Overseas Service and the Formation of the Flying Cruiser Squadron

Besides gunboats and "avisos," the cruiser was the most commonly used type of navy vessel overseas.[3] The cruiser also became the eponym of the Cruiser Squadron. In times of peace, the mission of cruisers was "to observe the power and sea interests of their country of origin," while in times of war "they were mainly used for reconnaissance, blockade duty, attacks on foreign commercial vessels and protection of own sea routes."[4] For the overseas service and consequently also for the Flying Cruiser Squadron, the German navy command almost always provided out-of-date vessels that were no longer useful for coastal defense in the event of war. With few exceptions this would not change until the beginning of World War I.[5]

In the era of Albrecht von Stosch (first chief of the Imperial German Navy, 1872–83), the brunt of operations abroad was borne mostly by smaller navy vessels that were permanently stationed overseas. Stosch's organization of the naval overseas service was based on the British concept of naval stations, just as were those of most other naval powers at this time.[6] Naval stations were "definite sea areas abroad where the German Reich (or any other naval power) permanently represented its interests through navy vessels without permanent bases."[7] In the 1873 Fleet Foundation Plan only two naval stations, the East Asian and the West Indian, were initially defined.[8] But as a result of the permanently growing requirements for the Imperial German Navy regarding the representation and enforcement of German interests overseas, several further naval stations were established in the following years. By the mid-1880s a disposition had developed that continued to exist until the beginning of World War I, even if not all naval stations were equipped with navy vessels continuously. Overall, the Admiralty divided the non-European sea areas into six zones: Asia, Australia, West America, East America, West Africa, and East Africa.[9]

When Lt. Gen. Georg Leo von Caprivi took office as the new head of the Admiralty in March 1883 and the first German colonies were acquired a few months later, the mission priorities of the navy changed. Caprivi was convinced of the imminence of war on two fronts, against France and Russia. He defined the defense of the German coasts as the primary military-political goal of the navy in the case of such a war. But given the rapidly growing requirements for naval forces in the course of colonial policy, Caprivi was forced to dispatch more vessels overseas than before. Between 1884 and 1894 the overseas service, the so-called political service of the Imperial German Navy, was dominated by the protection of the "dependencies" *(Schutzgebiete),* as Chancellor Otto von Bismarck called them. At the beginning, Caprivi relied on ad hoc task forces like the West African Squadron (1884–85) and the East African Cruiser Squadron (1885–86).[10] This strategy significantly weakened the strike capability of the home fleet. Therefore he finally decided to establish, with the Flying Cruiser Squadron, under the command of an admiral, a mobile task force that would call, preferably in a regular cycle, on the German dependencies and all other overseas waters where German interests were to be represented, or, as the *Handbook for Army and Navy* precisely laid down, that "can be dispatched to different places as required to show the flag or to conduct special tasks without being allocated to a specific naval station."[11] From January 1886 to April 1893, this unit was permanently on duty as "colonial police" and an "overseas fire department" on the coasts of Africa, Asia, South America, Australia, and the South Seas.

As early as the end of 1884, the Imperial German Government saw itself forced to quell a colonial rebellion in Cameroon. For this purpose, four navy vessels (two cruiser-frigates and two cruiser-corvettes) were dispatched to West Africa. With the dispatch of the West African Squadron under Rear Adm. Eduard Knorr, the military protection of the young German dependencies began. Bismarck and Caprivi realized that the German claim to power overseas was relatively easy to impose on indigenous peoples, through use of navy vessels and landing forces, but not against the other European great powers, namely, Great Britain and France. In a European war, Bismarck stated, the colonies could be defended only at the gates of Metz.[12] Even Bernhard von Bülow (who became foreign secretary in 1897) and Adm. Alfred von Tirpitz (named navy secretary the same year) did not disturb the cornerstone of this defense strategy when they took the political decision to direct the battleship construction program against Great Britain and so initiated "the great departure of 1897."[13] In the case of war, they argued, the dependencies' destiny would rest in the North Sea.[14] In fact, before World War I, the Imperial German Government at no time seriously considered defending the colonies in a European war with overseas cruisers, and the navy was never seriously capable of such action, even in conjunction with the later colonial forces.[15] The government never developed a concept for imperial defense, a practice the British had established in the second half of the nineteenth century.[16]

The establishment of the Flying Cruiser Squadron, consisting of *Bismarck, Gneisenau,* and *Olga,* in January 1886 off the coast of Zanzibar also seemed advantageous from the Foreign Office's point of view.[17] In consideration of the German Reich's maritime military resources, this was an adequate solution for the fulfillment of the navy's growing overseas tasks in the context of the nation's new colonial and overseas policy. After all, the three vessels of the Cruiser Squadron represented nearly a fifth of the entire German overseas fleet.[18] With the establishment of this unit, longer-term dispatches of further navy vessels from home waters to overseas naval stations could be avoided and the costs of these missions could be limited, both of which were fully consonant with the terms of Caprivi's overall strategy.

The "Chivy" around Half the Globe

Between 1886 and 1890 the Flying Cruiser Squadron primarily discharged colonial police tasks. The first two years were characterized by a continuous and rapid change of missions and places of action. In his memoirs Knorr stated that this "chivy" around half the globe "had exhausting and damaging effects on both human beings and vessels."[19] In the course of the year 1886, the Cruiser Squadron completed a first journey through the island world of the South Pacific. In addition to short stays in Australia, New Zealand, Tonga, and Samoa, *Bismarck, Gneisenau,* and *Olga* visited the young German colonies in the South Seas, namely, the Marshall Islands and the Bismarck Archipelago. At this time there existed in these places neither a German colonial administration nor police force. In the Marshall Islands there was only a consular administrator and in the Bismarck Archipelago an imperial inspector. In coordination with these two diplomatic representatives and the German vice-consul in Apia, who had embarked on board *Bismarck* in Samoa, Rear Admiral Knorr took over tasks of executive and judicial power. He settled several criminal affairs (mainly thefts), and on Jaluit he oversaw the condemnation and execution of a murderer.[20]

In June 1886, Knorr ordered a large-scale punitive expedition on the Gazelle Peninsula against the Tolai, who had rebelled against German colonial rule. He wanted to make a bloody example of the tribe, but it avoided fighting. The largest German punitive expedition in the South Seas until that point ended in fiasco, a fate that the British had already experienced many a time.[21] The landing corps, with its modern equipment, was powerless against a militarily far inferior but tactically clever opponent who did not wage a desperate battle but instead retreated in an orderly manner, skillfully taking advantage of the terrain to escape a pincer movement. In this manner, the Tolai clearly showed the Germans the limits of their display of power.[22]

After this failed punitive expedition in the Bismarck Archipelago the Cruiser Squadron moved to North China, where its vessels conducted an impressive maneuver for Governor General Li Hung-chang, one of the most influential Chinese reformist politicians. The objective was to support the lucrative arms deal with China. During the mission in East Asian waters, *Gneisenau* was replaced by its sister ship *Carola*. Then followed an interlude in East Africa, at the turn of 1886–87, to force the sultan of Zanzibar to acknowledge a treaty that defined the spheres of influence between Great Britain and the German Reich in East Africa. Furthermore, Knorr carried out the execution of a fifteen-year-old Somali who had killed an agent of the German East Africa Company (GEAC) in Kismayu at the end of 1886. In the course of this mission, the Cruiser Squadron was reinforced with the deployment of an additional cruiser-frigate, SMS *Sophie*. From then on, until its dissolution in 1893, the strength of the Flying Cruiser Squadron was four warships. During the deployment in the East African waters, serious controversy and questions of authority between the commander of the Cruiser Squadron and the German consul general to Zanzibar finally led to Rear Admiral Knorr's relief and his replacement by Commo. Carl Eduard Heusner.[23]

After several weeks in the docks of Cape Town, the Flying Cruiser Squadron made its next major deployment, to Samoa, which had been the focal point of German (primarily commercial) interests in the South Pacific for many years. Under the pretext of retribution for an attack on German citizens by indigenous people a few months before, the German consul general, Eduard Becker, with the assistance of a 220-strong landing corps, imposed a regime change:[24] he deposed the Anglo-Americanophile King Malietoa, arrested him, and replaced him with the Germanophile King Tamasese. Becker's British and American counterparts protested this violent regime change, but in the end they acted passively, as neither of them had military instruments of power at their disposal. (Both learned afterward that their governments had approved the German military action several days before. At this time, Samoa was not yet connected to the international telegraph network, and the only regular mail steamer between Apia and Sydney had left Samoan waters shortly before the action began.) Any resistance by the indigenous people was immediately quashed by the German marines, and recognition of Tamasese was, where necessary, "enforced through dread before the squadron."[25] In the short term this intervention was of particular benefit to German trade, but Commodore Heusner was not able to cut the Gordian knot of Samoan politics in this manner. The archipelago remained a pawn in the hands of the treaty powers, and the *furor consularis* continued unabated. Until the partition treaties of 1899 were signed, Samoa remained a permanent hot spot for, and bone of contention between, the great powers.[26]

The Suppression of the Arab Revolt in German East Africa
After the intervention in Samoa, the Cruiser Squadron was redeployed for several months to the East Asian station, where the vessels visited the German naval hospital in Yokohama and several Chinese and Japanese harbors for trade and political interests. Then, in mid-1888, the squadron moved to East Africa. The flagship, *Bismarck,* was replaced by the cruiser-frigate *Leipzig* in Aden; the other vessels went straight to Zanzibar. With the deployment of *Leipzig,* the squadron was marginally upgraded. *Leipzig* was the longest-serving cruiser-frigate in the Imperial German Navy, having been constructed in 1875, two years before *Bismarck*. In addition, *Leipzig* was much bigger and better armed than *Bismarck*. However, from the Admiralty's point of view it "by no means" had "any value for battle" with the home fleet "any more."[27] Therefore, it had been assigned to the political service. Just a few weeks after the flagship change, the longest and most comprehensive mission of the Flying Cruiser Squadron began—its contribution to the suppression of the Arab Revolt in German East Africa from August 1888 to May 1890.

Initially, Bismarck refused permission for a comprehensive intervention by the navy. He relied on the sultan, whose authority should, he felt, be strengthened. He would rather "abandon all the colonial efforts," he announced internally, "than approve military activities of the Reich in the interior of the country."[28] Bismarck's attitude to this question was consistent. From the beginning of his colonial policy, he had been strictly against establishing statist colonies, fearing that massive intervention in support of the GEAC would result in similar interventions in the interior of East Africa. However, there was another reason for his cautious position—his concern over the possibility of a military humiliation. The Reich had never before been confronted with a colonial rebellion of such extent. There were neither existing colonial forces nor a rapid-deployment force for overseas expeditions. And the naval forces on site—the Cruiser Squadron and its subordinated East African station vessels—were unsuitable for combat missions in the hinterlands, where there would possibly be no contact between the landing forces and the vessels for days. This applied not only in regard to East Africa but in general for missions overseas. Finally,

Rear Adm. Karl August Deinhard, who had taken over command of the Cruiser Squadron in August 1888, was ordered to protect only the GEAC's headquarters in Bagamoyo, to evacuate to Zanzibar all Germans who wanted to leave the mainland, and "to support the operations of the Sultan as much as possible without engaging too far."[29] Kaiser Wilhelm II also spoke with Bismarck against intervention on the East African mainland: "I would rather let the current rebellion cauterize and hold on Your Highness' proposal that we do not engage *militarily* further than the reach of our ship guns."[30]

But soon the political climate in Berlin started to change, in view of the threatening developments in East Africa. Although the chancellor of the Reich (publicly) continued to speak out against a punitive expedition in the hinterlands, he was determined not to abandon the dependency—the national and international loss of prestige would have been too severe. He had already explored through the Admiralty the possibility of a naval blockade of the East African coast in conjunction with Great Britain, which operated the most powerful naval force in the Indian Ocean. The chancellor sought to determine whether such a blockade would be "realizable and advisable" and finally began negotiations with the British government, after the Admiralty approved the proposal.[31] The blockade, officially, aimed to restore the sultan's authority on the East African mainland and, within the meaning of the Kongo Act, to combat the slave traders, whom Bismarck assumed to be the masterminds of the rebellion;[32] British prime minister Lord Robert Salisbury had in principle no choice other than to cooperate, as Great Britain was considered to be the leading nation in combating the slave trade.[33] Bismarck had no personal interest in combating slavery or the slave trade. For him it was merely a means to an end—on the one hand to convince Great Britain, Portugal, France, Italy, the Kongo State, and the Christian churches to support the blockade, and on the other hand to manipulate (in secret cooperation with the influential author Friedrich Fabri) public opinion in Germany and a majority in the Reichstag into supporting a colonial war in East Africa.[34]

The international naval blockade of the East African coast started on the morning of 2 December 1888 and lasted until 1 October 1889. It was directed against the export of slaves and the import of war materiel and extended along the whole mainland coast of the sultanate from the Rovuma River to Lamu—that is, along the "coasts of the German and British spheres of interest."[35] German, British, and Italian navy vessels participated. Their political and military leaders had no illusions regarding the effectiveness of the blockade; the coastal area was much too extensive and the number of available warships and smaller craft was much too small to stop the arms and slave trade. But this was no problem from the Imperial German Government's point of view. For Bismarck the political signal of this action, the "closed union of the European powers," was much more important than its military effectiveness.[36] Nevertheless, it became possible to strengthen the blockade slightly when, at the beginning of March 1889, the islands of Zanzibar and Pemba, the centers of the East African arms and slave trade, were also included.[37]

Shortly after the blockade's start, armed conflicts with the rebels occurred. The guns of ships offshore were not always enough to repel attacks, and landing parties from the warships had to interfere repeatedly. Unlike the rebels, however, the Germans suffered only minor losses. Until the beginning of March 1889, combat operations concentrated on Bagamoyo and Dar es Salaam. Both cities were largely destroyed in the process, and trade in those areas completely collapsed. At the end of March, Deinhard shelled Saadani and sent a landing party to burn Conduchi, where blockading craft had been fired at several times from the beach. However, military operations went only as far as the kaiser's orders mandated—no farther than the reach of the ships' guns, that is, a few miles into the hinterlands. They primarily focused on holding the GEAC's two remaining stations on the mainland, Bagamoyo and Dar es Salaam, as ordered.[38] The defeat of the Arab Revolt was possible only through the use of a colonial force under the command of Hermann von Wissmann.[39]

Dissolution of the Flying Cruiser Squadron, and Conclusion
In the years following the Arab Revolt, the Flying Cruiser Squadron rarely acted militarily. Noteworthy are its deployment in the second half of 1891 in the Chilean civil war, where it preserved German interests, and two naval demonstrations on the coast of German East Africa in 1892 and 1893.[40] After Bismarck's dismissal, Wilhelm II tried unsuccessfully several times to instrumentalize the Cruiser Squadron for naval-political purposes, to bring about the construction of new cruisers. In the early summer of 1891, for example, he intentionally delayed the Flying Cruiser Squadron's deployment to Chilean waters, and at the end of March 1893 he ordered its abolition, in both cases because he was angry that his cruiser construction plans had been rejected by the Reichstag once again.[41] This dissolution order marked the end of the only mobile striking force of the Imperial German Navy during its existence, even though this effect was not intended by the Imperial German Government at the time.[42] All other German overseas squadrons established between 1871 and 1914 had clearly limited operational areas.

With the deployment of the Flying Cruiser Squadron in January 1886, the Imperial German Government had for the first time a powerful instrument for representation and enforcement of German interests overseas. The squadron was not militarily strong enough to press German interests on site against the other great powers, but the government at no time seriously considered that option. From the beginning, the Flying Cruiser Squadron consisted only of unarmored, out-of-date vessels—sailing ships equipped with steam propulsion—while by the 1880s the other naval powers had already stationed overseas at least some modern ironclad vessels that were much superior in battle. As a general crisis-reaction force, the Flying Cruiser Squadron was always sent to overseas hot spots. It actually used force, however, almost without exception only against poorly armed indigenous peoples in Africa and the South Seas. Its commander in chief had a broad selection of measures of compulsion at his disposal, from demonstration to blockade to bombardment of coastal towns, but in most cases he sent landing parties for punitive expeditions ashore. These expeditions were intended to crush local, limited revolts against the German colonial rule and to make examples of the indigenous populations involved. But the successes achieved were minor, because the naval vessels and their landing parties could intervene only on an ad hoc basis and could not be permanently present at any given point. The same applied to the German vessels on African and Australian stations, mainly gunboats and small cruisers responsible for areas encompassing several thousand nautical miles and therefore often unable to cope with their tasks of colonial protection. Consequently, local revolts against the German colonial rulers often resurfaced as soon as the Cruiser Squadron or the station vessels had left local waters. Therefore, after the late 1880s the task of protection and enforcement of German colonial rule was gradually transferred to police units and colonial forces, which could operate in the interior.

NOTES   1 Viktor Valois, "Unsere Marine im Dienste der kolonialen Bewegung," *Ueberall: Illustrierte Zeitschrift für Armee und Marine* 12, no. 1 (1909/10), pp. 21–27; no. 2, pp. 112–17; no. 3, pp. 178–84; no. 4, pp. 243–48; no. 5, pp. 309–15; no. 6, pp. 404–407; no. 7, pp. 462–65; no. 8, pp. 536–40; no. 9, pp. 604–609; no. 10, pp. 675–79; no. 11, pp. 751–56; no. 12, pp. 846–50; here, no. 12, p. 850.

2 See Heiko Herold, *Reichsgewalt bedeutet Seegewalt: Die Kreuzergeschwader der Kaiserlichen Marine als Instrument der deutschen Kolonial- und Weltpolitik 1885 bis 1901* (Munich: Oldenbourg Verlag, 2013), pp. 79–215.

3 Gunboats and avisos were lightly armed, unarmored navy vessels. Sometimes gunboats were categorized as cruisers. See Max Foß, *Marine-Kunde: Eine Darstellung des Wissenswerten auf dem Gebiete des Seewesens* (Stuttgart, Ger.: Union Deutsche Verlagsgesellschaft, 1901), p. 185.

4 Quotes from Militärgeschichtliches Institut der Deutschen Demokratischen Republik, *Wörterbuch zur deutschen Militärgeschichte* (East Berlin, Ger. Dem. Rep.: Militärverlag der Deutschen Demokratischen Republik, 1985), vol. 1, p. 396.

5 Hans H. Hildebrand, Albert Röhr, and Hans-Otto Steinmetz, *Die deutschen Kriegsschiffe: Biographien —ein Spiegel der Marinegeschichte von 1815 bis zur Gegenwart* (Ratingen, Ger.: Mundus Verlag, w.y. [1999]), passim.

6 The North German Federal Navy already had resorted to this concept. See Stenographische Berichte über die Verhandlungen des Reichstages des Norddeutschen Bundes, *Gesetz betreffend den außerordentlichen Geldbedarf des Norddeutschen Bundes zum Zwecke der Erweiterung der Bundes-Kriegsmarine und der Herstellung der Küstenvertheidigung (Flottengründungsplan)* (Berlin: Verlag der Buchdruckerei der Norddeutschen Allgemeinen Zeitung, 1867), vol. 4, app. 106, p. 179.

7 Willi A. Boelcke, *So kam das Meer zu uns: Die preußisch-deutsche Kriegsmarine in Übersee 1822 bis 1914* (Frankfurt a. M., Fed. Rep. Ger.: Verlag Ullstein, 1981), p. 37.

8 Stenographische Berichte über die Verhandlungen des Reichstages [hereafter SBR], *Denkschrift betreffend die Entwicklung der Kaiserlichen Marine und die sich daraus ergebenden materiellen und finanziellen Forderungen (Flottengründungsplan)* (Berlin: Verlag der Buchdruckerei der Norddeutschen Allgemeinen Zeitung, 1873), vol. 29, app. 50, p. 239.

9 Admiralstabs-Karte der Auslandsstationen der Kaiserlichen Marine, w.y. [1901], Bundesarchiv [hereafter BArch] RM 5/6079K.

10 The official designation of this unit was "cruiser squadron." For better delineation of the officially eponymous successor units the phrase "East African" was added here, because this cruiser squadron had been deployed only to East African waters. This principle applies analogously to the additions of "Flying" and "East Asian" to its successor units.

11 Georg von Alten and Hans von Albert, eds., *Handbuch für Heer und Flotte: Enzyklopädie der Kriegswissenschaften und verwandter Gebiete* (Berlin: Deutsches Verlagshaus Bong, 1909–14), vol. 5, p. 606.

12 See, among others, Walther Hubatsch, *Der Admiralstab und die obersten Marinebehörden in Deutschland 1848–1945* (Frankfurt a. M., Fed. Rep. Ger.: Bernard & Graefe, 1958), pp. 33–34, and Heinrich Schnee, ed., *Deutsches Kolonial-Lexikon* (Leipzig, Ger.: Quelle & Meyer, 1920), vol. 2, p. 335.

13 Rolf Hobson, *Imperialism at Sea: Naval Strategic Thought, the Ideology of Sea Power and the Tirpitz Plan, 1875–1914* (Boston: Brill, 2002), p. 233.

14 See, among others, Volker R. Berghahn, *Der Tirpitz-Plan: Genesis und Verfall einer innenpolitischen Krisenstrategie unter Wilhelm II* (Düsseldorf, Fed. Rep. Ger.: Droste Verlag, 1971), p. 151; Christian Rödel, *Krieger, Denker, Amateure: Alfred von Tirpitz und das Seekriegsbild vor dem Ersten Weltkrieg* (Stuttgart, Ger.: Franz Steiner Verlag, 2003), pp. 82–96; and Alfred von Tirpitz, *Politische Dokumente*, vol. 1, *Der Aufbau der deutschen Weltmacht* (Stuttgart, Ger.: J. G. Cotta'sche Buchhandlung Nachfolger, 1924–26), p. 346. Also see "Aufgaben der deutschen Flotte im Kriege," *Nauticus: Jahrbuch für Deutschlands Seeinteressen* 1 (1899), p. 42; "Flotte und Kolonien," *Nauticus: Jahrbuch für Deutschlands Seeinteressen* 2 (1900), pp. 70–73; and Viktor Valois, *Deutschland als Seemacht sowie Betrachtungen marinepolitischen Inhalts* (Leipzig: Wigand, 1908), pp. 33–36. As early as mid-1890, Eduard von Liebert, the later governor of German East Africa (1897–1901), commented similarly when Chancellor of the Reich Bismarck explicitly confronted him with the question of how he would defend the East African dependency in a war against Great Britain. Liebert had never been posed this question. Finally, after some consideration he answered, "Then we have to land at the Thames estuary and defend East Africa there"—a notion that was considered completely absurd at that time. Quote from Eduard von Liebert, *Aus einem bewegten Leben: Erinnerungen* (Munich, Ger.: Lehmann, 1925), p. 135.

15 The operational orders for overseas cruisers explicitly declared that "the direct protection of the German overseas possessions [is] no task of the swimming [i.e., afloat] forces. They may only indirectly contribute to the protection of the colonies etc. through engaging the enemy forces and through threatening the enemy's routes." Quote from Erläuterungen und Ausführungsbestimmungen zu den Allerhöchst genehmigten Operationsbefehlen vom 1. Februar 1900, 1 February 1900, BArch RM 38/125, p. 73.

16 See, among others, William J. McDermott, *British Strategic Planning and the Committee of Imperial Defence, 1871 to 1907* (dissertation, University of Toronto, 1972); Greg Kennedy, ed., *Imperial Defence: The Old World Order* (London: Routledge, 2008); David Killingray, "Imperial Defence," in *The Oxford History of the British Empire,* ed. William R. Louis,

2nd ed. (Oxford, U.K.: Oxford Univ. Press, 2004–2007), vol. 5, pp. 342–53; Edward S. May, *Principles and Problems of Imperial Defence* (London and New York: S. Sonnenschein & Co., 1903); and Keith Neilson and Greg Kennedy, eds., *Far Flung Lines: Essays in Imperial Defence in Honour of Donald Mackenzie Schurman* (London: Frank Cass, 1997).

17 H. v. Bismarck to Monts, 27 December 1885, BArch RM 1/2732, p. 10.

18 *Rang- und Quartierliste der Kaiserlich Deutschen Marine,* vol. 1886, pp. 104–106. Also see Franz Siewert, "Unsere Marine im überseeischen Friedensdienst," *Deutsche Kolonialzeitung* 2, no. 11 (1885), pp. 345–47. Kennedy is wrong in asserting that the Foreign Office's files in the second half of the 1880s "are full of requests to a reluctant Admiralty to send cruiser squadrons to overawe the Zanzibari, East African and Samoan opposition"—there only existed this one Flying Cruiser Squadron that was from then on dispatched everywhere the Imperial German Government considered it necessary. Quote from Paul M. Kennedy, *The Rise of the Anglo-German Antagonism 1860–1914* (London: Allen and Unwin, 1980), p. 199.

19 Quotes from Eduard von Knorr, *Meine Erinnerungen,* BArch N 578/7-11, vol. 5 [hereafter Knorr, *Erinnerungen*], p. 45.

20 Ibid., pp. 10–41, BArch N 578/11; Knorr to Caprivi, 12 June 1886, BArch RM 38/5, pp. 126–35.

21 "Englische Strafakte in der Südsee," *Deutsche Kolonialzeitung* 3, no. 7 (1886), p. 197. For British naval missions in the South Seas generally, see John Bach, *The Australia Station: A History of the Royal Navy in the South West Pacific 1821–1913* (Kensington: Univ. of New South Wales Press, 1986), and Jane Samson, *Imperial Benevolence: Making British Authority in the Pacific Islands* (Honolulu: Univ. of Hawai'i Press, 1998).

22 Reinhard Scheer, Briefe an seine Eltern von Dezember 1884 bis Januar 1887, BArch MSg 1/2569, 21 June 1886; Knorr, *Erinnerungen,* pp. 36–41, BArch N 578/11; Oertzen to Bismarck, 21 June 1886, BArch R 1001/2976, pp. 75–77; Knorr to Caprivi (with enclosures), 21 June 1886, BArch RM 1/2732, pp. 143–76; Prittwitz to Knorr, 21 June 1886, BArch RM 38/5, pp. 171–72; Knorr to Caprivi, 15 July 1886, ibid., pp. 183–84; Alexander Krug, *"Der Hauptzweck ist die Tötung von Kanaken": Die deutschen Strafexpeditionen in den Kolonien der Südsee 1872–1914* (Tönning, Ger.: Der Andere Verlag, 2005), pp. 109–13; Reinhard Scheer, *Vom Segelschiff zum U-Boot* (Leipzig, Ger.: Quelle & Meyer, w.y. [1925]), pp. 102–104; Valois, "Unsere Marine im Dienste der kolonialen Bewegung," no. 11, pp. 752–54.

23 Knorr, *Erinnerungen,* pp. 47–104, BArch N 578/11; Arendt to Bismarck, 19 December 1886 (with enclosures), BArch R 1001/7164, pp. 22–44; Arendt to Bismarck, 15 December 1886, BArch RM 1/2449, pp. 152–61; Arendt to Bismarck (with enclosures), 10 January 1887, ibid., pp. 173–90; Knorr to Caprivi (with enclosures), 17 January 1887, BArch RM 1/2733, pp. 101–21; Knorr to Caprivi, 15 February 1887 (with enclosures), ibid., pp. 141–218; Brandt to Knorr, 6 August 1886, BArch RM 38/8, pp. 49–50; Knorr to Caprivi, 2 October 1886, ibid., pp. 102–105; Caprivi to Knorr (sail order with enclosures), 17 November 1886, BArch RM 38/14, pp. 5–12; Knorr to Caprivi, 20 December 1886, ibid., pp. 25–34; Emile de Groot, "Great Britain and Germany in Zanzibar: Consul Holmwood's Papers, 1886–1887," *Journal of Modern History* 25, no. 1 (1953), pp. 120–38; Fritz F. Müller, *Deutschland-Zanzibar-Ostafrika: Geschichte einer deutschen Kolonialeroberung 1884–1890* (East Berlin, Ger. Dem. Rep.: Rütten & Loening, 1959), pp. 262–65; Heinz Schneppen, *Sansibar und die Deutschen: Ein besonderes Verhältnis 1844–1966,* 2nd ed. (Berlin: Lit Verlag, 2006), pp. 171–80. For the official investigation of the conflict between Rear Admiral Knorr and Consul General Arendt, see files R 1001/7165 and R 1001/7166 at the German Federal Archive in Berlin-Lichterfelde.

24 On 24 August 1887, Apia was occupied by the landing corps of *Olga* and *Sophie*. The figure mentioned above is based on a force chart of the Cruiser Squadron's landing corps from August 1887, included in BArch RM 1/2431, p. 25. According to this force chart the Cruiser Squadron's flagship was equipped with a landing corps of 185 men (plus a twenty-one-strong boat guard), while the other three vessels each were equipped with landing corps of 110 (plus thirteen-man boat guards). In total, accordingly, the landing corps comprised 523 soldiers, with its eight-headed cadre (plus sixty men in the boat guards). Kennedy's specification of approximately seven hundred soldiers is much too high; see Paul M. Kennedy, *The Samoan Tangle: A Study in Anglo-American Relations 1878–1900* (Dublin: Irish Univ. Press, 1974), p. 69. The Cruiser Squadron's ship files (BArch RM 38/6) specify only vaguely, where at all, the numbers of troops deployed in the operations on Samoa.

25 Heusner to Caprivi, w.d. [end of September 1887], BArch RM 1/2431, p. 174.

26 The Samoan question is extensively discussed by Kennedy, *Samoan Tangle,* pp. 70–239. Also see Kennedy, "Germany and the Samoan Tridominium, 1889–98: A Study in Frustrated Imperialism," in *Germany in the Pacific and Far East, 1870–1914,* ed. John A. Moses and Paul M. Kennedy (St. Lucia: Univ. of Queensland Press, 1977), pp. 89–114.

27 Quotes from Entwurf einer Denkschrift der Admiralität zum Etat für die Verwendung der Kaiserlichen Marine auf das Etatsjahr 1889/90, 29 September 1888, BArch RM 1/1844, p. 18. This judgment also applied to all other vessels assigned to political service. Therefore it was a boast when Herbert von Bismarck characterized the Cruiser Squadron's vessels as "4 of our best vessels" in the Reichstag in mid-December 1888. Quote from H. v. Bismarck, 14 December 1888, SBR, vol. 105, p. 311. See Entwurf einer Denkschrift der Admiralität zum Etat für die Verwendung der Kaiserlichen Marine auf das Etatsjahr 1889/90, 29 September 1888, BArch RM 1/1844, pp. 18–19, 26–27, and Eugen Richter (Deutsche Freisinnige Partei), 27 November 1888, SBR, vol. 105, p. 17.

28 Comment of Rantzau from 18 September 1888, quoted in Schneppen, *Sansibar und die Deutschen,* p. 225.

29 Monts to Deinhard, 29 September 1888, quoted in Deinhard to Monts, 3 October 1888, BArch RM 1/2909, p. 91.

30 Wilhelm II to Bismarck, 1 October 1888, quoted in Bismarck to Monts, 1 October 1888, BArch RM 1/2440, p. 33 [emphasis original].

31 Bismarck to Berchem, 28 September 1888, quoted in Schneppen, *Sansibar und die Deutschen,* p. 233.

32 This estimation relied on reports of Gustav Michahelles, German ambassador to Zanzibar. See H. v. Bismarck to Monts, 25 October 1888, BArch RM 1/2909, pp. 79–80. For the Kongo Act, "General-Akte der Berliner Kongokonferenz vom 26. Februar 1885," in *Protokolle und Generalakte der Berliner Afrika-Konferenz 1884–1885,* ed. Frank T. Gatter (Bremen, Fed. Rep. Ger.: Übersee-Museum Bremen, w.y. [1984]), chap. 2, art. 9, p. 605.

33 Since 1822 Great Britain had campaigned very successfully, in part, for the suppression of the slave trade in the western Indian Ocean, where the islands of Zanzibar and Pemba were regarded as having long been the most important places for transshipment of slaves. See Erik Gilbert, *Dhows & the Colonial Economy of Zanzibar 1860–1970* (Oxford, U.K.: James Currey, 2004), pp. 60–65, and Raymond Howell, *The Royal Navy and the Slave Trade* (London: Croom Helm, 1987), pp. 1–180.

34 Dr. Friedrich Fabri (1824–91), director of the Barmen Rhine Missionary Society, was an energetic and well-known apologist for German colonialism. See, among others, Klaus J. Bade, *Friedrich Fabri und der Imperialismus in der Bismarckzeit: Revolution—Depression—Expansion* (Osnabrück, Ger.: Selbstverlag, 2005), pp. 530–47, available at www.imis.uni-osnabrueck.de; Jan-Georg Deutsch, *Slavery under German Colonial Rule in East Africa, c. 1860–1914* (Berlin: Habilitation, 2000), pp. 115–19; Maria-Theresa Schwarz, *"Je weniger Afrika desto besser": Die deutsche Kolonialkritik am Ende des 19. Jahrhunderts: Eine Untersuchung zur kolonialen Haltung von Linksliberalismus und Sozialdemokratie* (Frankfurt a. M., Ger.: Peter Lang, 1999), pp. 87–101, 166–74, 259–68; and Schneppen, *Sansibar und die Deutschen,* pp. 277–81.

35 H. v. Bismarck to Monts, 23 November 1888, BArch RM 1/2441, p. 49. This was the official—and, as Herbert von Bismarck stated, "adequate"—designation of the coastal zone to be blockaded.

36 Bismarck to Hatzfeldt, 17 October 1888, quoted in Schneppen, *Sansibar und die Deutschen,* p. 243.

37 "Die Ausrüstung und Verwendung der Blockadeboote des deutschen Geschwaders an der Ostküste Afrikas 1888/90 und das Leben in denselben," *Marine-Rundschau* 9, no. 7 (1898), pp. 1017–30; J. W. Otto Richter, *Tätigkeit der deutschen Marine bei Niederwerfung des Araberaufstandes in Ostafrika 1888/90: Eine Erzählung nach amtlichen Quellen und Privataufzeichnungen* (Altenburg, Ger.: Geibel, 1906), pp. 51–103. Also "Thätigkeit der Marine bei Niederwerfung des Araberaufstandes in Ostafrika 1888/90," *Marine-Rundschau* 10, no. 2 (1899), pp. 181–200; no. 3, pp. 362–72; no. 4, pp. 463–71; no. 5, pp. 614–30; no. 6, pp. 740–65; no. 7, pp. 806–17; here no. 4, pp. 463–71; no. 5, pp. 614–30; no. 6, pp. 763–65.

38 Johannes Hirschberg, *Neunzehn Monate Kommandant S. M. Kreuzer "Schwalbe" während der militärischen Aktion 1889/90 in Deutsch-Ostafrika,* ed. Hedwig Hirschberg (Kiel, Ger.: Lipsius & Tischer, 1895), pp. 25–69; Richter, *Tätigkeit der deutschen Marine,* pp. 75–103; *Thätigkeit der Marine* no. 6, pp. 740–45.

39 See, among others, Jutta Bückendorf, *"Schwarz-weiß-rot über Ostafrika!": Deutsche Kolonialpläne und afrikanische Realität* (Münster, Ger.: Lit Verlag, 1997), pp. 383–407; Tanja Bührer, *Die Kaiserliche Schutztruppe für Deutsch-Ostafrika: Koloniale Sicherheitspolitik und transkulturelle Kriegführung 1885 bis 1918* (Munich, Ger.: Oldenbourg Verlag, 2011), pp. 48–86; Hirschberg, *Neunzehn Monate Kommandant,* pp. 100–23; Rochus Schmidt, *Geschichte des Araberaufstandes in Ost-Afrika: Seine Entstehung, seine Niederwerfung und seine Folgen* (Frankfurt a. O., Ger.: Trowitzsch, 1892), pp. 64–217; Schneppen, *Sansibar und die Deutschen,* pp. 286–316; and *Thätigkeit der Marine,* no. 6, pp. 746–65, and no. 7, pp. 806–17.

40 For the Chilean operation, Ekkehard Böhm, *Überseehandel und Flottenbau: Hanseatische Kaufmannschaft und deutsche Seerüstung 1879–1902* (Düsseldorf, Ger.: Bertelsmann, 1972), pp. 38–46; Gerhard Wiechmann, *Die preußisch-deutsche Marine in Lateinamerika 1866–1914: Eine Studie deutscher Kanonenbootpolitik* (Bremen, Ger.: Hauschild Verlag, 2002), pp. 127–36.

41 Wilhelm II to Hollmann (cabinet order), 28 March 1893, BArch RM 3/3154, p. 140; Böhm, *Überseehandel und Flottenbau,* pp. 39–43. On the naval budget negotiations of 1890–91 and 1893–94, see François-Emmanuel Brézet, *Le plan Tirpitz (1897–1914): Une flotte de combat allemande contre l'Angleterre* (Paris: Librairie de l'Inde, 1998), vol. 1, pp. 37–38, 41–42, and Hans Hallmann, *Der Weg zum deutschen Schlachtflottenbau* (Stuttgart, Ger.: Kohlhammer, 1933), pp. 69–78, 87–91. Sondhaus is wrong in writing that the Cruiser Squadron was abolished only because the vessels were strained too much. *Leipzig*'s deteriorated condition and the estimated high costs of its repair were only a pretext, not the reason, for this decision of the kaiser; see Lawrence Sondhaus, *Preparing for Weltpolitik: German Sea Power before the Tirpitz Era* (Annapolis, Md.: Naval Institute Press, 1997), p. 206.

42 See, among others, Goltz to Hoffmann, 28 October 1894, BArch RM 92/3320, p. 19, and Report to the Sovereign from Admiral Knorr, 10 May 1897, BArch RM 5/915, pp. 31–32. Both the Cruiser Division and the later so-called East Asian Cruiser Squadron were always considered only as detached to East Asia, although both units were in fact stationed in the local waters from the beginning and Tsingtao was employed as the base of the Cruiser Squadron after the seizure of Kiaochow. Regardless, the East Asian naval station was permanently equipped with its own naval vessels, mainly small cruisers and gunboats, that were subordinated, respectively, to the Cruiser Division and the Cruiser Squadron. See, among others, Organisatorische Bestimmungen für die Flotte (Entwurf), 6, Absatz 2, w.d. [July 1903], included in BArch RM 3/3945, p. 26.

V *Powering the U.S. Fleet*
Propulsion Machinery Design and American Naval Engineering Culture, 1890–1945

WILLIAM M. MCBRIDE

In his summary of his travels in early-1830s America, Alexis de Tocqueville observed that "European inventions are sagaciously applied in America, improved, and wonderfully adapted to the country's needs."[1] One exception to this derivative relationship was American maritime technology. Tocqueville considered Robert Fulton and American steamships as representing a unique, progressive creation. He quoted an American sailor who said that Americans avoided building ships "to last long," because American ship design made "such quick progress that even the best of boats would be almost useless if it lasted more than a few years."[2] Such an expression of continuing technological progress was not atypical in nineteenth-century America. John Gast's popular 1872 painting "American Progress" is quite representative. It featured a classically dressed "America" floating westward, illuminating the darkness for pioneers, stage coaches, railroads, and ships, while carrying a telegraph wire and driving Native Americans before her.[3]

The early-nineteenth-century U.S. Navy, for various reasons, did not match the constant progress of steamships in the private sector. Fulton's *Demologos,* built during the War of 1812 as a steam-propelled gun battery for harbor defense, was the first steam warship of the U.S. Navy. It was destroyed by an explosion in 1829 before Tocqueville came to America. The British Royal Navy, the nineteenth century's predominant naval force, had been more active in pursuing steamship technology. This raises a question: In the case of naval technology, was the U.S. Navy dependent on European, specifically British, inventions, in keeping with Tocqueville's general observation?

The U.S. Navy was initially derivative regarding its professional culture. In its formative years it drew on the heritage of the Royal Navy. An interesting example is the brass button still worn on American naval officers' uniforms. The button contains American icons—an eagle and thirteen stars to represent the original thirteen colonies/states—but also three cannonballs representing the victories of Horatio, Lord Nelson, at the Nile, Copenhagen, and Trafalgar. However, in terms of ship design and engineering culture, American naval engineers and naval constructors eschewed external influences. They pursued design paths aimed at outclassing corresponding European designs, especially during the wooden age.⁴ This became a bit more difficult to do with the advent of metal ships, given, as William Thiesen has pointed out, the initial dearth of a metal-material culture within the American shipbuilding industry.⁵ Yet soon, and bearing out Tocqueville's perception that Americans regularly improved imported European technology, the American shipbuilding industry had created for metal ships innovative manufacturing techniques that drew European shipbuilders to America to copy them.⁶

U.S. Navy marine engineers (who designed ships' propulsion and auxiliary machinery) had a more complicated relationship with the Royal Navy. Some British technologies, such as the steam turbine, were adopted and modified. However, U.S. Navy marine engineers routinely set their own courses. Two important expressions of this independent American design culture were the development and installation of a turboelectric propulsion system in the 1916-program capital ships and the development of efficient and standardized, high-pressure, high-temperature (HPHT) steam propulsion systems during the 1930s. These were preceded by a triple-screw design by George Melville, the U.S. Navy's engineer in chief, for the *Columbia* class of commerce-raiding cruisers (1890). Melville considered his design superior in efficiency and tactical abilities to twin-screw ships and took British ship designers to task for ignoring the triple-screw approach. Melville, like other American naval constructors and marine engineers, perceived himself as part of a distinct American design tradition whose heritage included Benjamin Franklin Isherwood's steam machinery for the high-speed commerce raider USS *Wampanoag* (1869) and extended back to the Humphreys frigates authorized in 1794.⁷

The ultimate American technological "declaration of independence" was the pursuit, development, and manufacture of HPHT propulsion during the 1930s. HPHT was the final repudiation of British marine engineering influence and of any lingering sense of a derivative technological relationship with the Royal Navy. By 1944, American marine engineering designs and technology were being exported to the Royal Navy.⁸ The evolution and nature of American naval engineering culture can best be understood within a historical context that includes the pursuit of a unique warship design philosophy dating from the early republic, the overriding Pacific component of American naval strategy, the varying relationships and technology transfers between the Navy and American industry, and, to a certain extent, American engineering culture in general.⁹

American Naval Engineering Culture
In a 1917 address before the annual meeting of the American Society of Naval Engineers, the head of the Division of Design of the U.S. Navy's Bureau of Steam Engineering, Capt. C. W. Dyson, emphasized one important difference between contemporary European and American warship design—the American focus on the Pacific Ocean. The U.S. Navy operated where "the areas to be covered are great and

the distances to bases and from base to base in some cases are magnificent."[10] This focus necessitated warships with efficient hull forms and propulsion machinery as well as sufficient fuel to operate across that vast expanse. Conversely, the European "nations were providing for operations in confined waters such as the North Sea and Mediterranean, where they never were far from their bases."[11] Additional, complicating factors for American warship designers were rooted in an American naval culture that had since its inception defined normalcy in terms of strong ships with large guns, such as the forty-four-gun "superfrigates"—*Constitution, United States,* and *President*—authorized in 1794. American ship designers were always conscious of European navies—especially the Royal Navy, the nineteenth century's premier naval force—and the warships they designed and operated. Nevertheless, American naval architects and marine engineers consciously pursued exceptionalist designs as an expression of an American design culture and as a means to counter European power.[12]

As the nineteenth century came to a close, this same pursuit of what American naval officers and engineers perceived to be unique designs shaped desires in warships for the post-1883 "New Navy." The two *Columbia*-class cruisers (built in 1890–91) served the traditional American strategy of *guerre de course* and, like the earlier high-speed commerce raider *Wampanoag,* featured a propulsion-machinery design not found in the Royal Navy. The *Columbia*s were designed for high speed (twenty-two knots) to overtake passenger liners and Melville's novel, triple-screw drive was projected to allow them to cruise for 103 days at ten knots and to circle the earth without need for refueling or bases.[13] In reality, *Columbia* and *Minneapolis* never lived up to their billing as globe-circling commerce raiders. The estimated endurance of 24,720 nautical miles at ten knots was reduced in service to 7,083 nautical miles at 10.46 knots.[14]

The predreadnought battleships built after 1890 included such uniquely American design attributes as the superposed turrets—in the *Kearsarge* class (authorized 1895) and repeated in the *New Jersey* class (authorized 1899)—meant to maximize armored strength, survivability, and gun power. The collective, professional identity of a navy historically built on the perceived exceptionalist character of its ships extended to the new all-big-gun battleship, by which early-twentieth-century naval power would be measured. In 1902, Lt. Homer Poundstone called for the "biggest" battleship possible and, in conjunction with future admiral William Sims, designed USS *Scared-o'-Nothing,* which paralleled HMS *Dreadnought* in name and function. In the U.S. Naval Institute's 1905 prize essay, Cdr. Bradley Fiske argued for a class of large, powerful, high-speed "compromiseless" battleships to serve American long-range strategic commitments in the Pacific.[15]

The differences in engineering cultures that have existed among Britain, continental Europe, and America have been addressed by historians, and recent works have treated similar differences in naval architecture and shipbuilding.[16] The American geostrategic emphasis on the Pacific and on the long-range warships it required cast a long shadow across the twentieth century and was reinforced by the 1941–45 Pacific War. Until the design of the *Arleigh Burke* class of destroyers during the early 1980s, American naval architects continued to use hulls optimized for endurance rather than high speed or sea-keeping qualities.[17]

The exceptionalist nature of nineteenth-century American warship design—with its historical emphasis on hull strength (including armor), gun power, and endurance—was acknowledged by one of the leading naval architects in Britain, Professor J. Harvard Biles of the University of Glasgow. In a 1901 paper presented to the Institution of Naval Architects on recent American warship designs, Biles reported that American battleships had "more powerful guns and more of them than in other battleships."[18] Biles was struck by the "enormous [gun] battery of these ships [*Maine*, 1898], and with the great [armored] protection it has."[19] The American emphasis on gun power and strength was exemplified by the *Virginia* class (authorized 1899), which had an "equivalent weight of armament of 400 tons more than our battleships"; further, "their armour protection is thicker and more extended."[20] The traditional American pursuit of superior gun power also extended to cruisers. Of the *Pennsylvania* class (1901) Biles observed that "the Americans seem to prefer a dominating armament to other qualities."[21]

The shift the U.S. Navy undertook in 1890 toward a *guerre d'escadre* strategy marked a significant discontinuity within the intellectual history of the American naval profession. American naval officers and naval engineers (and to some extent, the U.S. shipbuilding industry) had to reinvent the technological basis of the Navy to function within a new strategic framework, different from that which had prevailed for most of the nineteenth century. This required the continued pursuit of exceptionalist warship designs, in keeping with the American naval tradition. However, now this tradition was influenced increasingly by engineering, technological, and scientific transfers from Europe, especially Britain.

The shift to metal warships removed Americans from their familiar wooden-material culture and forced them, initially, to rely on ideas and methods from Britain. Similarly, the rise of scientifically influenced naval architecture rooted in a formal educational—rather than artisanal—setting forced American naval constructors to pursue British and French education in naval architecture.[22] However, by the century's end, America's pursuit of a modern navy and the industrial base it required would foster innovation in metal ship construction that would rebound to Europe and change shipbuilding methods there.[23] The ability to manufacture thick, homogeneous armor, thanks to the relationship between the Navy and Andrew Carnegie, was another practice developed in the United States and sent abroad.[24]

American naval constructors, influenced by their European educations (at the Royal Naval College, Greenwich; the École d'Application du Génie Maritime; and the University of Glasgow), would be led, partly forced by circumstance but partly in fulfillment of their own wishes, to create their own American school of naval architecture. This would continue the American navy on its trajectory of technological exceptionalism, both in warship design (large, strong, heavily gunned ships) and in the field of ship propulsion (extreme economies devised to deal with the vast Pacific) into the twentieth century. Emblematic of this new American school of naval architecture was David W. Taylor, who stood first in his class academically at the Naval Academy (1885) and first in his class in the naval constructor course at Royal Naval College, Greenwich (1888). Although educated in Britain, Taylor's "routine work was characterized by a willingness to depart from the precedents established by European predecessors." An example was his design of a tow tank in the Experimental Model Basin at the Washington Navy Yard to allow the use of twenty-foot models rather than the twelve-to-fourteen-foot models used in such tanks in Europe. The larger models allowed for much more accurate prediction of ship powering requirements (i.e., the horsepower needed), which refined the design in the areas most critical for American ships—economy and range of operations.[25]

From the very first warships designed and built in America during the Revolutionary War to the superdreadnought battleships launched on the eve of World War I, American naval architects tended to build larger ships, within given ship types, than did European, especially British, designers. The first frigates of the Continental Navy were larger and faster than corresponding British ships. This trend continued with the forty-four-gun frigates designed by the Philadelphia constructor Joshua Humphreys to form the core of the six frigates (the other three were rated for fewer guns) authorized by the 1794 Naval Act to deal with Algerian corsairs. These "44s" were longer and faster than British frigates and employed American live oak, a very dense wood weighing fifty-five to seventy-five pounds per cubic foot.[26] The heavier scantlings of the Humphreys frigates enabled them to carry larger guns (typically twenty-four-pounders) and more of them, sometimes up to sixty; the nickname of "Old Ironsides" earned by USS *Constitution* was based in the material superiority of the live oak. After three American frigate victories over the Royal Navy in 1812, the Admiralty forbade its frigate captains from engaging *Constitution, United States,* or *President* in single-ship combat.[27] The pursuit of exceptionalist design qualities of the Humphreys frigates continued in the seventy-four-gun ships of the line authorized in 1813 and 1816. For example, USS *Ohio,* laid down in 1817, reflected wartime confirmation of the American criterion of giving "all ships the heaviest armament possible in a given rate."[28] According to Howard Chapelle, naval architect and maritime historian emeritus at the Smithsonian Institution, "it was decided that all American naval vessels should be superior in size and armament to their European counterparts."[29]

The exceptional nature of American sailing warships provided little guidance for the steam-powered, post-1883 "new" Navy that required propulsion efficiency for long-range Pacific operations. Interestingly, the roots for both the 1916 turbo-electric drive and the HPHT propulsion that would power the newly constructed U.S. warships employed during World War II were in the private sector, specifically the electric-power-generation industry. In both cases, there was resistance within the Navy and in the private shipbuilding industry to these new, "outside" technologies.[30]

Technology Transfer from the Private Sector
Owing to its limited engineering bureaucracy, the late-nineteenth-century U.S. Navy relied on the private sector for the design and construction of the complex technological components of its modern ships. This left the Navy vulnerable to the unsubstantiated performance claims and vagaries of its industrial suppliers and private shipyards. Naval engineers were not comfortable relying on the goodwill of the private sector to supply quality machinery. The Navy had no machinery or material specifications, nor did it have viable means, save for noting failures and excluding vendors, to ensure quality control. The technologically complex modern Navy, unlike the antiquated force of the 1870s, needed a testing laboratory. Congress responded to naval engineers' call for such a facility by authorizing the Engineering Experiment Station (EES) at Annapolis, Maryland, in 1903; it became operational in 1908.[31]

Although EES contributed to the increased material readiness of the Navy, the bulk of engineering innovation still came from the private sector. EES scanned this environment for useful technologies, instruments, and processes. This paralleled contemporary industrial practice, wherein nascent corporate research organizations did not invent new technologies but used the work of individual inventors, often in a creative synthesis.[32] In 1915 Lt. Cdr. H. C. Dinger underscored this reliance on the private sector:

> The Navy relies on the commercial engineering field for the excellence of the products from which the material matters of our naval forces are constructed. It relies on it for the development of tools, methods of work and the training of artisans by which our fighting weapons are produced in superior form and efficiency. Without a high state of engineering ability and progress in the country at large, the highest character of excellence in navy material can not be realized. The capacity of our commercial engineering plants is the principal asset of our naval engineering reserve of material.[33]

This "reserve of material" within commercial engineering plants, specifically the civilian electrical-power generating industries, would offer the U.S. Navy valuable developmental and operational experience with both the turboelectric drive and HPHT steam propulsion.

The introduction of the all-big-gun HMS *Dreadnought* in 1906 represented a quantum change in battleship technology. The Parsons marine steam turbines used in *Dreadnought* greatly reduced the internal hull volume required for propulsion machinery.[34] However, because of its direct connection to the propeller, the marine turbine brought a decrease in propulsion efficiency and steaming radius.[35] The first twenty-five U.S. battleships, all predreadnoughts and commissioned between 1895 and 1908, were powered by large and relatively economical reciprocating steam engines. The U.S. Navy could not afford any decrease in propulsion economy, but the turbine was nevertheless attractive, because its compact size offered potential improvements in the fighting efficiency of battleships—for instance, the installation of an improved armor design theretofore precluded by the size of reciprocating engines. As a result, turbines were installed in one all-big-gun battleship *(North Dakota)* of the *Delaware* class.

Widespread acceptance of the marine turbine depended on the development of a means to optimize the turbine-propeller system—turbines develop little useful power at slow shaft speeds, and their maximum power at speeds so high that propellers, because of a phenomenon known as "cavitation," cannot efficiently deliver thrust to the surrounding water. Until this mismatch could be resolved, the turbine would be limited to ships requiring high-speed operation—warships and passenger liners. In the U.S. Navy, where speed took second place to propulsion economy, high speed was not a primary design criterion for its battleships. As a result, the turbine's position was precarious; traditional American naval engineering culture reasserted itself and excluded turbines from the battleships of the 1910 program. Meanwhile, hydrodynamic limitations on propeller design shifted the focus on improvement in propulsive efficiency to the turbine. To regain the U.S. naval market, in 1909–10 turbine manufacturers increased the diameter of their turbines, reducing their rotative speed while maintaining the same level of power output.[36] Although reduced to several hundred rotations per minute, the speed of the turbines was still too high for optimum propeller efficiency. The turbine's overall propulsive efficiency, as translated into fuel economy and long-range operation, still remained less than that of a reciprocating steam-powered ship but was offset, to a point, by its compactness, which allowed for increased coal bunkerage and, as noted, improvements in other ship systems.

To solve the problems of low propulsive efficiency and propeller cavitation, marine engineers proposed to place a speed-reducing device between the high-speed turbine and an optimized, low-speed propeller. They pursued three paths to develop such a device. The first option was the mechanical reduction gear, taken up in Britain and the United States. The second was turboelectric drive, an idea investigated in Britain, Germany, and the United States. The third was hydraulic speed reduction, by means of the Föttinger Transformer, developed in Germany.[37]

In 1904 Charles Parsons, George Westinghouse, former engineer in chief George Melville, and John MacAlpine, a marine engineer, formed a consortium to develop a suitable mechanical reduction gear. Metallurgical and machining difficulties precluded producing geometrically accurate gear teeth able to withstand the tremendous pressure and torque involved in use with steam turbines. Melville and MacAlpine thought they could bypass this problem by designing a reduction gear that incorporated a "floating frame." Refinement of the design was retarded by the adverse economic climate of 1907, which forced George Westinghouse to reduce his funding for the project.[38] Working independently and drawing on British expertise in metalworking, Parsons pursued a fixed-frame, high-tolerance mechanical-reduction-gear assembly. This type of gearing required accurate machining technology, and it was not until 1910, almost thirteen years after the initial success of his *Turbinia*, the first turbine-powered steamship, that the Parsons Marine Steam Turbine Company was finally able to develop and test an experimental fixed-frame reduction gear in the thousand-horsepower propulsion plant of SS *Vespasian*.[39]

Around the same time, Hermann Föttinger in Germany produced a hydraulic speed-reduction device. Föttinger had originally developed an electromagnetic transmission system that provided an overall power-transmission efficiency of 87 percent (compared with 60 percent in direct-drive turbines) but had abandoned it because of its complexity and expense. Föttinger had more success with his next design, the hydraulic transformer, in which the turbine shaft rotated a waterwheel that forced water through a set of guide blades onto a larger waterwheel attached to the propeller shaft. This Föttinger Transformer, coupled to an AEG-Curtis turbine, was tested at the Vulcan Shipbuilding Company power plant for fourteen months before being installed in a specially built test boat in 1910.[40]

While Westinghouse, Parsons, and Föttinger worked on mechanical and hydraulic methods of speed reduction, William Le Roy Emmet, a prominent General Electric (GE) Company engineer motivated by an idea advanced by the electrical inventor Reginald Fessenden, proposed a turboelectric ship-propulsion system to eliminate the inefficiency of the directly connected marine steam turbine.[41] Emmet had been quite successful in the development and marketing of turbogenerator systems within the American electrical-power industry. However, industry could absorb only a limited number of turbogenerators. The U.S. Navy, on the other hand, was a growing organization and a wealthy potential customer, and Emmet sought to extend General Electric's entrepreneurial success to this new and lucrative market.[42] To break into the battleship propulsion market, however, GE had to compete against the Melville-MacAlpine gear of the Westinghouse Machine Company and overcome the strong influence of the private shipyards that were Parsons licensees and advocates of the directly connected turbine drive.

Emmet and General Electric had an uphill fight, since the Navy's Board on Construction had rejected Fessenden's turboelectric-drive idea in 1908. Secretary of the Navy George von Lengerke Meyer, however, as a favor to Emmet's brother-in-law, used the conditional endorsement of Engineer in Chief Hutch Cone, chief of the Bureau of Steam Engineering, to bypass the Board on Construction and refer the question of turboelectric propulsion to the line officers on the Navy's General Board. The General Board recommended installing the General Electric system in one of three new colliers for evaluation.[43]

The 1911 collier program pitted Emmet's GE turboelectric drive against a new Westinghouse-backed system with the Melville-MacAlpine reduction gear. The third collier authorized that year was equipped with a diesel submarine engine from the Electric Boat Company.[44] The entire financial risk of the experiment was carried by the competing companies.[45]

The May 1914 report of the trial of the turboelectric drive in the collier *Jupiter* justified Emmet's claims for the electric drive. *Jupiter*'s chief engineer (and the future chief of the Bureau of Engineering), Lt. S. M. Robinson, reported that the turboelectric drive was easily operated by relatively unskilled sailors, provided accurate speed control, and, most important, exceeded GE's guaranteed economy predictions by a phenomenal 18 percent.[46] The rival Westinghouse Melville-MacAlpine reduction gear system, in the collier *Neptune*, had failed its trial. The third collier, *Maumee*, did not perform anywhere near expectations, and the diesel engine was rejected.

In 1915, the U.S. Navy was faced with a choice among the proven success and economy of the turboelectric drive, the trouble-plagued Westinghouse Melville-MacAlpine reduction gear, and a modification, first introduced in 1912, of the inefficient direct-drive arrangement by the addition of a small reduction gear–equipped cruising turbine. To the officers of the Bureau of Steam Engineering, the geostrategic realities of the Pacific made the choice clear. In April 1915, Secretary Daniels announced the selection of the General Electric turboelectric system to power the new superdreadnought *California*.[47] The following year the Navy announced that all sixteen capital ships of the massive 1916 program would be powered by turboelectric drive.[48]

The selection of so unconventional a propulsion system provoked a variety of responses. Published statements in favor of the electric drive by such notable electrical experts as Nikola Tesla and Frank Sprague did much to sway public opinion in favor of the Navy.[49] Even shipping-industry publications, such as *Marine Engineering* and *Shipping Illustrated,* pointed out the financial motivation behind opposition to electric drive. The latter, which held "no brief for the electric drive," attributed the "incompetent criticism" the idea was receiving to the shipyards' loss of business as patent licensees of Curtis and Parsons turbines. When the electric drive moved from an experimental collier built in a government yard to battleships built under contract by private firms, "the shoe began to pinch."[50]

The dominance of turboelectric propulsion in the U.S. Navy was relatively short-lived, largely as a result of the weight restrictions placed on capital ships by the Five-Power Treaty that resulted from the 1921 Washington Naval Conference. The treaty, which measured naval power in terms of ship displacement (weight), restricted capital ships and aircraft carriers but placed no limits on other types of warships.[51] Renewed naval competition was possible, especially in the unrestricted category of cruisers displacing up to ten thousand long tons. The Harding and Coolidge administrations were chary of renewed naval competition in cruisers, but when the 1927 Geneva Conference failed, the United States pursued cruiser construction in earnest.[52]

The Move toward HPHT Steam Propulsion
While turboelectric drive powered the latest American battleships and aircraft carriers in the 1920s, improvements in reduction-gear technology, coupled with the threat posed by higher-speed Japanese capital ships, such as those of the *Kongo* class, resurrected the geared-turbine propulsion system and added higher speed to the traditional Pacific-based requirement of endurance. Both General Electric and Westinghouse pursued reduction-gear technology, and the Navy installed it on smaller warships, such as destroyers. Reduction gears became more efficient, eventually transmitting 2 to 3 percent more power than electric drive. By 1931, machining and metallurgical processes could produce compact and lightweight reduction gears with which turboelectric drive could no longer compete. The first electrically propelled battleship, USS *New Mexico* (ex-*California*), had its electric motors replaced with a GE mechanical reduction gear in 1931.[53]

For both turboelectric and geared-turbine propulsion systems, high-pressure, high-temperature steam offered increased efficiency. In the development of cruiser designs displacing under ten thousand tons as required by the Five-Power Treaty, weight savings, always important, became even more critical. The Bureau of Steam Engineering and its Annapolis Engineering Experiment Station worked to develop more-efficient, lighter propulsion machinery both for new construction and for replacement of older machinery in existing ships. In 1925, the chief of the Bureau of Engineering reported that

> higher pressures and higher temperatures are constantly being advocated, which means that the metals must be subjected to stresses never before attempted. Before such new materials can be incorporated in the design of machinery a vast amount of research and experimental work must be performed. The bureau is constantly taking advantage of the facilities offered at the experiment station at Annapolis in the way of testing and developing engineering materials. . . . There is no substitute for the activities of . . . [EES] for investigation, test, development, and research work in naval engineering.[54]

The claim that there "is no substitute for the activities" of EES reflects a Navy inward focus similar to that found in the history of the turboelectric drive. The civilian electrical-power industry was already utilizing HPHT machinery, made possible by the development of high-strength, heat-resistant alloys after World War I.[55]

The U.S. Navy's first foray into HPHT propulsion was in the 1926 design of the heavy cruiser *Louisville*. The Bureau of Engineering initially used 450 pounds per square inch (psi)—up from the existing 300 psi—as the design operating pressure of its steam propulsion machinery. In testimony before the General Board of the Navy in October 1938, S. M. Robinson, now a rear admiral and former chief of the Bureau of Engineering, would recall the case for HPHT steam propulsion in *Louisville* and the maelstrom of opposition this decision had engendered in the years since:

> At the present time, most of the opposition to the use of higher pressures and temperatures comes from the same people who about twelve years ago [for *Louisville* in 1926] were opposing just as strongly the use of 400 pounds of steam as compared to 300 pounds of steam. These same people, and they are the shipbuilders at the Bethlehem Shipbuilding Co., Newport News Shipbuilding Co., and the New York Shipbuilding Co., opposed the use of 400 pounds as strenuously as they are now opposing 600 pounds. . . . There are several reasons, but the principal one is that they have not had any experience with such pressures and temperatures. . . . They have practically no research laboratories for developing turbines so they are not in the position to go ahead and advance the art as are the people who build for shore [power] plants.[56]

Louisville, part of the first real naval building program since the world war, was a much less capable ship than it could have been, because it had been completed with a 300 psi steam plant. The attempt by the Bureau of Engineering to raise the steam pressure to 450 psi was a "modest improvement in steam conditions, not anything like what was being done ashore [in electrical power plants]."[57] According to Robinson, who had seen the turboelectric controversy at first hand as chief engineer in USS *Neptune,* the shipbuilders' opposition to abandoning the low-pressure machinery with which they were comfortable "was enormous" and was "put on the Secretary of the Navy, the General Board, the Chief of Naval Operations, and the Chief of the Bureau of Engineering. . . . Of course, the Design Division of the Bureau of Engineering were the only people on the other side because they were the only people who had studied this thing and the result of all this was . . . the shipbuilders were allowed to put in bids on 300 pounds of steam."[58]

The break for advocates of HPHT steam propulsion came as a result of actions taken against the shipyards under the Espionage Act. The "big three" American shipbuilding corporations—Bethlehem, Newport News, and New York Shipbuilding—held turbine licenses from Parsons, Ltd., for the fabrication of turbines. In 1935 the chief of the Bureau of Engineering, Rear Adm. Harold Bowen, pursued enforcement of the Espionage Act against the shipyards, which forced them to sever their ties with Parsons, because using its turbines required the transmission of American warship-design details to Britain, which violated the law. The shipbuilders were obliged to use domestic turbines.⁵⁹ This, according to Bowen, was "a vital step in the development of American naval power."⁶⁰

The American electric-power industry had pursued increasingly higher-pressure and higher-temperature steam until designs using steam at 650 psi and 850 degrees Fahrenheit were commonplace. The turbines and machinery for the electrical-power industry were manufactured by GE and Westinghouse, and their development was supported by their large, generously funded research-and-development laboratories. As a result, the United States had "in operation in our central power stations the most modern and efficient turbine installations in the world."⁶¹

Rear Admiral Bowen's use of the Espionage Act marked the beginning of a long, difficult campaign to revolutionize and standardize U.S. warship propulsion by designing and installing superheat-capable, high-pressure, high-temperature steam-turbine propulsion systems.⁶² Robinson and Bowen had to overcome opposition from some engineer officers within the Bureau of Engineering, from the line admirals and staff of the General Board of the Navy, and the significant financial and political lobbying of major industrial interests who argued that HPHT steam propulsion posed significant manufacturing risks. By November 1938, however, Bowen had routed senior officers who were critical of HPHT steam propulsion.⁶³

The Quintessential Cultural Expression

In 1967, the historian Lynn T. White argued that "engineers are the chief revolutionaries of our time."⁶⁴ Although acting on a much smaller stage than White had envisioned, both Robinson and Bowen, in keeping with the exceptionalist culture of American naval engineering, successfully overthrew the low-pressure ancien regime of British marine engineering. The new paradigm of efficient, high-pressure steam machinery standardized the propulsion technology of major U.S. combatant ships on the eve of World War II, and its technological life lasted well into the Cold War. More important than standardization was the excellent fuel economy this system offered, which in turn translated into marked increases in the radius of fleet operations. Had the opponents of HPHT steam propulsion succeeded in maintaining the status quo, the U.S. Navy would have been hard pressed to conduct combat operations of adequate scope and duration, especially in the Pacific, during World War II.

The vastness of the Pacific Ocean had driven U.S. warship design since the rise of the modern, steam-powered Navy during the 1880s. Propulsion-machinery efficiency, coupled with fuel capacity, determined a ship's radius of operations. American commercial interests in distant China and southeastern Asia, along with a lack of overseas bases, made propulsion efficiency much more imperative for the U.S. Navy than for the fleets of other maritime powers.⁶⁵ During the early 1930s, using the civilian electrical-power industry as a model and benefiting from its technological innovations, the U.S. Navy began serious development work on high-pressure, high-temperature steam propulsion machinery. By the late 1930s it had designed and tested a standard suite that it installed in most of its warships that would be used during World War II.

No other maritime power pursued this path. The Royal Navy, whose technical inquisitiveness and experimental expenditures had been praised by Rear Admiral Melville in 1902, by this time lacked the financial means and institutional energy to do so.[66] Interestingly, the engineer in chief of the Royal Navy took a very conservative position regarding propulsion innovation during the 1930s: "Let the Americans and Germans do it, and if it succeeds we will copy them."[67] Apparently, during the interwar years the British shipping industry in general was reluctant to embrace new technology, since it perceived that "marine engineering was changing in such a rapid and uncertain way."[68] However, as Nathan Rosenberg correctly observes, militaries do not delay in embracing new technologies within rapidly changing technological landscapes.[69] The Royal Navy had certainly not delayed during the period of rapid technological change of the latter half of the nineteenth century. By the 1930s, this was no longer the case.

The new high-pressure, high-temperature propulsion machinery formed the "background of propulsion engineering during World War Two," and its excellent fuel economy translated into a significant increase in the radius of fleet operations. To credit the U.S. Navy's successful, long-range naval war against Japan to this innovative propulsion plant would not be hyperbole. According to Vice Adm. Earle W. Mills, later chief of the Bureau of Ships, U.S. naval operations in the Pacific "would not have been possible without it."[70]

The superiority of American HPHT propulsion technology during World War II was noteworthy. For example, the *North Carolina*–class battleship *Washington* (a 1937 design), equipped with high-pressure, high-temperature steam propulsion machinery, burned 39 percent less fuel at low speeds and was 30 percent more fuel efficient overall than the British *King George V* class, designed in 1936.[71] In fact, the cruising radius of the *North Carolina* class was nearly double that of the *King George V* class at lower speeds and 20 percent greater at higher speeds. The effect of high-pressure, high-temperature steam propulsion on other classes of warships was even greater. In April 1942, Cdr. Paul F. Lee, an assistant American naval attaché to the United Kingdom, reported that

> [the limited cruising radius of their ships] is a very serious question with the British and is having a marked effect on their naval operations. Even in their newest ships the fuel consumption is at least 50% higher and in some cases almost 100% higher than we have in our modern designs. Due to war conditions the normal peacetime cruising radius of their ships has been reduced by as much as 50% in some classes. This latter, combined with the poor fuel economy, has given their ships a comparatively short cruising radius. They are now fully alive to the mistakes they made in their prewar designs.[72]

The period of British maritime technological supremacy had ended, and the words of the prewar British engineer in chief now proved prophetic. The Royal

Navy copied the U.S. Navy's high-pressure, high-temperature approach in the *Daring*-class destroyers for its 1944 program. Not only was the U.S. Navy emancipated from Britain in its engineering but the historical flow of technological innovation had been reversed. By the end of World War II, the British were using pressurized-casing boilers produced by the American firms of Foster Wheeler and Babcock & Wilcox.[73]

Such disparities in propulsion efficiency were not limited to the Royal Navy. The *North Carolina*–class battleships used only 0.64 tons of fuel per nautical mile at twenty knots, but Germany's *Bismarck* burned 0.83 tons of fuel per nautical mile at the same speed. This was a difference of approximately 30 percent. Japan's *Yamato* (1937), with a propulsion plant along British low-pressure lines, used 0.88 tons of fuel per nautical mile at eighteen knots.[74] Although exact figures are unavailable, *Yamato* would have used even more fuel at twenty knots, increasing its disadvantage vis-à-vis the American design.

High-pressure, high-temperature steam propulsion systems were the quintessential expression of American naval engineering culture. HPHT propulsion did not have the visibility or the broad utilitarian postwar spillover that radar enjoyed. However, it was essential to the successful prosecution of the worldwide American war effort. Tocqueville wrote that in a democratic society, "men's minds are unconsciously led to neglect theory and devote an unparalleled amount of application to the applications of science, or at least to that aspect of theory which is useful in practice."[75] The HPHT design was certainly useful in the Navy's prosecution of the war against the Axis. Its development was a combination of the visions of Admirals Robinson and Bowen of steam-turbine propulsion as a linear technological progression (more pressure, more temperature) arising from the technological trajectory of the electrical-power generating industry. It also was the result of the ability of these two men, especially Bowen, to wage a successful social-constructivist campaign in support of HPHT systems.[76] This campaign was successful, in large measure because of its consonance with a strong, deep-seated American naval engineering culture that embraced a collective memory of exceptionalism and was always mindful of the strategic challenges of Pacific operations.

NOTES 1 Alexis de Tocqueville, *Democracy in America,* ed. J. P. Mayer and Max Lerner, trans. George Lawrence (New York: Harper and Row, 1966), p. 277.

2 Ibid., p. 420.

3 Of interest is Michael L. Smith, "Recourse of Empire: Landscapes of Progress in Technological America," in *Does Technology Drive History? The Dilemma of Technological Determinism,* ed. Merritt Roe Smith and Leo Marx (Cambridge, Mass.: MIT Press, 1994), pp. 38–52.

4 Perhaps the most applicable definition of culture in the context of engineering within the Navy as an institution is "the body of intellectual and imaginative work, the stock of recognized (not necessarily organized) knowledge, representing experience recorded," as presented in Ian Inkster, "Technology in World History: Cultures of Constraint and Innovation, Emulation, and Technology Transfers," *Comparative Technology Transfer and Society* 5 (2007), p. 110.

5 William H. Thiesen, *Industrializing American Shipbuilding: The Transformation of Ship Design and Construction, 1820–1920* (Gainesville: Univ. Press of Florida, 2006).

6 Ibid., chaps. 5–8; and Lars O. Olsson, "'To See How Things Were Done in a Big Way': Swedish Naval Architects in the United States, 1890–1915," *Technology and Culture* 39 (1998), pp. 434–56.

7 See William M. McBride, "Nineteenth-Century American Warships: The Pursuit of Exceptionalist Design," in *Reinventing the Ship: Science, Technology and the Maritime World,* ed. Don Leggett and Richard Dunn (Surrey, U.K.: Ashgate, 2012), pp. 173–207.

8 For the shift in propulsion design in the *Daring* class, see Edgar G. March, *British Destroyers: A History of Development, 1892–1953: Drawn by Admiralty Permission from Official Records & Returns, Ships' Covers & Building Plans* (London: Seeley, 1966), pp. 465–66. High-pressure, high-temperature steam-turbine propulsion, as a symbol of American engineering emancipation from Britain, is addressed in Vice Adm. Harold T. Bowen, USN (Ret.), *Ships, Machinery, and Mossbacks: The Autobiography of a Naval Engineer* (Princeton, N.J.: Princeton Univ. Press, 1954), p. 51.

9 Also crucial to the Navy's success during World War II was underway refueling; see Thomas Wildenberg,

Gray Steel and Black Oil: Fast Tankers and Replenishment at Sea in the U.S. Navy, 1912–1992 (Annapolis, Md.: Naval Institute Press, 1996). Useful starting points to understand American engineering culture are Terry S. Reynolds, ed., *The Engineer in America: A Historical Anthology from Technology and Culture* (Chicago: Univ. of Chicago Press, 1991), and Monte A. Calvert, *The Mechanical Engineer in America 1830–1910: Professional Cultures in Conflict* (Baltimore, Md.: Johns Hopkins Univ. Press, 1967).

10 Capt. C. W. Dyson, USN, "The Development of Machinery in the U.S. Navy during the Past Ten Years," *Journal of the American Society of Naval Engineers* [hereafter *ASNE Journal*] 29 (1917), pp. 195–238, esp. p. 217.

11 Ibid. Also see Engineer in Chief Hutch I. Cone, USN, "Naval Engineering Progress" (lecture to the Naval War College, Newport, R.I., 9 August 1910), repr. *ASNE Journal* 22 (1910), pp. 1013–37, esp. p. 1019. In designing, toward the end of the nineteenth century, cruisers for commerce protection, the Royal Navy did not ignore steaming radius, although the characteristic routinely emphasized by naval constructor and historian David K. Brown in his authoritative history of Royal Navy warship design (including cruisers) is speed rather than endurance; see David K. Brown, Warrior *to* Dreadnought: *Warship Development, 1860–1905* (London: Chatham, 1997), esp. pp. 156–66. While Dyson's comments may be focused on battleships, what is interesting is his belief that American warships were designed to a unique criterion. The smaller steaming radius and relative inefficiency of Royal Navy capital ships compared with U.S. battleships became readily apparent during World War II. According to Vice Adm. Harold G. Bowen, chief of the U.S. Navy's Bureau of Engineering (1935–39), Adm. Sir John Tovey, Commander in Chief, Home Fleet, "was said to be much exercised over the fact that our [USS] *Washington,* a contemporary of the *King George V* [both authorized in 1937], was about thirty per cent more economical than his flagship"; Bowen, *Ships, Machinery, and Mossbacks,* p. 113. The May 1941 *Bismarck* chase also brought to light the Royal Navy's historical reliance on bases to which Dyson had referred. In his *The* Bismarck *Episode* (New York: Macmillan, 1949), Capt. Russell Grenfell, Royal Navy (RN), writes, "That no such organization [refueling at sea] existed in the British Navy can probably be ascribed to its two-century predominance among the fleets of the world having given it copious supply or fuelling bases in every ocean. In consequence, British naval officers had become unduly 'base-minded,' the shore stocks of fuel at one of Britain's numerous naval bases being uppermost in their thoughts when any question of mobility arose"; quoted in Bowen, *Ships, Machinery, and Mossbacks,* p. 110.

12 Exceptionalism, from which "exceptionalist" is derived, is defined by *Merriam-Webster* as "the condition of being different from the norm; *also:* a theory expounding the exceptionalism especially of a nation or region." Naval constructors and engineers of all countries attempted to design ships that were "superior" to their rivals', and American designers were no different. However, American naval constructors and engineers had a distinct and active design culture that guided their actions. This design culture was part of a larger naval culture that embraced particular strategic paradigms that were affected significantly by geostrategic factors; all of that in turn became part of the professional collective memory of the American naval officer corps. The results were ships that often were "different from the norm" found in other navies. "Exceptionalism" is a "loaded" term in modern historiography, implying national or cultural arrogance. This is not a part of the argument here for American exceptionalist design, engineering, or technology. For an introduction to historical exceptionalism, see Ian Tyrrell, "American Exceptionalism in the Age of International History," *American Historical Review* 96 (1991), pp. 1031–55. Also of interest is Erik van der Vleuten, "Toward a Transnational History of Technology: Meanings, Promises, and Pitfalls," *Technology and Culture* 49 (2008), pp. 974–94.

13 Coal and range data from Norman Friedman, *U.S. Cruisers: An Illustrated Design History* (Annapolis, Md.: Naval Institute Press, 1984), p. 40, as is the "most important" characterization. In his 1890 annual report, Secretary of the Navy Benjamin F. Tracy wrote that these cruisers "would exterminate the commerce of any country under the present conditions of commerce protection and would thus, under these conditions, also preclude an attack from a commercial state, however threatening in its demands, powerful in its armored fleet, or aggressive in its foreign policy"; quoted in ibid.

14 Lt. C. R. Bryan, USN, "The Steaming Radius of United States Naval Vessels," *ASNE Journal* 13 (1901), pp. 50–69, data on p. 62.

15 Lt. Homer Poundstone, USN, "Size of Battleships for U.S. Navy," U.S. Naval Institute *Proceedings* [hereafter *USNIP*] 29 (1903), pp. 161–74; Cdr. Bradley A. Fiske, USN, "American Naval Policy," *USNIP* 31 (1905), pp. 1–80. For the USS *Scared-o'-Nothing,* see Robert F. Wilson, "Sims, of the Successful Indiscretions," in *The World's Work,* vol. 34, *May to October, 1917, a History of Our Time* (Garden City, N.Y.: Doubleday, Page, 1917), pp. 333–40, esp. p. 339.

16 For examples of assessments of national characteristics in engineering, see Eda Kranakis, *Constructing a Bridge: An Exploration of Engineering Culture, Design, and Research in Nineteenth-Century France and America* (Cambridge, Mass.: MIT Press, 1997), and John K. Brown, "Design Plans, Working Drawings, National Styles: Engineering Practice in Great Britain and the United States, 1775–1945," *Technology and Culture* 42 (2000), pp. 195–238, passim, esp. p. 238. For shipbuilding and naval architecture, see Thiesen, *Industrializing American Shipbuilding,* and Larrie D. Ferreiro, *Ships and Science: The Birth of Naval Architecture in the Scientific Revolution, 1600–1800* (Cambridge, Mass.: MIT Press, 2007). Also of interest is Larrie D. Ferreiro, "Genius and Engineering: The Naval Constructors of France, Great Britain, and the United States," *Naval Engineers Journal* 110 (1998), pp. 99–119.

17 For an entrée into modern, comparative naval architecture, see Capt. J. W. Kehoe, USN, et al., "Comparative Naval Architectural Analysis of

NATO and Soviet Frigates, Part 1," *Naval Engineers Journal* 92 (1980), pp. 87–99; Kehoe et al., "U.S. and Foreign Hull Form, Machinery and Structural Design Practices," *Naval Engineers Journal* 95 (1983), pp. 36–53, esp. p. 36; and Kehoe, "Warship Design: Theirs and Ours," *Naval Engineers Journal* 88 (1976), pp. 92–100.

18 Professor J. H. Biles, Member of Council, "Ten Years' Naval Construction in the United States," *Transactions of the Institution of Naval Architects* [hereafter *INA Transactions*] 43 (1901), pp. 3–4.

19 Ibid., pp. 6–7.

20 Ibid., pp. 14–15.

21 Ibid., p. 8.

22 For the education of American naval constructors in the United Kingdom and France, see William M. McBride, *Technological Change and the United States Navy, 1865–1941* (Baltimore, Md.: Johns Hopkins Univ. Press, 2000), pp. 24–31.

23 See Thiesen, *Industrializing American Shipbuilding*, chaps. 5–8, and Olsson, "'To See How Things Were Done in a Big Way,'" pp. 434–56.

24 See B. Franklin Cooling, *Gray Steel and Blue Water Navy: Formative Years of America's Military-Industrial Complex, 1881–1917* (Hamden, Conn.: Archon Books, 1979).

25 Rodney P. Carlisle, *Where the Fleet Begins: A History of the David Taylor Research Center, 1898–1998* (Washington, D.C.: Naval Historical Center, 1998), pp. 49–50.

26 Ian W. Toll, *Six Frigates: The Epic History of the Founding of the U.S. Navy* (New York: W. W. Norton, 2006), pp. 58–61.

27 Ibid., p. 383.

28 Howard I. Chapelle, *The History of the American Sailing Navy: The Ships and Their Development* (New York: W. W. Norton, 1949), p. 316.

29 Ibid.

30 See William M. McBride, "Strategic Determinism in Technology Selection: The Electric Battleship and U.S. Naval-Industrial Relations," *Technology and Culture* 33 (1992), pp. 248–77.

31 See William M. McBride, "From Measuring Progress to Technological Innovation: The Prewar Annapolis Engineering Experiment Station," in *Instrumental in War: Science, Research, and Instruments between Knowledge and the World*, ed. Steven A. Walton (Leiden, Neth.: Brill Academic, 2005), pp. 215–51.

32 See John Kenly Smith, Jr., "The Scientific Tradition in American Industrial Research," *Technology and Culture* 31 (1990), pp. 121–31, esp. p. 126.

33 Lt. Cdr. H. C. Dinger, USN, "The Reserve Forces of Naval Material: Cooperation between the Navy and the Producers of Naval Material," *ASNE Journal* 27 (1915), p. 856.

34 One comparison placed the steam turbine at half the length and height and two-thirds the weight of a steam reciprocating engine delivering a comparable power output. See "Comparison of a Turbine and a Reciprocating Engine for the United States Navy," *Scientific American,* repr. *USNIP* 32 (1906), pp. 1615–16.

35 The high speed of the turbine caused the propeller to rotate at a speed above its optimum efficiency. Cavitation, with attendant propeller-blade erosion, was the result. See Rear Adm. C. W. Dyson, USN, "The Passing of the Direct-Connected Turbine for the Propulsion of Ships," *ASNE Journal* 31 (1919), pp. 555–76.

36 "A Marine Steam Turbine Reducing Gear," *Iron Age,* repr. *USNIP* 35 (1909), p. 1301.

37 For a brief description of each system, see William Hovgaard, *Modern History of Warships: Comprising a Discussion of Present Standpoint and Recent War Experiences for the Use of Students of Naval Construction, Naval Constructors, Naval Officers, and Others Interested in Naval Matters* (London: E. & F. N. Spon, 1920), pp. 378–81.

38 See Dyson, "Development of Machinery in the U.S. Navy," pp. 224–26; Francis Hodgkinson, "Progress in Turbine Ship Propulsion" (paper presented to the [U.S.] Society of Naval Architects and Marine Engineers, 14 November 1918), repr. *ASNE Journal* 31 (1919), pp. 193–94; and George Westinghouse, *Broadening the Field of the Marine Steam Turbine: The Problem and Its Solution (The Melville-MacAlpine Reduction Gear)* (Pittsburgh, Pa.: "Printed for Geo. Westinghouse," 1909).

39 C. A. Parsons and R. J. Walker, "Twelve Months' Experience with Geared Turbines in the Cargo Steamer *Vespasian*," *INA Transactions* 53 (1911), pp. 29–36; "Speed Reduction Gears for Marine Turbines," *Engineer,* repr. *USNIP* 36 (1910), p. 305.

40 "A Hydraulic Transmission Gear for Marine Turbines," *Engineering Magazine,* repr. *USNIP* 36 (1910), pp. 293–96.

41 Fessenden claimed to have offered his plans for an electric-driven ship to the Navy as early as 1899, and again in 1902 and 1904. In 1908, the Navy Department told him to take his idea to the "electric companies." See Fessenden to the Secretary of the Navy, 21 August 1911, record group 80, General Records of the Secretary of the Navy, National Archives, Washington, D.C. [hereafter RG 80], 1897–1915, file 24666-22.

42 Emmet was exhibiting "entrepreneurial alertness" in a Schumpeterian sense—the Austrian economist Joseph Schumpeter having emphasized the role of innovation in growth; see Inkster, "Technology in World History," p. 119. American naval expansion had absorbed an average of approximately 17 percent of the annual federal budget during Theodore Roosevelt's presidency; Roger Dingman, *Power in the Pacific* (Chicago: Univ. of Chicago Press, 1979), p. 3. In its business with the electrical-power industry, GE used the larger-capacity and more efficient impulse turbine developed by Charles Curtis. A five-thousand-kilowatt GE-Curtis impulse turbine was installed in Consolidated Edison's Fisk Street Station in Chicago in October 1903.

43 In September 1908, the U.S. naval attaché in Berlin reported on the claim for reduced fuel consumption in the new turboelectrically propelled submarine mother ship *Vulkan*. This report was in the

possession of the Bureau of Steam Engineering when it reviewed Fessenden's turboelectric-propulsion proposal. See *Board on Construction Endorsement on National Electric Signal Company Propelling Plant for Battleships Nos. 30 and 31, 25 January 1909*, RG 80, 1897–1915, file 26272-13, and Secretary of the Navy, memorandum to the General Board, 10 April 1911, RG 80, 1897–1915, file 24666-14. Also see Fessenden to Secretary of the Navy, 14 August 1908, RG 80, 1897–1915, file 26272-13a, and Engineer-in-Chief Cone, memorandum to the Secretary of the Navy, 3 February 1910, RG 80, 1897–1915, file 26840-208.

44 Rear Adm. C. W. Dyson, USN, "A Fifty Year Retrospect of Naval Marine Engineering," *ASNE Journal* 30 (1918), p. 297.

45 Secretary Meyer to Congressman Knowland, 21 April 1911, RG 80, SecNav, 1897–1915, file 26466-15.

46 Lt. S. M. Robinson, USN, "Operation and Trials of the U.S. Fleet Collier *Jupiter*," *ASNE Journal* 26 (1914), pp. 339–53.

47 See William Le Roy Emmet, *The Autobiography of an Engineer* (Albany, N.Y.: Fort Orange, 1931), pp. 167–68.

48 See McBride, *Technological Change and the United States Navy,* chap. 4.

49 See Tesla's statement in the *New York Herald,* repr. *USNIP* 43 (1917), pp. 798–800, and Frank J. Sprague's letter to the *New York Times,* 21 February 1917.

50 Articles from *Shipping Illustrated* and *Marine Engineering,* repr. *USNIP* 43 (1917), pp. 803–804. The inertia of these American shipbuilders is in stark contrast to the intellectual inquisitiveness and energy of Mitsubishi Nagasaki Shipyard in acquiring, studying, and mastering early steam-turbine theory and technology. See Miwao Matsumoto, "Reconsidering Japanese Industrialization: Marine Turbine Transfer at Mitsubishi," *Technology and Culture* 40 (1999), pp. 74–97.

51 Capital ships were defined as battleships and battle cruisers displacing more than ten thousand long tons and carrying guns whose bores exceeded eight inches.

52 For the cruiser competition, see McBride, *Technological Change and the United States Navy,* p. 160.

53 *Annual Report of the Secretary of the Navy, 1931* (Washington, D.C.: U.S. Government Printing Office [hereafter GPO], 1932), p. 313.

54 "Annual Report of the Chief of the Bureau of Engineering," in *Annual Reports of the Navy Department for the Fiscal Year 1925* (Washington, D.C.: GPO, 1926), p. 272. The Bureau of Steam Engineering became the Bureau of Engineering as a result of the June 1920 Naval Appropriations Act.

55 See Nathan Rosenberg, "On Technological Expectations," *Economic Journal* 86 (1976), p. 533.

56 Rear Adm. S. M. Robinson, USN, "Steam Pressures and Temperatures," p. 2, *Hearings before the General Board of the Navy,* 26 October 1938, microfilm, Nimitz Library, U.S. Naval Academy, Annapolis, Md.

57 Ibid.

58 Ibid., p. 3.

59 Bowen, *Ships, Machinery, and Mossbacks,* pp. 56–57.

60 Ibid., p. 57.

61 Ibid.

62 A superheat-capable boiler has a separate pressure vessel in which the steam is heated to a temperature above its saturation point, thereby increasing its thermal energy.

63 "Shake-Up in Navy Hits Sharp Critics of New Warships," *New York Times,* 4 November 1938, p. 1.

64 Lynn T. White, Jr., "Engineers and the Making of the New Humanism," *Journal of Engineering Education* 57 (1967), pp. 375–76.

65 Dyson, "Development of Machinery in the U.S. Navy," p. 217.

66 "Rear-Adm. George W. Melville, Engineer-in-Chief, U.S. Navy," statement, 10 December 1902, *Hearings before the Committee on Naval Affairs, House of Representatives, on Appropriation Bill Subjects* (Washington, D.C.: GPO, 1903), no. 8, p. 9.

67 The Royal Navy's engineer in chief, quoted in Bowen, *Ships, Machinery, and Mossbacks,* p. 100.

68 R. S. Sayers, "The Springs of Technical Progress in Britain, 1919–39," *Economic Journal* 60 (1950), pp. 289–90, quoted in Rosenberg, "On Technological Expectations," p. 530.

69 Rosenberg, "On Technological Expectations," p. 529.

70 Bowen, *Ships, Machinery, and Mossbacks,* p. 111.

71 The *King George V*–*Washington* comparison is based on comments by Adm. Sir James Somerville, RN, commander of Force H, which pursued the German battleship *Bismarck,* and by Adm. Sir John Tovey, RN, Commander in Chief, Home Fleet, both in Bowen, *Ships, Machinery, and Mossbacks,* p. 113.

72 Cdr. Paul F. Lee, USN, to Vice Adm. Harold G. Bowen, USN, repr. Bowen, *Ships, Machinery, and Mossbacks,* p. 114.

73 See note 8 above.

74 Fuel-consumption figures calculated from information in William H. Garzke, Jr., and Robert O. Dulin, Jr., *Battleships: Axis and Neutral Battleships in World War II* (Annapolis, Md.: Naval Institute Press, 1985), pp. 124, 292. While the Germans employed high-temperature, high-pressure steam in the *Bismarck* design, they used single-reduction rather than double-reduction gearing and thereby failed to take advantage of the increased thermal energy of the steam.

75 Tocqueville, *Democracy in America,* p. 429.

76 For a discussion of technological trajectory and social constructivism, see Henk van den Belt and Arie Rip, "The Nelson-Winter-Dosi Model and Synthetic Dye Chemistry," in *Social Construction of Technological Systems: New Directions in the Sociology and History of Technology,* ed. Wiebe E. Bijker, Thomas P. Hughes, and Trevor Pinch (Cambridge, Mass.: MIT Press, 1994).

VI Theodore Roosevelt, Social Psychology, and Naval Public Relations
The 1906 John Paul Jones Reinterment Ceremony

LORI LYN BOGLE

Naval historians struggle to assess fairly Theodore Roosevelt's impact on the U.S. Navy. They credit him for successfully using the Navy as his big stick in foreign policy, but they offer mixed evaluations of his overall contribution to the service itself. While he oversaw a number of improvements in recruitment, training, naval gunnery, and battleship design, his constant interference in the daily activities at the Navy Department caused considerable bureaucratic turmoil, especially because of his favoritism toward junior officers. Scholars generally agree that Roosevelt had considerable success during his first term in achieving his diplomatic and battleship-construction objectives but that after 1905 he mishandled the battle for appropriations that would have led to a more balanced fleet by the end of his presidency.[1] There is little argument among scholars, however, over Roosevelt's success in popularizing the service. Acting almost as a one-man public relations firm, Roosevelt, more than any president before or since, fired the national imagination regarding America's potential for naval greatness.[2] This paper looks at how Roosevelt used social psychology to turn a relatively insignificant event—the 1905 discovery of the body of John Paul Jones—into an international naval extravaganza that brought his sea-power message directly to the American public.

Theodore Roosevelt brought to the presidency two essential components for his naval publicity efforts: a great love for the Navy and a sophisticated understanding of how to influence public opinion. His love of the Navy had begun in childhood. "From my earliest recollection," Roosevelt told one of his biographers, "I have been fed on tales of the sea and of ships. My mother's . . . deep interest in the southern cause [her two brothers had served with the Confederate navy] . . . led her to talk to me as a little shaver about ships, ships, ships, and [the] fighting of ships, till they sank into the depths of my soul."[3] In 1882 he made a name for himself as an up-and-coming young historian with the publication of a cautionary tale on the nation's lack of naval preparedness, *The Naval War of 1812*. The book's critical success caught the attention of influential men who shared his belief that national prestige and international power required a strong navy. Without one, Roosevelt, Henry Cabot Lodge, Brooks Adams, John Hay, and other "Large Policy" men argued, the nation would not have the opportunity to fight wars against inferior races—wars needed to strengthen the American character with manly, fighting qualities. For nearly twenty years, Large Policy men encouraged one another's naval publicity efforts and helped finance Roosevelt's political career as he "rose like a rocket" into national prominence.[4]

Whether as a state assemblyman working on civil service reform, a New York City police commissioner, or Assistant Secretary of the Navy, Roosevelt was consistent. He promoted a powerful offensive fleet of capital ships that, supported by adequate coaling stations, would project America's power into areas of national interest. He may have micromanaged the service and alienated naval committees in the House and Senate, but he also energized all those around him by bypassing Congress and speaking directly to the American people about the nation's naval needs. In a well-publicized 1897 speech at the Naval War College in Newport, Rhode Island, "Washington's Maxim," Roosevelt reassured the nation that a large navy would not break with American traditional values or lead to war with a European power. "Those who wish to see this country at peace," Roosevelt argued, should "place [their] reliance upon a first-class fleet of first-class battleships rather than on any arbitration treaty which the wit of man can devise."[5]

Roosevelt's populist appeal in his Naval War College appearance was in keeping with late nineteenth-century scholarship on how leaders could maintain order as America transformed itself into a democratic mass society. The American founders generally defined "the public" as those with the education and financial means to participate in the free flow of ideas.[6] The so-called penny press of the 1830s, however, began to challenge the political power of the governing elite by producing increasingly cheaper newspapers and magazines that by 1880 had put timely information and analysis in the hands of Americans of all classes. While many applauded the expansion of democracy through mass media, others worried about the new power of the self-conscious, politically active masses, which grew larger by the year because of the rapid influx of new immigrants. By the late nineteenth century an outbreak of strikes and labor violence, coupled with corrupt "boss rule" in the nation's major urban centers, seemed to confirm elite fears that America was developing into a mobocracy. Educated members of the upper class turned to the new academic discipline of social psychology, popularly known as "crowd psychology," for solutions to the disruption of the social order (real or perceived) by the emergence of mass society.[7]

In 1895 the French criminologist Gustave Le Bon popularized social psychology with his best-selling *Psychology of Crowds* (or *The Crowd*). Building on the work of earlier scholars and cutting-edge studies on hypnosis and the subconscious, Le Bon argued that the masses (much like a crowd) possessed a highly suggestible "collective mind," prone to hysteria and imitation ("mental contagion"). Leaders, especially those with charisma and powerful speaking skills, could manage the masses and change public opinion with "absolute, uncompromising, and simple" emotional appeals and heroic imagery. The most effective leaders would demonstrate that they themselves were one of the crowd, physically able to hold their own with working-class men, before stepping forward as champions of the people. By beginning with traditional ideals and then slowly planting heroic imagery into the mass subconscious, a leader could manipulate the public "little by little" to support his modern-day policy initiatives. The images used need not be accurate, the political psychologist claimed, for "appearances have always played a much more important part than reality in history. . . . It is only images that terrify or attract [the crowd] . . . and become motives of action." In fact, "great power," Le Bon declared, would be given to heads of state who understood these principles and propagated their ideas with rituals and ceremonies and by "affirmation, repetition, and contagion."[8]

Critics challenged Le Bon's methodology. They also found simplistic his view of the masses behaving as a violent mob. More compelling was the work of social psychologists who described the general public as comprising a number of subgroups, some more reasoned than others and able to set the tone for the whole. Roosevelt agreed that there were a variety of publics. He divided the masses into distinct "races," or types (the race of hardworking farmers, the American race, or sometimes a particular ethnic group).[9] Roosevelt also studied the American sociologist Edward A. Ross, who claimed in his 1901 *Social Control* that there were thirty-three different ways in which a society could effectively control its people. Like Le Bon before him, Ross stressed the role of the hero and of emotional imagery in shaping public opinion. In addition, he argued that government could effectively manage the national will by regulating the press. Apparently Roosevelt was in agreement with the renowned scholar, for in 1905 he wrote Ross a glowing letter regarding Ross's work, prophesying that "public opinion if only sufficiently enlightened and aroused is equal to the necessary regenerative tasks and can yet dominate the future."[10]

Despite clear differences regarding the makeup of the crowd, Roosevelt's public-relations efforts reflected Le Bon's formula for governing a mass society with heroic imagery. Roosevelt established his credentials as a man of the people and as their heroic leader (an important step, according to Le Bon) by going to the West after a number of personal and political setbacks.[11] On the Dakota frontier he dressed as and lived the life of a cowboy, captured boat thieves, built a photography lab under his cabin (for publicity purposes), wrote of his heroic exploits in a number of hunting and wilderness books, and kept the New York papers apprised of his latest exploits.[12] He carefully and effectively crafted his public image, much as William Cody had his own alter ego, Buffalo Bill. Some historians have ridiculed Roosevelt's actions as the products of an out-of-control ego and an adolescent personality. Instead, his heroic self-depictions as, according to political scientist Bruce Miroff, "the cowboy of the Dakotas, the police commissioner patrolling New York's mean streets, the Rough Rider charging up San Juan Hill," and so forth, were all concerted efforts to make him appear to be a worthy leader and "the first great American hero of a new age of mass media."[13]

Once president, Roosevelt worked to distance himself from his former cowboy image and to rely, as Le Bon recommended, on the prestige of his high office for his public-relations efforts.[14] He quickly transformed himself into a mature statesman and saved heroic imagery for naval expansion (and other proposed policy measures) rather than for self-promotion. Building on public enthusiasm for the heroic Navy following the Spanish-American War, Roosevelt relied on his political prestige to preach sea power at monument dedications and historical commemorations, even events with little or no connection to the service, as well as at international naval parades (including the departure of the Great White Fleet), a series of world's fairs, and a number of other naval fêtes.[15]

One of the clearest demonstrations of Roosevelt's use of crowd psychology was the reinterment ceremony of John Paul Jones at the U.S. Naval Academy, in Annapolis, Maryland, in 1906.[16] The discovery of the Revolutionary War hero's grave the year before had given Roosevelt an excellent opportunity for naval publicity. Following the war and the disbanding of the Continental Navy, Jones had traveled abroad, hopeful that he could secure another naval commission at home once America re-formed its naval forces. In 1792, however, the forty-five-year-old hero died in Paris. A French official packed the corpse in alcohol, sealed it in a lead coffin, and interred it in a cemetery for foreign Protestants to await transport back to the United States.[17] America showed no serious interest in retrieving the body of John Paul Jones, however, until 1845, when a brief investigation seemed to prove that finding it would be impossible. Interest revived during the Spanish-American War, and several American research teams began searching for the grave. The ambassador to France, Gen. Horace Porter, and his investigators ultimately identified in archival records the correct tract of land. Porter was pained "beyond expression" to learn that this hero, whose "fame once covered two continents," had lain for over a hundred years in "ground once consecrated, but since desecrated"; the site had served as both a cesspool and a dumping ground for dead animals, and it was now covered with buildings and a street.[18] On learning of the discovery Roosevelt sent an urgent request to Congress for the thirty-five thousand dollars the ambassador needed to excavate. In 1905 Porter telegraphed the president that he had performed an autopsy on what had seemed the most likely corpse and had identified it with scientific certainty as the body of John Paul Jones.[19]

Roosevelt's excitement over the discovery of John Paul Jones's body could hardly be contained. Porter had delivered an extraordinary opportunity for the president to put Le Bon's ideas into action.[20] There was a problem, however. Prior to the turn of the century few in America had placed great importance on John Paul Jones, nor had Roosevelt been one of them. The public, of course, had admired Jones during and after the Revolution for his glorious, even audacious, victories over the British. The Navy, however, had not held him in very high esteem over the years. His exaggerated sense of personal honor, poor leadership skills, and questionable national loyalty while serving abroad prevented his being considered a model for professional officers to emulate.[21] Among Roosevelt's monographs on American history was one that dismissed Jones as merely a "daring corsair."[22] As Assistant Secretary of the Navy Roosevelt had claimed that his exploits did not "size up big enough" to be included in an anthology of American heroes.[23] Certainly, no one seriously considered Jones a contender for designation as "father of the Navy" until 1900, when a new, two-volume biography by Augustus C. Buell, *Paul Jones: Founder of the American Navy,* appeared. It would be revealed later that Buell, an engineer turned historian, had fabricated documents to provide seemingly irrefutable proof that Jones was the service's "father."[24]

When Porter discovered the lost corpse, however, Roosevelt overcame his qualms and proclaimed an importance for the Revolutionary War hero over that of any other naval officer. Roosevelt was well aware that Buell was out of step with contemporary historical thinking (though not, at this point, that his claims were bogus), yet quoted him during the 1906 reinterment ceremony. By doing so he firmly, almost inextricably, planted Buell's new interpretation in the national psyche. As Le Bon had written, appearances were more important than reality.[25] The crowd, the psychologist explained, responds best to "exaggeration in the sentiments of its heroes. Their apparent qualities and virtues must always be amplified."[26] Roosevelt was undoubtedly encouraged in this path by the near mass hysteria following the Spanish-American War surrounding the Navy's first modern celebrities. "Dewey Mania" and a "Hobson Craze" swept the nation when Adm. George Dewey and Lt. Richmond Pearson Hobson triumphantly returned to the United States.[27]

Public excitement surrounding the Jones discovery had been equally impassioned. Newspapers on both sides of the Atlantic described in graphic detail the opening of the casket and the process used to identify the remarkably well-preserved remains. To the disappointment of a number of cities vying for the honor, the Navy had announced that the body, when retrieved from France, would be taken for reburial at the Arlington Cemetery, just outside Washington, D.C. Roosevelt, who micromanaged almost every detail, agreed with Ernest Flagg, the architect in charge of the Naval Academy's classical renovation then under way, that "the ashes of the founder of the American Navy should repose in the midst of the institution [underneath the chapel] which is the cradle . . . of the Navy." By doing so, Flagg argued, "the Chapel will become what it ought to be, and what I have always hoped it would be, the Pantheon or Westminster Abbey of the Navy."[28]

John Paul Jones, who had once written that "my desire for fame is infinite," would have been quite pleased to see how America now celebrated his life and death. First honored in an elaborate ceremony in France, then brought to America by a U.S. Navy squadron, his casket arrived at Annapolis for a brief but dignified military and religious service before French and American pallbearers placed it in a temporary brick vault to await the full international commemoration scheduled for the following spring.[29] When Acting Secretary of State Alvey A. Adee heard that the Navy planned in the meantime to conduct a second autopsy, "he jumped from his chair and ran for the office of the Secretary of the Navy, where he burst in and bellowed that once America had accepted the body from France as Jones, it would forever remain Jones."[30] The *Baltimore Sun* agreed: "We refuse," an editorial charged, "to have the authenticity of the body questioned. We claim the bones of Jones, which have been formally christened, so that any possible mistake would have no effect."[31]

The president personally picked the anniversary of the naval hero's capture of HMS *Drake,* 24 April, as the date of the reinterment. At first Roosevelt had hoped to keep the occasion primarily a naval spectacular, incorporating elements of both the American and French fleets into the pageantry and strictly limiting participation by other branches of the government. But as the date of the commemoration approached, the value of including congressmen—who were then in the midst of debates on naval appropriations—became evident. Seven thousand people attended the three-hour ceremony in Dahlgren Hall, which showcased the grandeur of the Naval Academy's renovation and provided the president with a public ritual in which to sell the Navy to the American public.[32] Journalists and photographers retold the event for a national audience. The Navy further publicized the occasion when Congress authorized eleven thousand copies of an elaborately decorated 210-page commemorative volume, featuring details of the discovery (including graphic photographs of the decaying body) and the subsequent ceremonies, for distribution to the public.[33]

Roosevelt's remarks at the reinterment ceremony closely followed Le Bon's recommendations on how to craft speeches to change public opinion. Eschewing the example of muckrakers who exposed shortcomings and wrongdoing, Roosevelt included, per Le Bon, "energetic affirmations" and "impressive images" that were accompanied by only "summary arguments," unburdened by evidence.[34]

The ceremony opened with the flag-draped coffin at center stage, in front of a towering platform and speaker's podium and surrounded by midshipmen lining the walls of the Academy's spacious armory building, Dahlgren Hall. But clearly Theodore Roosevelt was the main attraction: "All eyes were on him and cameras shot at him from every corner of the gallery in the Armory," the Annapolis daily newspaper reported the next day. He first thanked the French nation for its help during the American Revolution, as well as General Porter for his "zealous devotion" in bringing Jones back to the United States, before launching into his main message, applying the lessons of the past to the nation's needs for the future, much as Le Bon had instructed.

> Every officer in our Navy should know by heart the deeds of John Paul Jones . . . [and] should feel in each fiber of his being an eager desire to emulate the energy, the professional capacity, the indomitable determination and dauntless scorn of death which marked [him] above all his fellows. . . . Remember, you here who are listening to me, that to applaud patriotic sentiments and to turn out to do honor to the dead heroes who by land or by sea won honor for our flag is only worth while if we are prepared to show that our energies do not exhaust themselves in words. . . . [T]ake to heart the lessons of the past and make things ready so . . . fighting men on sea and ashore shall be able to rise to the standard established by their predecessors in our services of the past.
>
> Those of you who are in public life [directing his comments to congressmen in attendance] have a moral right to be here at this celebration to-day only if you are prepared to do your part in building up the Navy of the present; for otherwise you have no right to claim lot or part in the glory and honor and renown of the Navy's past.[35]

Following other speakers, an international honor guard placed the naval hero's body under the main staircase in the school's dormitory, Bancroft Hall, to await the completion of its final resting place—an ornate marble sarcophagus reminiscent of Napoleon's tomb in France.

Roosevelt had not only produced a spectacle that demonstrated the tenets of Le Bon's crowd psychology; he had conducted a ritual that fit well with modern sociological principles. According to Joseph W. Bastien and David G. Bromley, rituals and ceremonies create stability by performing at least one of three important functions. First, they can "provide either continuity or movement."[36] That is, they connect the present to the past, or, as in the case of rites of passage, they can provide a transition to the future. Second, they can "enhance communality and solidarity within a group," by expressing commitment to a set of "common values and beliefs." Third, they often offer individuals involved opportunities to experience the "mystery and majesty" that "separate the ordinary from the extraordinary, the mundane from the important, the sacred from the profane. By so doing," Bastien and Bromley conclude, "ritual helps to create social order, and to link an individual's emotional life with collective experiences." Roosevelt accomplished all three with the John Paul Jones commemoration. The mystery and majesty surrounding the Revolutionary War hero's life and death and the later discovery of his remains linked the twentieth-century Navy to its past and allowed the president to refashion traditional ideas regarding the military, in much the way Le Bon had suggested, to support his vision of the Navy as a professional, progressive service prepared for offensive fleet action.

Newspapers heralded the commemoration as a complete success, but the enthusiasm surrounding the Revolutionary War hero, like that for Dewey, soon faded. After Roosevelt left office, Jones's body languished in its temporary tomb in Bancroft Hall, inspiring a reference in a somewhat impertinent ditty sung by midshipmen, "Everyone Works but John Paul"—who was, as the song had it, "pickled up in alcohol" and seemed to be "on a permanent jag."[37] In 1913 Congress finally appropriated the funds necessary to complete construction of a permanent resting place for the once-celebrated corpse. But the Academy chapel never became the Westminster Abbey of the Navy that Ernest Flagg had envisioned.[38] Even to this day, few visitors to the Yard are aware of where the body of the hero lies. Dark and eerie and with little interpretative information, the John Paul Jones crypt, seemingly hidden from tourists underneath the chapel, does virtually nothing to strengthen the nation's collective memory of its naval past. But in 1906 the myth of John Paul Jones as promoted by Theodore Roosevelt was considerably more powerful and helped the president secure his goal of popularizing the Navy.

Other naval extravaganzas soon followed. Roosevelt transformed the Jamestown world's fair that commemorated the first successful English colony in the New World into an "international, naval, marine, and military celebration."[39] He also sent the Great White Fleet around the world. He did so for a number of diplomatic and military reasons, but there is no doubt the voyage was also a publicity event—a global maritime pageant that elevated the Navy's officers, sailors, and even the battleships themselves to national heroes.[40] A number of domestic and international factors played a role in modernizing the U.S. Navy before, during, and after his presidency. Credit for the service's new popularity with the American masses, however, belongs to Theodore Roosevelt and his love of the Navy, his understanding of the psychology of the crowd, and his shrewd use of naval publicity to reach out to the masses. With or without congressional support, Theodore Roosevelt wisely and adeptly publicized an American fleet capable of offensive operations, as powerful nations jockeyed for position on the world's ocean highways.

NOTES   1 A good portion of the credit for naval advances at this time must also go to the pronavy attitudes following the Spanish-American War and the success of William McKinley's policies already in place when Roosevelt assumed the presidency. For more on Theodore Roosevelt's naval policies, see Harold and Margaret Sprout, *The Rise of American Naval Power: 1776–1918* (Annapolis, Md.: Naval Institute Press, 1966); Gordon Carpenter O'Gara, *Theodore Roosevelt and the Rise of the Modern Navy* (Princeton, N.J.: Princeton Univ. Press, 1943); Edward J. Marolda, *Theodore Roosevelt, the U.S. Navy, and the Spanish-American War* (New York: Palgrave, 2001); Matthew M. Oyos, "Theodore Roosevelt: Commander in Chief" (PhD dissertation, Ohio State University, 1993); and Henry J. Hendrix, *Theodore Roosevelt's Naval Diplomacy: The U.S. Navy and the Birth of the American Century* (Annapolis, Md.: Naval Institute Press, 2009).

2 How he did so is the subject of my current book project. The U.S. Navy's publicity efforts were not well coordinated until after World War I, when the

Navy League of the United States (founded in 1902) conducted sophisticated public relations efforts on behalf of the service; Dirk Bönker, *Militarism in a Global Age: Naval Ambitions in Germany and the United States before World War I* (Ithaca, N.Y.: Cornell Univ. Press, 2012), p. 203. For more on nineteenth-century naval public relations, see Mark R. Shulman, *Navalism and the Emergence of American Sea Power, 1882–1893* (Annapolis, Md.: Naval Institute Press, 1995); Lisle A. Rose, *Power at Sea: The Age of Navalism, 1890–1918* (Columbia: Univ. of Missouri Press, 2007); and Fred Harrod, *Manning the New Navy: The Development of a Modern Naval Enlisted Force, 1899–1940* (Westport, Conn.: Greenwood, 1978), and "Managing the Medium: The Navy and Motion Pictures before World War I," *Velvet Light Trap* 31 (Spring 1993), pp. 48–58.

3 Theodore Roosevelt, quoted in Ferdinand Cowle Iglehart, *Theodore Roosevelt: The Man as I Knew Him* (New York: Christian Herald, 1919), p. 122.

4 Julius W. Pratt, "The Large Policy of 1898," *Mississippi Valley Historical Review* (September 1932), pp. 219–42. Roosevelt's claim that he "rose like a rocket" in politics is from a letter to his son Theodore Roosevelt, Jr., on 20 October 1903, as quoted in Joseph Bucklin Bishop, *Theodore Roosevelt and His Time: Shown in His Own Letters* (New York: Scribner's, 1920), p. 19.

5 Theodore Roosevelt, quoted in Leon F. Litwack and Winthrop D. Jordan, *The United States: Becoming a World Power* (Upper Saddle River, N.J.: Prentice Hall, 1991), vol. 2, p. 545.

6 This was in keeping with the definition held by most Enlightenment philosophers. V. O. Key, *Public Opinion and American Democracy* (New York: Knopf, 1961), pp. 8–10.

7 The roots of social psychology (a subfield of political philosophy) can be found in the first half of the century, when a number of European scholars, including Charles Mackay, tried to explain how panics and revolutions spread from one location to another, much like viruses. See Charles Mackay, *Memoirs of Extraordinary Popular Delusions* (London: Richard Bentley, 1841), and Jaap Van Ginneken, *Crowds, Psychology, & Politics, 1871–1899* (New York: Cambridge Univ. Press, 1992), p. 5.

8 Gustave Le Bon, *The Crowd: A Study of the Popular Mind* (1896; repr. Mineola, N.Y.: Dover, 2002), pp. 35, 46, 77.

9 Thomas G. Dyer, *Theodore Roosevelt and the Idea of Race* (Baton Rouge: Louisiana State Univ. Press, 1992), passim.

10 Social psychologists, according to historian Eugene Leach, argued that the new "crowd-society," rid of certain revolutionary tendencies, could be directed "toward acts of heroism and patriotism that surpassed the spiritual resources of the individual members." Eugene E. Leach, "'Mental Epidemics': Crowd Psychology and American Culture, 1890–1940," *American Studies* (Spring 1992), pp. 5–29, and "Mastering the Crowd: Collective Behavior and the Mass Society in American Social Thought, 1917–1939," *American Studies* (Spring 1986), pp. 99–114. See also Daria Frezza and Martha King, *The Leader and the Crowd: Democracy in American Public Discourse, 1880–1941* (Athens: Univ. of Georgia Press, 2007).

11 Because Roosevelt's first use of heroic imagery had occurred over a decade before Le Bon, his initial efforts at shaping his public image most likely were influenced by his reading of scholars writing on the topic since the 1840s. Le Bon, however, popularized the research of others and reflected Roosevelt's understanding of the discipline in the 1880s. Roosevelt read French and commented on several of Le Bon's books in the 1890s. In 1914 the former president made a point of meeting with the popular scholar in Paris. See Van Ginneken, *Crowds, Psychology, & Politics*, passim.

12 The *New York Times* and other newspapers kept track of his Dakota exploits. "General Telegraph News: Roosevelt and the Grizzly," *New York Times*, 30 December 1884; "Theodore Roosevelt as a Hunter," *New York Times*, 24 December 1884; "Theodore Roosevelt: His Prompt Pursuit and Capture of Three Thieves in Dakota," *New York Times*, 25 April 1886; "Theodore Roosevelt in Dakota," *New York Times*, 29 October 1886.

13 Bruce Miroff, *Icons of Democracy: American Leaders as Heroes, Aristocrats, Dissenters, and Democrats* (Lawrence: Univ. Press of Kansas, 2000), p. 158.

14 Le Bon, *Crowd*, pp. 81–82. Certainly his expert use of photographs (and film), along with his ability to manage the press—daily press releases, trial balloons, and his knack for developing close, personal relationships with newspaper reporters—was important to his public relations as well.

15 See Lori Lyn Bogle, "TR's Use of PR to Strengthen the Navy," U.S. Naval Institute *Proceedings* (December 2007), pp. 26–31.

16 Another example is the building of the Panama Canal. J. Michael Hogan argues that Roosevelt responded to criticism of the project by transforming "the story of the canal into an inspirational tale of American power, ingenuity, and perseverance . . . [creating] a new generation of uniquely American heroes." See abstract to J. Michael Hogan, "Theodore Roosevelt and the Heroes of Panama," *Presidential Studies Quarterly* (Winter 1989), pp. 79–94.

17 The two most popular biographies are Evan Thomas, *John Paul Jones: Sailor, Hero, Father of the American Navy* (Waterville, Maine.: Thorndike, 2003), and Joseph F. Callo, *John Paul Jones: America's First Sea Warrior* (Annapolis, Md.: Naval Institute Press, 2009).

18 Ambassador Horace Porter to the Secretary of State, 14 April 1905, as quoted in U.S. State Dept., *Papers Relating to the Foreign Relations of the United States* (Washington, D.C.: U.S. Government Printing Office [hereafter GPO], 1906), p. 428.

19 "General Porter's Triumph," *New York Times*, 16 April 1905; Theodore Roosevelt to Charles J. Bonaparte, 1 August 1905, Theodore Roosevelt Papers, reel 338, series 2, Library of Congress, Washington, D.C. Engineers sank five separate shafts, and workmen sifted through hundreds of bodies—many

without coffins, stacked one on another—before uncovering five lead caskets. For more on the autopsy see N. L. Rogers et al., "The Belated Autopsy and Identification of an Eighteenth Century Naval Hero: The Saga of John Paul Jones," *Journal of Forensic Science* (September 2004), pp. 1036–49, and Matthew R. Weir, Lori L. Bogle, and Philip A. Mackowiak, "The Death of John Paul Jones and Resurrection as 'Father of the U.S. Navy,'" *American Journal of Nephrology* (January 2010), pp. 90–94.

20 Finding the body fit well with the psychologist's claim that the dead held the most powerful form of prestige. Le Bon, *Crowd*, p. 81.

21 James Bradford, *The Reincarnation of John Paul Jones: The Navy Discovers Its Professional Roots* (Washington, D.C.: Naval Historical Foundation, 1986), p. 7.

22 Theodore Roosevelt, *Gouverneur Morris* (New York: Houghton, Mifflin, 1888), p. 196.

23 Theodore Roosevelt to George Haven Putnam, 1 November 1897, in *The Letters of Theodore Roosevelt*, ed. Elting E. Morison (Cambridge, Mass.: Harvard Univ. Press, 1954), vol. 1, p. 705.

24 Alfred Thayer Mahan, however, had written an article that, seeming to suggest that Jones had possessed these values, may have influenced Buell to include them in his fabricated letters; Augustus C. Buell, *Paul Jones: Founder of the American Navy* (New York: Charles Scribner and Sons, 1900); E. Field, "Paul Jones, Founder of the American Navy, a History," *American Historical Review* (April 1901), pp. 589–90. Soon after the John Paul Jones reinterment ceremony, historian Anna De Koven exposed the Buell forgery in the *New York Times*. Anna Farwell De Koven, "A Fictitious Paul Jones Masquerading as the Real: The Accepted Life of the Naval Hero by A. C. Buell Pronounced to Be an Audacious Forgery," *New York Times*, 10 June 1906, magazine section, pp. 1–3. See also Lori Lyn Bogle and Joel I. Holwitt, "The Best Quote Jones Never Wrote," *Naval History* (April 2004), pp. 18–23.

25 Le Bon, *Crowd*, p. 35.

26 Ibid., p. 3.

27 Roosevelt was governor when the Dewey reception occurred, and he witnessed firsthand the elaborate decorations, fireworks, and military parade, as well as the dedication of the colossal Dewey Arch. Lt. Richmond Pearson Hobson had failed in his daring attempt to block Santiago Harbor by sinking the collier *Merrimac*, but that did not dissuade his adoring female fans from showering the handsome officer with kisses. "Kissing Hobson," as he became known, successfully ran for Congress and became a chief advocate of Roosevelt's Big Navy policies.

28 Ernest Flagg to Willard Herbert Brownson, 15 April 1905, Records of the Superintendent, Individual Exhibits, John Paul Jones, Special Collections, box 10, folder 1, Nimitz Library, U.S. Naval Academy, Annapolis, Md.

29 Henri Marion, *John Paul Jones' Last Cruise and Final Resting Place: The United States Naval Academy* (Washington, D.C.: George E. Howard, 1906), passim.

30 The story is related by Charles W. Stewart in an official memorandum. U.S. Navy Dept., "Memorandum Regarding the Early Investigation of the Burial Place of John Paul Jones," 4 November 1911, Naval War Records, ZB files, box 121, folder "John Paul Jones," Navy Department Library, Washington, D.C.

31 *Baltimore Sun* newspaper clipping, 2 May 1906, from John Paul Jones, Edwin Warfield Scrapbook, #2, Maryland Historical Society, Baltimore, Md.

32 The ceremony also reassured the officer corps that historical values of nobility and bravado that had made men like Jones effective in the past would not be lost as the service underwent modernization and adopted new corporate values now believed essential to true professionalism.

33 Charles W. Stewart, ed., *John Paul Jones: Commemoration at Annapolis, April 24, 1906* (Washington, D.C.: GPO, 1907).

34 Le Bon, *Crowd*, p. 128. It is interesting to note that Roosevelt as president rejected muckraking, the publicity efforts of other progressives. Roosevelt brought his naval publicity to the American people through Le Bon's method of prestige, ritual, and positive affirmation. He did not use the Great White Fleet as a muckraker would have, to demonstrate the flaws of the Navy. Instead he celebrated the American fleet and attempted to attach heroism and prestige to it; Theodore Roosevelt to Elihu Root, 4 September 1906, in *Letters of Theodore Roosevelt*, ed. Morison, vol. 5, p. 394.

35 Theodore Roosevelt quoted in Stewart, *John Paul Jones*, pp. 15–19.

36 Joseph W. Bastien and David G. Bromley, "Metaphor in the Rituals of Restorative and Transformative Groups," in *Ritual and Ceremonies in Popular Culture*, ed. Ray B. Browne (Bowling Green, Ohio: Bowling Green State Univ. Popular Press, 1980), pp. 48–60.

37 Andrew L. Pendleton, *The Silly Syclopedia* [sic]: *Containing "Daffynishuns" of the Words of the Slang Spoken by Midshipmen of the U.S. Naval Academy* (n.p.: Charles G. Feldmeyer, 1908), back matter.

38 Marion, *John Paul Jones' Last Cruise and Final Resting Place*, p. 65.

39 *The Official Blue Book of the Jamestown Ter-Centennial Exposition* (Norfolk, Va.: Colonial, 1907), p. 75.

40 Leroy G. Dorsey, "Sailing into the 'Wondrous Now': The Myth of the American Navy's World Cruise," *Quarterly Journal of Speech* (November 1997), pp. 447–65. For more on the Great White Fleet see Lori Lyn Bogle, "Why TR Sent the Great White Fleet," *Daybook* (October 2007), pp. 7–9; James Reckner, *Teddy Roosevelt's Great White Fleet* (Annapolis, Md.: Naval Institute Press, 1988); Robert A. Hart, *The Great White Fleet: Its Voyage around the World, 1907–1909* (Boston: Little, Brown, 1965); and Kenneth Wimmel, *Theodore Roosevelt and the Great White Fleet: American Sea Power Comes of Age* (Washington, D.C.: Brassey's, 1998). For more on international naval parades see Jan Rüger, *The Great Naval Game: Britain and Germany in the Age of Empire* (Cambridge, U.K.: Cambridge Univ. Press, 2007).

VII "The Committee of Four"
The "Blue Funk School," the CID, and the Myth of the German Peril, 1906–1909

ANDREAS ROSE

In August 1908—as the Anglo-German naval race was just about to reach its peak—the small Hessian town of Cronberg witnessed a royal encounter between Kaiser Wilhelm II and a representative of his uncle King Edward VII. Charles Hardinge, the British Permanent Under Secretary for Foreign Affairs, sitting on the billiard table and enjoying his after-lunch cigar with the kaiser, did not mince any words. He told Wilhelm in no uncertain terms that he held the German High Seas Battle Fleet to be "the only disturbing factor in international politics" and thus the prime culprit in the worsening of Anglo-German relations. "In England," Hardinge said, "it is perfectly clear that the German fleet will be in a few years' time superior to the Royal Navy," and would threaten the British Isles with the danger of invasion.[1]

The orthodox view among historians generally tends to share Hardinge's assessment.[2] His talks with Wilhelm II and the latter's determined refusal to reduce the German shipbuilding program even at the cost of war are commonly taken as clear evidence for the existence of a blundering German foreign policy—a policy that supposedly missed every opportunity that arose to come to terms with the United Kingdom, let alone to ease international tensions. Jonathan Steinberg, Volker Berghahn, and Paul Kennedy in the wake of the so-called Fischer controversy (and many others since) have forcefully posited that "Admiral Tirpitz and his clique did indeed dream of challenging the Royal Navy," resulting in a self-inflicted isolation of Germany.[3]

The established pattern of interpretation, therefore, reads as follows. By the end of the 1890s, Germany had embarked on the construction of a battle fleet, as a result of which Great Britain had no choice but to react to this "unique German threat" right "at her own front door" by regrouping the fleets of the Royal Navy and starting a hitherto unprecedented shipbuilding program. By launching "all big gun" ships of the dreadnought type, Britain followed the assumption of the American naval theorist Capt. Alfred Thayer Mahan that only capital ships counted in securing a state's national security needs and would be decisive not only in home waters but also in achieving the vital "command of the sea" in general. Furthermore, the supposed German peril at sea is said to have conveyed to London's political and diplomatic elites the need to abandon its policy of "splendid isolation" altogether. In other words, as one eminent political historian has summarized the causal nexus between the naval race and prewar diplomacy, "it was without doubt the construction of the German battle fleet" that forced Britain's hand and so "contributed significantly to the revolution of the states system before 1914."[4]

In recent years, however, naval historians in particular have challenged this orthodoxy. They have expressed their concern that the common notion of a German challenge triggering an inevitable British response is based on a rather too simplistic and too one-sided model of interpretation. If we take Great Britain generally as the epitome of a complex parliamentary system before 1914, it seems remarkable that political and diplomatic historians especially still believe in high politics, the primacy of foreign politics, and the activity of British diplomats in a rather strange vacuum separated from the "world outside," while recent naval historians have looked at the domestic realities behind London's naval policy and decision making. Naval historians, therefore, have warned against focusing unduly on German policies when explaining Britain's naval policy. Rather, they have identified a number of Anglo-centric explanations for Britain's naval policy. They have highlighted various constraints within the British parliamentary and financial systems, as well as within the British defense structure, and thus have opened a new perspective leading to reinterpretation of prewar international relations. As a result of intriguing archival findings, Jon Sumida, Nicholas Lambert, and Rolf Hobson have been able to show persuasively that Britain's naval policy can also be explained on its own terms, without constant necessity to invoke a German threat.

According to Sumida's and Lambert's research, the concentration of the British fleet in home waters in early 1905—certainly one of the key arguments of the conventional view—turns out to be far less a reaction to the German High Seas Battle Fleet than a result of technological developments, financial constraints, and industrial interests. In fact, as one hitherto neglected memorandum of March 1904 by Lord Esher, one of the most influential politicians of the time, reveals, it was due to modern telegraphy that the Admiralty could afford to concentrate its fleets in home waters rather than having to deploy them constantly on all seven seas:

> The Admiralty possess a well organized system of recording, in times of peace, the movement of ships all over the world. At any hour during the day the sea Lords are enabled to locate the position of any British or foreign vessel, and to calculate the precise effect upon our fleets of the movements of foreign ships of war. The Naval Branch is thus able from day to day to amend and alter plans for the distribution of the Fleet, as well as schemes of naval defence, should the country be suddenly and unexpectedly plunged into war.[5]

Whereas new and faster communication made the concentration of forces possible, concentration was also desirable financially, especially after the costly South African War. Moreover, for example, in the decision to build a North Sea naval base at Rosyth, a move that has long been taken as a clear countermeasure against the Kaiserreich, the German navy was not even mentioned.[6] Rather, the naval base primarily served the stagnant Scottish shipbuilding industry.[7] Considering the rising danger of torpedo attacks and the anticipated risks from rapidly improving submarines, the First Sea Lord, John A. Fisher, thought the harbor completely useless and declined to waste a penny on it.[8] Fisher, who has always been described as a Mahanite and a key witness for the Anglo-German naval race, seemed to have been influenced less by the Anglo-German concerns than by the Jeune École and his own observations of the French navy's testing of torpedoes and submarines during his time as chief of the Mediterranean station between 1899 and 1902.[9]

Mahan's views on the central importance of large battleships and decisive battles were certainly very popular in states that only recently had started building formidable fleets, such as the German empire, Japan, and the United States.[10] Yet the fact that Mahan's major work, *The Influence of Sea Power upon History,* served as a kind of "naval Bible" for the kaiser does not allow the conclusion that Mahan was the "most influential prophet of the new navalism" in Britain as well.[11] There his writings were often considered by naval experts like Julian Corbett or Richard Thursfield to be obsolete by modern standards, or, as in the case of Arthur Balfour, mere propaganda. Even Fisher held Mahan's work in lower esteem than has hitherto been believed and occasionally called his theories "passé" or even "nonsense."[12]

Another, and rather misleading, argument, which also stems in part from Mahan's belief in big battleships and large tonnages, refers to the tables of displacement repeatedly used in historical works. They are aimed at proving the dynamic effect of the prewar naval arms race, especially Germany's challenge of the "two-power standard." But the mere addition of numbers essentially ignores the fact that the standard was neither a natural law nor understood as an adequate instrument for estimating the "real strength" of a navy.[13] In fact, the standard represented rather a public instrument, an argument used by the Admiralty in public and parliamentary discussions to justify the skyrocketing costs resulting from technological innovations and new ship designs since the 1880s. Asked about the importance of displacement, naval correspondents like Herbert W. Wilson or Archibald Hurd would reply that these statistics were not suitable indicators of naval strength.[14] Captain Carlyon Bellairs, indeed, thought the tonnage theory outdated and absurd: "I know of no more foolish contention in our naval discussions than the plea that has been advanced by civilians like Lord Eversley, that tonnage is an accurate measure of fighting strength."[15] William White, one of the chief engineers of the Royal Navy, fully agreed.[16] As early as 1903 he published an article in which he called the use of displacement as a measure of power a relic of the age of sail. In his Cantor Lecture in February 1906 he referred to the difficulty of estimating naval strength under modern circumstances and concluded that tonnage was no longer an adequate indication of it. Instead, structural capacities like docking and coaling facilities, economies of scale, technological know-how, experience in the shipbuilding industry, and the diversity of units within fleets were of far greater importance.[17] Lord Selborne, a key witness to the conventional interpretation, thought tonnage data "completely worthless" for measuring the actual strength of a fleet. Nevertheless, in political and public discourse those data seemed indispensable.[18] Not without reason did Lord Ellenborough, one of the leading scaremongers about a possible German invasion, emphasize in the House of Lords that the only value of displacement tables was to persuade the people of an imminent German danger.[19]

For historical research, therefore, it is important to look closer at the hidden contemporary motives for presenting certain pieces of evidence to the public. These are overlooked all too easily. Similar caution is required when dealing with Lord Selborne's often-cited memorandum of December 1904 in which he justified the redeployment of fleets on grounds of a German danger. On closer scrutiny, however, it becomes obvious that he was less concerned about Germany than about foreign navies generally, especially the French and Russian navies, as well as the newly modernized U.S. Navy.[20] Only a year earlier, in October 1903, Selborne had been "in despair about the financial outlook, because these cursed Russians are laying down one ship after the other."[21] In his memorandum of December 1904 he called the German navy one "of the most efficient types," but the French stood "always in the forefront," whereas the American potential appeared to him "limitless."

Matthew Seligmann has recently supported the conventional view that Selborne and the Royal Navy perceived Germany alone as the foremost danger. In citing "the first Progress Report on the Committee of the Redistribution of the Fleet in Commission," however, he unfortunately omits a very revealing annotation by Selborne dated 21 November 1904. In this the First Lord of the Admiralty stated, "The worst case which can befall us under present conditions is for Germany to throw her weight against us in a middle of a still undecided war between us and France and Russia in alliance."[22] The redistribution of the Royal Navy, therefore, was anything but solely aimed at Germany. Far more was it the beginning of a flexible defense strategy against all naval rivals.

Taken together, the so-called revisionists have identified four major forces as decisive for Britain's naval policy, an insight that for the time being has fallen nearly entirely on deaf ears among political, particularly diplomatic, historians:[23] The first was the heavily felt financial burden of naval armament in the aftermath of the South African War, which drove home the necessity to cut costs and improve efficiency.[24] The second was the technological revolution, marked by telegraphic communication, higher speed, and inventions like the torpedo, the submarine, and the battle cruiser.[25] Third, British grand strategy did not focus only on Germany or the historically overrated two-power standard—which was an instrument to placate

Parliament—but aimed at sustaining an overall supremacy, over all modern fleets, especially over the French and the U.S. navies, and not through numbers but by mobility and quality.[26] The fourth was a more nuanced British vision of sea power, a view that—unlike those of new and rather inexperienced naval powers such as Japan, the United States, and Germany—was profoundly different from the popular writings of Alfred Thayer Mahan.[27] As noted, Mahan's emphasis on capital ships, tonnage, command of the sea, and decisive battles was even criticized by First Sea Lord Fisher, Julian Corbett, and others.[28]

One may, of course, respond that however persuasive this argument may be, we are still left with the question of why prewar British public opinion on the German navy was so much more emotionally charged than on other foreign navies. Jan Rüger's study of naval celebrations—work whose innovative integration of naval and cultural history allows him to demonstrate how sea power was constructed—shows us a possible way to account for the obsession of public opinion with German sea power. He sees the cult of the naval race as part of what can be called the theater of diplomatic relations before the First World War, a realm in which the demonstration of power and deterrence replaced actual facts.[29] Another possibility for dealing with increasing public hysteria and its effects on political decision making is to combine naval history with modern media history and the study of party and propagandistic politics. Traditionally, the emotional buildups in British and German public opinion have been interpreted in opposite ways. German public opinion has always been explained in terms of cynical manipulation by the press bureau or dangerous self-mobilization;[30] the influence of public opinion in England, in contrast, has usually been interpreted as positive and useful.[31] However, recent research on the press as a rising political actor in both Germany and England has stressed that the "similarities between the two countries" are more striking than the differences and that "political and cultural liberalism" in prewar Britain has often been "overestimated."[32] The press, therefore, should not be used as an expression of unfiltered perception.[33]

In any case, to reach analytically satisfying conclusions one needs to combine different approaches and identify an element that links the cultural sphere with decision-making processes. This could be done, for example, by contrasting the emotional public debate on science fiction, invasion and spy stories, plays, and press campaigns with the viewpoints of naval and military experts. Surprising differences are to be found between the expert risk assessments concerning the German battle fleet and public scares.[34] Just how little public opinion and its leading voices were mere accelerators and transporters of facts and perceptions but were rather independent political players with manifold contacts and their own agendas and (immense) political influence has been demonstrated in particular by Dominik Geppert's study of the "press wars" before 1914.[35]

The following considerations are based on all this recent research. It builds on Sumida's, Lambert's, and Hobson's results and combines them with findings of modern media and cultural history to draw attention away from the encounter at Cronberg toward the complex domestic background and in that way to provide further insight into Britain's prewar foreign and naval policy.[36]

"The Committee of Four"

Just before Hardinge and Wilhelm II met at Cronberg, from November 1907 to July 1908, a special subcommittee of the Committee of Imperial Defence (CID) dealt extensively with the perceived German naval menace. Historians have tended to interpret the convening of this subcommittee as further evidence of how London responded to the fourth German Naval Bill of the Reichstag in November 1907.[37] In fact, nothing could be farther from the truth. Archival material confirms that the special investigation had been decided on many months before the Naval Bill passed in the Reichstag, in response to public outrage and hysteria in the wake of the publication in 1906 of William Le Queux's science-fiction book *The Invasion of 1910*.[38] As for actual British naval opinion, however, men like Philipp Dumas, Adm. Louis Battenberg, and Lord Selborne saw no reason to investigate any further, because of the "overwhelming superiority" of the Royal Navy.[39]

At the end of 1906, Archibald Hurd, a freelance naval correspondent, also saw "absolutely no danger" coming from Germany.[40] Hurd firmly believed that the British position diplomatically as well as navally had never been stronger, with the three-power standard (i.e., a Royal Navy stronger than any three possible adversaries combined) now in reach. Only days before the subcommittee met, Fisher—always described by historians as a notorious enemy of Germany—remarked to the king, "England has 7 Dreadnoughts and 3 Invincibles, in my opinion better than Dreadnoughts, built and building, while Germany had not begun one!"[41]

Why then another investigation, when nothing had changed since November 1905, when, in the aftermath of the Norfolk Commission, Premier Arthur Balfour had declared Britain absolutely safe at home and abroad?[42] How to deal with public scares, during which Balfour had been heavily attacked for a "soporific" attitude?[43]

The answer is to be found first and foremost in Britain's domestic politics, or, to be more precise, in the change of government in 1906 that followed the landslide Liberal victory in parliamentary elections. Archibald Hurd, John Fisher, and Hugh Arnold-Forster, former parliamentary Secretary for the Admiralty and Secretary of State for War in the Balfour government, now replaced by that of Sir Henry Campbell-Bannerman, all concurred that German policies had little, if anything, to do with the establishment of the subcommittee. They were in full agreement that rather than the sudden emergence of a German threat, "pure party politics stood behind the Sub-committee."[44]

The Liberals—in particular, their left-wing majority—had won the elections on a ticket of promising social reforms and cutting armament expenditures. Their winning slogan had been "Retrenchment and Reforms." The smaller but more influential (owing to their dominance of key cabinet positions) Liberal imperialist faction around H. H. Asquith and Edward Grey fundamentally disagreed, on the basis of their concern for Britain's international security and social reform. Under such circumstances the traditionally strained relations between the service departments became even worse. From now on, they degenerated into what Charles Ardagh as director of military intelligence once called "two rival syndicates" fighting each other for tight budgets.[45]

The army, trying to improve its damaged reputation after the South African War, feared to lose its importance and social function within Britain and the empire. Thus many army officers, backed by the National Service League and the National Defence Association, fought for conscription.[46] The navy, feeling rather self-assured, popular, and never short of volunteers, was largely concerned with itself and Fisher's internal reforms. Fisher himself, of course, did not want the money his painful structural reforms had just saved to go for social benefits, and certainly not for the land forces. For him personally, but certainly also for the navy, a renewed investigation into Britain's security was not only a "waste of time" but a drain on scarce administrative resources.[47] For Arnold-Forster, therefore, it was only too logical to presume that the main driving forces behind the demand for a new debate came from the army camp, even more so because its traditional role had been defense of the British coastline.[48]

Deeply disappointed in the results of the former investigation under Balfour and confronted with an even more pacifist approach by radical liberalism, Lord Roberts, Britain's greatest war hero, and Charles Repington, a former army officer and military correspondent of the *Times,* with the support of the spectacularly rich Lord Lovat and Samuel Scott, founded a pressure group, known as the "Committee of Four," that agitated for conscription and a Prussian-like "million-men standard."[49] "The Nation," as Repington explained the committee's slogan at Aldershot, "must be a Nation in Arms or perish."[50] Acknowledging that tradition, political constellations, and the fiscal situation militated against an army a million strong, he called for a smooth, concerted, well-regulated, and persistent propaganda campaign. The Committee of Four won powerful pens to its assistance: John Strachey of the *Spectator,* himself a hobby soldier and high sheriff of a paramilitary unit in Surrey; the notorious anti-German Leo Maxse of the *National Review;* Arthur Gwynne of the *Standard;* and Cyril Pearson, proprietor of the *Daily Express,* the *Standard,* the *Evening Standard,* and *Morning Herald,* as well as the whole Northcliffe Press.[51] They all agreed with Repington's and Roberts's demands: "The Blueprint for reducing the value of the [Royal] Navy, is the bogey of invasion." The most valued enemy for a truly national British army was the glorious Prussian army.[52] If the prestige and budget of the army were to be increased, the British public had to be persuaded that the Royal Navy would no longer be capable of guaranteeing security. As Repington predicted to CID member and army reformer Lord Esher, "Until we have put an end to all that damned nonsense that is written about sea power, we shall never get our national army."[53]

Repington was in close contact with the army's leadership, but motives can also be found in his foreign-policy aims. As unofficial mediator in secret Anglo-French staff talks that had begun in early 1906, he strove for a foreign political security bloc with Paris, and if possible also with Saint Petersburg, to control the destinies of international relations. Russia, in contrast to his public utterances on Germany, he thought invincible, as he told his friend Colonel Raymond John Marker. Therefore he pleaded that the tsarist empire be co-opted and if necessary appeased, together with France, until Britain was militarily prepared for the worst or diplomatically safeguarded. In the meantime, the German empire served as a perfect bogeyman.[54] To this end he did not hesitate to distort information. For example, upon learning that the French general staff was still working on plans to invade Britain despite the Entente Cordiale, he alleged instead that the Germans were doing so.[55] In fact, the Kaiserreich by then had long abandoned all plans to invade the British Isles as completely unrealistic.[56]

With this program Repington and his fellow conspirators stumped the country. In countless speeches and articles for the *Times,* the *National Review,* and other influential papers, they pressed the government for army reform and tried everything they could to undermine Fisher's navy.[57] Together with Lord Northcliffe and the National Service League they promoted and paid for invasion stories, such as Le Queux's *Invasion of 1910* or Guy du Maurier's play *An Englishman's Home* (1909), and countless others. They did not even bar fabricating sensational "revelations" about German spies and arsenals supposedly hidden beneath the streets of London.[58] Although their revelations were both fictitious and preposterous, the propaganda and modern media manipulation through the tabloids worked.[59] It was sufficient simply to make countless unsubstantiated assertions, place them prominently in the press, and repeat them ad nauseam.[60] Soon "the newspapers of the breakfast table, the reviews of the clubs, even the 'society' journals teem[ed] with articles of more or less interest on naval topics."[61]

Repington's main forum for his blows against the so-called Blue Water School was the *Times*.[62] In March it published a full-page prospective invasion map that it encouraged every household to keep for reference. In an influential August 1906 article, "Moltke and Over-Sea Invasion," Repington even claimed that the operation in 1864 of Helmuth von Moltke "the Elder" against the small island of Alsen (or Als), separated from the mainland by the two-hundred-foot-wide Alsenfjord, had been a rehearsal for an invasion of the British Isles.[63] This charge was meant to be a "nasty jar for the Blue Water fanatics. . . . The only way out for them will be to declare that Moltke was an ass."[64] What followed was a heated debate lasting months, from which "no periodical, great or small," could escape and that provoked further invasion and spy stories.

While Repington lost no opportunity to stir up the people or to influence directly the Prince of Wales or the Secretary for War, Richard Haldane, to repeat an investigation of the German peril, his critics tried to deal with the allegations as objectively and coolheadedly as possible. The navy's advocates preferred reason to passion. Arnold-Forster (the CID secretary), George Sydenham Clarke, the naval historian David Hannay, Julian Corbett, and Repington's counterpart at the *Times*, the naval correspondent Richard Thursfield, argued in a very sophisticated manner, referring to weather conditions, water depths, tides, and loading capacities, as well as the special naval problems of protecting convoys against torpedoes or submarines and amphibious warfare.[65] Although today's reader would find that they succeeded in exposing the "Blue Funk School," as they called the Committee of Four, their contemporary impact was limited.[66] Their writings, it seemed, were simply too difficult for laymen, who were inclined to sensation. In fact, the more the "Blue Funk School's" assertions were objected to, the longer and harder its views were discussed and the more supporters it gained.[67] Repington rubbed his hands and made no secret of his wish that Thursfield and others would voice objections, by which he would gain more attention himself.[68]

The decisive factor was the emotional appeal, which was not to be offset even by subsequent clarification, as can be seen in the cases of Foreign Office officials like Eyre Crowe, who were deeply convinced by Repington's allegations.[69] What is striking is the passivity of the government. Neither Asquith, Grey, nor Haldane dealt with naval or military questions in detail. Even Haldane—who was, after all, Secretary for War—apparently saw no reason to calm the public. To the contrary, he rather reckoned in terms more of benefits for his military reforms than of the reasonableness of the assertions. Among high-ranking politicians, Balfour, who remained the leader of the Conservatives in the Commons, was the only one to recognize the propaganda coup being achieved by the Committee of Four.[70] In general, and in contrast to the agitation of the "mischief-makers," as Clarke called Repington and Roberts, objective arguments failed to excite the public.[71]

At the turn of 1906/1907, the debate gained momentum. Fisher and Clarke tried everything to contain the "Blue Funk School" and to prevent a further time-consuming and (in their eyes) useless investigation of the German peril.[72] Clarke had published his own series of articles, entitled "The Bolt from the Blue School," which Fisher distributed as a sort of memorandum within the Admiralty.[73] Fisher also suspected his personal archenemy, Adm. Charles Beresford, of being behind the repeated attacks of the Committee of Four. As it turns out, this was not pure invention. In fact, Beresford fought Fisher on all fronts and did not stop even at treason. On his orders his chief of staff, Frederick Sturdee, provided the Committee of Four with secret information on the distribution of the British fleets, as well as the strengths and weaknesses of individual units.[74]

Fisher strongly believed that all his critics, as well as Charles Hardinge—who, he knew, took the scaremongers at their word—were misguided: "The real truth is we have enormously increased both our readiness for war and our instant fighting strength." The First Sea Lord even thought it would be safe to abandon the dreadnought program for the current year:

> Again *and this requires to be most prominently and emphatically reiterated, ad nauseam.* We are not going to be frightened by foreign paper programmes (the bogey of agitators). . . . Our present margin of superiority over Germany *(our only possible foe for years)* is so great as to render it absurd in the extreme to talk of anything endangering our naval supremacy, *even if we stopped all shipbuilding altogether*!!![75]

If he thought the German empire theoretically a "possible" foe, in practice he was sure this was an unrealistic scenario: "For years and years to come it is simply impossible for Germany to cope with us single handed and she has no naval ally."[76] In other words, it was fortunate for the prospects of social reforms that Germany and not the rival sea power France was seen as a potential threat, because it meant that the British government could have it both ways, saving money and safeguarding British supremacy at sea at the same time.[77]

According to Nicholas Lambert and Jon Sumida, Fisher always planned Britain's supremacy at sea not only against Germany but against all naval powers. Moreover, to enforce his naval reforms he fought on several external and domestic fronts. This is why many older interpretations characterizing him primarily as a notorious anti-German focused on the High Seas Battle Fleet are somewhat hasty and unduly sweeping. Certainly he was full of doubts about the aims of the German navy, and, needless to say, from time to time he even had preventive strike in mind. But this mind-set affected not only Germany; he expressed similar thoughts about Russia and France as well.[78] Of far greater importance from a diplomatic point of view was the fact that he took great care that Berlin learn of his ideas, so as to discourage it from risking any adventures.[79] Any combined activity, however—for example, staff talks, or a landing operation with France—he strictly refused.[80] In this respect, the differences between Fisher and Repington, and between Fisher and the new political leadership, could not have been greater.[81] Again and again he stressed that the Royal Navy was fully capable of guaranteeing Britain's security.[82] Of course, these assurances were aimed at saving his reform program and the prestige of the navy and his own, especially in comparison to the land forces. Nevertheless, the weight of security data speaks for itself. The superiority of the Royal Navy undercut the unsustainable allegations of the scaremongers. For months Fisher, Julian Corbett, and Captains Ernest Slade and Charles Ottley from the Naval Intelligence branch tried everything "to smash the German bogey" and to prevent a further subcommittee—to them only a "master piece of funk."[83] Not only would its deliberations stir up the people, but its existence alone would certainly undermine the reputation of the navy, as the "1st, 2nd, 3rd, 4th, 5th . . . ad infinitum Line of Defence!"[84] Time and again they briefed Lord Tweedmouth, the First Lord of the Admiralty, journalists like Arnold White, and the king, as well as the crown prince, that Britain's position was in "every little particular magnificently splendid."[85]

In the end, however, Fisher found himself in a dilemma among public policy, the aims of the navy, and Parliament. The more he was attacked, and the more he stressed Britain's strength, the more the radicals demanded retrenchment. "We are so strong. It is quite true!" he admitted. But telling the truth could easily mean committing parliamentary suicide. "The real truth is, we don't want anyone to know the truth."[86] Tirpitz and Wilhelm II would know it anyway, but "we don't want to parade all this, because if so, we shall have parliamentary trouble." Fisher was referring to 150 radical members who had signed "one of the best papers" he had ever read calling for a cut in expenditure due to the Royal Navy's superiority.[87] Ironically, the pacifist left-wing Liberals understood the real balance of power far better than the Liberal imperialists. Against the background of the crushing defeat of Russia at Tsushima, Germany was logically regarded as the only remaining potential threat but not as the greatest, let alone "unique," danger. Therefore the Admiralty quite inevitably arrived at the "common sense conclusion that the outlying Fleets no longer require to be maintained at the strength that was admittedly necessary a year ago when France and Russia were our most probable opponents."[88]

Conversely, the advocates of conscription and a million-man army used and needed the German peril to buttress their case and to justify an entente with former imperial rivals. The defense of the empire alone would not suffice to persuade the public of the necessity of compulsory service or of a rapprochement with Russian autocracy. As Arnold-Forster knew, the very existence of Britain itself had to be at stake.[89] Nothing else would stir up the people to agree to such a sea change.[90] Repington himself admitted that the supposed German danger was a straw man: "The truth is . . . our superiority over Germany is so overwhelming, . . . that the Germans know it would be madness for them to provoke war."[91]

The German peril, therefore, united army advocates and conscriptionists, sensationalist journalists, writers of science fiction and spy novels, and younger diplomats and politicians, especially from the Liberal imperialist faction. They were in favor of a new course of abandoning "splendid isolation" and approaching the old rivals France and Russia. George Clarke did not doubt for a second that the main reason for the existence of a subcommittee on the German peril was to be found not in Wilhelmshaven, the home base of the German High Seas Battle Fleet, but among the "numerous writers in this country endeavouring for some time to create a German Scare."[92]

The Subcommittee and Julian Corbett's Expertise
On 27 November Edward Grey, H. H. Asquith, and Richard Haldane opened the inaugural meeting of the subcommittee of the CID, and almost immediately it turned into a farce. While the Tory government had worked hand in hand with the naval experts in the 1905 investigation and ultimately had tried to calm public hysteria, the Liberal imperialist faction now adopted a free-rider position. Instead of contributing to the public debate, they simply let rumors about an imminent German threat run without restraint. They did not even protest when Fisher himself was publicly denounced by Leo Maxse as a "traitor" who ought to be "hung at his own yard arm."[93]

The reason for the Liberal imperialists' passivity was twofold. Since 1895—and thus before the well-known caesura of the famous Kruger telegram in January 1896 and the first German Naval Law in 1898—Edward Grey had argued for a global alliance with Britain's most dangerous rivals, Russia and France, and if possible also with the United States. He thus aimed at killing not just two but three birds with one stone. First, he wanted to relieve the security threat to the empire, particularly on the northwestern frontier in Central Asia; second, he aimed at reducing defense budgets in favor of financing social reform; and third, he wanted to control global international relations in a shared hegemonic manner, without German hindrance.[94]

Germany—Grey was quite clear in this respect—seemed too dependent on Russia and thus too weak a potential partner to balance Russian aggressiveness.[95] A major obstacle to this strategy change was the radicals' refusal to cooperate with the Russian autocracy. "Painting the German devil on the wall," as Cecil Spring-Rice and others, especially in the liberal paper *The Nation*, noted, seemed likely therefore to help overcome radical stubbornness on this point.[96] One explicit power-political result was construction of a double standard concerning Russian and German, or Austrian, aggressiveness in the Balkans; the Foreign Office, manifestly behaving in a fashion "more Russian, than the Russians" brought international tension back to the continent.[97]

During sessions of the CID subcommittee, Lord Esher acted as the prime supporter of the "Blue Funk School."[98] As a typical Edwardian, he was deeply convinced of the inevitability of war, sooner or later, though he did not think that it would necessarily come in the form of a war against Germany. He even thought the idea of a German danger "to be absurd."[99] However, as a military reformer, he saw his task as preparation of Britain for the worst. He deemed Germany the perfect enemy for propaganda reasons and welcomed any public scare as a useful instrument to make the British people "warlike in spirit." In other words, he judged that riding an anti-German scare was for political and tactical reasons the best thing to do and advised Fisher to do the same. For him, clearly, the end justified all means; if the German peril helped to prevent the radicals from further retrenchment of naval spending, so much the better.[100] In October 1907, Esher wrote Fisher, "The German peril is a bogey. Granted. But it is a most useful one"—that is, for the army and the navy.[101] The calming results of the Balfour committee in 1905 had proved counterproductive for the martial spirit of the nation; now Esher pleaded for the establishment of an organized propaganda machine:[102]

> If history has any teaching for us, it is that our day of trial must come, and that without adequate preparation we cannot avoid the fate of other nations, who have relied upon their ancient traditions. . . . We require writers and lecturers, not labelled as paid agents, but with an appearance of independence. These men have to be paid. . . . The work is one of converting the nation to an idea which it is anxious to put aside as long as possible.[103]

In the Committee of Four—journalists like John Strachey, Leo Maxse, and Louis Garvin or novelists like Erskine Childers, Guy du Maurier, and William Le Queux, to name but a few—Esher found his "agents" without even paying them. For their purposes, real wonders were attributed to the German military machine. Repington, Roberts, Lovat, and Scott seriously claimed to believe that Germany could secretly load 150,000 soldiers, two hundred field guns, and seven thousand horses in a few hours and bring them to British shores, almost unnoticed and at a rate of twenty thousand soldiers per hour.[104] In view of the general experience of deployment of land forces from the sea and the great difficulties the Japanese had encountered against Russia in 1905, this was a fantastic assumption.[105] This was even more the case as the results from the maneuvers at Clacton upon Sea in 1904 spoke against it. At Clacton, under ideal conditions and against no resistance, British forces had needed at least thirty hours to get only twelve thousand soldiers ashore.[106] George Clarke, Julian Corbett, and Admirals Slade, Battenberg, and Philip Howard Colomb were well aware of the logistic and meteorological obstacles of landing operations.[107] To cross the 360 miles from Hamburg to the British coast a transport needed at least thirty hours. Everything in such an enterprise depended on secrecy, but the smoke of an invasion convoy (in that era of largely coal-fired ships) would be seen from a distance of at least thirty miles and thus would provide ample warning. Moreover, it was impossible to confiscate a large merchant fleet secretly—in this case more than 250,000 tons of shipping—for transport purposes. The loading of such a fleet would paralyze several harbors, international trade centers, for days.[108]

On 12 December 1907, Julian Corbett countered Repington's assertions before the subcommittee. Disappointed at the lack of a worthy intellectual challenge by Repington, who seemed to "know less about naval matters, than a sheet of paper," Corbett spread his superior knowledge before the committee.[109] Backed by Rear Admiral Slade, he rebuked the evidence of the German peril in a most complex manner, referring to all the modern aspects of naval warfare and the difficulties of amphibious operations. His verdict was devastating. Repington and his peers had neglected any difference between warfare by land and by sea, had evidently been not only influenced but misled by Mahan's popular writings on the eighteenth century, and lacked understanding of modern naval conditions. The prospect that a whole division could be wiped out by a few torpedo hits would in itself deter any enemy from an amphibious operation.[110]

How Mahan's way of thinking dominated Repington and his supporters could be seen, Corbett pointed out, in exaggerations in the public debate and by politicians alike on the issues of decisive battle, interior lines, battle fleets, capital ships and their tonnages, and command of the sea as the epitome of Britain's naval supremacy. On all these Corbett took a different position: "The task of the great fleets is merely to keep the enemy at a distance. To prevent an invasion no battleships, but [a] few operating flotillas are crucial. As for the future of naval warfare, it would depend mainly on new technologies, such as speed, torpedoes and submarine and the advantages in information and communication." A temporary loss of "command" did not automatically mean passing it over to the enemy; to the contrary, "in three of five major wars at sea," Corbett reported, "Britain had lost the command altogether and still prevailed." The assumption that Britain's fate was tied to "command" ignored the power of the strategic defensive, which had increased at least tenfold with the new technological developments. Concerning a possible threat by a German navy, Corbett stated, one must not forget Germany's geographical weaknesses. In contrast to Britain's past enemies, Germany depended in all its naval operations on a single small exit, easily blocked; for protection against Germany "second line forces" were more than enough. Finally, Corbett poked fun at the "continental school," mocking the claim that Germany could control the streets of Dover within forty-eight hours: "Splendid. That will end that [i.e., Germany's fleet]. Head in lion's mouth."[111]

Though Corbett's profound analysis was characterized by Haldane as "one of the most important state papers" he had ever seen, it failed to prevent the Liberal imperialists from adopting the Committee of Four's line.[112] Since then, and almost indiscriminately, many historians have tended to rely for these naval matters on statements of diplomats, politicians, journalists, and army officers. Even Repington and Roberts have not infrequently been treated as naval experts, for the simple reason that they commented on naval affairs.[113] However, historians more often than not have neglected to account for the professions of their witnesses or to examine their hidden motives and agendas.

Ironically, naval experts thought the German navy apparently less dangerous than their peers from the army did. For both groups, the deep rivalry between the two military branches was decisive. At the same time, Corbett and Slade brought forward plausible arguments, pointing to the fundamental differences between naval and land forces. Corbett's complex analysis, which can be only touched on here, at least offered a political alternative to the arms race, as well as, for historians, to the widespread interpretation of militarism preventing rational politics before 1914. Among contemporary politicians this alternative had been outlined only by Arthur Balfour, who, in contrast to his Liberal successors, had dealt extensively with naval and military matters. Therefore he was invited by the subcommittee to provide his insights from the first investigation of the German peril in 1905. The plenary session was visibly impressed by his statement, "lasting about an hour, quite perfect in form and language, and most closely reasoned." Privately, Esher noted in his diary that "not a question [was] put to him. Asquith, Grey, Haldane, [Lord] Crewe, [David] Lloyd George. All were equally dumbfounded."[114]

The essence of Balfour's remarks was that he stuck to his assessment of May 1905. British security, he concluded, would be ensured by the Royal Navy, and even the most recent inventions would benefit Great Britain more than any other nation.[115] Moreover, Balfour stressed that despite rapprochement with Saint Petersburg, he saw Russia as the most dangerous enemy of the empire.[116] A German attack, on the contrary, he thought quite unlikely and conceivable only if the Germans stood with their backs to the wall and feared for their very existence.[117] Admiral Slade described Balfour's speech as "most excellent," as one "in which he summed up the whole situation in a most remarkable manner."[118] Esher too could not help but underscore Balfour's "masterly knowledge."[119] Given the overwhelming evidence, Esher and Haldane had finally to admit that England had nothing to fear even from a Franco-German alliance.[120]

Conclusion

The rather reassuring facts regarding Britain's safety and supremacy led neither to a relaxation of the Anglo-German antagonism within the political arena nor to a naval agreement.[121] Again and again, attempts to reach an understanding failed, be it before the second disarmament conferences at the Hague;[122] in December 1907, when Germany, Britain, and France tried to conclude a North Sea Convention;[123] in the spring of 1908, when both Tirpitz and Wilhelm II refused to challenge Britain's naval supremacy; or in summer 1908, when Hardinge and Edward VII went to Cronberg.[124] According to conventional wisdom, it always was "Germany's refusal to limit shipbuilding, that 'blocked' any understanding."[125] As for Cronberg, however, where, as Wolfgang Mommsen posits, Wilhelm II supposedly missed "a great opportunity" to change the history of the world, at least three things become obvious.[126]

First, Hardinge's viewpoint was based on public stereotypes, not on sound intelligence; second, he, and even more the Liberal imperialists, totally lacked naval expertise; third and above all, there was no pressure on the British side for an understanding with Germany. The allegedly "missed opportunity," therefore, appears illusory. As if the CID's expert testimony and even the reassuring reports of his own diplomats in Germany concerning the Kaiserreich's devastating financial problems did not exist, Hardinge asserted that it was a "common notoriety, that in three or four years' time Germany would have more dreadnoughts than Great Britain."[127] Thus, on this view, Germany alone was to blame for the worsening of Anglo-German relations. Hardinge even conveyed the impression to the kaiser that the British coastline stood open to invasion and sold that idea as the official belief and fear of the British Admiralty.[128] He thus explicitly adopted the propaganda of the Committee of Four, which had already been proved wrong. Where a display of firm resolution, determination, and confidence might have deterred Wilhelm II, Hardinge thus inadvertently promoted the false impression in Berlin that Britain would sooner or later give way.

Without question, at Cronberg Wilhelm II once more behaved clumsily and foolishly. He even boasted that he had "given it properly" to Hardinge (although other witnesses of the interview described it as a "cozy" and "polite" conversation).[129] Nevertheless, whatever the atmosphere of that conversation, for scholarly study it remains "one thing to show that Germany blundered and had dangerous aims, quite another however to prove that these really caused the outcome, or that, had Germany not made them, the overall outcome would have been drastically changed."[130] As Christopher Clark has remarked, much historiography "and . . . popular present day awareness" has been marked by a "perplexing tendency" to "accept implicitly the notion that British colonial expansion and British perceptions of British rights constituted a natural order, in the light of which German objections appeared to be wanton provocations."[131]

In any case, consideration of the domestic side of British foreign and naval affairs and the context of Britain's parliamentary system seems to be a desideratum even today. Whereas the domestic side of the Kaiserreich has been well researched and in great detail, we still know surprisingly little about Edwardian Britain as concerns interservice rivalry, party politics, and, equally important, the media as power-political actors with an agenda of their own—but no responsibility. As concerns the construction of the German fleet, we have shown that there was neither anything revolutionary about the building of a German battle fleet nor any inevitability of German action and British response. On one hand, this is because Germany's navalism mainly followed the pattern of naval expansion by all the great powers. On the other hand, Britain's Liberal leadership knew that German naval armament did not constitute an existential threat to British security—or at least it could have known, had it taken advantage of service expertise as Balfour had done before—and it could have communicated the experts' advice to calm the public.

Against this background, the change of government in 1906 and the generational change within the Foreign Office appear with particular importance. The new diplomatic elite around Charles Hardinge, Arthur Nicolson, and Eyre Crowe no longer had the same relaxed attitude toward Germany that Thomas Sanderson or Frank Lascelles had taken; at the same time, the political leaders of the Liberal imperialists also had a different outlook from what the left-wing radicals or their conservative predecessors had. All in all, it can be said that diplomatic action was driven more by domestic and partisan interests than has hitherto been accepted and the reasons for the failure of détente politics were far more complex.

Foreign and defense issues have to be taken into account, as well as the traditional rivalry of the service departments, the press as a political player in itself, and the rather complicated situation in partisan relations, especially as concerns radicalism and imperial liberalism. Not without reason did the left-wing periodical *The Nation* suspect partisan interests behind the anti-German hysteria, calling it the "great Grey bogey." Not only journalists like James Garvin confirmed this straw man but also diplomats like Cecil Spring-Rice, Arthur Nicolson, and even Edward Grey himself, who repeatedly spoke of an imminent German danger.[132] Therefore it seems that the magazine had more than adequate grounds for its eloquent conclusion that "it is the writers, not the sailors, who have largely poisoned the Anglo-German situation."[133]

A new concentration on the domestic side and the public sphere in Britain would raise many new questions. For example, does Corbett's rather relaxed interpretation of the "command of the sea" and his precise analysis according to which Britain had nothing to fear even from a Franco-German alliance, and in fact enjoyed a superior defensive position, mean that an important alternative for Britain's crisis management in 1914 existed? Perhaps in these years the dominance of politics over the military or naval experts—usually seen as Britain's particular advantage in contrast to the continental powers—proved disadvantageous.

NOTES This paper draws partly on research carried out for my PhD thesis (*Zwischen Empire und Kontinent: Britische Außenpolitik vor dem Ersten Weltkrieg* [Munich, Ger.: Oldenbourg, 2011], pp. 171–236, 385–423) and partly on that for a postdoctoral project, funded by the Swiss National Foundation on British Military Journals, on the expectations of war from 1880 to 1914: "'Readiness or Ruin' die britischen Militärzeitschriften und der Krieg der Zukunft (1880–1914)," in *Vor dem Sprung ins Dunkle: Die Debatten in den Militärzeitschriften des Deutschen Reiches, Frankreichs und Großbritanniens über den Krieg der Zukunft, 1880–1914,* Stig Förster, ed. (Paderborn, Ger.: Schöningh, 2015), pp. 275–440.

1 Wilhelm II to Bülow, 12 August 1908, in *Die Große Politik der Europäischen Kabinette: Sammlung der Diplomatischen Akten des Auswärtigen Amtes,* ed. Johannes Lepsius et al. (Berlin: Deutsche Verlagsgesellschaft für Politik, 1925) [hereafter GP], vol. 24, no. 8225, pp. 125–26; no. 8226, pp. 126–29; Bernhard Fürst von Bülow, *Memoirs* (Boston: Little, Brown, 1931), vol. 2, pp. 309–10; "Lord Hardinge's Report," *Times* (London), 10 November 1924; David Stevenson, *Armaments and the Coming of War: Europe 1904–1914* (Oxford, U.K.: Clarendon, 1996), p. 171.

2 John Röhl, *Wilhelm II.: Der Weg in den Abgrund 1900–1941* (Munich, Ger.: C. H. Beck, 2008), pp. 677–88; Wolfgang J. Mommsen, *War der Kaiser an allem schuld? Wilhelm II. und die preußisch-deutschen Machteliten* (Munich, Ger.: Ullstein, 2002), pp. 140–41; Matthew S. Seligmann, *Spies in Uniform: British Military and Naval Intelligence on the Eve of the First World War* (Oxford, U.K.: Oxford Univ. Press, 2006), p. 1; Arthur Marder, *Anatomy of British Sea Power, 1885–1905* (Hamden, Conn.: Archon Books, 1964), p. 496; Paul M. Kennedy, *The Rise of the Anglo-German Antagonism, 1860–1914* (London: Ashfield, 1980), p. 279; George Monger, *The End of Isolation: British Foreign Policy, 1900–1907* (London: Nelson, 1963), p. 176; Zara Steiner and Keith Neilson, *Britain and the Origins of the First World War* (Cambridge, U.K.: Cambridge Univ. Press, 2003), pp. 51–52; Magnus Brechtken, *Scharnierzeit 1895–1907: Persönlichkeitsnetze und internationale Politik in den deutsch-britisch-amerikanischen Beziehungen vor dem Ersten Weltkrieg* (Mainz, Ger.: Verlag Philipp von Zabern, 2006), p. 369; Annika Mombauer, *The Origins of the First World War: Controversies and Consensus* (London: Longman, 2002), p. 6; Volker Ullrich, *Die nervöse Großmacht 1871–1918: Aufstieg und Untergang des deutschen Kaiserreichs,* 3rd ed. (Frankfurt am Main, Ger.: Fischer, 2007), p. 209. For an extended historiographical discussion see Andreas Rose, *Zwischen Empire und Kontinent: Britische Außenpolitik vor dem Ersten Weltkrieg* (Munich, Ger.: Oldenbourg, 2011), pp. 171–88.

3 Steiner and Neilson, *Britain and the Origins of the First World War,* p. 53.

4 Klaus Hildebrand, "Staatskunst und Kriegshandwerk: Akteure und System der europäischen Staatenwelt vor 1914," in *Der Schlieffenplan: Analyse und Dokumente,* ed. Hans Ehlert et al. (Paderborn, Ger.: Schöningh, 2006), p. 28; Brechtken, *Scharnierzeit,* p. 58; Ivo N. Lambi, *The Navy and German Power Politics* (Boston: Allen and Unwin, 1984), p. 290. As concerns the inevitability of the dreadnought: Marder, *Anatomy of British Sea Power,* pp. 457–67. More doubtful: Charles Fairbanks, Jr., "The Dreadnought Revolution: A Historiographical Essay," *International History Review* 13, no. 4 (1991), pp. 246–72; Nicholas Lambert, *Sir John Fisher's Naval Revolution* (Columbia: Univ. of South Carolina Press, 1999), passim, esp. p. 1; Ruddock Mackay, *Fisher of Kilverstone* (Oxford, U.K.: Oxford Univ. Press, 1973). For Gregor Schöllgen, the naval race is overrated only after 1911; the previous years the naval race was, he concludes, "the pivotal aspect in international relations"; Gregor Schöllgen, "Großmacht als Weltmacht," *Historische Zeitschrift* 248, no. 1 (1989), p. 93 note 32.

5 Esher, memorandum on National Strategy, 27 March 1904, Balfour Papers, Add. 49718, British Library, London [hereafter BL].

6 Kerr to Selborne, 11 March 1902, cited by Lambert, *Sir John Fisher's Naval Revolution,* p. 34.

7 Maconochie (MP) to Selborne, 30 December 1904, and reply, 31 December 1904, *Times* (London), 3 January 1905.

8 Mackay, *Fisher of Kilverstone,* pp. 337–38.

9 Theodore Ropp, *The Development of a Modern Navy: French Naval Policy 1871–1904,* ed. Stephen A. Roberts (dissertation, Harvard University, Cambridge, Mass., 1937; repr. Annapolis, Md.: 1987).

10 For Mahan's views, Kennedy, *Rise of the Anglo-German Antagonism,* p. 420f.

11 Arthur Marder, *From Dreadnought to Scapa Flow: The Royal Navy in the Fisher Era, 1904–1919* (Oxford, U.K.: Oxford Univ. Press, 1961), vol. 1, pp. 344, 364–68; William Langer, *The Diplomacy of Imperialism* (New York: Knopf, 1960), p. 423; Paul Kennedy, "Mahan versus Mackinder," in *Militärgeschichtliche Mitteilungen* 2 (1974), p. 39; Kennedy, *Rise of the Anglo-German Antagonism,* p. 237; Steiner and Neilson, *Britain and the Origins of the First World War,* p. 52; Jonathan Steinberg, "The German Background to Anglo-German Relations," in *Foreign Policy under Grey,* ed. Francis H. Hinsley (Cambridge, U.K.: Cambridge Univ. Press, 1977), pp. 193–215.

12 Balfour to Mahan, 20 December 1899, Balfour Papers, Add. 49742, BL; Nicholas Lambert, "Admiral Sir John Fisher and the Concept of Flotilla Defence, 1904–1910," *Journal of Military History* 59, no. 4, p. 646; Rolf Hobson, *Maritimer Imperialismus: Seemachtsideologie, seestrategisches Denken und der Tirpitzplan 1875 bis 1914* (Munich, Ger.: Oldenbourg, 2004), pp. 170–71. Other skeptics were Lord Esher (the First Lord of the Admiralty), George Joachim Goschen, and Admirals Philip Howard Colomb, Prince Louis of Battenberg, and Edmond Slade.

13 Brechtken, *Scharnierzeit,* p. 69.

14 Herbert W. Wilson, "The New German Navy," *Harper's Monthly Magazine* 103 (June–November 1901), p. 534; Excubitor [Archibald S. Hurd], "Our Position of Naval Peril," *Fortnightly Review* 82 (1907), p. 247.

15 Bellairs, 6 December 1906, cited in "The Standard of Naval Strength," *Journal of the Royal United Service Institution* 51, no. 1 (1907), p. 128.

16 White, 6 December 1906, cited in ibid., p. 168.

17 White, letters to the editor, *Times* (London), 22 January 1903, and "Modern Warships" (Cantor Lectures, 19 February 1906), repr. *Journal of the Society of Arts* 54 (1905/1906), p. 868.

18 Selborne to Lansdowne, 7 December 1901, Lansdowne Papers, LANS/PL 1, BL; Selborne to Balfour, 12 May 1904, Balfour Papers, Add. 49707, BL; Balfour to Lansdowne, 26 October 1904, Balfour Papers, Add. 49698, BL; Lambert, *Sir John Fisher's Naval Revolution,* pp. 17–21.

19 Lord Ellenborough, "The Possibility of Fleets and Harbours Being Surprised," *Journal of the Royal United Service Institution* 49, no. 2 (1905), p. 793.

20 Selborne, memorandum, 6 December 1904, cited in George D. Boyce, ed., *The Crisis of British Power: The Imperial and Naval Papers of the Second Earl of Selborne, 1895–1910* (London: The Historians' Press, 1990), vol. 2, no. 62, pp. 184–90.

21 Selborne to Balfour, 28 October 1903, Sandars Papers, MSS Eng.hist.c.715, Bodleian Library, Oxford, U.K.

22 Lord Selborne, marginalia dated 21 November 1904, ADM I/7736, The National Archives, Kew, U.K. [hereafter TNA]. For this misinterpretation see Matthew Seligmann, "Switching Horses: The Admiralty's Recognition of the Threat from Germany, 1900–1905," *International History Review* 30 (2008), pp. 242–46, and "New Weapons for New Targets: Sir John Fisher, the Threat from Germany, and the Building of the HMS *Dreadnought* and HMS *Invincible,* 1902–1907," *International History Review* 30 (2008), pp. 303–31. For further evidence on this I am very thankful to Katherine Epstein.

23 For Mark Hewitson, all are revisionists who do not explicitly accept that Germany alone was to blame for the First World War. Mark Hewitson, *Germany and the Causes of the First World War* (Oxford, U.K.: Berg, 2004), p. 11.

24 An example is the harbor at Rosyth: Maconochie (MP) to Selborne, 30 December 1904, and reply, 31 December 1904. Also Kerr to Selborne, 11 March 1902; Archibald S. Hurd, "The Navy First," *United Service Magazine* 148 (1903), pp. 117–26; Mackay, *Fisher of Kilverstone,* pp. 337–38.

25 Esher, memorandum, 27 March 1904. See Jon T. Sumida, *In Defence of Naval Supremacy: Finance, Technology and British Naval Policy, 1889–1914* (London: Routledge, 1993); Sumida, "British Naval Administration and Policy in the Age of Fisher," *Journal of Military History* 54 (1/1990), pp. 1–26; Sumida, "Sir John Fisher and the *Dreadnought:* The Sources of Naval Mythology," *Journal of Military History* 59 (10/1995), pp. 619–38; and Sumida, "British Capital Ship Design and Fire Control in the Dreadnought Era: Sir John Fisher, Arthur Hungerford Pollen, and the Battle Cruiser," *Journal of Modern History* 51, no. 2 (1979), pp. 205–30.

26 Lambert, *Sir John Fisher's Naval Revolution,* and "Admiral Sir John Fisher and the Concept of Flotilla Defence," pp. 639–60. "The Sea-Power of the United States was seen as the new power to dispute the overlordship of the sea"; *Naval and Military Record,* 9 April 1903, p. 5.

27 Ropp, *Development of a Modern Navy;* Hobson, *Maritimer Imperialismus.* Older but also recent works, however, have always extrapolated from the kaiser's belief in Mahan to the British way of thinking: Kennedy, "Mahan versus Mackinder," p. 39; Kennedy, *Rise of the Anglo-German Antagonism,* pp. 237, 420–21; Marder, *From Dreadnought to Scapa Flow,* vol. 1, pp. 344, 364–68; Langer, *Diplomacy of Imperialism,* p. 423; Steiner and Neilson, *Britain and the Origins of the First World War,* p. 52; and Steinberg, "German Background to Anglo-German Relations," pp. 193–215. For Japan see Sadao Asada, *From Mahan to Pearl Harbor: The Imperial Japanese Navy and the United States* (Annapolis, Md.: Naval Institute Press, 2006), and J. Charles Schencking, *Making Waves: Politics, Propaganda, and the Emergence of the Imperial Japanese Navy, 1868–1922* (Stanford, Calif.: Stanford Univ. Press, 2005), pp. 128–29. For the United States, Reto Proksch, *Alfred Thayer Mahan: Seine Thesen und sein Einfluss auf die Außen- und Sicherheitspolitik der USA* (Frankfurt am Main: Peter Lang, 2002).

28 Fisher to Tweedmouth, 5 October 1906, cited in Arthur Marder, ed., *Fear God and Dread Nought: The Correspondence of Admiral of the Fleet Lord Fisher of Kilverstone,* vol. 2, *Years of Power, 1904–1914* (London: Jonathan Cape, 1959), no. 51, pp. 95–97; Balfour to Mahan, 20 December 1899, Balfour

Papers, Add. 49742, BL; Thursfield to Sydenham, 11 August 1898, Thursfield Papers, TT/NAVAL/JRT/2/190, News International Archive, London; Lambert, "Admiral Sir John Fisher and the Concept of Flotilla Defence," p. 646; Hobson, *Maritime Imperialismus*, pp. 170–71. Mahan's seminal works were *The Influence of Sea Power upon History 1660–1783*, published 1890; *The Influence of Sea Power upon the French Revolution and Empire 1783–1812* (1893); and *The Life of Nelson: The Embodiment of Sea Power of Great Britain* (1897).

Tonnage was mainly viewed as a totally irrelevant and "worthless" measure; Selborne to Lansdowne, 7 December 1901; Selborne to Balfour, 12 May 1904, Balfour Papers, Add. 49707, BL; Balfour to Lansdowne, 1904; Lambert, *Sir John Fisher's Naval Revolution*, pp. 17–21; Wilson, "New German Navy," p. 534; Excubitor, "Our Position of Naval Peril," p. 247; Bellairs, 6 December 1906; White, 6 December 1906. Far more important than tonnage or the concentration on capital ships seemed to be the modern mix of ships and their technology; White, letters to the editor, *Times* (London), 22 January 1903, and "Modern Warships," p. 868.

29 Jan Rüger, *The Great Naval Game: Britain and Germany in the Age of Empire* (Cambridge, U.K.: Cambridge Univ. Press, 2007).

30 Geoff Eley, "Reshaping the Right: Radical Nationalism and the German Navy League, 1898–1908," *Historical Journal* 21 (1978), pp. 327–54; Eley, "Sammlungspolitik: Social Imperialism and the Navy Law of 1898," in *From Unification to Nazism: Reinterpreting the German Past* (London: Allen and Unwin, 1986), pp. 110–53; Eley, *Reshaping the German Right: Radical Nationalism and Political Change after Bismarck* (Ann Arbor: Univ. of Michigan Press, 1991).

31 Thus at Marder, *Anatomy of British Sea Power*, p. 465; Kennedy, *Rise of the Anglo-German Antagonism*, p. 251.

32 Frank Bösch, *Öffentliche Geheimnisse: Skandale, Politik und Medien in Deutschland und Großbritannien 1880–1914* (Munich, Ger.: Oldenbourg, 2009), p. 470.

33 Compare Gottfried Niedhart, "Selektive Wahrnehmung und politisches Handeln: Internationale Beziehungen im Perzeptionsparadigma," in *Internationale Geschichte*, ed. Winfried Loth and Jürgen Osterhammel (Munich, Ger.: Oldenbourg, 2000), pp. 141–58.

34 Rose, *Zwischen Empire und Kontinent*, pp. 82–101, 189–273, 385–423.

35 Dominik Geppert, *Pressekriege: Öffentlichkeit und Diplomatie in den deutsch-britischen Beziehungen (1896–1912)* (Munich, Ger.: Oldenbourg, 2007); Rose, *Zwischen Empire und Kontinent*, pp. 27–107.

36 Rose, *Zwischen Empire und Kontinent*, pp. 385–423.

37 Steiner and Neilson, *Britain and the Origins of the First World War*, pp. 51–52; Samuel Williamson, *The Politics of Grand Strategy: Britain and France Prepare for War, 1904–1914* (Cambridge, U.K.: Cambridge Univ. Press, 1969), pp. 91–92; Nicholas D'Ombrain, *War Machinery and High Policy: Defence Administration in Peacetime Britain* (Oxford, U.K.: Oxford Univ. Press, 1973), pp. 220–24; Kennedy, *Rise of the Anglo-German Antagonism*, pp. 442–43; John Charmley, *Splendid Isolation? Britain and the Balance of Power 1874–1914* (London: Hodder and Stoughton, 1999), p. 350; Matthew Seligmann, *Naval Intelligence from Germany: The Reports of the British Naval Attachés in Berlin 1906–1914*, vol. 152 (Aldershot, U.K.: Navy Records Society, 2007), p. 105; Marder, *From Dreadnought to Scapa Flow*, vol. 1, p. 136.

38 See "Notes on Invasion," supplied to Mr. Balfour, June 1907; note by secretary, August 1907; both CAB 3/2/1/42A, TNA; Dumas, 3 October 1907, pp. 121–22, British Documents on Foreign Affairs [hereafter BDFA], F/XX, no. 59.

39 Dumas, Report 3/07, 29 January 1907, cited in Seligmann, *Naval Intelligence from Germany*, no. 24, p. 60; Dumas, Report 7/07, 6 March 1907, cited in ibid., no. 26, p. 81.

40 Archibald Hurd, "A Dreadnought Naval Policy," *Fortnightly Review* 80 (1906), p. 1017; Distribution and Mobilization of the Fleet, 1905, Cd. 2335 and Arrangements Consequent on the Redistribution of the Fleet, 1905, Cd. 2430.

41 The first German dreadnought, *Nassau*, was not launched until March 1908 and the first German battle cruiser, *Von der Tann*, not until March 1909. Günther Prochnow, ed., *Deutsche Kriegsschiffe in zwei Jahrhunderten* (Preetz, Holstein: Ernst Gerdes, 1964), vol. 1, pp. 52, 110. "We have 123 Destroyers and 40 Submarines, the Germans have 48 Destroyers and one Submarine. The whole of our Destroyers and Submarines are absolutely efficient and ready for instant battle"; Fisher to Edward VII, 4 October 1907, cited in Marder, *Fear God and Dread Nought*, vol. 2, no. 90, pp. 139–43.

42 For a first investigation on the Norfolk Commission see Rose, *Zwischen Empire und Kontinent*, pp. 202–17.

43 Charles Repington, *Times* (London), 19 May 1905; Strachey, *Spectator*, 20 May 1905, p. 737.

44 Mary Arnold-Forster, *Memoir of H. O. Arnold-Forster* (London: E. Arnold, 1910), p. 345; Fisher to White, 25 December 1904, cited in Marder, *Fear God and Dread Nought*, vol. 2, no. 10, p. 50; "'XYZ' who is Sir John Wolfe-Barry, writes in *The Times*, and he knows no more about marine engines than this sheet of paper"; Fisher to the Prince of Wales, 15 April 1906, in ibid., no. 37, p. 78f.

45 Ardagh, memorandum on the (so-called) Scheme of Authorized Defence, 19 January 1907, p. 8, WO 32/218, TNA; Agite, "The Influence of Submarine Warfare on British Naval Supremacy," *United Service Magazine* 151, no. 5 (1904), pp. 483–91.

46 Though the Army War Council did not fight for conscription, many of its members privately believed in some form of conscription, and they instead secretly assisted Roberts's league. On this see Rhodri Williams, *Defending the Empire* (New Haven: Yale Univ. Press, 1991).

47 Fisher to Edward VII, 4 October 1907; Slade to Corbett, 5 November 1907, 14 November 1907, 18

November 1907, and 21 November 1907, Corbett Papers, CBT/6/5, National Maritime Museum, Greenwich, U.K. [hereafter NMM]; Fisher to Corbett, 7 November 1907, Richmond Papers, RIC/9/1, NMM; Slade, Sub-Committee of Imperial Defence, 22 October 1908, p. 226, CAB 16/3A, TNA; Fisher to Spender, 11 February 1908, Spender Papers, Add. 46390, BL.

48 Arnold-Forster, *Memoir of H. O. Arnold-Forster,* p. 345; Selborne, *Times* (London), 26 February 1903.

49 Repington to Maxse, 15 October 1907, cited in Andrew Morris, ed., *The Letters of Lieutenant-Colonel Charles à Court Repington CMG Military Correspondent of* The Times, *1903–1918* (London: Sutton, 1999) [hereafter Morris, Repington Letters], no. 48, p. 126.

50 Spring-Rice to P. Spring-Rice, 20 September 1900, cited in Stephen Gwynn, ed., *The Letters and Friendships of Sir Cecil Spring-Rice* (London: Constable, 1929), vol. 1, p. 325.

51 *Times* (London), 15 March 1906; J. B. G. Tulloch [Capt.], "Is a National Army Necessary for the British Isles?," *Journal of the Royal United Service Institution* 51, part 1 (1907), pp. 184–98. For John Strachey: Amy Strachey, *St. Loe Strachey: His Life and His Paper* (London: V. Gollancz, 1930), pp. 191–202, 240–44, 247–56, 285–89.

52 Repington to Marker, 19 July 1906, in D'Ombrain, *War Machinery and High Policy,* pp. 219–20 note 35.

53 Repington to Esher, 22 November 1906, Esher Papers, ESHR 4/2, Churchill College Archive Centre, Cambridge, U.K.

54 Repington to Hutton, 13 March 1907, in Morris, Repington Letters, no. 42, pp. 116–17; Repington to Marker, 14 April 1907, in ibid., no. 43, p. 117; Repington to Maxse, 11 March 1908, Maxse Papers/458, West Sussex Record Office, Chichester, U.K.; Repington to Garvin, 15 March 1908, Maxse Papers/458, West Sussex Record Office, Chichester, U.K.

55 Repington to Roberts, 20 November 1907, in Morris, Repington Letters, no. 51, pp. 129–30.

56 Compare Jonathan Steinberg, "The Copenhagen Complex," *Journal of Contemporary History* 3 (1966), p. 28; Gerhard Ritter, *Staatskunst und Kriegshandwerk: Das Problem des Militarismus in Deutschland* (Munich, Ger.: Oldenbourg, 1960), vol. 2, p. 195; Charles Repington, *The First World War* (London: Constable, 1921), vol. 1, p. 10; Repington, 27 November 1907, Sub-Committee of the C.I.D., p. 33f, CAB 16/3A, TNA. One informant (among others) for Repington was Major Huguet; Repington to Roberts, 20 November 1907; see also RM 5/1609–10, Bundesarchiv Militärarchiv Freiburg.

57 Repington to Roberts, 28 July 1906, Roberts Papers, R 62/3, National Army Museum, London; Repington to Roberts, 15 August 1906, Roberts Papers, R 62/6, ibid.; Repington to Roberts, 23 October 1906, Roberts Papers, R 62/7, ibid. For Spender see Repington to Roberts, 29 January 1908, cited in Morris, Repington Letters, no. 58, p. 139.

58 *Times* (London), 29 August 1906; Rose, *Zwischen Empire und Kontinent,* pp. 82–101.

59 Rose, *Zwischen Empire and Kontinent,* pp. 82–101.

60 Repington to Marker, 25 July 1906, Marker Papers, Add. 52277B, BL. Within the next few months appeared Walter Wood, *The Enemy in Our Midst*; L. Cope Cornford, *The Defenceless Islands*; Ernest Oldmeadow, *The North Sea Bubble*; Patrick Vaux, *The Shock of Battle*; and Lionel Yexley, *When the Eagle Flies Seaward*; see *Times Literary Supplement,* 5 October 1906, p. 339. Until 1914 more than a hundred invasion stories were published.

61 "The Truth about the Navy," *Edinburgh Review* 1 (1907), p. 170.

62 *Times* (London), 29 and 30 August 1906, 1 September 1906, 4 September 1906, 5 September 1906, 7 September 1906, 8 September 1906, 15 September 1906, 17 September 1906, 20 September 1906, 22 September 1906, 4 October 1906, 8 October 1906, 9 October 1906, 13 October 1906, 16 October 1906, 27 and 28 December 1906, 8 January 1907; *National Review* 11 (1907), pp. 468–84; *United Service Magazine* 12 (1907), pp. 248–51; *Quarterly Review* 7 (1908), p. 295; *Spectator,* 29 September 1908, pp. 438–40; George Sydenham Clarke, *My Working Life* (London, Murray: 1927).

63 *Times* (London), 29 August 1906, p. 6.

64 Repington to Marker, 25 July 1906.

65 Clarke to Thursfield, 22 October 1906, Thursfield Papers, News International Archive, London; Charles Dilke, "Clarke on Defence," *Nation,* 13 July 1907, p. 733. David Hannay, "Invasion or Raid?," *Macmillan's Magazine* 84 (1901), pp. 311–20.

66 Navalis [Richard Thursfield], *Times* (London), 4 September 1906, 4 October 1906, 9 October 1906, 16 October 1906; H. O. Arnold-Forster, letter to the editor, *Times* (London), 5 September 1906; David Hannay, *Times* (London), 15 September 1906, 8 October 1906. About Moltke's motives see Arden Bucholz, *Moltke and the German Wars 1864–1871* (Basingstoke, U.K.: Palgrave, 2001), pp. 91–92, and War Office, Note, 10 December 1907, WO 106/47B, ID/8, TNA.

67 *Times* (London), 5, 14, 20 September 1906 and 4, 8, 9 October 1906; Charles Repington, letter, *Times* (London), 13 October 1906, 27 and 28 December 1906, and 8 January 1907; Clarke to Ewart, 16 October 1906, Ewart Papers, NRAS 1054/81/C, National Archives of Scotland, Edinburgh; *Times* (London), 27, 28 December 1906.

68 Charles Repington, "The Blue Water School," *Times* (London), 1 December 1906, 8 January 1907; Crowe, Minutes, 10 February 1908, British Documents on the origins of the First World War, ed. by G. P. Gooch et al., [hereafter], BD VI, no. 80, pp. 115–17, p. 117. Fisher to Edward VII, 23 October 1906, cited in Marder, *Fear God and Dread Nought,* vol. 2, no. 56, pp. 102–105; Repington to Roberts, 28 November 1906, Roberts Papers, R 62/10, National Army Museum, London.

69 Crowe, Minutes, 10 February 1908, BD VI, no. 80, pp. 115–17, p. 117. For Harding's view see Fisher to Edward VII, 23 October 1906; Repington to Roberts, 28 November 1906.

70 Balfour to Clarke, 14 September 1906, Balfour Papers, Add. 49702, BL; Clarke to Balfour, 20 September and 15 November 1906, BL.

71 Clarke to Balfour, 20 September 1906.

72 Fisher to White, October 1906, cited in Marder, *Fear God and Dread Nought,* vol. 2, no. 52, p. 97f; C.W. Radcliffe-Cooke, "The Invasion-Scare: A New View," *Nineteenth Century* 3 (1907), pp. 395–405; Reginald Hennell, "Organization of Power Traction," *Journal of the Royal United Service Institution* 4 (1907), pp. 413–14; Charles Dilke, "Official Opinion on Defence," *United Service Magazine* 10 (1907), pp. 31–33; John Leyland, "Invasion and Imperial Defence," *Nineteenth Century* 12 (1907), pp. 935–48.

73 George Clarke, "The Bolt from the Blue School," *Times* (London), 19 February 1907, 15 March 1907, 29 March 1907; Admiralty, memorandum, n.d., Add. 49711, BL.

74 Repington to Roberts, 22 October 1907, cited in Morris, Repington Letters, no. 49, pp. 127–28; Beresford to Repington, 17 November 1907, Roberts Papers, R 62/23, National Army Museum, London.

75 Fisher to Tweedmouth, 16 October 1906, cited in Marder, *Fear God and Dread Nought,* vol. 2, no. 55, p. 101.

76 Fisher to Tweedmouth, 26 September 1906, cited in ibid., no. 49, pp. 90–93.

77 Fisher to Tweedmouth, 4 October 1906, cited in ibid., no. 50, pp. 93–95.

78 Fisher to Selborne, 29 October 1904, cited in ibid., no. 4, p. 46.

79 Fisher to Corbett, 28 July 1905, cited in ibid., no. 24, p. 63.

80 Fisher to Edward VII, 4 October 1907. Instead he proposed a Copenhagening. Ibid., p. 168 note 2. His consequent attitude against amphibious operation during the war among other things led to the breakup with Churchill over the disastrous Gallipoli expedition. *Times* (London), 12 July 1920.

81 Grey to Haldane, 8 January 1906, Haldane Papers, MSS 5907, National Library of Scotland; Repington to Marker, 14 June 1906, Marker Papers, Add. 52277B, BL.

82 Fisher to Beresford, 30 April 1907, cited in Marder, *Fear God and Dread Nought,* no. 74, p. 122.

83 Fisher to Corbett, 28 September 1907, cited in ibid., pp. 137–38.

84 Fisher, memorandum, July 1904, p. 3, Battenberg Papers, MB1/T5/31, University of Southampton Library.

85 Fisher to Tweedmouth, 5 October 1906.

86 "We shall have 4 Dreadnoughts ready to fight before a single foreign Dreadnought is launched. But we don't want to say this. We have 3 Invincibles building, which some people think stronger than Dreadnoughts—this is also a secret—and we have a pledge to lay down 3 more Dreadnoughts next year. Practically 10 Dreadnoughts. . . . We are more than equal to any combination." Fisher to Unknown, 3 January 1907, cited in Marder, *Fear God and Dread Nought,* no. 61, pp. 110–12.

87 Fisher to Edward VII, 4 October 1907. For Wilhelm II, see Fisher to Tweedmouth, 26 September 1906. See also Metternich to Bülow, 3 March 1908, cited in GP, vol. 24, no. 8185, pp. 37–38.

88 Admiralty, "The Home Fleet," December 1906, cited in Marder, *From Dreadnought to Scapa Flow,* vol. 1, p. 71.

89 H. O. Arnold-Forster, Diary, 21 May 1907, Arnold-Forster Papers, Add. 50353, BL; Repington to Marker, 14 April 1907; Repington to Mrs. Haldane, 27 February 1908, cited in Morris, Repington Letters, no. 60, pp. 141–42.

90 Arnold-Forster, Diary, 21 May 1907.

91 Repington to Hutton, 13 March 1907.

92 George Clarke, "Distribution of Our Naval Forces," secret, early 1907, Clarke Papers, Add. 50836, BL. In August 1907 he thought a further investigation necessary, because the press was campaigning against Germany, to stir up the people; George Clarke, Note, August 1907, p. 1, CAB 3/2/1/42A, TNA.

93 Fisher to Esher, 7 October 1907, cited in M. V. Brett, ed., *The Journals and Letters of Reginald, Viscount Esher,* (London: Ivor Nicholson & Watson, 1934–38), vol. 2, p. 145; Fisher to Cawdor, 4 December 1907, cited in Marder, *Fear God and Dread Nought,* vol. 2, no. 97, pp. 151–52; Bertie to Grey, 22 November 1907, BD VI, no. 73, p. 106.

94 Grey to Buxton, 31 December 1895, cited in H. C. G. Matthew, *The Liberal Imperialist, The Ideas and Politics of a Post-Gladstonian Elite, (*Oxford: Oxford Univ. Press, 1973), p. 202.

95 Rose, *Zwischen Empire und Kontinent,* pp. 69–81.

96 "The statesmen have simply been driven to find the material equivalents for a vicious, but really pointless, war of words"; *Nation,* 29 February 1908, cited in Metternich to Bülow, 29 February 1908, R 5777, Politisches Archiv des Auswärtigen Amtes, Berlin.

97 Dillon to Spring-Rice, 28 August 1909, CASR 1/33, Churchill College Archive Centre, Cambridge, U.K.

98 Arnold-Forster to Maxse, cited in Morris, Repington Letters, introduction, p. 19.

99 Esher, memorandum, 27 March 1904. "'The Bolt from the Blue' upon which Lord Roberts' case is founded, is absurd"; Esher, 16 November 1907, cited in Brett, *Journals and Letters of Reginald, Viscount Esher,* vol. 2, p. 257.

100 Esher to Ewart, 9 October 1900, Ewart Papers, NRAS 1054/3, National Archives of Scotland, Edinburgh.

101 Esher to Fisher, 15 October 1907, cited in Brett, *Journals and Letters of Reginald, Viscount Esher,* vol. 2, p. 251; Fisher to Esher 1 October 1907, Esher Papers, ESHR 10/42, Churchill College Archive Centre, Cambridge, U.K.; Mackay, *Fisher of Kilverstone,* p. 355; "Invasion," note by Lord Esher, 23 July 1908, p. 2, CAB 1/37, TNA.

102 Notes on Invasion supplied to Mr. Balfour, Balfour to Clarke, 2 July 1907, p. 10, CAB 3/2/1/42A, TNA; Report of the Sub-Committee on Invasion, 15 July 1908, p. 2, CAB 1/37, TNA; Esher to Knollys, 6 November 1908, cited in Brett, *Journals and Letters of Reginald, Viscount Esher,* vol. 2, p. 357.

103 Esher to Roberts, 28 August 1907, Roberts Papers, R 29/15, National Army Museum, London.

104 Notes on Invasion, 2 July 1907, pp. 6–8, 10–13.

105 Günther Ortenburg, *Waffen der Millionenheere 1871–1914* (Bonn, Ger.: Weltbild, 1992), pp. 208–209.

106 *Times* (London), 27 December 1906.

107 Balfour to Clarke, 20 July 1907, p. 32, Richmond Papers, RIC/9/1, NMM; Clarke, p. 33; Slade, 16 August 1907, p. 17, Corbett Papers, CBT/6/5, NMM; Notes on Invasion, 2 July 1907, pp. 12–13.

108 Slade, Sub-Committee of Imperial Defence, 22 October 1908, p. 226; Clarke, August 1907, pp. 2–4, CAB 3/2/1/42A, TNA.

109 Slade to Corbett, 12 December 1907, Corbett Papers, CBT/6/5, NMM.

110 Corbett, Roberts, memorandum, 17 November 1907, p. 37, Richmond Papers, RIC/9/1, NMM; Alfred Thayer Mahan, *Naval Strategy: Compared and Contrasted with the Principles of Military Operations on Land* (Boston: Little, Brown, 1911), p. 113.

111 Corbett, 12 December 1907, appendix XVI, memorandum by the DNI on invasion in reply to the memorandum presented by Lord Roberts and Colonel Repington, pp. 21–22, CAB 16/3A, TNA.

112 Fisher to Balfour, 23 December 1907, Balfour Papers, Add. 49712, BL.

113 Christian Wipperfürth, *Von der Souveränität zur Angst. Britische Außenpolitik und Sozialökonomie im Zeitalter des Imperialismus* (Stuttgart: Steiner, 2004). Howard Weinroth, "Left-Wing Opposition to Naval Armaments in Britain before 1914," *Journal of Contemporary History* 6, no. 4 (1971), pp. 93–120.

114 Esher to Balfour, 29 May 1908, cited in Brett, *Journals and Letters of Reginald, Viscount Esher,* vol. 2, p. 317f.; Arnold-Forster to Balfour, 28 September 1908, Balfour Papers, Add. 49723, BL; Selborne to Brodrick, 14 January 1908, Selborne Papers, Folder 3, Bodleian Library, Oxford, U.K.

115 Mr. A. J. Balfour before the Sub-Committee on Invasion, 29 May 1908, pp. 3–5, CAB 3/2/143A, TNA.

116 Balfour to Esher, 25 May 1908, Balfour Papers, Add. 49719, BL.

117 A. J. Balfour before the Sub-Committee on Invasion, 29 May 1908.

118 Slade, Diary, 29 May 1908, Slade Papers, MRF/39, NMM.

119 Esher to Balfour, 29 May 1908.

120 "Invasion," note by Lord Esher, 23 July 1908, p. 2; compare Fisher to Edward VII, 4 October 1907; Slade, memorandum, 16 August 1907, p. 28f, Corbett Papers, CBT/6/4, NMM.

121 Crowe to Dilke, 15 October 1907, Dilke Papers, FO 800/243, TNA; Sir Edward Grey, *25 Years, 1892–1916* (London: Hodder and Stoughton, 1925), vol. 1, p. 149; Dumas to Lascelles, 3 February 1908, BD VI, no. 80, pp. 115–17; Volker R. Berghahn, *Germany and the Approach of War in 1914,* 2nd ed. (London: n.p., 1993), p. 67; Niall Ferguson, *Der falsche Krieg: Der Erste Weltkrieg und das 20. Jahrhundert* (Stuttgart, Ger.: Jahrhundert, 1999), pp. 109; Hildebrand, "Staatskunst und Kriegshandwerk," pp. 30–31; Paul G. Halpern, *A Naval History of World War I* (London: Routledge, 1995), pp. 7–10; Steiner and Neilson, *Britain and the Origins of the First World War,* p. 68; Grey, memorandum, 23 July 1908, Grey Papers, FO 800/92, TNA.

122 Crowe to Dilke, 15 October 1907.

123 Grey, *25 Years,* vol. 1, p. 149.

124 Ibid., p. 68; Grey, memorandum, 23 July 1908.

125 Kennedy, *Rise of the Anglo-German Antagonism,* pp. 450–52; Imanuel Geiss, "'Weltpolitik': Die deutsche Version des Imperialismus," in *Flucht in den Krieg? Die Außenpolitik des kaiserlichen Deutschland,* ed. Gregor Schöllgen (Darmstadt, Ger.: Wissenschaftliche Buchgesellschaft, 1991), pp. 166–67; Berghahn, *Germany and the Approach of War in 1914,* p. 134., p. 175; Mommsen, *War der Kaiser an allem schuld?,* p. 140.

126 Mommsen, *War der Kaiser an allem schuld?,* p. 140.

127 Hardinge, memorandum, 16 August 1908, BD VI, no. 117, p. 187. For financial problems, Goschen, Report 1906, BDFA F/XXXIV, no. 94, pp. 122–26; Report 1907, ibid., no. 123, pp. 123–30; Cartwright, Report 1908, ibid., no. 137, pp. 268–76; Goschen to Grey, 23 June 1906, ibid., no. 77, pp. 100–101. Compare FO 371/75/711, TNA; Ferguson, *Der falsche Krieg,* p. 115.

128 Röhl, *Wilhelm II.,* pp. 678–79.

129 Bernhard von Bülow, *Denkwürdigkeiten,* Franz Stockhammer, ed. (Berlin: Ullstein), vol. 2, pp. 322–23.

130 Paul W. Schroeder, "International Politics, Peace, and War, 1815–1914," in *The Short Oxford History of Europe: The Nineteenth Century,* ed. T. C. W. Blanning (Oxford, U.K.: Oxford Univ. Press, 2000), p. 196.

131 Christopher Clark, *Kaiser Wilhelm II: A Life in Power* (London: Penguin, 2000), pp. 182–83.

132 Garvin to Prothero, 12 November 1908, cited in Anthony Morris, *The Scaremongers: The Advocacy of War and Rearmament, 1896–1914* (London: Routledge and Kegan Paul, 1984), p. 264. In May 1908 Spring-Rice received a letter saying that Britain needed "another war scare like in 1887 to get the vote for the navy bill"; Unknown to Spring-Rice, May 1908, Spring-Rice Papers, FO 800/241, TNA; Spring-Rice to Chirol, 21 June 1907, cited in Gwynn, *Letters and Friendships of Sir Cecil Spring-Rice,* vol. 2, p. 101; Spring-Rice to Maxse, 3 June 1908, Maxse Papers/458, West Sussex Record Office, Chichester, U.K.; Nicolson, Memoradum, 9 December 1912, cited in Erwin Hölzle, *Die Selbstentmachtung Europas: Das Experiment des Friedens vor und im Ersten Weltkrieg* (Göttingen, Ger.: Musterschmidt, 1976), p. 156. Keith M. Wilson, *The Policy of the Entente: Essays on the Determinants of British Foreign Policy, 1904–1914* (Cambridge, U.K.: Cambridge Univ. Press, 1985); Metternich to Bülow, 4 January 1909, cited in GP, vol. 28, no. 10249, p. 57f.

133 See note 97 above.

There is no question whatever that the first desideratum in every type of fighting vessel is speed. It is the weather gauge of the olden days. You then fight just when it suits you best. Some people don't want it for Battleships, but they are wrong, because both strategy and tactics demand speed.

SIR JOHN FISHER, *NAVAL NECESSITIES,* 14 MAY 1904

We build mighty vessels at gigantic cost, which are obsolete almost before they leave the stocks, even if we can be sure, as we cannot always be, that they will float when they get to sea.

TIMES (LONDON), 31 AUGUST 1877

[W]hat probable advantage does a fleet obtain by arriving ten days sooner, if it must get behind batteries on coming of an opponent who has preferred offensive power to speed?

CAPT. ALFRED T. MAHAN, USN,
U.S. NAVAL INSTITUTE *PROCEEDINGS,* JUNE 1906

VIII *Differing Values?*
The Balance between Speed, Endurance, Firepower, and Protection in the Design of British and American Dreadnoughts

ANGUS ROSS

By the turn of the twentieth century, the larger navies of the world, all of which were in Europe, were facing an unprecedented dilemma. The main component of sea power, the battleship, was becoming increasingly costly to develop and maintain, with a seemingly exponential rise in the size and complexity of each successive generation. As a consequence, these intricate machines were becoming far more dependent on dockyard resources and logistical support than ever before, the major costs being the large crews and the regular dockings required to keep their steel hulls and fittings in good condition. To make matters worse, the prevailing "Mahanian" naval doctrine of the day held that these ships should be kept together as a concentrated fleet, because it was the combined power of the whole fleet that maximized the probability of success in a decisive battle and therefore produced the deterrent value that was so prized by statesmen.[1] The combination of these three factors led to a marked reluctance by most powers either to split their fleets or to allow them to stray too far from the likely field of battle, which in the British case, if history was anything to go by, would be in either the approaches to the English Channel or the Mediterranean.

At the same time, however, the mercantile nature of the industrial age and its associated "scramble" for resources and possessions overseas had created an increasing demand for naval imperial policing and diplomacy duties abroad. Support and defense of overseas possessions, not to mention the commerce that plied between them, were ill matched to the idea of battleship predominance. In fact, and as John Beeler has described, prior to the advent of the *Royal Sovereign* class in the 1890s, a true oceangoing capital ship was simply not feasible from a technological point of view, even assuming that sufficient funds were available.[2] This constraint brought about an additional need for whole classes of "cruising ironclads"—or "cruisers," as they became known—an essentially new type but one whose speed and endurance also put it in demand as a scouting vessel for the battle fleet. Essentially, these were the successors to the numerous frigates of Napoleonic times. Considerably cheaper at the outset than capital ships, these vessels were destined to grow in complexity and size as their utility became evident. These classes would also be "over and above" any continuing need to meet obligations with regard to battle fleets.

To offset the resultant fiscal pressures, there was a natural tendency to use ships of older, less sophisticated classes on the imperial beat as "station" cruisers. This followed the rationale that a cruiser, obsolescent for a scouting commission in a fleet pitted against first-class European opposition, could still serve with credit abroad, where the likelihood of encountering sophisticated opponents was considerably reduced. For a while this policy worked well, but with the advent of faster, long-range armored cruisers developed by France in the 1890s specifically for distant-waters operations, the days of a ship living out its twilight years in glorious isolation abroad looked to be numbered.[3] Unfortunately too, for many of the colonialist nations, sharp growth in imperial responsibilities had led to many scores of these vessels being so employed, and the prospect of being forced to replace them all in short order with first-rate armored cruisers was daunting. This development more than any other had led to the massively increased financial draw on naval budgets and all the attendant political scrutiny that followed.

In the case of Great Britain, with the world's largest navy, there were some additional slants on this problem. On the plus side, it had an unrivaled network of coaling stations and dockyards all around the world upon which it could draw. This gave it a degree of confidence in operations abroad that would have been difficult for an opponent to match. In terms of ship design, this network meant that the Royal Navy was less tied than other fleets to the constraints arising from building endurance and self-sufficiency into its warships. The downside, however, was that the sheer volume of the Royal Navy's worldwide commitments was increasing at the fastest rate of any first-rate navy, and hence the problem of wholesale modernization at increasingly frequent intervals was grossly exacerbated in its case. The historian Jon Sumida has eloquently captured the scale of the difficulties it faced by noting that the costs of running the Royal Navy increased 65 percent in the seven-year period from 1889 to 1896, while in the following seven-year period, from 1897–1904, the unit costs of capital ships doubled.[4] Similarly, in each of the same two periods the costs of first-class cruisers quadrupled and those of dockyard facilities quintupled. Perhaps worse still, these statistics implied that to remain on the cutting edge, the entire battle fleet and the overseas cruiser complements of the Royal Navy effectively needed to be replaced every seven years. Small wonder that the chancellor of the exchequer, Austen Chamberlain, insisted to the cabinet in April 1904 that "however reluctant we may be to face the fact, the time has come when we must frankly admit that the financial resources of the United Kingdom are inadequate to do all that we should desire in the matter of Imperial defence."[5]

The First Sea Lord of the day, Adm. Sir John "Jackie" Fisher, had been thinking about these difficulties for many years.[6] A fervent navalist with a strong sense of patriotic duty, he differed from most of his naval colleagues in that he realized early on that the economies being demanded by the nation's political leadership were necessary for the nation's continuing health.[7] In short, if maritime primacy was to be preserved, the only responsible way was to achieve these savings by adopting a radically different vision of future naval warfare—a vision he believed advances in technology were on the verge of delivering. Specifically, Fisher questioned the continuing soundness of all the accepted naval missions. Whether operating defensively or offensively as a blockading force, the battle fleet looked to be increasingly threatened in coastal waters by the torpedo, while, as discussed, the station cruiser and commerce protector abroad were similarly under threat from the sheer speed and operational agility of modern armored-cruiser squadrons. Worse still, however, was Britain's manpower and training situation—because of the growth in the number of older cruisers scattered around the world, a large percentage of the navy's crews were committed abroad on stations where they could learn little about the techniques and drills associated with modern warfare, or anything of fleet maneuvers. To Fisher this was an unforgivable waste in an era where naval warfare was increasingly characterized by extreme suddenness.[8] He believed that the Royal Navy simply could not afford to keep such a high percentage of its human capital essentially "untrained" in the art of modern naval warfare; besides, he needed these men at home to man the revolutionary new fleet he was about to develop.

For Fisher was working on a truly comprehensive reform program for the Royal Navy that sought to prepare it for the new era. Underpinning these reforms was the idea that Great Britain could no longer afford to provide a dedicated platform type for each of its naval missions, nor was doing so necessarily sound tactically. The speed and endurance of modern ships were opening the door to more versatile types. Furthermore, by the judicious use of the new technology and better training, he believed, it was possible to change radically the way in which these missions were addressed and still provide the savings demanded by the Treasury.[9]

In facing these same difficulties, the United States entered with an entirely different perspective. For one thing, it possessed a much smaller navy, well behind those of the "big four" European powers, and it lacked the worldwide resources that allowed the British effectively to give things like endurance and reliability lower priority in their warships. For America, the key was building influence in proportion to its steadily increasing status as a world power, and that meant battleships. But these battleships had to be affordable, preferably numerous, and, above all, able to support themselves overseas. Although the United States did not have worldwide naval responsibilities of anything like the scope of Britain's, its battle fleets were likely, thanks to quirks of geography and the sheer size of the Pacific Ocean, to have huge distances to travel to their operating areas.[10] The formula in the case of the United States, therefore, was subtly different—yes, there were concerns over increasing naval expenditure, but the development of its fleet had been effectively expansive from the start, and the issue was simply the management of a rate of naval expansion appropriate for the nation's continuing fiscal health. Unburdened by rampant imperial expenditures or cruiser complications faced by their British counterparts, American naval planners also had the luxury of looking at the capital-ship problem in much more depth.

Conventional wisdom has encapsulated these differences in the following way. The U.S. Navy, with its primarily defensive outlook, built its battle fleet to a fairly conservative pattern, to be employed in the defense of American interests primarily in the West Indies and the Atlantic but also to be sent across the Pacific in defense of the Philippines. The result was a slow transition into the dreadnought era, a transition during which numbers, overall firepower, armored protection of the main battery, and reliability and endurance of the propulsion plant remained the primary drivers in ship design. Implicit here is the belief among the Americans that they did not really need to think "outside the box." This was in stark contrast to the situation in Great Britain, where increasing global responsibilities and the simultaneous need for savings encouraged enormous innovation in the fields of propulsion and tactics and gave the ascendancy to fast, turbine-driven capital ships armed with large guns and novel fire-control systems.

As a result historians have dismissed the American dreadnought debate as rather inconsequential: the Americans were slow into the game, did not understand the dynamics of running a first-class navy, were hampered by overly influential technical bureaus, or perhaps all three. Such opinions might seem logical interpretations were it not for the fact that in almost every case the U.S. Navy's operators, engineers, and naval architects debated and discussed the very same innovations as their counterparts across the Atlantic and in parallel with them. That they subsequently came to such different conclusions with regard to U.S. naval needs is therefore significant and worthy of comparative analysis. The aim of this paper is to examine the American decision making here more closely, looking for crucial differences in emphasis. In the interests of brevity, the survey of the British debate will generally assume knowledge of the extensive and mature scholarship available, elaborating only the appropriate high points.

The Fisher Revolution: Speed and Lethality in All Things
The British story is dominated by three factors, essentially interlinked. Absolutely paramount was the need to make economies in the running of the Royal Navy; this was nonnegotiable. As has already been mentioned, the chief instigator of the reforming movement, Admiral Fisher, saw that speed, or more specifically improved responsiveness, was the key to gaining greater utility from his major units. In essence, by building a type of capital ship that was faster and had longer legs, he hoped that he could effectively replace both the large ships of the battle line and the

numerous station cruisers with power-projection platforms of a single class, able to be dispatched at will to trouble spots around the world. The advantages would be a smaller number of more-powerful ships, crewed by, overall, fewer but better-trained personnel. In other words, he was aiming for a more multipurpose core for the Navy, a more efficient way of using his resources. Of course, a lot of other things had to fall into place—capable submarines for flotilla defense at home and the wireless communications necessary to direct these ships, to name but two—but it is important to grasp at the outset the sheer audacity of the idea. It was basically a complete reversal of the Mahanian concentration edict in response to new needs brought on by a changing, industrial-age naval situation.

Besides savings and speed, the next obvious quality needed was lethality. These new ships would have to deal with all comers in distant waters, even if that meant avoiding battle until the circumstances could be made favorable. There was no point in dispatching them, otherwise. Obviously speed was important, but an ability to engage and destroy an enemy at a range at which he would be unable to reply, or even threaten, was the other, vital part of the scheme. Only then could armor protection be reduced enough to make the desired speeds possible in a reasonably sized hull. To achieve this lethality therefore, the most powerful, long-range gun possible was needed, but not only this. There also had to be an associated fire-control system to control these guns, so that effective hits could be made at extreme ranges. Fisher, with his knowledge of the gunnery world and his close association with inventors like Arthur Pollen, was confident that such a capability was an imminent probability in 1904.[11] It also explains his desire for a uniform-caliber, all-big-gun configuration. After all, if the tactics were based on engaging the enemy at extreme range, what was the point of a mixed battery, the bulk of which would be useless at such ranges? Besides, to save manpower and weight, the calibers had to be consolidated; there really was no other option. Thus, the key points here are that the British revolution was essentially driven by three main factors: savings, speed (reactivity), and lethality—in that order. This is stressed because, as we shall see, the situation was very different on the other side of the Atlantic.

Although Fisher had long been outspoken on the subjects of speed and gunnery efficiency, it was the intricate combination of all these factors as a coherent whole, backed up by all the necessary material and managerial reforms, that was so stunning about the package presented to the Admiralty Board in October 1904. At a stroke, it made more sense of the manpower and officer-training adjustments that had already been started. Many would deplore the manner of its release as theatrics, and indeed there was a clear desire to shock and make an impact; nevertheless, there was also a hard, businesslike practicality involved that needs to be understood. For one thing, the interconnected nature of the reforms required that the package be implemented as a whole; to release individual measures piecemeal would have risked incoherence and worse. Second, Fisher clearly understood that he needed to be in a position of supreme power in the service before he could risk disclosure of his aims. Only in that way could he hope to control matters so as to ensure their safe passage. As he himself put it, "The new great scheme of reform which will emerge from the Admiralty like Minerva from the brain of Jupiter, full grown and armed against all objectors! Napoleonic in its audacity, Cromwellian in its thoroughness!"[12]

All these points made the Royal Navy's experience very different from the equivalent situation in America. Since the U.S. Navy was not facing such draconian economies as had necessitated the British comprehensive reforms, its naval hierarchy was able to devote far more attention to the minutiae of the capital-ship issue. Second, there was no position of supreme power in the naval hierarchy equivalent to that of the First Sea Lord. By design, that power was effectively shared by boards of experts in the technical bureaus, the Naval War College (which put forward and evaluated operational suggestions), and the senior officers on the General Board (who brought things together for the good of the Navy as a whole). Although Admiral of the Navy (as he was styled in honor of his 1898 victory at Manila Bay) George Dewey might have had great influence within some quarters of the government, it would have been inconceivable for him to have enjoyed the sort of individual and direct influence that Fisher expected (and achieved) over the design and building of warships.[13]

Indeed, the responsibilities of the First Sea Lord, only recently upgraded, at Fisher's insistence, by an order in council dated 10 August 1904, were a matter of controversy even within the Royal Navy. Specifically, the distribution of business within the Admiralty Board had been altered to give the First Sea Lord broad responsibilities for the "Preparation for War; all large questions of Naval Policy" and, second, "the Fighting and Sea-going Efficiency of the Fleet, to include the Distribution and Movements of all Ships in Commission."[14] Many of Fisher's opponents resented this as a brazen grab for power, arguing, not without reason, that the loose wording here effectively sidelined the well-proven Admiralty Board system. As Reginald Custance put it, "This is an entirely new departure, which virtually makes him supreme over all his colleagues, since those words cover everything."[15] In most cases, it was the abrasive and aggressive techniques that Fisher used to get things done that caused the backlash, almost more than his actions themselves. In the case of the fast, all-big-gun battleship, for example, opinions had already been polarized by earlier reforms in naval personnel and the Admiralty Board, to the extent that it was now difficult for any subsequent idea to be judged solely on its own merits. This has to be continually borne in mind when comparing the Fisher era in Great Britain with what was going on in other nations' navies.

Another factor that is pertinent while reading Fisher is the fact that his flamboyant and combative style tended to get the better of him on occasions. This led him to some notable inconsistencies on even major issues where clarity should have been at a premium. For example, on the merits of the battleship, at one point he seems to be advocating their complete replacement by his "super cruisers" and submarines, blustering that

> the Battleship of olden days was necessary because it was the one and only vessel that nothing could sink except another battleship. Now, every battleship is open to attack by fast torpedo craft and submarines. . . . ALL THIS HAS BEEN ABSOLUTELY ALTERED! . . . The battlefleet is no protection to anything or any operation during dark hours and, in certain waters is no protection in daytime, because of the submarine. Hence what is the use of Battleships as we have hitherto known them? NONE![16]

It is therefore surprising that elsewhere in the very same document he insists that the "Battleship of 21 knots," along with his cruisers, was one of the four "essential" vessels of the modern navy, whose building program in turn should be "absolutely restricted" to these four types.[17] Why, given that his "super cruisers" were also to be built, did Fisher allow this compromise? Hints only come later, with the question, "Hence the history and the justification of the type of new battleship now proposed: for what else is it but a glorified armored cruiser?"[18] The full truth, however, requires some more detailed research, through which it is revealed that what Fisher really wanted was to combine the two types over time to produce a "fusion type," or in modern parlance, a fast battleship.[19]

Similarly, on the subject of the ideal gun he seems to vacillate between the merits of the rate of fire of the medium-sized, quick-firing battery and the destructive power of the big gun. As late as 1902, for example, he is still extolling the virtues of the rate of fire of the battery as a whole, as compared with the destructive power of larger calibers: "The armament we require is the greatest number of the largest quick firing guns. . . . [T]hey call it secondary armament; it is really the primary armament!"[20] Only a couple of years later, however, he takes an entirely contrary view: "To make good shooting at 6,000 yards and above, the guns must be fired slowly and deliberately. Hence the use of a large number of guns disappears, and the advantage of a few well-aimed guns with a large bursting charge is overwhelming."[21] Admittedly, ongoing developments in gunnery were changing the perceptions of a great many at the time, but this sort of thing is nonetheless confusing. The point to these examples is that to clarify things it is always worth trying to detect the longer-term trends beneath Fisher's rhetoric or, better still, seeking corroborative evidence from some of the many experts he consulted, in order.

Since the British debate effectively begins with the release of Fisher's "scheme" on his appointment as First Sea Lord in 1904, it is worth examining this source document in some detail.[22] On the subject of the first factor, savings, he was unequivocal: "The British Empire floats on the Navy! So we must have no doubt whatever about its fighting efficiency and its instant readiness for war! To ensure this and at the same time *to effect the economy which the finances of the country render imperative* there must be drastic changes!"[23] Fisher had been explicitly chosen as First Sea

Lord for his ideas about how money could be saved, so the only arguments were about his chosen methodologies for doing so. In short, as already noted, he saw the multitudes of obsolete vessels then being used around the empire on detached duties as a colossal waste of manpower and resources. These ships were unfit for fighting and too slow to escape: "a single armored cruiser would overtake and gobble them up one after the other."[24] The real calamity, though, was "the deterioration of the officers and men who serve in these isolated vessels."[25] In proposing to withdraw and scrap these vessels Fisher looked forward to releasing a large reserve of manpower for his nucleus crews and first-rate vessels—manpower that could then be trained and kept current with the ways of the modern fleet. Reducing the overall manpower required was also a key part of his savings strategy.

The main objections were predictable—not so much concern on the part of the Admiralty at seeing its budget trimmed but fearfulness of the impact that a reduction in the overall number of hulls might have on British influence abroad. As this matter has a bearing on the argument used against proposals for a smaller number of larger battleships in the United States, it is worth examining the logic involved. For example, and in the same letter of protest quoted earlier, Custance made the point that many ships of types that would be considered "old" under Fisher's criteria had in fact given useful service to both sides in the recent Russo-Japanese War; furthermore, he argued, there was a whole range of secondary tasks in wartime to which such ships would be ideally suited, tasks that these reforms seemed to overlook.[26] Implicit within this criticism was an imputation that the Admiralty was out of touch: "This is undoubtedly due to neglect of the study of war and to attaching too much importance to *materiel*."[27] Custance reiterated the same objections a month later in more detail, reinforcing his arguments with the not-unreasonable point that since the newer armored cruisers were becoming so valuable in the overall naval strength, there would likely be a marked reluctance to allow them to fulfill the tawdry, if vital, tasks of the detached cruisers overseas.[28] This was an argument that Fisher stubbornly refused to answer, insisting instead on the potential efficiencies of the nucleus-crew system should war come.[29]

In an even more serious objection, Sir William White, a previous Constructor in Chief of the Navy and the architect of the first truly modern battleship, questioned the details of Fisher's assumptions about savings.[30] White's objection hit hard at the basis of Fisher's reforms, asserting that savings of the magnitude claimed were in fact possible only through accompanying measures that actually reduced the maintenance and support of the fleet and by taking which Fisher would be guilty, no matter what was claimed, of effectively "hollowing-out" the Royal Navy's overall resilience.[31] Furthermore, he pointed out that Fisher, as a longtime member of the Admiralty Board, was as guilty of waste as anyone, having been a willing party to refits and other expenditures on the very vessels that were now being discarded and that now he apparently so vehemently derided as wasteful.[32] Finally, he claimed, the low figures Fisher had cited for the *Dreadnought* estimates had in fact been obtained by subterfuge—by the deliberate ordering of subassemblies in prior years as a way of concealing the true costs.[33] White's main point, however, was less personal and amounted to opposition to the dropping of the time-honored British strategy of "laissez faire" shipbuilding—that is, letting your opponent suffer the uncertainties of innovation while you bide your time, confident in your overall ability to "outbuild" quickly any innovation that looks promising.[34] There is no record of a specific response to these charges, but there is little doubt that they greatly resonated among Fisher's critics.

Finally, and as a way of firmly tying together the debates on the two sides of the Atlantic, mention must be made of Captain Mahan's influential reflections on the Russo-Japanese naval events.[35] Among his many points, Mahan came out strongly against the tendency toward larger and more-complex battleships, arguing, like many of his counterparts in Britain, that this "is . . . a mistake; for it means one of two things: fewer ships, or a larger national budget."[36] Since the latter was not an option, the inference to be drawn was obvious. Mahan goes on to explain that to afford the latest designs, nations are forced to "prematurely relegat[e] to the dump vessels good in themselves, but unable to keep up with the ones last built. . . . This wilful premature antiquating of good vessels is a growing and wanton evil."[37] Since this charge was aimed squarely at the heart of Fisher's savings strategy and came from such a respected figure in naval circles, it was bound to enliven the debate. Lord Brassey, arguing in the *Times* from a similar standpoint, added yet another slant by reminding his readers of the inevitable risk of packing too much capability in a decreasing number of ships—that should one become disabled, its loss would be proportionately higher in terms of overall fleet capability.[38] (While correct in principle, this argument does not, of course, address how far the opposite "larger number, less capable" idea ought to be taken and what the risks of that might be.) Fisher was dismissive but maddeningly vague in his own defense.[39]

On the question of speed, the British debate became particularly acrimonious. Fisher, of course, was unequivocal. In his original proposals he advocates high speed for every type of fighting vessel, explaining that "strategy demands it—so as to get the deciding factor quickest to the decisive point; and tactics demands it, to afford choice of range at which action is to be fought."[40] For Fisher, it was all about providing more options. If you were faster, you could dictate the course of the action to suit your own particular capabilities. The slower fleet simply did not have this opportunity. There were, of course, other considerations—specifically, what should be sacrificed to gain this speed advantage. While Fisher was apt to dismiss this problem rather cavalierly, going so far as to advocate unarmored ships if necessary, a more considered position was put forward in a War Course lecture by one of his "experts," Capt. E. J. W. Slade.[41] Slade made the point that each naval situation must be viewed on its own merits to come to the right decisions. Strong and slow ships were likely to be "overkill" if their strength were out of proportion to the threat that could be brought against them and nugatory if the enemy could evade them. Similarly, fast but weak ships were of no use against a powerful enemy. Speed therefore should not be bought at the expense of fighting strength but through the improvement of material and design, even if this were more costly.[42] In essence Slade was explaining that the country had no choice but to afford ships of the *Dreadnought* and *Invincible* classes, because they represented the best compromise that naval science had yet come up with to deal with Britain's naval situation.

The opponents of large fast ships, however, argued that the price was indeed too high, that too many smaller vessels were being sacrificed to produce the new generation. Custance went farther, refuting the tactical advantages of speed and claiming that it was only an advantage in that it gave its possessor the option of running away.[43] How much of this was intended as a personal slight against Fisher it is difficult to tell, because a seasoned sailor of his stature could hardly have failed to acknowledge some advantages. Custance later rethought his position, then claiming that since Fisher's battle cruisers were too powerful to be detached, they basically represented battleships in which fighting strength had been sacrificed to speed.[44] This turned out to be prophetic, although Fisher's supporters would argue that under such circumstances the battle cruiser would be misemployed. What was clear, however, was that a possible ambiguity of the concentration doctrine as it might apply to these powerful new vessels existed and needed clarification. Finally, and after some analysis of the recent battle of Tsushima, Custance further refined his view that the battle cruisers were too much of a compromise and introduced the idea that ships should be armed to fight at all ranges. Speed, after all, was never a weapon, and the aim should always be to endow a fleet with superior offensive power.[45] In this last point Custance basically talked past the Fisher camp, which would likely have agreed with him on the question of offensive power, pointing out that all along it had actually advocated speed and offensive power in equal measure.

Mahan took a rather different stance. While endorsing the view that fighting power was paramount, he also contended that since battleships were designed to work together as fleets, the value of faster individual ships was somewhat academic, since their speed would have to be reduced to that of the slowest in the line.[46] Accordingly, there should be no undue effort to make accommodations for greater speed. Although reasonable at first glance, this is a strangely misleading position, since on literal extrapolation it is clear that there could never be any naval progress at all if the qualities of the previous generation were always to be taken as given. How would advances ever be made unless successive generations began to move in the right directions? That this problem was vexing to the British is illustrated by the fact that no less an authority than Brassey saw fit to devote an entire chapter of his 1906 annual to a discussion of both positions.[47]

Extraordinarily, though, at no time did anyone question the type of propulsion needed to gain this extra speed. It would appear that, by the time Fisher's design committee met, another group had already considered the results of the comparative trials between HMS *Amethyst* and HMS *Topaze* and had all but recommended that all future Royal Navy warships be turbine powered.[48] The full trials report has yet to be located, but an extract reproduced in a contemporary periodical reveals that at ten knots the reciprocating plant was the more economical, while at twenty the reverse was true; the crossover point appeared to be about fourteen knots.[49] On the basis of this finding and the facts that a turbine installation was smaller, smoother running, easier to maintain and operate, and less prone to failure, the committee reported that for wartime use the turbine plant was likely to be superior. Certainly by 1905 Fisher, along with the director of naval construction and the engineer in chief, seemed completely convinced, mainly on account of the weight and manpower that would be saved, although they had reservations about the plant's maneuvering abilities, particularly when operating astern.[50] The perceived superiorities had also been endorsed by some remarks from the director of naval intelligence and a further evaluation visit to the turbine steamer *Queen*.[51]

The other part of the speed equation—the impact that high-speed, powerful turbines might have on the endurance and radius of action of battleships—played no significant part in the discussion either, but it would be wrong to say that endurance did not feature in the deliberations or that the British built their ships primarily for the short ranges of the European theater.[52] Fisher, after all, had designed his ships to travel over great distances at high speed to bring decisive naval power to bear anywhere in the world. The advantage he had was the most extensive coaling-station network in the world, support that no other naval planner could take for granted. As a result, endurance took a position of lesser prominence than reactivity. This priority, as well as the desire to save on operating costs by a reduction in engine-room crews, greatly strengthened the case for turbines in Britain.

Julian Corbett, however, added another twist to the argument, one that, given his unique perspective and access to Fisher, may be the most accurate.[53] Recognizing the dilemma above, Corbett invited his readers to consider the impact that British moves might have on potential opponents.

> By a policy of high speed we involve them in a strategical dilemma. They must either increase their speed so as to equal us in the vital area of our home waters, and so render our Imperial defense easy by reducing their Radius of action; or they must sacrifice their position at home and contend with us in the oceanic areas, where we are particularly strong in coal supply, and able thereby to neutralize their assumed superiority in radius of action.[54]

The implication here is obvious: by utilizing their superior strategic position, the British could force any potential competitors to make choices that were unfavorable to their own programs—provided, of course, that Britain was able to maintain its shipbuilding advantages.

The third factor, that of the right combination of guns on these ships, was almost as contentious as speed. As already explained, Fisher was inconsistent here; in fact, there is evidence that he had long vacillated between the need for true armored cruisers, specialized for long-range commerce raiding and speed of response, on one hand, and an all-medium-caliber battleship, on the other.[55] This latter type of vessel was one in which a speed advantage would be generated by reductions in the main armament, on the assumption that it was the powerful, secondary battery of quick-firers that really counted. Prior to developments in gunnery and armor that improved the prospects for heavy guns, such a ship seemed a viable compromise. Employing a more numerous quick-firing battery in lieu of the slow-firing main armament of the battleship would save weight that could be translated directly into more speed or better protection.[56] The problem, after all, with the traditional battleship was that its very slow rate of fire from its few large guns made it vital that every shot count—something that was simply not possible at the time. In contrast, the strengths of the medium-caliber battleship or armored cruiser were tied to the "shredding effects" possible with their preponderance of quick-firing guns. These guns had a vastly superior rate of fire, which happily also made them more accurate to aim and hence, potentially more likely to hit the enemy.[57] Best of all, though, this could likely be achieved without any real advances in gunnery techniques being necessary.

Given that the medium-caliber battleship could be expected to enjoy at least a small advantage in speed and handiness over a conventional predreadnought, coupling this with the rate-of-fire advantage might offer possibilities. In Fisher's mind, it might have enabled these vessels, even with only a slim margin of speed, to dictate the pace of the engagement. At the same time, the fact that such ships were less expensive and handier might enable them to be built in sufficient numbers to undertake some imperial duties as well. They would certainly be quite sufficient to overcome all but the fastest armored cruisers afloat. Thus, although different in origins, both the large armored cruiser and this sort of battleship actually offered similar strategic advantages.

By 1905, however, the calculus had changed completely. In the face of the depressing fact that medium-caliber guns were simply not strong enough to penetrate battleship armor at the longer battle ranges expected, attention had returned to the heavy gun and the rationale for a medium-caliber battleship had fallen away. If the heavy gun could be made superior on all counts (accuracy, hitting power, and rate of fire), it would probably be a logical extrapolation of Fisher's ideas to merge the versatility (and savings potential) of a uniform-caliber platform with the hitting power of the heavy gun.[58] All Fisher would need was a reasonable assurance from his colleagues that no insuperable obstacles existed to the solution of the problems of accuracy and rate of fire for the heavy gun, an assurance that seems to have been provided by his design committee at the time.[59] This confidence probably explains his uncharacteristically clear stipulations in *Naval Necessities*. On the uniform-caliber idea he cites the advantages of a smaller quantity of a single type of ammunition and the need to stock spare parts and equipment (not to mention the manpower and training savings) for only a single type of gun.[60] As for the rationale for the heavy gun, it seems to have been that to hit at long range, a slow and deliberate fire was necessary, which was by nature better suited to the heavy battery, provided sufficient guns could be carried.[61] Suddenly the uniform-caliber all-big-gun ship looked the obvious candidate.

Although Fisher does not explicitly mention it, another major driver toward a uniform-caliber armament was the problem of spotting. When the secondary armament was wholly distinct from the main battery, such issues did not arise—that is, the hits and misses (or, explosions and splashes) of the two could be readily distinguished from a distance. However, with the tendency in the years immediately prior to *Dreadnought* to increase the caliber of the quick-firing secondary battery in response to the expected increase in battle ranges and improvements in protective armor, this problem became acute. The British *King Edward* class, for example, mounted no fewer than three types of medium-to-heavy gun (twelve-inch, 9.2-inch, and six-inch), all of which, through quirks of muzzle velocity and design, were perfectly capable of long ranges. They were, however, quite different guns and required correspondingly different ballistic corrections. Yet if they were firing simultaneously, it would be almost impossible for a spotter in the heat of battle to identify the fall of shot of each caliber and thereby apply the right corrections. A committee specifically convened to investigate this problem confirmed "the impossibility of controlling two natures of guns as they require different ranges and deflections."[62] To minimize the effects of this problem, the doctrinal guidance was issued to suppress fire from the secondary battery when the main guns were firing. So now not only was the secondary battery unlikely to be effective at battle ranges, but it was likely not to be firing at all. Small wonder then that Fisher felt that it could be omitted entirely.

Others, however, had different views. Both Custance and Mahan criticized the move to all big guns because of the consequent loss of the "hail" of projectiles from secondary quick-firers. The latter echoed an early Fisher view by contending that the secondary battery "is really entitled to the name primary because its effect is exerted mainly on the personnel."[63] This view, though no doubt true only a few years earlier, had been made outdated by dramatic improvements in armor plate.

Perhaps the most authoritative word on the matter came from an Admiralty pamphlet, *The One Calibre Big Gun Armament for Ships*.[64] Although written later by the director of naval ordnance, Capt. John Jellicoe, to explain to doubters why the Admiralty was pressing ahead with follow-on *Dreadnoughts,* it makes clear that the information had been largely available to the Committee on Designs back in 1905 but had been kept secret at that time.[65] In this pamphlet Jellicoe made the following claims for the superiority of the twelve-inch gun:

- That a twelve-inch shell could penetrate Krupp nine-inch armor at nine thousand yards, whereas the figure for the six-inch was a mere six hundred yards.
- That improved hydraulics had made the twelve-inch as easy to operate as the smaller weapon.
- That those navies expressing a preference for mixed batteries had done so only because they lacked effective fire control.
- That a "hail" of hits was not much use against a modern, well-protected ship.
- That a mixed-caliber battery greatly impaired the efficient firing of the main battery.
- That since the early hits would all be twelve-inch (i.e., the main battery), that battery would dominate the course of the engagement and therefore its capability should be maximized.

As if that were not sufficient, Jellicoe endorsed a uniform-caliber arrangement for the planned *Indefatigable* class, citing the shell-splash problem and the needed reduction or simplification of requirements for manpower, ammunition, and training.[66] It is little wonder that Fisher felt reassured.

To sum up, the British debate was rancorous and personal, and the fact that it became so polarized at an early stage arguably prevented a more measured and dispassionate discussion of the truly important issues at stake. There was no doubt that Fisher enjoyed immense power—or at least that the system in Britain was susceptible to domination by strong personalities. Some have said that this was a great advantage in terms of innovation, in that contentious reforms could be driven through to a point where educated choices could be made. An almost equal weight of opinion, however, would dissent, pointing to the fact that in this case, absent a pause to gather the majority opinion, the seeds of failure were sown early. After all, resentment and bitterness at being ignored caused the detractors to dismiss out of hand even the better parts of the scheme. As for its methodology, to achieve savings was the indisputable driving factor, with speed and lethality adjusted to accommodate a more "general purpose" design. Protection was an order of magnitude in importance below these three—whatever could be afforded once speed and lethality had been satisfied. Fisher, after all, believed that speed was protection in and of itself.

For America, the Key Was Combat Power

If the need for savings and the desire for speed bounded and characterized the British capital-ship debate, the same could not be said of its American counterpart. The strategic circumstances were so markedly different in the United States that a completely new set of priorities came to the fore. The first and most obvious difference was the size and status of the U.S. Navy at the time. Unlike its counterpart in Britain, it was not all-powerful or beloved by the nation it served. The United States was a newly rising power on the international stage, only recently convinced of the need for sea power in the pursuit of its national goals. As such, its navy had some way to go to attain the same degree of domestic recognition—a situation that manifested itself as a mixed blessing. While naval spending was not automatically the focus of attention from Congress and the Treasury whenever the need for savings arose, naval officers were constantly in the business of selling the naval case. That said, there seemed to be an understanding everywhere that the Navy ought to expand; the only issue was ensuring that this expansion took place in such a way as to make the most efficient use of every dollar.

Thus, even though Congress felt bound to impose fairly stringent fiscal limitations on what was possible, these limitations were perceived far more positively in America, as a set of choices and not as an onerous contraction on capabilities and activities. The differences that this made in institutional terms were enormous and cannot be overemphasized. While the Royal Navy was constantly on the defensive, closing ranks to protect capabilities that seemed under threat and inclining to the worst in parochialism and brooding introspection, the U.S. Navy's decision makers were under no such pressure. Their sole aim throughout this period was to ensure that what money did become available produced the best possible naval capability. For them, frank and open discussions of options were the norm, and for as long as it took to gather the necessary facts. They were not constantly looking over their shoulders to see what their competitors were doing. While there were moments of frustration and disagreement along the way, the mood overall was more optimistic. Politically, this state of affairs was undeniably assisted by having a strong ally in the White House, in the person of Theodore Roosevelt.[67]

In terms of strategy, the problems facing American naval planners at the time can be seen from an examination of some of the many "Summer Problems" posed to the students of the Naval War College course in Newport, Rhode Island. In the 1901 academic year, for instance, the notional enemy power from Europe was Germany (referred to as "Black"), which was depicted as intent on moving against the Panama Canal area after attaining a lodgment in the Caribbean.[68] Since such an attempt was likely to constitute a casus belli, the American fleet strategy recommended by the students was to force battle early, even if the fleet were unready, so as to prevent Germany from attaining that lodgment. The students recognized that the outcome was likely to be poor if Germany were able to muster the bulk of its fleet and so further recommended that, first, the U.S. Navy be sized to be at least a match for Germany, which meant a considerable expansion; and second, that the battle fleet consist of powerful, modern battleships with sufficient speed and strategic mobility to concentrate efficiently.[69] Numbers, battleship strength, and mobility looked to be at a premium. So while the need for strategic speed was arguably similar to the British situation just described, almost everything else was markedly different.

In addition, and given the position of inferiority of the United States with respect to its likely competitors, at least for the time being, it was also important that such units as the United States had should be made to count. In fleet terms, this meant a rigid adherence to the edicts of concentration, and in naval construction terms the procurement of resilient and powerful ships that could stand, unit for unit, against the best that the European navies could offer. Everything else had to be secondary to that aim. This meant, paradoxically, that qualities like speed, while desirable, tended to be viewed as things that should not be bought at the expense of gun power or protection. For the smaller navy, the issue was the chance of survival in battle, not the speed with which the enemy could be brought to the point of decision.

Similarly, long-range gunnery, while much more important to the Americans than speed, was viewed as something that should be pursued only to the point at which it impinged on either survivability or the delivery of sufficient units to the fleet. Unlike the British, the Americans did not anticipate the luxury of decisively outranging their opponents—they fully expected to take and inflict hits at whatever ranges were doctrinaire for the times. On a more positive note, however, the Americans, not having to rationalize ship types to replace scores of outdated cruisers, were at liberty to look searchingly at the theoretical qualities desired of the major ship types. This included their own examination of the four types deemed indispensable in Fisher's *Naval Necessities*. In the end, though, the American debate would be framed first and foremost by combat power, both offensive and defensive, followed by numbers, with everything else a distant third. These boundaries made these years a very different experience for them than for the British.

Against this backdrop appeared one of the earliest attempts to upgrade the offensive combat power of American battleships, an article in the U.S. Naval Institute's journal *Proceedings* by Lt. Matt Signor in 1902.[70] In a very clearly constructed piece of reasoning, Signor described a potential battleship armed with just four large, triple turrets and a series of three- and five-inch torpedo-defense guns. Two of the turrets were mounted in the traditional way, fore and aft, while the other two were "wing," or beam turrets, on either side of the superstructure—an arrangement not dissimilar to the later British *Dreadnought* and *Invincible* classes. As for the caliber of the guns to be mounted, Signor discussed an all-twelve-inch layout, although by virtue of the improved availability of the end turrets—that is, they could more likely be brought to bear in most tactical situations—Signor argued for thirteen-inch guns fore and aft and ten-inch on the wings, for the same displacement as an all-twelve-inch ship.

He explained the overall advantage of such an arrangement as simply the improved availability of armor-piercing guns—that is, guns large enough to penetrate armor—when compared with the conventional, predreadnought arrangement. Its six- and eight-inch guns being only marginally effective at battle ranges, the predreadnought really only had four effective "ship-killing" guns in a fleet action. His arrangement, however, would "contain twelve armor piercing guns, of which in squadron action nine will almost always be available."[71] Furthermore, guns concentrated in turrets, he maintained, could be better protected with less overall armor than could the broadside batteries of the predreadnought, thus saving weight. In all but name, therefore, he was arguing for a dreadnought-type ship. Surprisingly, though, he did not emphasize the advantages of uniform-caliber firing with respect to spotting, a point that had been convincingly argued by his British counterparts.

Although Signor was at pains to point out that he was no authority on ship design but simply laying out certain salient "features," or themes, his proposal attracted comment from readers who were qualified.[72] Later the same year, Professor P. R. Alger, a leading gunnery expert and regular contributor to the technical columns in *Proceedings*, cast doubt on whether so heavy a battery could be carried by so small a ship and also on the efficacy of the triple-gun-turret arrangement; however, he came out broadly in favor of the overall arrangement of the battery, albeit with twin twelve-inch turrets all around.[73] More significantly perhaps, a future Chief Constructor of the Navy, David Taylor, while reiterating Alger's concerns about displacement, came out in favor of the turret arrangement as the most efficient way of protecting the main battery. Further, he promoted the variable-pitch propeller as a simple "fix" to allow the high-revolution steam turbine to be adopted for these battleships.[74] One by one the relevant pieces were falling into place and, at this point, faster than they were for the British; alas, that was not to continue.

At the same time, however, Mahan was advising the new president of his views on the qualities to be insisted on in any battleship buildup.[75] Here, well ahead of his more famous remarks after Tsushima, he used the same arguments against size and speed—specifically that since battleships were designed to operate with others of their kind, the aim should be homogeneity of capabilities across the fleet, and so any large "step" increases in size and speed would be unwise. The flaws in this argument have already been pointed out, but absent any particular reason to strive for higher speed (as was the case in Britain) and in a navy anxious to expand its size and influence, it may have been persuasive.[76] It is not clear what prompted Mahan's letter to Roosevelt in the first place, although discussion resulting from the Signor article cannot be ruled out. It is also significant that the Bureau of Construction and Repair (BuC&R) did not entirely agree. Its chief expressed the opinion that since warships had been steadily increasing in size and capability in all the major navies, it would probably be unwise for America not to follow suit.[77]

By the time of the 1903 Summer Problem, the Naval War College had other concerns that were causing a reexamination of the importance of speed. The Navy's torpedo school, the College's analysis of the Summer Problem noted, had reported successful runs of 4,200 yards, with Whitehead torpedoes traveling at eighteen knots. Reports such as these led to two main tactical concerns.[78] First, it was clear that the torpedo was fast becoming a powerful naval weapon, one that might soon offer ship-killing capabilities at a potentially greater range than the heavy gun. In light of the primacy of the battle line as the offensive element of most navies, one of the early lines of thinking was simply to adapt torpedoes for launch by battleships, as an adjunct to the main battery, and adjusting fleet tactics accordingly. This new task, however, would produce new design pressures on capital ships. For one thing, the need for precise positioning to guarantee a hit while remaining outside the gunnery range of the enemy would likely put speed and maneuverability at a premium in any torpedo-wielding battleship. In the words of the report, "If the fleet possessing them [torpedoes] has superior speed, it will decide the battle."[79] Elsewhere in the same document, however, the Naval War College assessed the American battle fleet, with its average of fifteen knots, as a full three knots slower than its Black counterpart.[80] It was clear therefore that before mounting torpedo tubes on U.S. battleships it would be most desirable, from a tactical standpoint, to increase their speed.

At the same time, the prospect of being forced to fight at longer ranges to avoid these torpedoes was causing more discussion on the accepted way of arming battleships. Up to this point, shortcomings in the rate of fire of the main battery had been compensated for by mounting a battery of increasingly powerful quick-firing guns on the broadside. This was fine when the battle ranges were expected to be short, in which case the relative lack of penetrating power of quick-firers would not be exposed. If, however, the decisive ranges were going to be longer, this secondary battery, as Signor had pointed out, would need reevaluation. In short, would a secondary battery be the best use of the available displacement, or could the weight it represented be more profitably employed to increase endurance, speed, or protection —or all three? Anticipating these dilemmas, the students in the 1903 problem were invited to consider a paper, "Considerations as to the Advisability of Suppressing the Secondary Battery in Battleships," that addressed all these options.[81] Noting that the move toward an all-big-gun ship was gaining traction overseas, the Summer

Problem participants endorsed this sentiment and proposed that future U.S. battleships be "armed with as many heavy guns as possible, relying solely on the 3″ for torpedo-boat defense."[82]

It comes to light in later correspondence that the students at the 1903 problem thoroughly discussed a fairly detailed proposal for an all-big-gun battleship on the lines of the Signor vessel, and most of them were in favor.[83] The architect of the proposal, Lt. Cdr. Washington I. Chambers, added the following endorsements: that the modern twelve-inch gun had to be considered to be as rapid and accurate in fire as the lesser calibers, that the best way to protect guns was the turret, and that a profusion of intermediate calibers firing simultaneously would interfere with the accuracy and control of the main battery.[84] Chambers's design featured three twin twelve-inch turrets in a triangular arrangement at either end of the ship. In war-gaming tests comparing it with the predreadnought *Connecticut* class, the new vessel came out as superior, so much so that the General Board recommended to the Secretary of the Navy (SecNav) in October of the same year that the all-big-gun proposals be studied.[85] The board stopped short, however, of an outright endorsement of "such a new and untried type."[86] But by January 1904 it was officially urging SecNav to direct BuC&R to produce a tentative design for "a battleship with twelve heavy turret guns, none of which shall be less than 10″ . . . the secondary battery being not above 3″." The aim would be to "show the practicability of the idea" so that "a more accurate opinion can be formed of the tactical qualities of such a ship."[87]

Another study, by Lt. Homer C. Poundstone, was coming to the same conclusion as were Chambers and the Naval War College, that the utility of the intermediate battery was becoming questionable. The paper was originally sent directly to President Roosevelt in December 1902, in protest at the continuing displacement limitations being imposed on battleships; a modified version was published in the June and September 1903 editions of *Proceedings*.[88] It must therefore have been taken into account in the College's discussion of the Chambers design and probably added weight to a later observation by Admiral Dewey that "some officers regard it as the Battleship of the future."[89] Significantly, in the first version of his paper, Poundstone insisted that to have "better speed and good coal endurance," as well as an "effective battery and its protection," battleships had to have large displacements—in excess of eighteen thousand tons. Small battleships would involve "serious sacrifices" in one or all of these desiderata, because the building of a battleship was always a compromise.[90] This view, clearly aimed at the congressionally imposed limits on battleship displacement, was diametrically opposed to Mahan's on the balance between numbers and size that the president had received only weeks earlier.[91]

On the question of armament, Poundstone opened by "failing to see the logic, necessity or practical use in carrying a mixed battery of pieces so nearly the same caliber." On the question of the seven-inch, he contended that it would be unable to penetrate even intermediate armor at anything more than the closest battle ranges; the eight-inch gun, although it had performed well in the Spanish-American War, was similarly afflicted. In fact, the only possible reason for the inclusion of the eight-inch weapon would seem to have been that "we doubt whether it [the seven-inch gun] will really do what we designed it for."[92] Poundstone therefore proposed the adoption of an all-quick-firing battery of eleven- and nine-inch guns (though in a later paper prepared soon afterward, probably with the help of Cdr. William S. Sims [who had a reputation as a gunnery expert and reformer], he came out in favor of a solely eleven-inch battery).[93] At the end of the *Proceedings* version of the paper, he makes reference to events in England (specifically the design of the *Lord Nelson* class, with its intermediate battery of turreted 9.2-inch guns) as greatly reinforcing his case.[94] Although he arguably only "nips" at the problem by simply increasing the caliber of the intermediate battery toward that of the main one, without being as decisive as Chambers and Signor, his reasoning—the increasing range of torpedoes and the improved lethality of the modern quick firing gun absolutely necessitating longer-range combat—mirrors their thinking completely.[95]

The Americans, then, were coming to the same realizations as their British counterparts about the relative uselessness of the secondary battery in a modern engagement. Both were concerned about the increasing range of torpedoes, and both realized the value of longer-range engagements, but whereas the British had become acutely aware of the problem of long-range hitting and had emphasized effective fire control at an early stage, in the American debate this appeared to be less of an issue. The emphasis there seemed to be on simply increasing the power of the battery such that whatever hits were achieved would penetrate and tell. On the subject of speed too the positions were subtly different, although it would be wrong to say that the Americans did not desire higher speeds. If for Britain the force of Fisher's personality almost guaranteed the official adoption of speedy vessels, in America opinion was divided. The innovators (Chambers, Poundstone, and the Naval War College) seemed to want to use the weight saved by the uniform-caliber battery for better speed and endurance; the strategist (Mahan) and the General Board were more cautious.[96] Most significant of all, perhaps, was the fact that all these detailed discussions took place in the United States well ahead, up to two years ahead, of the convening of Fisher's design committee. The U.S. Navy cannot therefore be characterized as being slow into the game.

Unfortunately, however, the reformers lacked anyone with the tenacity and sense of urgency of Jackie Fisher and who, also like Fisher, possessed the executive authority necessary to make things happen. For example, although Admiral Dewey had urged SecNav in January 1904 to have BuC&R draw up plans for an all-big-gun ship, this did not actually happen for another eighteen months, despite frequent reminders.[97] Ostensibly this delay was owing to the heavy workload being placed on the naval architects by the expanding fleet, but reading between the lines of one of the replies from Rear Adm. Washington Capps (Chief Constructor, BuC&R) to SecNav in September of that year gives one the feeling that this work had been done before (in the design stages of the *Connecticut* class). As the approach had been rejected at that point in favor of a more conventional design, there might have understandably been reluctance to, in effect, do this work again.[98] It is difficult to imagine Admiral Fisher either contenting himself with this explanation or being invited to wait for so long.

Whatever the reason, the first set of plans was received by the General Board only in July 1905, which gave it no choice but to recommend "repeat" battleships of the *Connecticut* class for the 1904/1905 program, although it clearly expressed a preference for an all-big-gun arrangement.[99] Citing the Russo-Japanese experience and acknowledging the improvements in the rate of fire of heavy guns, the General Board declared that "we should not defer making this change in the armament of battleships" and recommended that "the battleship be given a battery of heavy turret guns, none of which shall be less than 10″, and at least 4 of which shall be 12″, without intermediate battery."[100] Unfortunately, between this letter and the final receipt of the plans, Congress had renewed the sixteen-thousand-ton displacement limit for the next year's ships, against the urging of the Navy, a development that no doubt contributed to delay by grossly complicating BuC&R's problem.[101] Capps, however, got around this restriction masterfully by pioneering a "superfiring" arrangement for a four-turret, all-twelve-inch main battery for the 1905/1906 ships, with no intermediate battery, in what was effectively little more than a *Connecticut* hull.[102]

This eighteen-month hiatus, though it delayed the ships, did nothing to stem the debate. In the 1904 Summer Problem at Newport, the Naval War College students looked again at the issues of torpedoes, speed, and all-big-gun armament. Like their counterparts in Fisher's team, they began to discuss the divergent functions of battleships and armored cruisers, although their conclusions were quite different. While they favored the development of an armored cruiser that "would be a battleship without an intermediate battery," armed solely with four turreted twelve-inch guns and an offensive battery of torpedoes, they envisaged that these ships would operate as adjuncts to a conventional battle line, not as speedy replacements for it. In other words such ships would be primarily torpedo carriers, using their speed to keep out of harm's way while positioning for a torpedo attack against the enemy fleet.[103] This was completely the opposite of Fisher's conclusion that such ships could best meet the British strategic dilemma by replacing both battleships and cruisers completely, leading smaller, power-projection fleets about the empire.

On the subject of battleships, the 1904 course endorsed the previous year's all-big-gun proposal but further noted that a reduction in the numbers of calibers carried would greatly simplify the internal organization of a ship and make gunnery spotting easier. Overall armor protection could also likely be reduced, since there would be no broadside battery to protect, just the four or five large turrets and the conning position.[104] So, in some aspects they were converging on the British position, but not with respect to speed. They thought it "doubtful that a speed of more than eighteen knots was desirable in battleships," while in terms of priorities, protection was of the first importance, followed by a "fair speed."[105] As explained above, however, this more conservative viewpoint has to be understood against a probability of fast divisions of torpedo-carrying armored cruisers operating with future battle fleets.

The year 1905 marked something of a landmark on both sides of the Atlantic —and in fact of the globe. For the British, the *Dreadnought* and *Invincible* plans would be approved and the former ship laid down, to be complete and running trials eleven months later. Meanwhile, in the Far East, the decisive battle of Tsushima would be fought, from which would come all sorts of stimuli for almost every conceivable naval controversy, the speed and all-big-gun debates not excepted. In America, the year began with another move in the battleship-size debate, this time from a new source. Perhaps in response to Poundstone's earlier pleas for policy guidance, Cdr. Bradley A. Fiske, in a prize-winning essay entitled "American Naval Policy," ventured the opinion that the ships of the U.S. battle fleet were incorrectly designed.[106] The problem was more fundamental than simply the size of their guns, the scope of their protection, or the speed at which they moved, although these all had parts to play. Unlike the British, Fiske believed that U.S. Navy ships were more likely to be engaged in fights with other navies in fleet engagements. America was largely self-sufficient in materiel and hence seaborne trade did not have the same strategic value in Washington as it did in London.[107] At the same time, the country's policies, generally hostile to colonialism—notably the 1823 Monroe Doctrine, warning European states against colonialization or interference in the Western Hemisphere—were likely to be antagonistic to many of the colonial powers and could therefore act as a catalyst for foreign naval interventions in support of rival policies. This situation threw up different necessities in terms of design and put a premium on strength. Essentially echoing Poundstone, Fiske argued that American warships would need speed and offensive power in equal measure and that their displacement would have to be increased accordingly.[108]

Fiske thus accepted the need for large ships; furthermore, he argued, they would be more economical in the long run than they appeared on paper. Homogeneity within a fleet was unattainable, owing to rapid advances in technology; beyond the common sense of grouping ships of similar performance in squadrons, striving for homogeneity should not be allowed to restrain overall progress.[109] In this he was in stark disagreement with Mahan. There was no doubt that the article struck a chord, enough to encourage him to supply some specifics in a later article,

"Compromiseless Ships."[110] Here, in another pointed attack on Mahan on the questions of numbers and size, he settled on a displacement of around twenty thousand tons, a figure later given technical endorsement by a naval architect.[111]

In retrospect, an implication of all this would seem to have been that the usual process—Congress setting moderate (but arbitrary) size limits and naval architects struggling to shoehorn in all the other parameters—would have to be reversed. But Fiske now asserted that it should not be the responsibility of naval officers to second-guess Congress on which ships it was likely to authorize. Naval officers should simply recommend, he held, the best possible combination of dimensions and power according to their professional instincts and leave it to others to determine what was affordable.

The Naval War College's students evidently agreed. At the 1905 Summer Problem, they compared the likely performance of the *Connecticut* and *South Carolina* classes with the 1903 "all-big-gun" ship, concluding that "the [1903] design supplies the best battery, and with the simplification of calibers and the attendant advantages of ammunition stowage and supply, better fire control and more concentrated all round fire, is much superior. Such battleships should be built and the displacement [limits] increased to allow it."[112] In a letter to SecNav in September, the General Board attempted to prioritize the various demands on the battleship, stating that the "battery is the all important element" in these ships' design. That issue settled, "the best possible speed should be achieved on a given displacement."[113] This is a significant statement, as it is one of the only instances where the Navy's thinking on the relative priorities among these various commodities is expressed. The same letter reiterated that "the board has resisted an increase in size for speed alone, but, if the uniform big gun battery is accepted then an increase in size is justified." Finally and more specifically: "Therefore irresistibly drawn by the example of other navies, our experience and conclusive evidence that battleships need a uniform 12″ battery, to gain sufficient [room] we need 18,000 tons."[114]

Interestingly, BuC&R felt that the General Board had not gone far enough, claiming that eighteen thousand tons was an insufficient increase in size. On the basis of their experience with the design of *South Carolina,* its analysts maintained that fitting more than four twin twelve-inch turrets would involve a very large increase in displacement, which in their opinion would not be worth pursuing at the time.[115] A few months later, however, and presumably based on more unfavorable comparisons with *Dreadnought,* the General Board was pressing for a twenty-thousand-ton ship, turbine driven and with a secondary battery increased to six-inch guns.[116] Fiske's "compromiseless" ship was fast becoming a reality.[117]

There is no doubt, however, that one of the more important differences in a practical sense between the British and American programs was the slow progress of the latter. The British and American all-big-gun ships were authorized by their respective governments within days of one another, but the building of the American vessel took far longer.[118] The British had a "demonstrator" to play with, in the form of HMS *Dreadnought*, from the fall of 1906 and were thus able to start answering comparative questions on the efficacies of the all-big-gun battery and turbine propulsion by early 1907; the same was not true in America until late 1909 at the earliest.[119] In reality, moreover, no useful comparisons could be made for another year, when the large, turbine-driven *North Dakota* joined the fleet—effectively a full four years behind the British. By that time the Royal Navy already had seven dreadnought battleships and three battle cruisers in commission. Of course, this was exactly the benefit that Fisher had originally anticipated by his forcing the pace with *Dreadnought*.[120]

The upshot of this was that only in one year, 1906/1907, did the British have to order ships on blind faith. In America this "speculative period," without a ship to provide some answers, went on for considerably longer, which in practice meant that the next three classes (six ships in all) had to proceed to building without the benefit of practical experience. It really was not until the tendering for the *New York* class (BBs 34 and 35) in 1910–11 that the characteristics of the design could be directly influenced by firsthand, seagoing knowledge. The effect on the overall process was dramatic, in that any changes that were then felt necessary were immediately questioned on the basis of a lack of precedent in the intervening years; a case in point was the reversion to reciprocating engines for the two *New York*s, making the U.S. Navy appear far more conservative than it actually was.

In that intervening period the debate continued. In 1907, another prominent reformer, Commander Sims, publicly joined the chorus for the larger, all-big-gun ships, specifically targeting Mahan's recommendations as being in error.[121] In a journal article Sims reinforced the "Fisherite" belief that a faster fleet would always be able to dictate the course of the battle, and he reasonably asked what possible reason the United States could have, while all other important navies were building large, twenty-knot battleships, for knowingly placing its future fleet at a disadvantage by building sixteen-knot ships with about half the heavy-gun power.[122] He explained that by concentrating the same gun power in a much shorter battle line, the larger ship made tactical sense in terms of ease of handling in battle. He refuted Mahan's concerns over the alleged effects of the loss of funnels and uptakes, a major factor in the latter's support for massed small-caliber fire (as presumably allowing more deck space for routing smoke exhaust, a major factor in boiler efficiency). He rejoined with the gunnery specialist's plea for a uniform-caliber battery so as to ease handling and spotting problems. Given the weight of evidence now accumulating that the large caliber gun was superior, a well-written article by so widely recognized an expert in the field of gunnery as Sims was bound to be influential. It was therefore no surprise that by the beginning of 1907 Mahan had acknowledged that the president's mind was made up.[123]

Significantly, though, it was not on the issue of speed that the decision was made. While Sims had extolled the virtues of greater speed as he had gone along, his article particularly emphasized the superior fighting power of the large, all-big-gun ship and the possibility that its superior capability could be had for an initial expense equivalent to that of the alternative, cost less to run, and require fewer men. The implication was that the impact on fleet numbers might not be as crippling as Mahan had suggested.[124] These points were picked up by the General Board in its recommendations to SecNav on the subject of all-big-gun ships, adding that although the *Louisiana* and *South Carolina* classes would form a good squadron, the time was ripe to make the next advances in protection and gun power, which would mean larger ships.[125]

Equally, it was the issue of protection rather than a lack of any wider "dreadnought-like" qualities that brought about the extended 1908 Summer Problem at Newport, later to be called the "Battleship Conference." Having been passed a letter sent to SecNav by Cdr. Albert Key that pointed out numerous shortcomings in the design of the *North Dakota*, the president instructed both the General Board and the College to comment.[126] The Navy Department, however, saw an opportunity for a wider discussion and promptly convened a conference to be held at the War College over the summer season, so as to benefit from student input. Key's most serious allegations were all in the field of gunnery and protection: first, that the armor protecting the class's secondary battery was inadequate; second, that turret guns would have offered superior protection; and third, that the main armor belt on the hull was of the incorrect size and in the wrong place, making the ship vulnerable, particularly in a seaway. For these reasons it was ill suited, in his opinion, for its primary mission, which was to fight other battleships.[127]

The conference's work was divided into three broad sets of committees: those looking at the *North Dakota* design; those considering the next class, comprising *Florida* and *Utah* (BBs 30 and 31); and those considering future classes. In something of a Pyrrhic victory for the Sims and Key camps, most of the charges against the *North Dakota* design were upheld but were deemed relatively minor and not worth the extra time and expense to remedy. The conference largely endorsed the design as it stood, recommending no substantive changes, even though its participants acknowledged that the secondary battery was insufficiently protected and too low in the ship to be fought in all weathers.[128] They cautioned, however, that "there is no absolute protection," although most committees did endorse studies aimed at increasing the thickness and coverage of the casemate armor in future classes (from five to eight inches), even suggesting "a reduction in speed to accept armor improvements—but not below 18 knots."[129] On the subject of speed, Adm. Caspar F. Goodrich (then commandant of the Washington Navy Yard but previously commander of the Pacific Squadron) was of the opinion that in the *North Dakota* armor had been sacrificed for speed. He believed this a bad idea for battleships and one that ought not to be repeated. In fact, he went as far as maintaining that the builders had simply wanted to "best" the British *Dreadnought,* an inappropriate objective.[130] It would seem therefore that whatever Sims might have wanted, speed was near the bottom of the priorities in most naval minds when it came to battleships.[131]

In its recommendations to the Navy Department for the battleships of the 1909–10 program (the *Wyoming* class), the General Board reiterated the conference's recommendations that the battery and its protection were all important and that displacement should be allowed to increase to accommodate these needs. Specifically, it recommended a twenty-five-thousand-ton ship with ten twelve- or fourteen-inch twin turrets.[132] At this point the era of restrictive displacements was effectively at an end and the age of American battleships stronger and bigger than anyone else's was about to begin. Of course, perhaps the most important change to come out of the conference was an institutional one—future designs would be submitted to a board of officers considered best qualified to criticize and modify them before acceptance. In practice the General Board assumed this responsibility, from 1909 on. (The effects of this, which were not to be felt for some years, are largely outside the remit of this work and will not be discussed further.)

The final major distinction between the American debate and what took place in Britain was the significance of endurance as a desired quality in battleships—or more specifically, the power plant required to gain endurance and performance in an adequate balance. The early turbines were "high revving" and notoriously inefficient in terms of fuel consumption at slower speeds. This created a problem in marine applications where cruising and maneuvering at moderate speed for a high percentage of the running time was envisaged. It was not a concern for commercial operators of fast mail steamers, where almost continuous high speed was the norm. For them the turbines looked the perfect answer—providing higher speeds, less vibration, and lower maintenance requirements than reciprocating plants. Naval applications, however, were problematic: the highest possible speed was desirable for the odd occasions in which ships were required to pursue enemies, but most classes operated at a whole range of speeds, with perhaps a preponderance of moderate to slow speeds for cruising or patrolling. For this, the early steam turbines were a poor choice, particularly if endurance and self-sufficiency were prized by the navy in question.

As has already been discussed, for the British, with their predominant desire to save on running costs and their perceived strategic need to project power quickly in response to situations abroad, the turbine looked a workable answer, particularly given their numerous coaling stations and bases abroad. For them, endurance was of less concern, and there was even the prospect of using speed to force reductions in the available endurance of less-well-supported competitors.[133] This may be the reason that when Fisher recommended turbine propulsion for all classes of warship, it passed with almost no dissent. The Americans, however, coming late onto the naval stage and without a large spread of colonial possessions and bases, had to look very critically at anything that seemed likely to reduce the radius of action of their units and make them more dependent on base support.

The first mention of this as a potential concern comes in the 1906 Summer Problem at Newport, where the students were grappling with the huge distances involved in countering a Japanese move against the Philippines. Some of the questions asked of them by the organizers reflected the American strategic dilemmas: "What speed should be ordered for the voyage from the Atlantic to the Philippines, via the Panama canal?" "How should the battlefleet and the 12″ Armored cruisers be used?"[134] The outcome, however, was uncharacteristically noncommittal; the participants concluded that they had insufficient knowledge of turbines to make a decision. They noted that the British were developing turbine-powered capital ships, but they also noted the poor cruise economy of such a plant.[135] By the fall of that year, however, the matter had been somewhat taken out of their hands, in that the General Board, no doubt feeling pressure from observers comparing the U.S. battleships with the *Dreadnought,* recommended that the 1906 ships were to "have the latest type of engines adopted by any power for a battleship and to attain a trial speed of 21 knots. The armament, fuel endurance and armor protection to be equal to that of any battleship of similar size now built or building."[136] In practice, and in lieu of any definitive experience, this meant turbines—and so it was that the second *Delaware*-class vessel, *North Dakota,* received Curtis turbines, while the follow-on class, the *Floridas,* were specifically designed to receive Parsons units.[137] This would give the U.S. Navy an unrivaled opportunity to compare both turbines and reciprocating plants in similarly sized vessels.

Unfortunately, the very slow rate of shipbuilding in the United States meant that the first two ships did not run trials until 1909–10, by which time three more classes had been authorized and designed without benefit of experience to guide the Navy in its choices of machinery.[138] This sort of thing was evidently a source of great frustration to Admiral Dewey.[139] In the meantime, however, the claims for the superiority of turbines were becoming more strident. There is evidence that the Royal Navy's *Amethyst* trials were widely reported in the United States, as was the German experience with *Lübeck,* fitted with Curtis turbines.[140] Both sets of trials indicated that higher speed and lower overall coal consumption could be expected from turbine-driven vessels, and other benefits as well, even though at slower speeds the turbine ships were clearly less economical to operate. Another report, comparing the dimensions and weight of the turbine plant of the scout cruiser *Salem* with those of the reciprocating plant of the battleship *Vermont,* with similar shaft horsepower, came out heavily in favor of the turbine installation.[141] A much more influential piece of evidence, however, was a report filed by Commander Sims after visiting *Dreadnought* in Portsmouth, England.[142] Sims recounted that his host, the commanding officer, Reginald Bacon, had maintained that the turbine decision had been made in May 1905, to achieve the advantages of a smaller, simpler plant (fewer moving parts); less propulsion-plant weight overall, and concentrated lower in the ship; lower coal consumption at higher speeds; and ease of operation, with accordingly a smaller complement of engineers.[143] It was small wonder then that the General Board, in developing recommendations for the 1907 ships, specified that bidders were to provide data for both turbines and reciprocating plant over a whole range of speeds.[144]

Meanwhile the engineer's viewpoint, in the absence of definitive battleship trials, was perhaps typified by a short article for the American Society of Naval Engineers by Lt. W. G. Diman comparing the utility of the two installations for naval purposes.[145] Diman pointed out that much of the simplicity of early turbine installations would be lost if they were made practical for the wide range of naval speeds. As a result, and given that the turbine failures were likely to require dockyard support, he concluded that "at the present time it has not shown a great enough advantage in all round work to warrant its taking the place of the reciprocating engine."[146] Unfortunately for the turbine enthusiasts, the early trials with *North Dakota* in 1909 tended to confirm these thoughts. Comparative trials with its reciprocating sister *Delaware* bore out the predicted 30 percent drop in endurance. In a rather blunt summation, a Lieutenant Commander Price maintained that "15–30% fuel consumption at 12–15 knots above [the] consumption in a sister ship in the same fleet at the same speed is too dear a price to pay for a possible ¼ knot more top speed."[147]

Both BuC&R and the Bureau of Engineering (BuEng) agreed. In a letter of recommendation for the power plants of the next class after the six ships already mentioned—that is, the *New York* class, BBs 34 and 35—the two bureau chiefs, writing jointly and quoting exhaustively from the trial results, demonstrated that a turbine-powered battleship could not get from the West Coast to the Philippines without refueling, whereas a reciprocating ship could, with ease.[148] For these reasons and others similar to those cited by Diman, they recommended that the Navy award the contract for BB 35 *(Texas)* to the Newport News Shipbuilding and Drydock Company, which had tendered a reciprocating-plant bid. There is no doubt that this letter had the intended impact. In its recommendations to SecNav the General Board had originally, on 14 December, recommended the adoption of turbines for *Texas,* on the basis of improved reliability at high speed. This document was summarily withdrawn, however, and replaced by a counter-recommendation for a reciprocating plant, quoting information in the chiefs' letter.[149]

The potential of the turbine plant still attracted supporters, but the fears over endurance at moderate speeds had won through for the time being.[150] In the words of a future chief of BuEng, "A careful study of the performance of the *North Dakota*

. . . had assured the Bureau that no great economy of propulsion could be expected so long as the turbine builders adhered to what was at that time current turbine practice . . . sacrificing propeller efficiency in order to obtain a high turbine efficiency and so as to be able to hold down weight and space."[151] The answer was an efficient form of reduction gearing, but this would take years to develop. To force the turbine companies in this direction the bureau took the decision to support bids with reciprocating engines until the companies responded.

In sum, the American preference for a powerful offensive battery, in well-protected positions on ships of adequate dimensions, made a good deal of sense against the background of Fiske's strategic assumptions. Fiske made the case that whereas Britain, with its huge imperial responsibilities, had an urgent need to protect its global trade on a diminishing naval budget, the United States needed a navy prepared for very different eventualities. Uninterrupted trade was likely to be less of a factor in its own national survival, while, conversely, its own national policies were likely to be more antagonistic to the established powers. As a rule therefore, the U.S. Navy could expect to have to face other navies directly, not just their cruisers abroad. This meant that a powerful battleship fleet, stressing offensive power and sound protection, would likely be at a premium. As a result, these two qualities were never to be compromised, whereas everything else was negotiable. Speed, while certainly desirable, was not the "first desideratum," as it had been for Fisher. Endurance and self-sufficiency, however, were deemed much more important in a navy without a global support system than they had been for Fisher. These factors led to a far more critical assessment of the benefits and limitations of turbine propulsion. Finally, while the U.S. Navy certainly discussed the intended characteristics of its ships in great detail, in the end the slowness of its shipbuilding hampered the accumulation of practical experience and hence prevented more-educated decisions.

So, what conclusions can we draw from these two stories? The first, interestingly enough, reinforces the significance of strategy. While similar in many respects, these two cases were actually driven by very different strategic needs. This meant that the qualities sought from the emerging technologies were correspondingly different in each case. Great Britain had long been the world's largest maritime power and owned the most extensive array of colonial possessions ever amassed. As a result, it had dockyard facilities and coaling stations in all the important areas of the globe. The British were aiming to use the new technology as a way to make needed savings in their naval budget while still retaining overall naval primacy. Their plan was to develop an improved responsiveness in a few large and powerful ships that, if correctly placed in key locations, might obviate the need for large numbers of isolated "station" cruisers positioned everywhere that a British presence might be needed. In so doing, they hoped to gain fleet efficiencies by training their crews in groups of modern vessels, while achieving substantial savings in ships and manpower overall. At the same time, this reversal of the Mahanian edict to concentrate the fleet dealt conveniently with another of the exclusively naval problems of the day, that of the troubling vulnerability of battleships to low-cost torpedo craft in coastal waters. By taking the big ships out of dangerous waters altogether and using them instead on the deep oceans, the torpedo threat could be effectively neutralized, at least for the time being.

To do this, the Royal Navy had to meet some very specific technological needs. To gain the necessary responsiveness, it needed sustained high speed and proven hitting power over immense ranges—and it had to have both! Either alone was insufficient. The demand for high speed would necessitate a reduction in weight, which, if the offensive power was also to be optimized, had to come at the expense of the ship's protection (armor). If the ship's protection were reduced, the resulting vulnerability would have to be offset, and that is where the drive for long-range hitting came from. The theory went that if you could effectively hit your opponent at a range where he could not reply and keep out of his range (and so out of trouble) with superior speed, then you really did not need any armor at all. In essence the British aimed to use speed strategically to shrink the world, and tactically (combined with very big guns) to dictate how engagements would be fought. For this they needed turbine propulsion, a proven long-range gunnery fire-control system, and a method of controlling these ships on a global basis; these three things became the prerequisites for the proposed Fisher sea-control revolution. Given their primacy, geostrategic position, and, as noted, available facilities worldwide, endurance was much less of a concern for them. The other part of the puzzle was an effective flotilla-defense system in home waters to replace the departed battle fleet, and for this Fisher envisaged a network of interconnected submarines. Global sea control with battle cruisers and anti-invasion defense with submarines were thus the two vital pillars of his naval strategy.

By contrast, the United States was building a first-rate navy from a position of inferiority; it had no infrastructure around the world to support fleets away from home and no economies to be achieved by decommissioning older ships. Strategically speaking, its overseas trade was a relatively unimportant driver in sizing its fleet, since, and unlike Great Britain, it was largely self-sufficient in resources. As a result, and in view of the nation's anticolonialist policies, its naval leaders believed that their main fighting ships were much more likely to have to fight others of their kind in fleet actions, in response to challenges to the Monroe Doctrine. They also expected that such battles would come down to short-range slugging matches in which gun power and protection would be at a premium. Since the U.S. Navy was likely to be smaller than its opponent, it would have to remain concentrated, comprise powerful, well-built battleships, and be much more self-sufficient than the British when deployed. As a result, it stressed the qualities of good protection, offensive power, and endurance over everything else. Speed was much less a factor. Although officers like Sims, in particular, shared the British views on large, fast, all-big-gun ships, their recommendations tended to go unheeded, simply because this British vision of ocean protectors did not fit the American strategic circumstances. What was important for the fleet was to keep concentrated and to survive in battle; thus the sacrifices in speed and responsiveness necessary to achieve these ends were made.

The second great difference between the two cases related to the impact of personalities and institutional structures on the actual progress of naval reform. When we look at the British situation, it is difficult not to see a dominant reformer (Fisher) completely taking over the system and driving it to his own personal beat. Some would say that this was a strength in terms of innovation, and certainly it allowed one set of reforms to gain traction quickly, but because the changes were so quick and necessarily forced, great segments of the service population were simply bypassed or remained unconvinced.

Equally, programs like Fisher's require meticulous long-range planning and a degree of consistency in execution that were simply lacking. While Fisher started in the right way, with his personnel and fleet-disposition reforms in his run-up to 1904, once he was ensconced as the First Sea Lord his inconsistencies came to the fore, particularly in the more technical arguments. As a result, the many potential allies who had been overlooked or browbeaten were determined, and eventually able, to muster a credible opposition that, although unsuccessful while he was in office, slowed things down once he had left. The battle cruiser was a case in point. Devoid of its champion and with its strategic rationale diminished by external factors by the time it finally emerged, this class of ship would be misemployed as an adjunct to the battle line, a role for which it was simply unsuited.[152] In short, the Royal Navy was poorly prepared as an institution to deal with a volcanic personality like Fisher, who managed to polarize opinions to an unhealthy degree. The ultimate result was that his promising reforms fell short in a number of key areas.

By contrast, in the American case there was no single, dominant personality (although some, like Sims, shared many of the traits that had brought Fisher to prominence in Great Britain). In fact, the American institutional system, a network of powerful bureaus and boards, each controlling a different aspect of the naval procurement process, was specifically designed to ensure that this could not happen. The result was a far more considered, albeit slower, process that took equal account of all the necessary angles. No one aspect was allowed to predominate through force of advocacy alone. While the system had its faults, it arguably gave its navy a better-researched product at the end of the day. It would certainly be wrong to claim that the Americans were slow and unresponsive to the dreadnought-era innovations. As this article perhaps has shown, there was in the United States no shortage of pioneering brilliance, as seen in Washington Capps's innovative use of superfiring turrets to get around displacement limitations—a move that created a fashion that was to endure for decades. Nor was there any shortage of moral courage, as evidenced by the Bureau of Engineering's persistence in achieving the best power plant for the U.S. Navy, even to the point of forcing turbine manufacturers to consider its unique needs or face rejection. In every area, American naval architects analyzed key developments carefully and with extraordinary foresight, fitting them around their own strategic needs and looking for valid improvements. When such improvements were found, they were pursued with vigor.

The problem, though, was in the time that it took for the system as a whole to respond. Without an enormous military-industrial complex behind it, the multifaceted approval process was simply unable to capitalize on its superior analysis in a timely and positive way, once the path became clear. The result was a much slower transformation overall, which caused the operators to claim that the ship-design system was unresponsive to their needs. In truth, however, the design analysis in this case was ultimately correct—the British battle-cruiser revolution would not have been a good fit for the American strategic situation, and it is to the Americans' credit that they were not swept along by it, as the Germans were. Far from stifling innovation, therefore, the exacting American process was actually more searching than that of the British. It effectively ensured that, before proceeding, any proposed innovations were sound, having been properly analyzed and deemed unlikely to lead into strategic "blind alleys." Each system had its strengths, but the American process deserves more credit than it has received for ultimately leading to a broadly durable vehicle for the support of its navy in the remainder of the twentieth century.

NOTES 1 The term "Mahanian" refers to sea power's most famous prophet, Alfred Thayer Mahan of the United States. His explanation of the merits of concentration with regard to battle fleets is perhaps most notably expounded in his *Naval Strategy: Compared and Contrasted with the Principles of Military Operations on Land* (London: Sampson Low, Marston, 1911), esp. p. 8.

2 See John Beeler, *Birth of the British Battleship: British Capital Ship Design, 1870–1881* (Annapolis, Md.: Naval Institute Press, 2001). In particular, chapter 3 outlines the technological difficulties with the plant, and chapter 10 the difficulties with endurance and the provision of adequate coaling supplies and dry docks.

3 For a good summation of this threat, see Theodore Ropp, *The Development of a Modern Navy: French Naval Policy, 1871–1904* (Annapolis, Md.: Naval Institute Press, 1987), pp. 240–53, 284–98.

4 Jon T. Sumida, *In Defence of Naval Supremacy: Finance, Technology and British Naval Policy, 1889–1914* (Boston: Unwin Hyman, 1989), esp. chap. 1, pp. 3–35.

5 Chancellor of the Exchequer, "The Financial Position," 28 April 1904, Cabinet Papers, CAN 37/70, The National Archives / Public Record Office, Kew, United Kingdom [hereafter TNA]. Also cited in Sumida, *In Defence of Naval Supremacy*.

6 Adm. Sir John Arbuthnot Fisher (1841–1920), first Baron Fisher of Kilverstone, joined the Royal Navy in 1854, served in the China and Egyptian wars, in the latter in command of HMS *Inflexible*, the *Dreadnought* of its day. Promoted rear admiral in 1890, he embarked on a nine-year stint in procurement and shipbuilding positions. He commanded the Mediterranean Fleet in 1900–1902, making great strides to improve operational effectiveness. He was First Sea Lord from October 1904 to January 1910 and again from October 1914 to May 1915.

7 A good example of how he saw the relationship between the empire, the navy, and the economy as crucial for the health of Great Britain can be found in his "Notes by Sir John Fisher on New Proposals for the Committee of Seven," written in Portsmouth on 14 May 1904 and reproduced in P. K. Kemp, ed., *The Papers of Admiral Sir John Fisher* (London: Ballantyne for the Navy Records Society, 1960) [hereafter *Fisher Papers*], vol. 1, p. 18.

8 For Fisher's thoughts on the "suddenness" of modern naval warfare requiring "an instant readiness for war," see Kemp, *Fisher Papers,* vol. 1, pp. 16–27, and also a letter to Lord Selborne written in April 1904; see Arthur J. Marder, ed., *Fear God and Dread Nought: The Correspondence of Admiral of the Fleet Lord Fisher of Kilverstone,* vol. 1, *The Making of an Admiral, 1854–1904* (London: Jonathan Cape, 1952), pp. 310–11.

9 Although it would be improper not to mention Arthur Marder's classic five-volume work on the Fisher era—*From the Dreadnought to Scapa Flow: The Royal Navy in the Fisher Era, 1904–1919* (London: Oxford Univ. Press, 1961–70)—as it is the starting point for most subsequent interpretations, its message has been greatly enriched and in some cases corrected by subsequent works. Notable among these have been Jon Sumida's aforementioned *In Defence of Naval Supremacy,* which challenged Marder's geopolitical basis for the development of the dreadnought and the battle cruisers, arguing that the need for financial economy was what really drove Fisher to rethink the business of sea control. Nicholas Lambert takes this one step farther by introducing the concept of "flotilla defense," explaining that Fisher's faith in the emerging technology of the submarine provided the home-defense capability necessary to allow the capital ship to become a reactive defender of the worldwide periphery. Lambert first expounded his theories in a pair of articles written in 1995. The more important here is "Admiral Sir John Fisher and the Concept of Flotilla Defense," *Journal of Military History* 59 (October 1995), pp. 639–60. His whole plan is laid out in a later, book-length monograph, *Sir John Fisher's Naval Revolution* (Columbia: Univ. of South Carolina Press, 1999). This article and monograph have been steadily enriched by subsequent work, notably Sumida's "Gunnery, Procurement and Strategy in the Dreadnought Era," *Journal of Military History* 69, no. 4 (October 2005), pp. 1179–87, which goes into great detail on the gunnery and its fire-control aspects, and Lambert's own "Transformation and Technology in the Fisher Era: The Impact of the Communications Revolution," *Journal of Strategic Studies* 27, no. 2 (June 2004), pp. 272–97, which introduced previously missing wireless command-and-control aspects.

10 See George Baer, *One Hundred Years of Seapower: The U.S. Navy, 1890–1990* (Stanford, Calif.: Stanford Univ. Press, 1994), chap. 2, pp. 27–48, for a concise explanation of the American sea-power dilemma.

11 Fisher himself was a gunnery specialist, having been commanding officer of HMS *Excellent,* the Naval Gunnery School, at Whale Island, Portsmouth, in 1883–85. He had also been the director of naval ordnance from 1886 to 1891, latterly as a rear admiral. Arthur Hungerford Pollen was the British inventor who first recognized the need for an analog computer system to calculate the "range future" position of a moving ship to facilitate ship-versus-ship gunnery engagements. Starting work in 1900, his "Argo clock" system showed promise and attracted Fisher's support. Unfortunately, it was to be dogged by small errors in its calculation logic that produced unacceptable sighting data, a problem that took years to fix. For a good discussion of the importance of Pollen's system to Fisher's scheme and the current dichotomy in scholarly opinion on the subject, see a review essay by Jon Sumida, "Gunnery, Procurement, and Strategy in the Dreadnought Era." It reviews John Brooks, *Dreadnought Gunnery and the Battle of Jutland: The Question of Fire Control* (New York: Routledge, 2005).

12 See a letter from Fisher to the journalist Arnold White (a Fisher favorite) dated 21 August 1904, two months before Fisher takes office as First Sea Lord, in Marder, *Fear God and Dread Nought,* vol. 1, p. 326. This description is later repeated in his reforming document *Naval Necessities* to emphasize the need to consider the whole package.

13 Adm. George Dewey, U.S. Navy, had commanded the U.S. squadron that destroyed the Spanish fleet at anchor in Manila Bay in 1898. This action had done much to bring the U.S. Navy to the forefront as a naval power. In 1900, he was appointed as the first president of the Navy's General Board, a new advisory body working for the Secretary of the Navy, a post that he held until his death in 1917.

14 See the full wording reproduced in Barfleur [Rear Adm. Reginald Custance], "A Retrograde Admiralty," *Blackwood's Edinburgh Magazine* 177 (May 1905), pp. 601–602.

15 Ibid., p. 602. Rear Adm. Reginald Custance, lately the director of naval intelligence (1899–1902), was perhaps the most fluent of Fisher's opponents in the press and became the leader of the "syndicate of discontent" pledged to oppose his reforms on principle. In this article Custance accuses Fisher of deliberately undermining the authority of the other board members, in particular the controller, thus effectively turning the Admiralty into a dictatorship so that he could force his reforms through. There is evidence that the article particularly incensed Fisher. A good synopsis of the two men's disagreements over this period can be found in Matthew Allen, "Rear Admiral Reginald Custance: Director of Naval Intelligence, 1899–1902," *Mariner's Mirror* 78, no. 1 (February 1999), pp. 61–75.

16 Kemp, *Fisher Papers,* vol. 1, pp. 30–31.

17 Ibid., pp. 22, 30.

18 Ibid., p. 31.

19 In fact, in the first year of his tenure as First Sea Lord he authorized a rather secret subcommittee within his "committee on designs" charged specifically with assessing the merits of a "fusion type" (i.e., of battle cruisers and battleships). See "Navy Estimates Committee 1906–7," 10 January 1906, pp. 18–23, Fisher Papers, FP 4711, FISR 8/6, Churchill College Archives, Cambridge, United Kingdom [hereafter Churchill Collection]. Although his committee did not agree with him and was unable to recommend so expensive a ship as what he had in mind, Fisher continued to press for such "fusions" for the remainder of his tenure.

20 See "Extracts from Confidential Papers, Mediterranean Fleet," 30 December 1901, p. 10, FP 4702, FISR 8/1, Churchill Collection.

21 Kemp, *Fisher Papers,* vol. 1, "Types of Fighting Vessels," p. 74.

22 The document in question, entitled *Naval Necessities, Volume 1,* dealt with the wholesale scrapping of obsolete warships, types of future fighting vessels to be discussed, reorganization of the fleets, and a nucleus-crew system. It is reproduced in its entirety in Kemp, *Fisher Papers,* vol. 1. An original text (unedited) is in the Churchill Collection*,* FISR 15/4.

23 Kemp, *Fisher Papers,* vol. 1, "Organization for War," p. 17 [emphasis original].

24 Ibid., p. 30.

25 Ibid.

26 [Custance], "Retrograde Admiralty," pp. 606–607.

27 Ibid., p. 607 [emphasis original].

28 In truth, if also in hindsight, such resistance was undoubtedly a part of the story surrounding the misemployment of the battle cruisers in World War I. See Reginald Custance, "Admiralty Policy Historically Examined," *Blackwood's Edinburgh Magazine* 177 (June 1905), p. 743.

29 See a letter to Captain Fortescue (aide-de-camp to the king), in *Fear God and Dread Nought: The Correspondence of Admiral of the Fleet Lord Fisher of Kilverstone,* vol. 2, *Years of Power, 1904–1914,* ed. Arthur J. Marder (London: Jonathan Cape, 1959), p. 71. Fisher in effect diverts the criticism without addressing it, calling it a triviality that has been magnified out of all proportion to its impact on the whole scheme of reform.

30 William H. White, a naval architect who rose to be the chief constructor in 1881, served with the Admiralty for seventeen years. During that time he was responsible for harmonizing the great variety of ships then serving the navy; he introduced the landmark *Royal Sovereign* class (the first predreadnought) and was subsequently responsible for over forty other battleships in carefully designed classes of similar ships that successfully and incrementally improved on their respective predecessors. See his letter "Admiralty Policy and the New Naval Estimates," *Nineteenth Century* 59 (April 1906), pp. 601–18.

31 Ibid., pp. 602–604.

32 Ibid., p. 607.

33 Ibid., p. 615.

34 Ibid., p. 613.

35 Capt. Alfred T. Mahan, "Reflections, Historic and Other, Suggested by the Battle of the Japan Sea," U.S. Naval Institute *Proceedings* [hereafter *USNIP*] 32 (June 1906), pp. 441–71.

36 Ibid., p. 461.

37 Ibid.

38 Lord Brassey, *Times* (London), September 1906, p. 5, col. A. Lord Brassey (1836–1918), a politician, philanthropist, heir to a railway contractor fortune, and prominent naval commentator of the time who gave his name to the most respected naval annual of the period, was a tireless advocate of a larger number of less capable ships.

39 See a letter to Lord Tweedmouth, First Lord, 5 October 1906, in *Fear God and Dread Nought,* ed. Marder vol. 2, pp. 96–97.

40 Kemp, *Fisher Papers,* vol. 1, "Types of Fighting Vessels," p. 28.

41 See Capt. E. J. W. Slade, "Speed in Battleships," May 1906, pp. 4–9, FP 4718, FISR 8/8, Churchill Collection. Captain (later Admiral) Slade (1859–1928) was specifically chosen by Fisher for the War College position, later (in 1907) succeeding Charles Ottley as director of naval intelligence, again with Fisher's insistence.

42 Ibid., p. 8.

43 [Custance], "Retrograde Admiralty," p. 603.

44 Custance, "Admiralty Policy Historically Examined," p. 743.

45 See Reginald Custance, "Lessons from the Battle of Tsushima," *Blackwood's Edinburgh Magazine* 179 (February 1906), p. 164, and "The Growth of the Capital Ship," *Blackwood's Edinburgh Magazine* 179 (May 1906), pp. 594–95. Similar sentiments were also expressed by Adm. Sir Cyprian Bridge; see *Times* (London), 2 March 1906, p. 4, col. C.

46 Mahan, "Reflections . . . Suggested by the Battle of the Japan Sea," pp. 452–53.

47 "The Problem of Speed: Both Sides of the Question," *Brassey's Naval Annual 1906, (*Portsmouth, U.K.: J Griffin & Co., n.d.), chap. 9, pp. 144–55.

48 These two ships were Gem class, third-class protected cruisers, completed in the spring of 1905. *Amethyst* was fitted with Parsons turbines, while its sister had a standard reciprocating plant. Both vessels were subjected to exhaustive propulsion trials aimed at determining the advantages and disadvantages of the turbine installation.

49 "Report from the Institution of Naval Architects, Speech by Lord Glasgow," *Nature* 71 (20 April 1905), p. 594.

50 Committee on Design, proceedings of Friday, 13 January 1905, in *Fisher Papers,* ed. Kemp, vol. 1, p. 233.

51 See apps. F and G to the Committee on Design report, *Fisher Papers,* ed. Kemp, vol. 1, pp. 272–78.

52 This viewpoint appears in an engineering article discussing progress in warship propulsion over the period 1905–17; see Capt. C. W. Dyson, USN, "The Development of Machinery in the U.S. Navy during the Past Ten Years," *Journal of the American Society of Naval Engineers* 29 (1917), p. 217. This was to become a fairly universal theme of the early postwar histories, though Fisher had clearly planned from the outset to use his ships for long-range power projection.

53 Julian (later Sir Julian) Stafford Corbett (1854–1922) was a prominent naval historian and geostrategist who was a member of Fisher's "brain trust." Trained as a lawyer, Corbett had no military background, which tended to act against him. He did, however, have the trust of Fisher, who arranged for him to join the faculty of the newly developed War College in Portsmouth in 1905. Corbett wrote his most famous work, *Some Principles in Maritime Strategy,* in 1911. Corbett was not infatuated with the search for decisive battle or with the strategic offensive. In general, he favored the strategic defensive, with an emphasis on the offensive at the operational level. Corbett's strategic defense advocated such measures as an intense local offensive, the projection and support of land forces (where the decisive actions would be taken), various types of blockades, and attacks on trade. For these purposes dispersed naval forces, acting against the periphery of the enemy, could be valuable. This view brought him into contrast with Mahan.

54 See Corbett, "The Strategical Value of Speed in Battleships" (lecture to the Royal United Services Institute, repr. *RUSI Journal* 51, no. 2 [July–December 1907], pp. 824–33). This work was instigated by Fisher himself, in response to criticism of his reforms. Fisher was delighted with the article and congratulated Corbett on it; see Marder, *Fear God and Dread Nought,* vol. 2, p. 120.

55 See, for example, his account of his experiences with his flagship, *Renown,* in maneuvers during which the ship's speed enabled him to "mop up" all the "enemy" cruisers, in two expansive letters on the benefits of speed in large warships written to Lord Selborne when Fisher was First Sea Lord; Marder, *Fear God and Dread Nought,* vol. 1, pp. 170–79. HMS *Renown* was officially a second-class battleship, having only ten-inch guns in its main battery, as opposed to the usual 13.5-inch, and a large battery of six-inch quick-firers. The weight saving gave the ship a handy two-knot speed advantage over its larger brethren, however. It was built on Fisher's own recommendation as Controller of the Navy in 1892. The Admiralty writ large, however, was not convinced; see Sumida, *In Defence of Naval Supremacy,* p. 40.

56 This was more than just a theoretical concept at this stage. Other navies, in particular that of the Germans, were actively developing all-medium-caliber battleships to take advantage of the supposed accuracy and rate of fire of quick-firing ordnance. For a good description of the rationale behind the 1899 building of SMS *Kaiser Karl der Grosse,* see Ropp, *Development of a Modern Navy,* pp. 297–99.

57 For a discussion, see Sumida, *In Defence of Naval Supremacy,* pp. 40–50.

58 For a good contemporary discussion of the merits and otherwise of the six-inch versus twelve-inch batteries in ship-killing terms, see Navalis, "Do Dreadnoughts Only Count?," *Fortnightly Review*

59 (June 1909), pp. 1096–99. While acknowledging the impressive rate of fire of the quick-firers, the pseudonymous author argues that "there can be no comparison between the destructive force of these and that of a large shell discharged from the 12″ guns." Thus, and with the prospect of better fire control in the dreadnought type, he concludes that the all-big-gun decision for *Dreadnought* was the right one.

59 For more detail see the Admiralty pamphlet *The One Calibre Big Gun Armament for Ships,* June 1908, p. 10, FP 4881, FISR 8/31, Churchill Collection.

60 Kemp, *Fisher Papers,* vol. 1, "The Guns of the Battleship and Armored Cruiser," pp. 32–33.

61 Ibid., p. 74.

62 Matthew Seligmann cites the results of trials held in 1904 on board HMS *Victorious* ("Report of the Committee on Control of Fire in Action") in his "New Weapons for New Targets: Sir John Fisher, the Threat from Germany and the Building of HMS *Dreadnought* and HMS *Invincible, 1902–1907,*" *International History Review* 30, no. 2 (June 2008), p. 310. Since the trial report was widely circulated at the time, it is almost impossible that Captain Jellicoe, then Fisher's main gunnery adviser, would not have been aware of it.

63 Mahan, "Reflections . . . Suggested by the Battle of the Japan Sea," p. 460. But see also Custance, "Lessons from the Battle of Tsushima," pp. 162–63.

64 See note 59 above.

65 Captain (later Admiral of the Fleet, Lord) Jellicoe (1859–1935) joined the navy in 1872, becoming a gunnery specialist in 1884 and serving with distinction in the Egyptian conflict and Boxer Rebellion. He was special assistant to the director of naval ordnance (DNO) in 1888 and served in 1897, as a captain, on the Admiralty Ordnance Committee. Fisher's most trusted gunnery adviser, he was appointed as DNO in 1905–1907 and oversaw the whole big-gun controversy. Jellicoe was to command the Grand Fleet during World War I, on Fisher's express wish.

66 "Armament for the 1908–09 Armored Cruiser," FP 4850, FISR 8/27, Churchill Collection.

67 Theodore Roosevelt (1858–1919) became the twenty-sixth president of the United States in 1901 and was in office throughout the period under investigation. Roosevelt was something of a naval enthusiast, having written on the naval war of 1812 and having been an influential Assistant Secretary of the Navy for a year in 1897 in the run-up to the Spanish-American War. It helped that he saw naval power as the instrument through which America's rightful status in the industrial age was to be achieved. In short, he was a confirmed believer in the merits of a "big navy."

68 "1901 Summer Problem," pp. 1–14, Record Group [hereafter RG] 12, Naval Historical Collection, Naval War College, Newport, R.I. [hereafter NHC NWC].

69 Ibid., pp. 14, 25.

70 Matt. H. Signor, "A New Type of Battleship," *USNIP* 28, no. 1 (March 1902), pp. 1–20.

71 Ibid., p. 10.

72 Ibid., p. 3.

73 P. R. Alger, "Discussion on 'A New Type of Battleship,'" *USNIP* 28, no. 2 (June 1902), pp. 269–72.

74 David Taylor, "Discussion on 'A New Type of Battleship,'" *USNIP* 28, no. 2 (June 1902), pp. 272–75. David Watson Taylor (1864–1940), who would later to rise to the rank of rear admiral and the office of chief constructor, was a naval architect and engineer who had served as a constructor since 1886. He is most remembered for his work in hydrodynamics and hull forms, employing America's first hydrodynamic tank. In 1909 he served as the chief of the Bureau of Construction and Repair. For the issue of applying the fast-spinning steam turbine to ship propulsion, see chapter 5 of this collection, "Powering the U.S. Fleet: Propulsion Machinery Design and American Naval Engineering Culture, 1890–1945," by William M. McBride.

75 See Mahan, memorandum to President Roosevelt, 16 October 1902, on the subject of numbers versus power of units, forwarded to the president of the General Board by the president's secretary the same day; General Board [hereafter GB] file 420.6, "Battleships," box 73, RG 80, National Archives and Records Administration, Washington, D.C. [hereafter NARA]. This letter is reproduced (without endorsements) in Robert Seager and Doris Maguire, eds., *The Letters and Papers of Alfred Thayer Mahan* (Annapolis, Md.: Naval Institute Press, 1975), vol. 3, pp. 38–40.

76 Morison suggests that Mahan's name alone—that is, his reputation—was probably worth more than any amount of technical papers from BuC&R. See Elting E. Morison, *Admiral Sims and the Modern American Navy* (Boston: Houghton Mifflin, 1942), p. 164.

77 BuC&R Chief Constructor A. T. Bowles, first endorsement, 22 October 1906, GB file 420.2, RG 80, NARA.

78 Tactics Committee report, "1903 Summer Problem," pp. 67–68, RG 12, NHC NWC.

79 Ibid., main report, p. 46.

80 Ibid., "Comparison of Fleets," p. 40.

81 Ibid., part VIII.

82 Cuniberti's 1903 paper in *Jane's Fighting Ships,* "An Ideal Battleship for the British Fleet," was cited specifically here. Ibid., p. 72.

83 See Admiral Dewey (General Board president) to the Secretary of the Navy in reference to these blueprints, 26 January 1904, GB file 420.2, RG 80, NARA. A copy of the plans for the ship is in an unmarked brown envelope in box 73 of that record group.

84 See Chambers to Captain Sperry (of the Naval War College) explaining his blueprints, 1 February 1904, GB file 420.2, RG 80, NARA. This memorandum, which covered and explained the blueprints, was enclosed under a Naval War College reply to the General Board letter of 26 January. Washington Irving Chambers, later a captain, was an important innovator during this period, particularly in the field of naval aviation. Recruited to the faculty at the Naval War College by Mahan, Chambers held strong

opinions on the application of technology and the importance of education in an officer's career. After tests of his 1903 battleship proposal proved favorable, he pursued the idea of the all-big-gun ship doggedly until the concept was accepted. By 1910, however, he had switched his attention to the promotion of naval aviation. For a biography, see Stephen Stein, *From Torpedoes to Aviation: Washington Irving Chambers and Technological Innovation in the New Navy, 1876–1913* (Tuscaloosa: Univ. of Alabama Press, 2007), esp. chap. 11.

85 Stein considers the Chambers design truly revolutionary, the only one to anticipate gunnery engagements at long ranges. He also credits it as the inspiration for Poundstone and Sims, whose work he considers far less groundbreaking, in that they did not necessarily dispense with the secondary battery; Stein, *From Torpedoes to Aviation,* pp. 137–39. But this last deduction is questionable; plenty of evidence shows that both Poundstone and Sims were aware of the futility of secondary batteries in an era of well-protected ships (see notes 92 and 121, below).

86 The General Board's minutes for 16 October 1903 record an extraordinary piece of institutional legerdemain—the reading of a draft letter to SecNav (later sent on the 17th) and a decision that while the minutes were to report a favorable opinion of the design, the official report would not. "General Board: Proceedings," (microfilm) M1493, roll 1 (1900–1906), drawer 53A/05, NARA.

87 See Admiral Dewey to SecNav, 24 January 1904, GB file 420.2, RG 80, NARA.

88 Lt. Homer C. Poundstone, USN, "Size of Battleships for the U.S. Navy," *USNIP* 29 (June 1903), pp. 161–74, and "Proposed Armament for Type Battleship of U.S. Navy with Some Suggestions Relative to Armor Protection," *USNIP* 29 (September 1903), pp. 377–411.

89 Dewey to the Secretary of the Navy, 26 January 1904.

90 Poundstone, "Size of Battleships for the U.S. Navy," pp. 164–65.

91 Mahan to president, 16 October 1902 (see note 75 above).

92 Poundstone, "Proposed Armament for Type Battleship," pp. 382–83.

93 Morison points out that Poundstone was an "old friend and classmate" of Admiral Sims, then the director of target practice and a renowned gunnery expert who was also in favor of a uniform-caliber, large-battery ship (see below). It is likely that the two colluded on this paper; Morison, *Admiral Sims and the Modern American Navy,* p. 159. This possibility is supported by Robert F. Wilson, "Sims, of the Successful Indiscretions," *World's Work* 34 (May–October 1917), p. 339, claiming that the two of them together came up with the blueprints for Poundstone's all-big-gun ship *Scared-o'-Nothing.*

94 Poundstone, "Proposed Armament for Type Battleship," p. 409.

95 For another secondary interpretation of the events see Norman Friedman, "The South Carolina Sisters: America's First Dreadnoughts," *Naval History* (February 2010), pp. 16–23. See also, by the same author, *U.S. Battleships: An Illustrated Design History* (Annapolis, Md.: Naval Institute Press, 1985), esp. chap. 2.

96 For example, the Naval War College's recommendation after the 1903 summer discussions on the issue of suppressing the secondary battery stated that not only should the United States arm its future battleships with "as many heavy guns as possible, relying solely on the 3″ for torpedo defense" but "the weight saved should be used to get 21 knots speed and better endurance"; "1903 Summer Problem," pp. 72–76, RG 12, NHC NWC.

97 Dewey is on record as asking SecNav at least three times for a reply to his 17 October 1903 letter: on 29 January 1904, 29 September 1904, and finally 10 June 1905. GB file 420.6, "Battleships," 1900–1906 file, box 73, RG 80, NARA.

98 See BuC&R endorsement to SecNav, 27 September 1904, on the General Board letter of 29 January 1904, GB file 420.6, "Battleships," 1900–1906 file, box 73, RG 80, NARA. Stein claims that Capps dropped the idea when he assumed office; Stein, *From Torpedoes to Aviation,* p. 138. Rear Adm. Washington Lee Capps (1864–1935) joined BuC&R in 1892, having studied naval architecture since he had been a junior officer. He was well known to Dewey, having been with him at the battle of Manila Bay, in the aftermath supervising the salvage of Spanish warships. Promoted to rear admiral in 1903, Capps served as Constructor of the Navy and head of BuC&R until 1910.

99 It is evident that the controversies over the mixed armament of USS *New Hampshire,* the battleship authorized that year, reached as high as Roosevelt. The president, who was in correspondence with Commander Sims on the matter, specifically asked his gunnery expert for his opinion on the uniform-caliber, all-big-gun ship. See Roosevelt to Sims, 5 October 1904, in Elting E. Morison, ed., *The Letters of Theodore Roosevelt,* vol. 4, *The Square Deal, 1903–1905* (Cambridge, Mass.: Harvard Univ. Press, 1951), p. 973.

100 See GB to SecNav, 28 October 1904, "Types to Be Authorized at 1904 Congress," GB file 420.2, "Building Program," 1900–1908 file, RG 80, NARA.

101 See wording of congressional act reproduced in BuC&R's description of BBs 26 and 27, *South Carolina* and *Michigan*: "Two First-class Battleships carrying the heaviest armor and most powerful armament for vessels of their class upon a maximum trial displacement of not more than 16,000 tons." BuC&R letter 19421-E.41, 10 November 1905, GB file 420.2, "Building Program," 1900–1908 file, RG 80, NARA.

102 This has been well covered by Friedman, "South Carolina Sisters," pp. 20–23. BuC&R submitted the plans for these two ships to the General Board on 8 July 1905; GB file 420.6, "Battleships," 1900–1906 file, box 73, RG 80, NARA. (The plans are missing in this file.)

103 "1904 Summer Problem," RG 12, NHC NWC, esp. pp. 18–23, Tactics Committee, for a description

of the ship and its role. This was endorsed by the overall report, on p. 67.

104 Ibid., pp. 35–37.

105 Ibid., p. 52.

106 Bradley A. Fiske, "American Naval Policy," *USNIP* 31, no. 1 (March 1905), pp. 1–79 (the prizewinning essay for January 1905). Commander (later Rear Admiral) Fiske (1854–1942) was a noted technical innovator who had written extensively on professional matters and had worked specifically on a range finder for battleship guns. He was serving with the Bureau of Ordnance at the time and would later rise to be SecNav's aide for operations (precursor to the Chief of Naval Operations) during World War I. Poundstone had originally complained that "the United States has no established naval policy"; *USNIP* 29 (September 1903), p. 436.

107 Fiske, "American Naval Policy," pp. 9–11.

108 Ibid., pp. 34–36.

109 Ibid., pp. 38–39.

110 Bradley A. Fiske, "Compromiseless Ships," *USNIP* 31, no. 3 (September 1905), pp. 549–53.

111 Richard D. Gatewood, "Approximate Dimensions for a Compromiseless Ship," *USNIP* 32 (1906), pp. 572–83. Gatewood mathematically derives a figure of 20,200 tons.

112 "1905 Summer Problem," part III, p. 10, RG 12, NHC NWC.

113 See General Board to SecNav, 30 September 1905, "Bearing of Size on the Possibilities for the Main Battery and Speed Attained," GB file 420.6, "Battleships," 1900–1906 file, box 73, RG 80, NARA.

114 Ibid.

115 See BuC&R, third endorsement to General Board's 30 September 1905 letter, GB file 420.6, "Battleships," 1900–1906 file, box 73, RG 80, NARA.

116 See General Board to SecNav, dated 9 January 1907, GB file 420.6, "Battleships," 1907 file, box 73, RG 80, NARA.

117 The *Delaware* class (BBs 28 and 29), authorized in March 1907, was the first U.S. battleship design intended to eclipse all comers.

118 The *Dreadnought* estimates (1905–1906) were approved in the House of Commons on 2 March 1905; "The Navy Estimates," *Times* (London), 3 March 1905, p. 12, col. 2. *Michigan* and *South Carolina* were authorized in Congress a day later, on 3 March 1905.

119 HMS *Dreadnought* began running trials on 15 September 1906, completing contractor's trials by 18 October. It was commissioned into the fleet on 3 December 1906.

120 See, for example, Fisher's letter to the First Lord, the Earl of Tweedmouth, 26 September 1906: "10 Dreadnoughts practically built or building in two years!! What is there to touch this in foreign shipbuilding programmes?" Marder, *Fear God and Dread Nought*, vol. 2, pp. 90–93.

121 William S. Sims, "The Inherent Tactical Qualities of All-Big-Gun, One-Caliber Battleships of High Speed, Large Displacement and Gun-Power," *RUSI Journal* 51 (March 1907), pp. 261–88. This article was reprinted from the U.S. Naval Institute *Proceedings,* where it had appeared as a direct response to Mahan's "Reflections" on the Russo-Japanese War (note 35 above). William Sowden Sims (later admiral) (1858–1936) was perhaps the most influential of the American reformers. A gunnery expert and director of target practice at the time of writing, he also had the president's ear and was unafraid to use it. He was, however, hindered by his low rank at the time (commander) and so lacked the executive power of his counterpart in Britain, Admiral Fisher. He was also an unabashed Anglophile, which tended to act against him, particularly when advocating British-style reforms in the U.S. Navy. Sims earnestly believed in the merits of the large, all-big-gun ship with the speed necessary to dictate the terms of battle. He had been advocating them since working with Homer Poundstone on the original 1902 plans.

122 Ibid., p. 271.

123 See Mahan to William Henderson, 19 January 1907, acknowledging that the preponderance of service opinion has come out in favor of the dreadnought type; Seager and Maguire, *Letters and Papers of Alfred Thayer Mahan*, p. 204.

124 Sims, "Inherent Tactical Qualities of All-Big-Gun, One-Caliber Battleships," p. 287.

125 See General Board to SecNav, 9 January 1907.

126 Cdr. Albert Key commanded USS *Salem,* a scout cruiser that was undergoing yard work alongside the completing *North Dakota;* Key took the opportunity to examine the ship in detail. A copy of his letter, dated 18 June 1908, is reproduced in the 1908 summer conference papers, vol. 1, app. A, RG 8, NHC NWC. Another copy can be found in GB file 420.6, "Battleships," 1908 file, attached to SecNav to General Board, 2 July 1908, box 73, RG 80, NARA. President Roosevelt's letter to SecNav, dated 30 June, is reproduced in Elting E. Morison, ed., *The Letters of Theodore Roosevelt,* vol. 6, *The Big Stick, 1907–1909* (Cambridge, Mass.: Harvard Univ. Press, 1952), p. 1101.

127 The other allegations concerned the dubious placement of the number-three turret between the engine and boiler rooms (thus necessitating magazine cooling) and the alleged inferiority of the U.S. twelve-inch gun to those of France, Japan, and Great Britain. See "1908 Summer Conference," vol. 1, app. A, RG 8, NHC NWC.

128 James Reckner argues that although the reformers gained tacit acknowledgment of some of the defects in *North Dakota,* the discussion "did not properly address the issue of practical remedies." *North Dakota* was probably too far along in construction to make substantive changes; the case for *Florida* is less clear-cut. See James Reckner, *Teddy Roosevelt's Great White Fleet* (Annapolis, Md.: Naval Institute Press, 1988), pp. 130–31.

129 See the report of the General Board (app. F) and Committee 1 on the design of new ships (app. J), "1908 Summer Conference," vol. 1, RG 8, NHC NWC.

130 For Admiral Goodrich's letter, dated 12 August 1908, see "1908 Summer Conference," vol. 2, app. H, RG 8, NHC NWC.

131 Sims had made a last-ditch effort to induce the president to have both the conservative viewpoint and Sims's own reported to him for decision—and thereby to overturn the conference recommendations—but in the end, facing considerable professional and financial pressure, the president had little choice but to accept the majority view and approve the *Delaware* and *Florida* classes with only minor changes. See his letters to SecNav on 15 and 28 August, in Morison, *Letters of Theodore Roosevelt,* vol. 6, pp. 1174, 1199. See also Morison, *Admiral Sims and the Modern American Navy,* pp. 210–11.

132 See General Board letter to SecNav, dated 26 September 1908, "Types of Battleships to build," GB file 420.6, "Battleships," 1908 file, box 73, RG 80, NARA.

133 See Corbett's reasoning in note 54 above.

134 "1906 Summer Problem," questions 18 and 22, RG 12, NHC NWC.

135 Ibid., part III, p. 12.

136 See General Board to SecNav, 2 October 1906, "Types to Be authorized at 1906 Congress," GB file 420.2, "Building Program," 1900–1908 file, RG 80, NARA.

137 The *Delaware*s were too far along in the design process and had insufficiently long engine spaces to receive the Parsons installation.

138 Friedman, *U.S. Battleships,* p. 69.

139 See, for example, his letter to SecNav of 9 January 1907, where, citing the British lead, he urges the secretary to demand better from BuC&R. GB file 420.6, "Battleships," 1907 file, box 73, RG 80, NARA.

140 The *Amethyst* trials (originally reported in the *Times* on 13 December 1905) were written up in *Machinery* 12 (September 1905–August 1906), pp. 296–98. This article reported a crossover point, in terms of efficiency, around fourteen knots, but the author (Lester French) made much of the fact that at speeds above this *Amethyst* had a far greater radius of action than its piston counterpart. The *Lübeck* trial reports, originally in the *Nautical Gazette,* then in Professor Alger's "Professional Notes," *USNIP* 32 (1906), pp. 370–71, were similarly glowing, claiming superior overall coal consumption across a range of operating speeds between ten and twenty-three knots.

141 Alger, "Professional Notes," pp. 1615–16. (This article was originally attributed to the journal *Scientific American.*)

142 Sims (Bureau of Navigation) to General Board, 12 January 1907, GB file 428, "Foreign Vessels," 1900–1910 file, RG 80, NARA.

143 Captain Bacon was considered something of an authority on the matter. In addition to his experience at sea with the ship on trials, he was a close friend and confidant of Admiral Fisher and had served on the *Dreadnought* design committee.

144 General Board to BuC&R, 25 April 1907, GB file 420.6, "Battleships," 1907 file, box 73, RG 80, NARA. The board asked for specifications for turbines with cruising plant, for turbines without cruising plant, and for reciprocating engines, at ten, twelve, fourteen, and sixteen knots.

145 W. G. Diman, "The Turbine and Reciprocating Engine for Naval Purposes," *Journal of the American Society of Naval Engineers* 21 (February 1909), pp. 19–26.

146 Ibid., p. 26.

147 See Price to SecNav (via Lieutenant Commander Price's commanding officer), 1 October 1910, GB file 420.6, "Battleships," 1910 file, box 73, RG 80, NARA.

148 See BuC&R letter 26110-E.21 (signed by both BuC&R and BuEng), 6 December 1910, GB file 420.6, "Battleships," 1910 file, box 73, RG 80, NARA. The letter quotes endurance at twelve knots of only 5,606 miles for the turbine ship (as opposed to 7,060 for the reciprocating ship), whereas the distance to Manila from San Francisco is 6,238 miles, and from Seattle 5,978.

149 The General Board, in an endorsement of 14 December to BuC&R letter 26110-E.21 (note 148), disagrees, making the case for turbines on the bases of reliability, commonality with previous classes, and the likelihood of improvement in endurance. The board on 17 December canceled this endorsement and replaced it with a simple recommendation for the reciprocating plant, "based on the views of the Chief Constructor and the Engineer in Chief." GB file 420.6, "Battleships," 1910 file, box 73, RG 80, NARA.

150 For a more positive viewpoint see a letter written by Capt. Allen Gleaves of *North Dakota* to SecNav (via his fleet commander), dated 6 February 1911, General Correspondence of SecNav, file 26529, *North Dakota,* box 1288, RG 80, NARA. Gleaves points out that the turbine was at an immature stage of development and that improvements could be expected that, in view of its ease of operation, would make it a natural choice. He also argues that turbine ships are better gun platforms, because of less vibration.

151 See a summary article written after the fact by Charles Dyson, "Development of Machinery in the U.S. Navy during the Past Ten Years," pp. 195–238. This article clearly explains how the inefficiencies of the early turbines (in endurance particularly) made them unsuitable for the strategic problems facing the Navy at the time. Charles Wilson Dyson (1861–1930), was a noted marine engineer who wrote extensively for technical journals. He was head of the BuEng Design Division over the crucial years of 1906–18, where he had an unrivaled view of some of the greatest advances in marine propulsion ever seen. There is little reason to question his authority on the subject.

152 Arguably the only time the fast, all-big-gun ship (battle cruiser) was used in the manner that its creators intended occurred when two were dispatched to the South Atlantic in November 1914 to intercept Vice Adm. Maximilian von Spee's South East Asia Cruiser Squadron. The result was a classically lopsided victory, exactly as Fisher had always envisaged. For the remainder of the war, however, there being no global commerce-raiding threat, the ships were employed with the Grand Fleet, often with disastrous results.

IX Innovation for Its Own Sake
The Type XXI U-boat

MARCUS O. JONES

The origins of this article lie in a new study of the Nazi German economy by Adam Tooze, a fragment of which argues that the need to overcome the technological deficit built by the Western Allies in antisubmarine warfare from 1939 triggered a major shift in U-boat design and production after 1943.[1] Tooze points out that an emphasis on technological solutions to strategic and operational problems had by that point become a hallmark of the Nazis', and especially Hitler's, thinking. (Other examples were the Tiger and Panther tanks at Kursk, both of which types proved dysfunctional as platforms, and neither of which proved decisive to the outcome.) So interpreted, the Nazi penchant for imputing to innovation the means to solve a whole class of operational and strategic problems seems to resemble "technological fixes" in other fields of innovation.[2] In so arguing Tooze writes off the findings of Richard Overy, who points to the failure of the regime to develop positive relationships between industry and the war effort as reflecting a "peculiar irrationality of the 'Nazi social system.'" Tooze highlights the research of Ralf Schabel on jet-engine development in the aircraft industry, research asserting that exaggerated technological expectations resulted from Germany's hopeless strategic dilemma and that the systems themselves, while quite promising, were rushed into mass production and combat without adequate testing or development. Interestingly, he then characterizes Adm. Karl Dönitz's decision to embrace the Type XXI submarine in 1943, under the technocratic direction of Albert Speer's ministry, as reflecting both the increasing unreality of German armaments propaganda and a progressively more authoritarian cast of the German war economy.

While agreeing entirely with Tooze's identification of a strong relationship between Nazi Germany's broad strategic and economic problems and the technological innovations seen as panaceas for them, this paper argues that the U-boat Type XXI was nonetheless not nearly so unrealistic a solution as his account suggests, nor as reflective of a grossly dysfunctional culture of innovation as other commonly cited cases may be. If one assumes Nazi Germany's essentially flawed strategic decision to interdict the Allies' commerce traffic in the Atlantic, then the German navy, under the technological and operational constraints then prevailing, had no better option than to develop a platform that accomplished what the Type XXI promised. This revision of Tooze's case arises from the assumption that the culture of naval architecture and engineering before 1943, organized around largely traditional methods of design and construction, was wholly inadequate to Germany's strategic problems. In the absence of more promising alternatives, the decision to subordinate the shipbuilding industry ruthlessly to innovative technocratic priorities appears more rational than otherwise. It may also serve as a cautionary example of the extent to which social explanations of technological adaptation must include appreciation of the iron operational constraints on military effectiveness.

Naval warfare is arguably more revealing of the intimate connections among technological trends and broader political, economic, and military circumstances than is warfare of nearly any other kind. As Karl Lautenschläger has argued, "naval warfare in general is sensitive to changes in technology, because it is platforms as well as weapons that are necessary for combat at sea. Whereas armies have historically armed and supported the man, navies have essentially manned and supported the arm."[3] Determination of the reasons for the paths of innovation taken, as well as the pace and character of innovation itself, has bedeviled historians of technology for generations. Every military technological innovation is shaped by a complex of influences, but most notably by some conception, however well or poorly understood, of the operational scheme within which it is intended to fit.

The technologies that defined Germany's Atlantic campaigns had their roots in expectations about future conflict that seemed entirely reasonable in the 1930s but proved woefully misguided when the full implications of Hitler's strategic ambitions became apparent by 1942. In the decade before the war, the nascent Kriegsmarine envisioned a limited naval war primarily against France, and after 1938, England. The prevailing operational scheme, which found its strongest exponent in Adm. Erich Raeder, then commander in chief of the navy, emphasized a balanced fleet comprising heavy and light elements to threaten enemy naval and commercial interests in a dispersed manner. The primary role of submarines in this concept was twofold: to serve in a fleet-support and screening capacity, for which a limited number of larger, longer-range, and faster submarines would be required; and to conduct a commerce war of limited range and intensity against French, and later English, maritime assets in the eastern Atlantic, for which a large number of smaller, cheaper, and easily produced boats was necessary. Although some elements within the German naval command in the mid-1930s, notably Admiral Dönitz, envisioned a strategy of commerce interdiction that emphasized an autonomous role for U-boats, the then-prevailing doctrine saw the U-boat as but one of a broad mix of assets in a balanced fleet. Most importantly, and to the extent that the anti-commerce strategy of Dönitz could be said to have shaped procurement decisions in the late 1930s and early phases of the Second World War, the notion of wolf-pack tactics against convoys made the acquisition of as large a number as possible of comparatively simple, inexpensive, medium-sized submarines a priority in naval planning. However, at no point before 1942/43 could the German navy be said to have enjoyed a substantial priority in German armaments production. As a result, the German navy began the war with scarcely more than two dozen oceangoing submarines, and not before 1942, arguably past the critical point of balance in its commerce war against Britain, did it have a number sufficient to mount consistent group operations.

As those familiar with the course of the Atlantic war until May 1943 understand, initial German success was gradually eclipsed by superior Allied technology, code breaking, organization, and especially shipbuilding capacity—arguably the most decisive single element in determining the outcome of the naval war. On the tactical level, where the platforms themselves were decisive, the increasing number and effectiveness of Allied convoy escorts and countermeasures, especially electronic means of detection, led to unacceptably high losses of the Types VII and IX U-boats that made up the bulk of the German fleet. According to the commander of the U-boat force, Dönitz, losses to mid-1943 amounted at most to 13 percent of the deployed boats. The severe setbacks that the fleet suffered in early 1943 amounted to some 30 to 50 percent of the deployed force, with losses in May 1943 of forty-three boats, or more than a boat a day on average.[4] The limited utility of conventional diesel submarines had become irrefutably obvious. If defensive tactics could deny the submarine surface mobility and compel it to rely on its subsurface capability for survival, then it became nearly useless as an offensive weapon. Defensive platforms detected U-boats with radar, sonar, high-frequency direction finding ("Huff Duff"), and—most effectively—roving aircraft, which became increasingly common by late 1943. Aircraft or surface ships could then prosecute the contact, compelling the boat to dive and holding it down long enough for a convoy to lumber away. With its slow surface and even slower submerged speed, a conventional Type VII or IX U-boat was hard pressed to develop a second attack angle, and then only if antisubmarine units were not hounding it.

In a draft assessment of the naval strategic situation in September 1942, the Kriegsmarine High Command starkly expressed its first noteworthy reservations about whether the U-boat campaign could have the desired decisive effect on the Allies' capacity to sustain their war effort, a finding based as much on the vulnerability of existing platforms to Allied countermeasures as on anything else.[5] Although the finding was stricken, the final report acknowledged that "not one war in history was won by the use of a single weapon," a caution reflecting the simple fact that Germany could not sink enough tonnage fast enough to overcome the enormous American shipbuilding capacity.[6] Although Hitler had declared on many occasions that he considered U-boat warfare crucial for the overall war effort, not until after the surrender of the Sixth Army at Stalingrad did he seize on it as the sole remaining offensive potential available to the Third Reich and accord it a meaningful priority in war production.

These circumstances lay behind the radical shift in platform design and production priorities after 1943. The essential question facing the strategic leadership after the midyear debacle was whether to abandon the Atlantic—which would amount to an almost inconceivable admission by professional officers of the strategic bankruptcy of their service—or to redouble the effort and shift the terms on which commerce warfare was waged through evolutionary advances in platform survivability and effectiveness.[7] Dönitz, commander in chief of the German navy as of January 1943, opted for the latter, with the full backing of Hitler. The platform that would bring about this transformation was the Type XXI submarine.

Historians have generally thought of the Type XXI—along with other systems like the Me 262, V-1 and V-2 rockets, and the Tiger tank—as an example of *Wunderwaffen*, wonder weapons. Since 1945 many have fixated on the revolutionary military technologies that the Third Reich developed in the last two years of the war.[8] The cultural impetus behind the concept, as implicitly or explicitly acknowledged by historians in the uneven and largely enthusiastic literature on the subject, was an irrational faith in technology to prevail in operationally or strategically complex and desperate situations—a conviction amounting to a disease, to which many in the Third Reich were prone in the latter years of the Second World War.[9] To the extent that it shaped decision making, faith in the *Wunderwaffen* was a special, superficial kind of technological determinism, a confidence in the power of technology to prevail over the country's strategic, operational, and doctrinal shortcomings. To the extent that leaders, officers, engineers, and scientists after 1943 believed innovation to be the answer to Germany's strategic dilemmas, they displayed a naive ignorance of how technology interacts with cultural and other factors to influence the course of events. In particular, they reflected a willful ignorance of the extent to which even substantial technological superiority has proved indecisive in human conflict throughout history.[10]

The origins of the Type XXI program lay in a test platform built in 1939–40 by a brilliant propulsion engineer, Helmuth Walter, who intended it to serve as a prototype of a genuine submarine weapon.[11] Submarines to that point, their name notwithstanding, had actually been little more than extremely slow, vulnerable, largely helpless torpedo boats capable of brief submergence. The underwater speed and endurance of standard U-boat types were insufficient to stalk and close on typical convoys, though they traveled at speeds of only eight knots or less, and were barely adequate against slower formations; U-boats were forced to spend the bulk of their time on the surface, vulnerable to all manner of countermeasures. Walter's test bed, designated *V80,* achieved an impressive twenty-eight knots submerged and seemed to address the need for a genuine high-speed underwater platform. The boat suffered from a range of thorny technical problems, however, most notably the type and quantity of fuel required by the closed-cycle Walter engine—highly volatile Perhydrol, or hydrogen peroxide. To power the boat the Perhydrol was reduced by chemical processes, generating extremely high-pressure gases that spun a propeller-geared turbine at nearly twenty thousand revolutions per minute. A submarine operating such a closed-cycle system could remain submerged as long as its fuel supply permitted. However, the Walter turbine required colossal amounts of fuel to meet even modest performance parameters, far outstripping the bunkerage capacity of existing U-boat designs. Walter, ever inventive, therefore conceived of a U-boat with a pressure hull of a figure-eight form: the top half would house the machinery, weapons, and the crew, while the bottom would contain the large amount of fuel necessary to power the turbine. The design draft was designated the Type XVIII.

In a November 1942 meeting on U-boat design projects, the director of naval construction, Heinrich Ölfken, along with a pair of engineers, Friedrich Schürer and Klaus Bröking, happened on the idea of utilizing the Walter architecture to house a conventional electric propulsion system able to drive the boat at underwater speeds higher than those attained by existing designs.[12] The lower loop of the figure eight, where Perhydrol would have been stored, afforded space for an enormous increase in battery capacity, effectively triple that of a conventional Type IX U-boat.[13] The massive battery plant would run a powerful electric-drive system, necessitating diesel power to charge the batteries much less often than current boats required. Preliminary testing revealed that the performance of the hybrid design, although it fell far short of the prototype Walter boat, far exceeded that of existing platforms, especially underwater. Admiral Dönitz, still commander of the submarine force, agreed that the concept merited further development and approved additional design work and testing. Theoretical calculations and modeling were complete by January 1943; five months later, the naval staff was provided with a preliminary design draft.

The resulting boat, designated Type XXI, displaced some 1,620 tons and was capable of a submerged sprint of eighteen knots sustained for an hour and a half, a moderate speed of from twelve to fourteen knots for ten hours, and silent running at five knots for sixty hours. Most importantly, it was designed from the outset to incorporate the sensors, countermeasures, and other devices understood by that point to be indispensable in the commerce war: water-pressure-controlled automatic depth-keeping equipment, an improved passive listening array, active sonar, a radar-search receiver, effective active radar, and a snorkel. Dönitz presented the Type XXI design to Hitler at a conference on 8 July 1943 to win his approval for the additional allocations of resources and labor required to realize a production program. Having persuaded Hitler, Dönitz issued an order on 13 August for the full-scale transition to building *"Elektroboots."* Initially, he had intended the Type XXI to replace the outmoded Type IX, but after the catastrophic performance of his boats in May 1943 he determined that it should take the place of the Type VII convoy-attack boat as well.

One cannot exaggerate the importance of the experience of the U-boat service in May 1943 to Dönitz's decision to shift production to an entirely new platform in wartime. As the officers and sailors who manned the U-boat fleet, and who had fought so doggedly, now found, no amount of willpower or doctrinal ingenuity on the basis of existing boat types could overcome the collective effects of the countermeasures the Allies employed so well by 1943. The obsolescence of the German navy's U-boats, which in the early years of the war had been the scourge of the British war effort, had come about so quickly and completely that Germany was compelled in the circumstances of a failing war to attempt a leap in submarine capability simply to have any hope of affecting the Battle of the Atlantic. In other words, Dönitz argued, his submariners had no choice but to innovate further, on the basis of their disadvantage. Thus understood, the capabilities of conventional U-boats by 1943 represented a "reverse salient" in a technological system (in this case, the interlocking network of technologies and practices of a maritime commerce war as a whole)—that is, "components in the system that have fallen behind or are out of phase with the others."[14] In technological terms, the reverse salient is the weak link that impedes progress. The concept has its origins in descriptions of warfare, where it refers to a section of an advancing military front that has fallen behind the rest, typically becoming the point of weakness in an attack and a zone, a sack, of vulnerability in defense, a lagging element that prevents the rest of the force from fulfilling its objective. Until the reverse salient is corrected, an army's progress comes to a halt. "When a reverse salient cannot be corrected within the context of an existing system, the problem becomes a radical one, the solution of which may bring a new and competing system."[15]

Even had Germany produced a large number of Type XXI boats in time to field them during the war, or brought forth any at an earlier date, it is doubtful whether they could have corrected the salient and fulfilled the promise of the *Wunderwaffen*. Historians have spilled much ink to argue how revolutionary a technology the Type XXI was and how qualitatively different would have been the terms on which the Battle of the Atlantic was fought had Nazi Germany sent substantial numbers of these high-performance platforms to sea. But a sober consideration of the new boat's capabilities in the context of existing Allied countermeasures makes plain that it would not have shifted the terms as much as Dönitz and the rest of the German leadership hoped. The Type XXI offered no expansion of missions beyond the three basic ones performed by submarines between the outbreak of the First World War and the launch of nuclear-powered USS *Nautilus* in 1954: coastal defense, naval attrition, and commerce warfare.

To be sure, the class certainly stood to enhance the ability of the German submarine force to fulfill its missions more effectively. But it could not have enabled the force to perform the other three significant roles of submarines that arose later in the twentieth century: projection of power ashore, fleet engagement, and assured destruction. Only the nuclear submarine, with its ability to remain submerged as long as the crew could feed itself and remain sane, offered navies the means of fulfilling those tasks, and then only in conjunction with technologies as yet undeveloped during the war. Most importantly, the Type XXI would have done nothing to solve the target-acquisition problem, arguably the single greatest obstacle to success in the U-boat campaign against Allied shipping. Without long-range patrol aircraft to detect convoys and fix their positions, submarine commanders had to rely on what could be glimpsed from atop the conning towers of their tiny craft. Limiting the effective range of observation was not only the submarine's low freeboard but the generally miserable weather of the North Atlantic Ocean. Even patrol lines of U-boats strung out across large areas frequently missed sizable convoys, and the vast majority lumbered by anyway. Only the Luftwaffe, which Hermann Göring guarded with jealousy and bile, could address that deficiency. For these reasons, it is important to understand the Type XXI as an evolutionary technological development of existing undersea warfare technologies, as opposed to a platform of the kind that changes entirely the nature of naval power altogether.[16]

However, in the design and production of the Type XXI lay evidence of innovation greater than that represented by the platform itself. The two principal shortcomings in the German navy's approach to commerce interdiction in the Atlantic lay, first, in its resource disadvantage in the war economy relative to the other services —an inferiority that was itself a function of the lesser strategic significance of the Atlantic war for the Nazi regime—and second, in the capacity constraints of the German shipbuilding industry. The former shortcoming was addressed to some extent on a political level in mid-1943, when Dönitz secured Hitler's acknowledgment of the importance of the U-boat war and approval for the Type XXI program, along with his promise, however nebulous, to resource it adequately. Dönitz dealt with the latter in a more radical manner. No amount of political capital could extract a higher unit productivity from the already-stretched shipbuilding industry, which was understood by that point to be essential to turning the tide of the Atlantic war. Certainly, one could not reasonably expect Type XXI submarines to be produced at the same rate as earlier types, or anything like it, as the new design was far larger, more complex, expensive, and resource and manpower intensive than its predecessors. A transformation of shipbuilding itself was essential.

In 1942, German U-boat construction, which by this point accounted for the bulk of total shipbuilding capacity, was organized around largely traditional methods of design, engineering, and production. The navy enjoyed a preeminent position in defining standards and regulating construction processes, as well as generally warm relations with the traditional shipyards, all of which guaranteed a high level of quality but did not meet the demands of mass production in a materiel-intensive war effort. That unsuitability was apparent as early as 1941, when the minister for munitions, Fritz Todt, broached the possibility of setting up a "Main Committee" for shipbuilding, based on the promise of industrial self-regulation, to centralize and make more efficient U-boat production. Rudolf Blohm, head of the enormous Blohm und Voss shipyards and an archreactionary capitalist, chaired the new organization, along with Ernst Cords of Krupp Germaniawerft. A key obstacle to higher rates of production at acceptable cost was the navy's custom of ordering boats on a quarterly basis; true mass production of the requisite components, large and small, required larger orders over lengthier periods of time, for which manufacturers could plan and invest on an appropriate scale.[17]

The committee quickly brought about a partial and largely successful reorientation of production of the conventional Type VIIC, the standard U-boat class of the war. Noteworthy in these early reforms were the establishment of long-series production and the subcontracting of major-component manufacture on a provisional basis to inland steel-construction firms—the latter being a critical, often-overlooked precedent of the Type XXI program. Moving production of major subcomponents to inland subcontractors permitted the specialization of manufacturing processes and reduced the time a U-boat spent in the slips during assembly, important for increasing shipyard throughput and for reducing the yards' vulnerability to Allied strategic bombing.

As already described, with Dönitz's appointment as commander in chief of the German navy in January 1943, just prior to the disastrous convoy battles of May, came a major shift in the orientation of the U-boat fleet. Dönitz was persuaded that nothing short of an industrial miracle would supply enough Type XXI boats to tip the balance of the Atlantic war. In a devil's bargain, therefore, he relinquished the navy's traditional strict control over ship design, engineering, and construction to Albert Speer's armaments ministry, which at that point was expanding its control into every corner of the German war economy. Speer's price for the manpower and raw materials to mass-produce the new class of submarine was the subordination of the dockyards to his ministry. Even with the backing of his powerful organization, however, the best initial estimates for an accelerated development program foresaw the arrival of the first boats only in late 1944, with series production beginning in March 1945.[18] Conventional U-boats had generally required between two and two and a half years to mature from concept to serial production; assuming that a conventional development curve applied as well to the Type XXI—an optimistic assumption, since it was a far larger and more complex boat—the earliest the new class could join the fleet would be 1946. A breathing space for the Allies of more than two years would presumably mean the loss of the Atlantic entirely.

To close the time gap, Speer resolved to break the conservative engineering and construction culture of the established dockyards with a radical program of modular construction and dispersed, serialized component manufacturing. In July 1943 he appointed Otto Merker, an impetuous forty-year-old industrial engineer with extensive experience in automobile and fire-engine manufacturing, to head the Main Committee for Ship Construction. Merker proposed that the new class of U-boats be assembled from eight large, prefabricated sections weighing between seventy and 130 tons apiece, assembled inland by firms that had been to that point, in most cases, rolling and shaping plate steel for pressure hulls. The advanced design and engineering work for the new class and the detailed planning for its production were assigned to a new, centralized organization called the Ingenieurbüro Glückauf, established in Blankenburg/Halberstadt to take over tasks traditionally handled by the yards of individual shipbuilders. Intense Allied bombing and communication difficulties drove the decision both to centralize the Ingenieurbüro and to situate it far from the waterfront. Nearly 50 percent of all German steel firms were to be involved to varying extents in manufacturing and assembling the hull sections and machinery for the new boats; many of the vendors had never before performed high-precision finished work and would require substantial technical direction to meet the exacting standards of pressure-hull construction. The prefabricated sections were to be transported by barge on inland waterways to three final assembly points: Blohm und Voss in Hamburg, Deschimag in Bremen, and Schicau in Elbing, east of Danzig. Utilizing such methods, Merker claimed, the first Type XXI could be launched by 1 April 1944, with production rising to thirty boats per month by autumn of that year. In fact, with the entire organization leaning ruthlessly toward the lofty production targets, the first copy was launched—amid great fanfare—less than three weeks late, on 19 April 1944, the day before Hitler's birthday.

Nonetheless, the Type XXI U-boats had almost no impact on the outcome of the Second World War, save perhaps to absorb large amounts of manpower and resources that might have been devoted more wisely to the manufacture of aircraft, armored vehicles, artillery, and munitions. Indeed, a senior engineer in the naval shipbuilding program estimated that a single Type XXI submarine consumed a volume of armaments-grade steel equivalent to some thirty tanks, a meaningful offset for the war in light of the much shorter production time for an armored vehicle.[19] By that logic, the program cost the war effort some five thousand tanks, a very consequential figure, and could be said to have hastened the defeat of Germany on the

Eastern Front. The new class hardly seemed a formidable prospect at the outset, at any rate. The first copy, assembled hastily as a showpiece for the führer's birthday, leaked so badly upon launching that it required pontoons to remain afloat; following the ceremony, it was towed immediately to dry dock for extensive repair.

The extraordinary complexity of the new boats, the novelty of the tactical concepts they made possible, and the difficulties of training new crews to man them in the mine-infested waters of the Baltic—to say nothing of the vagaries of producing them as the Western Allies relentlessly bombed German production centers—ensured that none of the roughly eighty produced by the end of 1944 was fit for action on delivery. Only two sallied forth on war patrols before the end of hostilities; neither sank an enemy vessel. Early Type XXI hulls suffered from defective diesel-engine superchargers, faulty hydraulic torpedo-loading systems, trouble-prone steering systems, and countless other deficiencies, making them decidedly less of a threat than originally foreseen. The improvised character of the boats' production made addressing these early shortcomings daunting. Basic to modern naval shipbuilding—and among the greatest challenges to effective platform development throughout the history of modern military procurement—is the feedback loop from the fleet back to the design bureau and shipyard about the actual operation of a vessel on patrol and in combat. Almost no early iteration of a ship class emerges from the slipways in a form optimized for its mission, and countless changes, large and small, factor into subsequent iterations.[20] The very processes that ensure the efficiency of serial production make such loops challenging, if not impossible, to establish. It had been this concern that lay at the core of navy objections to the abdication of authority over shipbuilding to the Speer organization, and it proved a major reason for the checkered early history of the program.

Certainly, the authors of the production concept had enormous obstacles to surmount to realize its potential.[21] As has been noted, few of the inland firms tasked with constructing the hull segments and machinery could initially meet the standards required, at least under the fraught circumstances of a failing war and the ruthless timetables established by Speer's organization. The tolerances involved in submarine construction were and remain extremely exacting. Type XXI hull sections were initially delivered to the shipyards with deviations of up to three centimeters in some cases and had to be torn apart and reconstructed properly—with massive outlays of time and effort—in the ways. Pressure testing revealed potentially lethal defects in the welding of the first boats, a result of poorly fitting components, new inspection standards, and construction methods unfamiliar to the facilities performing them. But the design agency, engineering staff, and shipyards addressed and overcame these problems by autumn 1944.

However, easily the greatest impediment to full realization of the serial production process, as postwar assessments make clear, was the intense and devastating Allied bombing campaign against its key components, especially the shipyards and installations at the waterfront.[22] The increasing vulnerability of the shipbuilding industry to bombing had made it necessary to scatter and move production away from launch sites. Enormous resources and labor were devoted to the construction of an elaborate inland system of barges and cranes to transship the boat segments to the finishing yards. The delivery system never really functioned smoothly, and in any case a sizable administrative apparatus was required to oversee the just-in-time process. The ingenuity of the Merker organization was never adequate to the challenge of Allied strategic bombing, the downstream effects of which were felt at every point.

Conclusion

As Tooze sensibly points out, "the disappointment of the XXI programme was due to the familiar problems of pushing a revolutionary new design straight from the drawing board into mass production, without extensive testing."[23] He faults the Speer ministry in particular, for clinging stubbornly to the system of dispersed sectional construction, arguing that an evolutionary approach to production, instead of a revolutionary new one, would have likely yielded more favorable results. Indeed, the engineer Friedrich Schürer raised such concerns in late 1943, as the joint complications involved in both a radical new platform and novel methods of engineering and production became increasingly clear. He suggested that the construction of the first boat proceed in a conventional, customized fashion, to develop experience with the platform itself. As Merker pointed out, however, to build the first Type XXI by conventional means would require no less than eight months, while the sectional method, however flawed, would require only four. The entire apparatus of dispersed sectional construction, moreover, was scheduled to commence operation in April 1944.[24] Merker's argument cuts to the entire point of the program—time was of the essence. The desperate operational and strategic circumstances of the German naval campaign in the Atlantic necessitated no less than an all-or-nothing approach to the production of the only platform that offered any prospect of success against an overwhelming Allied technological and materiel advantage.

As Dönitz well understood, a small number of even superlative boats would have produced little change in the Atlantic. The only hope for an effective naval interdiction strategy lay in building the Type XXI in numbers similar to, or greater than, those in which the Type VIIs had been constructed before 1943, thereby overcoming simultaneously the Allied superiorities in technology and in materiel. As we have seen, that goal was not achieved. But even so, it is astounding that a platform as complex and resource intensive—by the standards of any combatant nation—as the Type XXI could move from the drawing board to the water in a year, and by a radically new manufacturing process. The technology of the platform itself ultimately amounted to no more than an incremental or evolutionary improvement in the German ability to close the Atlantic; it most probably would not have realized the extraordinary effectiveness hoped for by its proponents then and admirers today. But the innovative method of constructing the new class represented a revolutionary transformation of economic practice in a war defined primarily by the mobilized productive potentials of the combatants.

NOTES   This chapter previously appeared as an article in the *Naval War College Review* (Spring 2014).

1 Adam Tooze, *The Wages of Destruction: The Making and Breaking of the Nazi German Economy* (London: Allen Lane, 2006), pp. 611–18.

2 See the definition, building on the enthusiastic notions of Alvin Weinberg about nuclear power and the guarded optimism of John G. Burke in his reflections on engineering education, in Lisa Rosner, ed., *The Technological Fix: How People Use Technology to Create and Solve Problems* (New York: Routledge, 2004), pp. 1–3. A technological fix is a useful innovation intended to solve a problem but that frequently distracts attention from other or better solutions or leads to worse problems. The record of such fixes in areas as wide-ranging as horticulture and computer networking demonstrates that initial assumptions are rarely, if ever, fulfilled, and that technological fixes generally wind up as partial solutions to complex problems.

3 Karl Lautenschläger, "Technology and the Evolution of Naval Warfare," *International Security* 8, no. 2 (Fall 1983), p. 5; Phillips Payson O'Brien, ed., *Technology and the Evolution of Naval Combat in the Twentieth Century and Beyond* (Portland, Ore.: Frank Cass, 2001).

4 Bundesarchiv-Militärarchiv [hereafter BA-MA] RM6/374, Die deutsche Seekriegführung, 6 August 1945. Dönitz's interim solution to the high losses—reallocation of assets to other theaters and truncated patrol patterns—amounted to a temporary strategic abandonment of the Atlantic war.

5 Frigattenkapitän Heinz Assman, "Entwurf der Lagebeurteilung vom 20. September 1942," cited in Werner Rahn, "Der Seekrieg im Atlantik und Nordmeer," in *Das Deutsche Reich und der Zweite Weltkrieg,* vol. 6, *Der globale Krieg: Die Ausweitung zum Weltkrieg und der Wechsel der Initiative 1941 bis 1943,* ed. Militärgeschichtliches Forschungsamt (Stuttgart, Ger.: Deutsche Verlags-Anstalt, 1990), p. 304.

6 "Lagebetrachtung vom 20. Oktober 1942: Stand und Aussichten der U-bootkriegs, Anlage 1," in *Die deutsche Seekriegsleitung,* vol. 3, *Denkschriften und Lagebetrachtungen,* ed. Michael Salewski (Frankfurt am Main, Ger.: Bernard & Graefe, 1973), p. 303.

7 The author gladly concedes that there are grounds to argue that either a strategic abandonment of the Atlantic to the Western Allies or a less-intensive spoiling strategy of limited commerce interdiction and harassment would have been a more sensible alternative to the decision to redouble the effort. Such concerns belong in another venue; for strategic context, see Werner Rahn, "Strategische Optionen und Erfahrungen der deutschen Marineführung 1914 bis 1944: zu der Chancen und Grenzen einen mitteleuropäischen Kontinentalmacht gegen Seemacht," in *Deutsche Marinen im Wandel: vom Symbol nationaler Einheit zum Instrument internationaler Sicherheit,* ed. Rahn (Munich, Ger.: Oldenbourg, 2005), pp. 220–25.

8 A good introduction is provided by Ulrich Albrecht, "Military Technology and National Socialist Ideology," in *Science, Technology and National Socialism,* ed. Monika Renneberg and Mark Walker (New York: Cambridge Univ. Press, 1994), pp. 88–125.

9 Serious scholarship on the *Wunderwaffen* and the interconnections of technology, politics, military research and development, the armaments industry, and the administrative organization of the Third Reich remains limited to Ralf Schabel, *Die Illusion der Wunderwaffen: die Rolle der Düsenflugzeuge und Flugabwehrraketen in der Rüstungspolitik des Dritten Reiches* (Munich, Ger.: Oldenbourg, 1994), and Michael J. Neufeld, *The Rocket and the Reich: Peenemünde and the Coming of the Ballistic Missile Era* (New York: Free Press, 1995).

10 George Raudzens, "War-Winning Weapons: The Measurement of Technological Determinism in Military History," *Journal of Military History* 54, no. 4 (1990), pp. 403–34. Raudzens's conceptual confusions and imprecisions notwithstanding, his argument underscores how strongly wedded many in the modern age of military conflict have become to technological panaceas.

11 Emil Kruska and Eberhard Rössler, *Walter-U-Boote,* Wehrwissenschaftliche Berichte (Munich, Ger.: J. F. Lehmann, 1969), vol. 8. On Walter, see Karl Günther Strecker, *Vom Walter-U-Boot zum Waffelautomaten: die Geschichte eines großen deutschen Ingenieurs und der erfolgreichen Konversion seiner Rüstungsfirma* (Berlin: Köster, 2001).

12 Ölfken, cover letter to a staff lecture, 30 November 1943, p. 123, BA-MA RM 7-98.

13 Abschrift, Typ XXI Enstehungsgeschichte, 25 June 1943, 0143, BA-MA N379-146.

14 Thomas Parke Hughes, "The Evolution of Large Technological Systems," in *The Social Construction of Technological Systems: New Directions in the Sociology and History of Technology,* ed. Wiebe E. Bijker, Thomas P. Hughes, and Trevor J. Pinch (Cambridge, Mass.: MIT Press, 1987), p. 73. Similarly, "as the system evolves toward a goal, some components fall behind or out of line. As a result of the reverse salient, growth of the entire enterprise is hampered, or thwarted, and thus remedial action is required"; Hughes, *Networks of Power: Electrification in Western Society, 1880–1930* (Baltimore, Md.: Johns Hopkins Univ. Press, 1983).

15 Hughes, "Evolution of Large Technological Systems," p. 75.

16 See Seekriegsleitung IIIa to I op, 24 June 1943, pp. 425–26, BA-MA RM 7-98, for a penetrating and refreshingly frank German "red team" analysis of the limitations of the Type XXI as a prospective undersea platform. Such dissenting assessments by senior naval staff personnel reveal a rejection of the basic operational and tactical suppositions of the new program. Of greater historical significance, however, is the argument that the doctrinal and technological prerequisites for defeating a Type XXI–like threat were by 1945 already securely in place; see Owen R. Cote, Jr., *The Third Battle: Innovation in the U.S. Navy's Silent Cold War Struggle with Soviet Submarines,* Newport Paper 16 (Newport, R.I.: Naval War College Press, 2003), pp. 13–18.

17 Ölfken and Arendt, "Die Baumethoden der deutschen U-Boote," 28 March 1948, p. 18, BA-MA N518-5.

18 Hauptamt Kriegsschiffbau, Aktenvermerk, 13 October 1943, pp. 18–19, BA-MA N379-146. As the note makes clear, a conventional construction path for the first boat was considered and rejected.

19 Heinrich Waas, "Eine Besprechung über den U-Boot-Krieg bei Hitler in der Reichskanzlei im Herbst 1942 und ihre Bedeutung für den Kriegsverlauf," *Geschichte in Wissenschaft und Unterricht* 38 (1987), p. 692.

20 Memorandum to Admiral Fuchs, re Organisation K-Amt, 19 June 1944, BA-MA N379-146.

21 The U.S. Navy began designing and constructing nuclear-powered attack submarines in large modular segments in the late 1980s and encountered problems nearly as debilitating as those to which the Type XXI production method gave rise. The construction yards at Electric Boat and Newport News required years to work the kinks out of what has since become a smooth process. See William J. Brougham, "Accuracy Control Risk Management for Modular Submarine Hull Construction" (master's thesis, MIT, Cambridge, Mass., 1999).

22 On the scale of the problem during the war, see "Über die Besprechung des Ob.d.M. mit dem Führer auf dem Berghof vom 4.–6. Mai 1944," 17 May 1944, pp. 242–45, BA-MA RM 7-189.

23 Tooze, *Wages of Destruction,* p. 616.

24 Hauptamt Kriegsschiffbau, Aktenvermerk, 13 October 1943. See also Dr. Heinrich Ölfken, Vortag, pp. 126–27, BA-MA RM 7-98.

X FREQUENT WIND, *Option IV*
The 29–30 April 1975 Helicopter Evacuation of Saigon

JOHN F. GUILMARTIN, JR.

The 29–30 April 1975 helicopter evacuation of Saigon, technically "Option IV" of Operation FREQUENT WIND, remains to this day the largest helicopter airlift ever. According to the official tally, 1,373 Americans and 6,442 non-Americans were taken from the city by helicopter, along with 989 Marines of the ground security force who had been inserted at the beginning of the evacuation.[1] As I will argue later, the figures are surely low and their precision illusory. So is the accuracy of their categorization. "Americans" lumps together civilians and, I presume, American military personnel who were not part of the ground security force (GSF). "Non-Americans" includes Vietnamese and friendly third-country nationals. More important, it lumps together Vietnamese deemed particularly at risk in the wake of communist victory, who were on prioritized lists of evacuees, and others, civilian and military, who gained entry to the evacuation staging areas through connections, force, or blind luck. Tragically, those in the second category vastly outnumbered those in the first.

Still, while we left behind many who should have been evacuated and evacuated many who would not have been high on anybody's prioritized list, we—by which I mean military helicopter crews; helicopter crews and ground personnel of Air America, the Central Intelligence Agency's (CIA's) airlift organization; the ground security force Marines; members of the embassy staff and civilian volunteers who helped maintain order in the staging areas; and ships' crews and operations personnel who maintained the helicopters and imposed a degree of order on the operation—did a magnificent job of rapidly transporting large numbers of people under difficult conditions. To the list of those deserving kudos, I would add the crews of Air Force, Navy, and Marine fighter and attack aircraft who provided fire support as needed—mostly it wasn't, with one significant exception of which I am aware—and the crews of the command-and-control aircraft and tankers who supported them. Certain of those in senior command billets deserve kudos as well, notably Rear Adm. Donald Whitmire, commander of Task Force (TF) 76; Brig. Gen. Richard E. Carey, who controlled all Marine helicopter assets; and Col. Alfred M. Gray, Jr., commander of the 4th Marine Regiment, which provided the ground security force.

It should be clear from the length of the above list that Option IV—the focus of this paper—was a complex operation but only part of the Saigon evacuation. There was a maritime component to FREQUENT WIND, Option III, which accounted for over two thousand evacuees. The South Vietnamese navy mounted its own remarkably successful evacuation. The South Vietnamese air force (VNAF) got out a significant number of its personnel and their families in an extemporized last-minute evacuation by fixed-wing aircraft and helicopter. Of direct relevance to Option IV, Air Marshal Nguyen Cao Ky, retired but still chief of the VNAF, intervened in the early morning hours of 29 April, taking off in his personal UH-1 Huey helicopter, scrambling VNAF A-1H fighter-bombers from Can Tho air base to the south, and personally directing them in suppressive attacks on North Vietnamese rocket batteries shelling Saigon's Tan Son Nhut airport, the site of the primary evacuation terminal.[2] Also of relevance, the crew of a VNAF AC-119K side-firing gunship took off from Tan Son Nhut at about the same time and spent the balance of the night suppressing communist fire around the airfield before making the ultimate sacrifice at 0700 (7 AM), shot down by an SA-7 shoulder-fired, heat-seeking missile.[3]

As the above preamble suggests, the helicopter evacuation of Saigon was not only a complex operation but one in which decision makers at all levels in the chain of command had to deal with uncertainty and the unexpected to an uncommon degree. There is much to be learned from a close examination of Option IV, and to that we now turn.

The story begins with the January 1973 Paris Peace Accords, essentially a cease-fire, which permitted North Vietnam to keep and sustain sizable forces within South Vietnam, while the American military presence was restricted to fifty officers assigned to the Defense Attaché Office (DAO) in Saigon and 159 Marines assigned as guards to consular offices in Da Nang, Nha Trang, Bien Hoa, and Can Tho.[4] The DAO was housed in the old Military Assistance Command Vietnam (MACV) headquarters on Tan Son Nhut airfield. Manned by 1,200 American civilians and 3,500 Vietnamese, in addition to the fifty officers, it was charged with orchestrating American support to South Vietnam, and it reported to the ambassador. On 29 March 1973, MACV was decommissioned and replaced as the senior U.S. headquarters in Southeast Asia by the U.S. Support Activities Group (USSAG, pronounced "you sog"), based at Nakhon Phanom Royal Thai Air Force Base, Thailand, and commanded by Lt. Gen. John J. Burns, U.S. Air Force (USAF), who also commanded Seventh Air Force.

By the time the cease-fire went into effect, we had augmented the South Vietnamese armed forces with a massive infusion of arms and equipment and reserved the right to resupply and to replace worn-out or destroyed equipment. The communists were bound by similar restrictions, but predictably they ignored them, so in the final analysis South Vietnam's survival depended on America's willingness to provide continuing economic and logistical support and to intervene militarily should the communist forces blatantly violate the terms of the treaty. Indeed, President Richard Nixon had secured the acquiescence of the South Vietnamese president, Nguyen Van Thieu, to the terms of the accords with a promise of military intervention should that become necessary.

On the positive side of the balance, by 1973 the guerrilla struggle was over in the South, with the Saigon government the victor. Though South Vietnam's military and civil institutions were penetrated by communist agents, the Viet Cong had effectively ceased to exist as a force in the villages. In the countryside, President Thieu's 1970 land reforms had leveled out the differences between the very wealthy and wretchedly poor, and the introduction of improved strains of rice had produced the beginnings of real agrarian prosperity.[5] True, communist forces occupied large chunks of South Vietnamese territory, but mostly in sparsely populated areas of the Central Highlands occupied during the 1972 Easter Offensive.

On the negative side of the balance, Soviet and Chinese support for North Vietnam remained strong, and congressional action had progressively curtailed U.S. military activity in the rest of Indochina, giving communist forces a free hand in their struggle with increasingly enfeebled government forces in Laos and Cambodia. With the threat of American bombs gone, the communist forces improved the Ho Chi Minh Trail, paving much of it and installing a gasoline pipeline running from North Vietnam into the Central Highlands. The communist-occupied zones of the South, though of little value politically or economically, would serve as useful jumping-off positions for a general offensive. The war was increasingly unpopular with the American intelligentsia; and news media and the public had largely lost interest. Against this political backdrop, Congress, with the antiwar faction calling the shots, progressively reduced economic aid to South Vietnam. Last and far from least, President Nixon's resignation in August 1974 sharply reduced the chances of U.S. military intervention to preserve South Vietnam.

The beginning of the end came in mid-December 1974, with a North Vietnamese attack on the provincial capital of Phuoc Long, north of Saigon. The town was lost on 6 January after a bitter struggle, becoming the first provincial capital to fall permanently into communist hands.[6] The place itself was of little strategic importance, and with the wisdom of hindsight it appears that a primary purpose of the attack was to gauge the American response. There was none, meaning a green light for the offensive that followed.

The next blow came in Cambodia on 1 January, with the beginning of the Khmer Rouge's anticipated dry-season offensive. It struck the eastern perimeter of Phnom Penh, throwing the Forces Armées Nationales Khmères into disarray. Unlike the loss of Phuoc Long, the Khmer Rouge offensive elicited an American response, albeit a defensive one. Only a massive application of American airpower had kept Phnom Penh from falling in 1973, and in 1974 the forces of Gen. Lon Nol's government had unexpectedly hung on by their teeth, but it was widely anticipated that Cambodia might fall in 1975. Joint U.S. Navy, Marines, and Air Force planning to evacuate from Phnom Penh not only Americans but Cambodians deemed particularly at risk in the event of communist victory and friendly third-country nationals had been under way since 1973. Indeed, two Air Force H-53 squadrons—the 21st Special Operations Squadron (21st SOS) and the 40th Aerospace Rescue and Recovery Squadron (40th ARRS)—had been retained at Nakhon Phanom in eastern Thailand for precisely that purpose. The preferred evacuation plan—EAGLE PULL—hinged on the use of Marine CH-53s of squadron HMH-462 (HMH for Helicopter Marine Heavy) embarked on the assault carrier USS *Okinawa* (LPH 3), assigned to TF 76 and operating in the Gulf of Thailand. The Air Force helicopters were insurance should the fall come before TF 76 could deploy. In either case, air support would be provided by Thailand-based USAF fighter-bombers, AC-130 side-firing gunships, and OV-10 forward-air-control aircraft. As in all such cases, the authority to order the evacuation and responsibility for in-country planning fell on the American ambassador.

The ambassador to Cambodia, the Honorable John Gunther Dean, was a man of foresight, courage, and competence. His staff had kept him abreast of evacuation planning from the outset, and with the start of the Khmer Rouge offensive he collapsed his up-country intelligence nets, recalling Americans and their Cambodian assets to the provincial capitals and from there to Phnom Penh. They were flown out by commercial air until communist rockets and the congressional ban on the use of U.S. military forces in Cambodia forced reliance on contract airlift (Air Force C-130s on loan to civilian contractors), steadily reducing the number of potential evacuees. Still, the number of projected evacuees was large, and it swelled as the Khmer Rouge drew closer to Phnom Penh. The Navy responded by dispatching from Hawaii a second Marine H-53 squadron, HMH-463, embarked on the attack carrier USS *Hancock* (CV 19). It arrived just in time.

On 9 April Ambassador Dean notified the military authorities that EAGLE PULL would go down on the 12th. On the day of the evacuation, Dean spent his last fifteen minutes in the embassy on the telephone with Premier Long Boret, pleading for the release of eight hundred Cambodians deemed particularly at risk. The premier refused, saying, in essence, "It's our country. We'll go down fighting." Dean stood at attention as his security detail lowered the flag, got into his limousine, and departed for the landing zone (LZ). His foresight had reduced the number of evacuees to the point that a single LZ in Phnom Penh sufficed, and the operation went off without a hitch. Two HH-53Cs from the 40th ARRS inserted and extracted the Marine command-and-control team that had been forward deployed to Nakhon Phanom. Marine H-53s inserted and extracted Marines of the ground security force and took out 276 evacuees.[7] CH-53s of the 21st SOS orbited over Phnom Penh, unneeded. Air Force OV-10s watched overhead, ready to direct suppressive air strikes. None were required. Its job done, TF 76 departed for Subic Bay in the Philippines on the 15th, arriving at midday on the 17th.

Meanwhile, things had gone badly in South Vietnam. On 10 March, communist forces attacked Ban Me Thuot in the Central Highlands. They were well supplied with tanks and artillery and protected by an antiaircraft umbrella featuring SA-2 radar-guided surface-to-air missiles and shoulder-fired SA-7 heat-seeking missiles that effectively neutralized the VNAF in daylight.[8] The day after the attack on Ban Me Thuot, President Thieu called his senior military commanders to a meeting in the Independence Palace and informed them of his intention to abandon the northern half of the country, pulling back to defend the south.[9] A sensible plan on paper, it failed to take into account the impact on troop morale in an army whose soldiers' families lived close to their units. Some units fought well; others simply melted away.

President Thieu gave the order to abandon the Central Highlands on 14 March. Ban Me Thuot fell on 18 March, and any hope of orderly withdrawal dissolved in the panic that ensued. The attack in the Central Highlands was followed by a major drive in northernmost South Vietnam; Da Nang fell on 29 March, again amid scenes of chaos. In Da Nang Harbor, cargo ship SS *Pioneer Contender,* hired by Military Sealift Command to take off evacuees and now loaded to the gunwales, was boarded by terror-stricken soldiers of the Army of the Republic of Vietnam (ARVN), who raped the women and seized control of the vessel's decks. The captain and crew locked themselves in the bridge. Five days later a small Marine boarding party rescued the crew and reestablished order. An astonishing seventeen thousand persons were aboard.[10] A final civilian Boeing 727 flight into Da Nang was mobbed by fleeing ARVN soldiers, who tried to force their way on board and were driven off by force as it took off from a taxiway. The landing gear failed to retract, jammed by the body of a soldier who had climbed into a wheel well; the crew proceeded to Tan Son Nhut at low altitude with the landing gear extended. When the aircraft came to a halt, several soldiers dropped still alive from the wheel wells, saved by their crushed compatriot. Cartoonist Jeff McNelly was to catch the bitter irony of the moment in his depiction of a parked Boeing 727 with a pair of lifeless legs dangling from a wheel well—wearing Uncle Sam's striped trousers and star-spangled spats.

By 9 April, communist spearheads had reached the eastern approaches to Saigon at Xuan Loc. There the ARVN 18th Division, reinforced by elements of the Airborne Brigade, made an epic stand, fighting the equivalent of three North Vietnamese divisions to a standstill, but it was too little and too late.

As all this was going on, a flood of refugees descended on Saigon, including—as had been the case in Cambodia—survivors of the up-country intelligence nets, though their concentration this time was chaotic and ill coordinated. Various American agencies compiled lists of Vietnamese with whom they had worked and so were deemed at risk in the event of a communist takeover and arranged for their billeting.

A plan for an evacuation of Saigon had been on the books since the summer of 1974, under the code name TALON VISE, later changed to FREQUENT WIND.[11] It had five options: Option I, evacuation by civilian airlift from Tan Son Nhut; Option II, evacuation by military airlift; Option III, evacuation by sealift; and Option IV, evacuation by military helicopter. An Option V, involving the movement by road of 130,000 evacuees to the port of Vung Tau for evacuation by sea, escorted by the remnants of the ARVN elite forces, was briefly considered but dropped.[12]

Option I proceeded more or less automatically as long as commercial aircraft could use Tan Son Nhut, though it was severely hampered by the embassy and the Saigon government's insistence on punctilious enforcement of the dictates of American and South Vietnamese emigration and immigration law. Option II would proceed in parallel with Option I and would take over when the military situation dictated. Option III involved seaborne evacuation from the port of Saigon; by the time of implementation, it relied on a single tank landing ship and three large barges towed by two hired deep-sea tugboats now moored at the Saigon docks. Option IV would depend on Task Force 76. The Navy and Marines took their commitment to Option IV seriously, but a lack of meaningful guidance from the embassy left them at sea, both literally and figuratively. General Burns at Nakhon Phanom, who would be in overall command of the operation once the ambassador gave the order to execute, was no better off.

As the North Vietnamese juggernaut closed on the capital, Admiral Whitmire, General Carey, Colonel Gray, and their staffs had little to work with in terms of anticipated numbers of evacuees, availability of air support and the constraints placed on it, or timing. The principal cause was the refusal of the ambassador, the Honorable Graham Martin, to confront the reality of the situation. An able diplomat with a distinguished record and a long-standing commitment to the American cause in Southeast Asia, Martin was a forceful personality with courtly manners and an icy reserve. Hardworking to an extreme, he was capable of fierce loyalty to subordinates but demanded unswerving obedience in return. Autocratic in style, he did not take challenges to his views lightly.[13] By the spring of 1975, he was not in the best of health.

Since June 1973, when he assumed his post, Martin had fought hard for the public support and congressional funding that South Vietnam needed to survive. For reasons readily understandable in terms of the political realities he faced, Martin sought to put the best face on the political and military situation and insisted that his subordinates do likewise.[14] But what began as a strategy for dealing with Congress and the news media came to dominate the embassy's perception of reality.

By the spring of 1975, the ambassador was surrounded by an inner circle that accepted and fed his predispositions. As South Vietnam's army disintegrated, the embassy clung to business as usual. In fairness to Martin, he was not alone in his slowness to appreciate how critical the situation had become; in American diplomatic and military circles generally, not until the withdrawal of South Vietnamese forces from the Central Highlands in panic-stricken rout after the fall of Ban Me Thuot did the notion that South Vietnam might collapse before the onset of the wet monsoon begin to gain acceptance.[15] For his part, the ambassador was aware of the existence of plans for evacuation but restrained his subordinates' desire to make overt preparations for evacuation for fear of unleashing the kind of chaos that had swept Da Nang.

Some preparatory measures for a helicopter evacuation were taken, notably by military officers of the DAO staff in organizing procedures for evacuees under Options I and II that would apply also to Option IV. The establishment of an evacuation center in the DAO compound, ominously code-named "Alamo," and in the adjacent DAO compound annex and the marking of nearby helicopter pads were central in this regard.[16] Air America, the CIA's contract airline, which operated a fleet of UH-1s out of Tan Son Nhut as well as an assortment of fixed-wing transports, made critical contributions to Option IV preparations. Air America pilots identified and marked thirteen rooftop helipads from which evacuees could be extracted and moved to the DAO compound for evacuation.[17] DAO communications officers had ordered a satellite communications terminal, a novelty in 1975. It arrived in Saigon the day after Da Nang fell and was promptly set up.[18]

As Option I merged into Option II, DAO personnel wrestled with the bureaucratic strictures imposed by the embassy and South Vietnamese authorities, and the pace of evacuation remained glacial, despite the availability of abundant airlift. Not until 19 April did personal intervention with the ambassador by General Burns and Adm. Noel Gayler, Commander in Chief, U.S. Pacific Command, produce relief —infants accompanied by parents were no longer required to have passports and full emigration papers.[19] The tempo of Option II briefly surged, but again it was too little and too late.

The next, crucial, development came as the result of the actions of Brig. Gen. Richard Baughn, USAF, the senior Air Force officer assigned to the DAO, under Maj. Gen. Homer Smith, U.S. Army. Baughn, a veteran of P-51 missions over Europe as a young lieutenant in 1944–45, had flown F-105s over North Vietnam in 1965–66; he was a seasoned military professional with few illusions.[20] He had arrived in Saigon in the summer of 1974 and had been disturbed by what he perceived as lassitude, an attitude of business as usual, in the embassy and an unwillingness on the part of the ambassador and his staff to face military reality. Shortly thereafter a retired French colonel visiting Vietnam, a paratroop veteran of the French war, paid Baughn a courtesy call. Baughn asked a favor of him: Would he report back in six months with his assessment of the situation? Six months later to the day, the colonel presented himself in Baughn's office with a grim prognosis, highlighting inefficiency, graft, and corruption in the ARVN command structure and their adverse effects on morale.[21] His bleak assessment was no doubt in Baughn's mind as he considered the deteriorating situation.

On or about 9 April, Baughn, increasingly concerned about the prospects of imminent ARVN collapse and the inadequate preparations for evacuation, contacted Maj. Gen. Kenneth Houghton, commander of the 3rd Marine Division on Okinawa, through military channels—in defiance of Ambassador Martin's ban on outside communication without his knowledge—and stated an urgent need for staff coordination between the Marines and DAO. In apparent response to Baughn's request, Col. Al Gray, commander of the 4th Marines and the man responsible for ground security arrangements in the event of an evacuation, flew in by helicopter with a small staff on the 11th.[22] Baughn and Gray met the next day and jointly concluded that the time for action had come; Gray, who had been monitoring the situation on the ground through frequent trips into Saigon from Admiral Whitmire's flagship, had needed little convincing. He and Baughn drafted a message to send up the military chain of command over Baughn's signature emphasizing the need for Marines on the ground in Saigon and the urgent need to begin plans for a helicopter evacuation. It went out unseen by the ambassador—who read it in the communications center in the early morning hours. He hit the ceiling and called Secretary of Defense James Schlesinger, demanding and securing Baughn's immediate expulsion from Saigon.[23] Baughn had fallen on his sword, but his principled act of disobedience marked the start of serious preparation for Option IV.

Admiral Whitmire and Brigadier General Carey flew into Saigon on the 13th and, accompanied by Colonel Gray, had their only meeting with Ambassador Martin. Gray was later to characterize the meeting as "brief and thoroughly unproductive."[24]

The ambassador continued to live in a world of real fears and illusory hopes, but Baughn had broken the logjam. Task Force 76 reached Subic Bay in the Philippines around midday on the 17th, only to be alerted for deployment the following afternoon with orders to be "on station and prepared for action" off Saigon by the 20th.[25] The order came without warning, and many crewmen ashore on liberty were left behind.

The 9th Marine Amphibious Brigade, comprising Marine assets committed to Option IV, was activated on the 18th, commanded by Brigadier General Carey, an aviator. Several days earlier, the Navy/Marine command structure responded to the magnitude of the projected evacuation by requesting the deployment of ten Air Force H-53s from Nakhon Phanom to the attack carrier USS *Midway* (CV 41). Despite the Navy's unease about the unfamiliarity of Air Force helicopter crews with deck handling procedures and its reluctance to clog *Midway*'s flight deck (unlike their Marine equivalents, Air Force H-53s lacked folding rotor blades and could not be struck below unless the blades were removed, a lengthy procedure), the transfer was made on the 20th, the day the battle of Xuan Loc ended. Threatened with being surrounded, the remnants of the ARVN 18th Division withdrew from Xuan Loc, accompanied by what was left of the Airborne Brigade.[26] Saigon was seemingly ripe for the taking, but for reasons still unknown today the North Vietnamese paused.

To insert the GSF and extract evacuees Brigadier General Carey now had available forty-four H-53s (thirty-four Marine CH-53Ds, eight Air Force Special Operations CH-53Cs, and two Air Rescue HH-53Cs) and twenty-seven CH-46s, of which he planned to launch forty and twenty-four, respectively.[27] In addition, Carey had at his disposal six UH-1E command-and-control helicopters and eight AH-1J gunships.[28] The H-46s were to be committed in pairs carrying fifteen Marines each, "Sparrow Hawk" teams to reinforce the GSF as needed or to rescue the crews and passengers of downed extraction helicopters. The gunships were to provide fire support as needed. As events would prove, it was a good plan with adequate flexibility.

The military was not the only player in the helicopter evacuation. Though not written into FREQUENT WIND, Air America, answerable to the CIA and thus to the ambassador, had a small fleet of UH-1 Hueys in South Vietnam. In anticipation of an evacuation, Air America had taken thirteen Hueys out of storage, raising the available total to twenty-eight. Of that total, Air American chief executive officer Paul Velte had promised the CIA to have twenty-four available for an evacuation. To Velte's credit, he traveled to Saigon to oversee operations personally, arriving on 7 April.[29] As the naval armada gathered off the coast, Air America helicopters provided shuttle service between Saigon and the fleet, and they would continue to do so until the bitter end.

In the days ahead, commanders, staffs, and aircrews afloat waited for the order to execute. For the Marine and Air Force helicopter crews, the drill was the same, day after day: get up before dawn, man and run up their aircraft in preparation for a dawn launch, then stand down when the word didn't come.

As a result of frantic efforts on the part of DAO officers and Marines flown in by Air America to provide additional security, plans for the evacuation were in place.

Bus convoys were organized to pick up evacuees from their billets throughout the city and deposit them at the DAO compound at Tan Son Nhut. The evacuation order was to be given at midnight so the buses could roll through deserted streets. To signal that the evacuation was on, American-operated Radio Saigon would play the song "I'm Dreaming of a White Christmas."

The bulk of the evacuees would come out of the DAO compound. Only two hundred or so evacuees were anticipated from the embassy, for which the rooftop helipad—which could accommodate nothing larger than a CH-46—would suffice. The embassy parking lot was big enough for an LZ capable of handling an H-53 but was blocked by a large tree, the removal of which the ambassador forbade. Initial guidance from Washington stipulated a minimal ground security force of a reinforced rifle company. Colonel Gray, who had made frequent trips into the city to gauge the situation, demurred, deeming a company grossly inadequate. His superiors backed him up.[30] The GSF would consist of Regimental Landing Team 4, established 19 April and, being based on 2nd Battalion, 4th Marines, was known as "2/4."

The size of the security force posed problems, because many of the GSF Marines were not billeted on the same ships as the helicopters that would transport them to their destinations, and because Marine CH-53Ds had relatively small fuel capacities.[31] Mating up Marines and helicopters thus required an elaborate "cross-decking" operation in which the helicopters would take off, pick up their Marines, return to top off their fuel, then proceed in to the LZs. This cycle would take some three hours to complete.[32] Further complicating planning was the requirement that the helicopter flow was not to begin until air support was overhead. While some of this cover was to be provided by attack carriers operating relatively close offshore, the bulk would come from Air Force runways in Thailand, requiring some two hours of lead time. The timing depended on a common schedule based on "L-hour"—which to the Marines meant the time the helicopters would touch down in the LZs but to the Air Force meant the time when sorties would launch, a misunderstanding that would be sorted out only on the day of the evacuation.[33] Helicopter ingress and egress ground tracks were assigned for the insertion and extraction sorties. The helicopter stream would ingress up the western edge of the Saigon River at 5,500 feet, then make a sharp left turn over the Newport Bridge before descending into the DAO compound. Egress would follow the same ground track.[34]

Intelligence indicated that the communists were unlikely to mount a major effort to halt the evacuation, and aircrew intelligence briefings conveyed the impression that the operation would be mounted in a permissive environment.[35] The rules of engagement (ROE) were extraordinarily restrictive. I have not been able to locate the ROE in written form, but I remember them as significantly more constraining than "do not fire unless fired upon." The phrase "unless in imminent danger" sticks in my mind. A partial exception involved special ROE for IRON HAND antiradiation, hunter-killer F-4s; in a detailed set of rules that ran to two sheets of teletypewriter printout, these aircraft were allowed to engage radar-directed antiaircraft artillery or SA-2 surface-to-air-missile batteries in a defensive reaction if the situation warranted.[36]

Meanwhile the communist noose grew tighter. The South Vietnamese Joint General Staff's last situation map, drawn on the 21st, showed Saigon ringed by no fewer than thirteen North Vietnamese divisions to the east, north, west, and southwest. An SA-2 unit was shown approaching from the north.[37] I cannot say whether the intelligence on which the map was based was shared with U.S. forces, but am inclined to doubt it.

On 27 April, communist rockets hit Saigon for the first time since 1973. There were only three 122 mm rockets, and they did little damage, but the handwriting was on the wall. Sorties into Tan Son Nhut by big Air Force four-engine C-141 transports that had been moving an unprecedented number of evacuees were terminated.[38] Option III would henceforth depend on turboprop C-130s based in the Philippines.

At this point the ambassador seemed torn between the desire to get as many Vietnamese out as possible and fear of causing panic through overt preparations for evacuation. The inertia was broken on 28 September by an attack on Tan Son Nhut by three—or five, the sources are in disagreement—AT-37s, flown by North Vietnamese pilots trained by a VNAF defector. The attack interrupted the flow of C-130s, but two made it in at about 2000 hours (8 PM), loaded up, and departed safely. By this time Ambassador Martin was demanding a mass airlift and requested sixty C-130 sorties for the 29th. His request was approved, and the first three C-130s landed at Tan Son Nhut shortly before midnight. For reasons that are difficult to imagine, they carried fifteen-thousand-pound BLU-82 bombs. One of the pilots announced the nature of the cargo on the ground-control frequency; his transmission was no doubt intercepted by North Vietnamese radio operators.

The BLU-82s (pronounced "bluey eighty-twos") were based on a commercial butane tank filled with high-yield slurry explosive. Extracted from the ramp of a C-130 by parachute, it descended the same way. Originally intended to clear helicopter LZs in heavy jungle, it detonated with devastating effect. The VNAF had used BLU-82s to considerable effect in the final month of the war, taking out the headquarters of the North Vietnamese 341st Division during the battle of Xuan Loc.[39]

It took the Vietnamese ground crews time to unload and store the huge bombs, and it was after 0300 before the C-130s could begin loading evacuees. Two had loaded and were taxiing for takeoff when communist rocket batteries opened up on Tan Son Nhut. The rocket barrage was aimed at the VNAF side of Tan Son Nhut, where it destroyed three AC-119K gunships and several C-47 transports, but barrage rockets are notoriously inaccurate.[40] One hit in the DAO compound, killing two Marines. One of the C-130s took off empty from a taxiway. Another, providentially the rearmost aircraft, was hit in the wing root and set afire. The passengers and crew ran from the burning aircraft and scrambled on board the lead C-130. It took off, again from the taxiway, its crew and passengers witnesses to a fiery display.[41] Option II was toast.

Shortly thereafter, Air Marshal Ky took off from his Tan Son Nhut compound in his personal UH-1 helicopter, scrambled A-1 fighter-bombers from Can Tho, and directed them in the first preemptive strikes on the rocket batteries. A VNAF AC-119K side-firing gunship took off at about the same time and spent the rest of the night engaging communist forces around the airfield. Landing shortly before dawn, it refueled, rearmed, and took off again, only to be shot down by an SA-7 at about 0700. As dawn broke, a swarm of VNAF aircraft took off from Tan Son Nhut's runways and taxiways (or tried to take off—there were several crashes), littering the field with jettisoned fuel tanks and ordnance.

Coincidentally, President Gerald Ford had convened a meeting of the National Security Council at 0700 Saigon time. Ambassador Martin had asked for a continuation of the fixed-wing airlift, and Secretary of State Henry Kissinger supported his position. The Chief of Staff of the Air Force, Gen. George Brown, and Secretary of Defense Schlesinger disagreed, arguing that it was past time to order Option IV into action.[42] In the meantime, General Smith had taken matters into his own hands and ordered preparations for Option IV. Ambassador Martin temporized, visiting Tan Son Nhut in his armored limousine at 0900. He was met by General Smith, who argued that further fixed-wing operations from Tan Son Nhut were out of the question. Smith had a telephone link with the White House, and Martin asked to use it. Precisely what happened next is unclear; the most likely scenario is that President Ford, after consultation with his staff, got on the line and gave Martin a direct order to implement Option IV. Martin gave the order at 1048. It was transmitted at 1051 and reached the aircrews at 1100.[43] At Radio Saigon the staff put a cassette recording of "White Christmas" on the air and departed. Bus convoys began to roll—some sources imply that they were already rolling, perhaps in response to General Smith's earlier order—on streets now swarming with Vietnamese. Convoys were mobbed, and one had to be abandoned. Several diverted to the embassy, unexpectedly increasing the number of refugees there. The situation at times bordered on the absurd. A convoy under Marine captain Anthony Wood was diverted to the ambassador's residence to pick up his dog, then was halted at the gate to Tan Son Nhut by an ARVN officer who refused it entry. Wood contacted Colonel Gray by radio. Gray, in turn, contacted a Marine AH-1J gunship and directed it toward the gate, then asked Wood if he could direct an airstrike. Wood replied in the affirmative and apprised the Vietnamese officer of his overhead firepower. The

Vietnamese officer relented, in return for what he really wanted—entry into the compound for a ride out.[44]

General Burns and Admiral Whitmire ironed out the L-hour misunderstanding with USSAG, adopting the Navy definition, and cross-decking got under way. Air Force aircraft took up their stations overhead, including a radio-stuffed C-130 Airborne Battlefield Command, Control, and Communications (ABCCC) aircraft to monitor the helicopter flow. At 1305, General Carey and Colonel Gray and their staffs flew into the compound by UH-1E. A small team of Marine air-traffic controllers under Maj. David Cox flew into the compound at the same time and took up their post on the roof of a DAO building that afforded a good view of the helicopter approach path to the east-northeast.[45] There they would do a magnificent job of cycling helicopters into available LZs until they were withdrawn shortly before the GSF was extracted at about 2130.

Meanwhile, things had not gone well for Air America. Its personnel had begun helicopter operations at about 0900 on the 29th, shuttling evacuees from the rooftop pads to the DAO compound and on occasion out to the fleet. Then, at 1000, VNAF personnel invaded the Air America ramp and began stealing Hueys at gunpoint. Air America supervisors armed themselves and restored order, but not before six helicopters had been stolen, one of them crashing on takeoff. Chief Pilot Carl Winston contacted his pilots and told them to land on rooftop helipads and await orders. Then, as Option IV came to life, Air America received another setback when Velte learned that a large fuel truck he had spotted near the DAO compound had been ordered removed by the fire marshal. It was finally located by helicopter search but proved to have a weak battery and could not be started. Air America Hueys would have to refuel on Navy ships, requiring an hour's round-trip. By midafternoon Air America was down to thirteen Hueys. Assuming a military helicopter evacuation, each of them shuttled evacuees to the DAO compound until it reached minimum fuel, then headed for the fleet with a load of evacuees, refueled, and returned.[46] To the best of my knowledge, the evacuees they extracted went uncounted.

The first wave of twelve Marine H-53s from HMH-462 began touching down in the DAO compound LZs at 1506, quickly unloaded their Marines, took on loads of evacuees, and departed. They were followed by a second wave of twelve HMH-463 H-53s. A third wave consisting of nine Air Force H-53s, seven "special ops" and two rescue, led in by an element of three HMH-463 '53s, followed and began touching down at about 1530.[47]

At about 1515, as the third wave proceeded up the Saigon River, chatter on multiple radio channels reported that a communist 57 mm antiaircraft battery to the east was engaging the helicopter stream. Shortly thereafter, those monitoring tactical frequencies heard an excited transmission on the guard channel, the common emergency frequency: "Protective reaction! Protective reaction!" The transmission had been made by Air Force captain Jay A. Suggs, leader of an IRON HAND flight of four F-4s from Udorn Royal Thai Air Base. Suggs's "backseater," an electronic warfare officer, had acquired the battery's radar and vectored him in to engage with a radar-homing Shrike missile. As Suggs turned toward the battery, its commander, no doubt warned by early-warning radar farther north, turned his radar off. According to the ROE that eliminated the battery as a valid target, but Suggs had acquired the gun position visually. He free-fired the Shrike, using it as a marking rocket for his wingmen, who took out the battery with cluster-bomb units. He had stretched the ROE to the limit and beyond. There is no evidence that the battery fired again.[48]

As the third wave initiated its descent into the DAO compound, the three H-53s of its final element were "painted" (detected) by the acquisition radars of no fewer than three SA-2 sites, well within range to the north-northeast of the city. The sites never launched.[49]

From this point, the operation took on a life of its own. Although the official histories skirt the issue, the flow of helicopters to and from the evacuation points was largely dictated by events, many of them unexpected, and by the decisions of individual pilots. The exceptions included the elements headed by Gray, who kept close tabs on his GSF Marines; by Carey, who kept equally close tabs on his lift assets, particularly those needed to get Marines in and out; and by the Navy flight controllers, "air bosses," and flight deck personnel, who controlled their landing pads and flight decks with a combination of ruthless decisiveness and remarkable flexibility. Attempts by ABCCC to monitor the helicopter flow and track the number of evacuees broke down early in the evacuation and were never resumed.[50]

Shortly after the arrival of the initial GSF elements in the DAO compound, General Carey learned that there were two thousand evacuees in the embassy. That was unexpected. Carey responded by directing H-53 as well as H-46 sorties into the embassy. The tree in the parking lot went down, providing an H-53-capable LZ—one that, however, required a seventy-foot vertical climb and descent, posing a hazard and reducing lift capability. The embassy was surrounded by a mob that swelled as the day wore on, and between 1900 (7 PM) and 2100 Carey transferred three platoons of 2/4 from the DAO compound to the embassy.[51] The impression that the embassy was a bottomless pit of Vietnamese evacuees took hold.

Operations from the compound proceeded with remarkable efficiency despite additional unanticipated occurrences. For example, three LZs marked out on the softball diamond were oiled down to suppress dust; tracers set the oil on fire, and several Marine '53s from the third wave had to return to the fleet empty. Started belatedly, evacuation operations stretched on into the hours of darkness, which fell suddenly and with tropical finality shortly after 1900. From that point, Saigon was illuminated by the light of burning buildings—some ten to a dozen in all—and flashes of lightning from a large thunderstorm to the northwest of the city.[52] Mercifully, the sky overhead held clear. Had it not, the consequences would have been horrible.

Predictions of a permissive environment were half-true at best. In addition to the 57 mm battery mentioned earlier, a 37 mm battery to the west of Tan Son Nhut attempted to engage the helicopter stream descending toward Tan Son Nhut after dark; fortunately, it was unable to depress its barrels sufficiently to pose a threat. An AC-130 acquired the site but was denied permission to open fire by General Burns.[53] An element of two HH-53s—the author's—was engaged at about 2015 by three 12.7 mm positions between the turning point to the DAO compound and the compound itself. The helicopters replied with 7.62 mm fire, suppressing the enemy guns.[54] Meanwhile, North Vietnamese SA-7 teams had infiltrated the city; a published Marine Corps photo of the operation shows an SA-7 passing through the main rotor of an H-53 in daylight. The author's H-53 was engaged by an SA-7 at about 2030; decoyed by M-50 flares, it missed astern by sixty feet.[55] There were other instances.

These incidents are not evidence of North Vietnamese intent to shut down the evacuation. The failure mentioned above of SA-2 batteries to fire is indicative in this respect. They are, however, in my opinion, evidence of a plan to disrupt the evacuation with serious loss of life and embarrassment to the United States, if it could be done with reasonable deniability. The SA-7s could have gotten into the city only on North Vietnamese orders. The same can be said of the 12.7 mm anti-aircraft heavy machine guns. The actions of the 57 mm battery are self-explanatory. Whatever design the communists may have had, the actions of American aviators frustrated it. Option IV's major failures—the belated launch order prominent among them—were products of high-level American indecision.

By 2250 the DAO compound had been cleared of evacuees, the buildings wired for demolition, and the last of the GSF evacuated. The embassy continued to bleed evacuees. Noting a halt in the helicopter flow, General Carey learned that Admiral Whitmire, concerned for the well-being of the fatigued helicopter crews, had halted the evacuation, planning to renew it at first light. Carey flew to Whitmire's flagship, USS *Blue Ridge* (LCC 19), and in a heated exchange with Whitmire got the decision reversed. But it was too late. Those on high—just who and how high is open to debate—had decided that Ambassador Martin was supporting an endless evacuation of Vietnamese pouring into the embassy. It was the final, bitter, legacy of Martin's disconnect with reality. The fact was that by midnight the crowd outside the embassy had dissipated and things were well in hand.

At 0327, President Ford ordered that there would be nineteen more extraction sorties into the embassy and that the nineteenth would bring out the ambassador, ending the evacuation. At 0458, a CH-46 with the call sign "Lady Ace 09," piloted by Marine captain Jerry Berry, hovered on the embassy's rooftop pad until assured that the ambassador was on board, then departed.[56] On board was Army major Stuart Herrington, a member of the DAO staff and a veteran of the war in the countryside against the Viet Cong in the early 1970s. That morning Herrington, fluent in Vietnamese, had recruited the Vietnamese of the embassy fire department to maintain crowd control within the embassy compound, which they had done with panache. The quid pro quo was that their families would be among the first evacuees, which they were. As Lady Ace 09 lifted off the rooftop, Herrington looked down and saw the firefighters themselves, in their yellow slickers, sitting in ordered rows waiting for evacuation.[57] They were among the four hundred or so left behind, including a number of South Korean businessmen and their families. A half-dozen more sorties would have done it. It was, and is, a blot of shame on the honor of the United States of America.

Also left behind were eleven Marines under Maj. James Kean, officer in charge of the embassy's Marine security guard. Kean and his men retreated to the rooftop pad and barricaded themselves in, thwarting with barricaded doors, broken glass, and tear gas desperate attempts to force the pad from the stairwell below. They were taken off by a CH-46 of Marine Medium Helicopter Squadron 163 at 0753 the next morning. Option IV was over.[58]

What can we learn from this? Some lessons are obvious—one is that competent contingency planning is hugely important. Another is that individuals can make a difference, particularly at the upper to middle levels of the chain of command—Ambassador Dean, Brigadier General Baughn, Colonel Gray, and Air America's Paul Velte come to mind in a positive sense, and Ambassador Martin in a negative one. The same applies farther down the chain of command: the effectiveness of Major Cox and his small team in controlling the flow of helicopters into the DAO compound made a huge contribution to success. Some are less obvious—for example, that too much communications capability at the highest levels of command can be a negative as well as a positive influence. President Ford's order to Ambassador Martin to order Option IV is on the plus side of the ledger, but the order from Washington to halt prematurely evacuation operations from the embassy goes on the negative side. Finally, and most encouragingly, Americans low on the chain of command demonstrated, once again, their ability to think on their feet and make time-critical decisions based on the best information available to them—even if it means violating orders. Captain Suggs's neutralization of the 57 mm battery is perhaps the most prominent example, but it was hardly the only one.

NOTES
1 Ray L. Bowers, *The United States Air Force in Southeast Asia: Tactical Airlift* (Washington, D.C.: Office of Air Force History, 1983) [hereafter Bowers, *Tactical Airlift*], p. 644.

2 Four VNAF A-1Hs of the 518th Fighter Squadron based at Can Tho were involved in suppressing communist fire around Tan Son Nhut. The first element of two, led by Maj. Troung Phung with Captain Phuc as his wingman, responded to Marshal Ky's scramble order. The second element, flown by Maj. Dinh Van Son and Lt. Ngoc Tuong Van, arrived after Marshal Ky had landed and worked closely with the AC-119K, using its flares to find targets; "Untold Stories of Vietnam [sic] War," VNAF MAMN (VNAF Model Aircraft of Minnesota), www.vnafmamn.com/.

3 The AC-119K of the 821st Attack Squadron, piloted by Lt. Tran Van Hien and Lieutenant Thanh, landed just before dawn to refuel and arm. The squadron commander advised against taking off, but the crewmen insisted and were shot down; ibid.

4 Lt. Col. Thomas G. Tobin, USAF; Lt. Col. Arthur E. Laehr, USAF; and Lt. Col. John F. Hilgenberger, USAF, *Last Flight from Saigon,* ed. Lt. Col. David R. Mets, Monograph 6, vol. 4 USAF Southeast Asia Monograph Series (Washington, D.C.: U.S. Government Printing Office, 1978), p. 5.

5 These realities were appreciated by North Vietnam's leaders, as evidenced by an account of an exchange in mid-to-late 1970 between Lao Dong, party general secretary; North Vietnamese leader Le Duan; and an American "agent of influence" visiting

Hanoi. Summarized in *Indochina Chronology* 19, no. 3 (August–October 2000), pp. 28–29, in an article bearing the imprimatur of editor—and surely author—Douglas Pike.

6 For the fall of the South, Cao Van Vien, *The Final Collapse: Indochina Monographs* (Washington, D.C.: U.S. Army Center of Military History, 1983). General Cao was the last chief of the Joint General Staff of the South Vietnamese Army.

7 Bowers, *Tactical Airlift,* p. 635.

8 The VNAF lost twenty-seven or twenty-eight AT-37s in the last three weeks of the war, almost all to SA-7s. Lt. Gen. John J. Burns, USAF, oral history interview by Hugh N. Ahmann, 5–8 June 1984, January 1986, Oral History Interview K239.0512–1587, USAF Historical Research Center, Maxwell Air Force Base [AFB], Alabama [hereafter Burns interview], p. 404.

9 Cao, *Final Collapse,* pp. 76–80. General Cao was at the meeting.

10 Author's recollection of coverage in the *Bangkok Post* and scuttlebutt at Nakhon Phanom air base, where I was based at the time. The dates and numbers are from Maj. George R. Dunham, USMC, and Col. David A. Quinlan, USMC, *U.S. Marines in Vietnam: The Bitter End, 1973–1975* (Washington, D.C.: History and Museums Division, Headquarters U.S. Marine Corps, 1990) [hereafter Dunham and Quinlan, *Bitter End*], pp. 90–92, which passes over the lurid details.

11 William P. Leary, "Last Flights: Air America and the Collapse of South Vietnam" (George Jalonick III and Dorothy Cockrell Jalonick Memorial Lecture, University of Texas at Dallas, 13 August 2005, Special Collections Department, Eugene McDermott Library, Dallas, Texas) [hereafter Leary, "Last Flights: Air America"], p. 4, has the TALON VISE plan published on 31 July 1974, citing Tobin, Laehr, and Hilgenberger, *Last Flight from Saigon,* p. 9, which does not give a specific date but suggests the summer of 1974.

12 Option V was seriously considered as late as 13–15 April; Burns interview, pp. 388–92; Col. Robert A. Reed, "End of Tour Report, 1 July 1974–30 June 1975," p. 3, USAF Historical Research Center, Maxwell AFB, Alabama. Reed was USSAG / Seventh Air Force deputy chief, Operations Plans Division.

13 Burns interview, p. 391. See David Butler, *The Fall of Saigon: Scenes from the Sudden End of a Long War* (New York: Simon & Schuster, 1985), pp. 143–49, for a balanced and generally sympathetic profile of Martin substantiating this characterization.

14 Martin from the beginning prohibited contact with the press by military embassy staff personnel without his explicit permission; Maj. Stuart A. Herrington, USA, *The Third Indochina War 1973–1975: A Personal Perspective,* Air Command and Staff College Report 1040-80 (Maxwell AFB, Ala.: May 1980) [hereafter Herrington, *Personal Perspective*], pp. 101–102.

15 For the ARVN collapse, Lt. Gen. Phillip B. Davidson, USA (Ret.), *Vietnam at War: The History 1946–1975* (New York: Oxford Univ. Press, 1991), pp. 767–794. Cao, *Final Collapse,* for the South Vietnamese perspective. Col. Gen. Tran Van Tra, *History of the Bulwark B2 Theatre,* vol. 5, *Concluding the 30-Years War* (Ho Chi Minh City, 1982), trans., Foreign Broadcast Information Service Southeast Asia Report 1247 (2 February 1983) for a North Vietnamese view.

16 The evacuation center was set up on 1 April. Tobin, Laehr, and Hilgenberger, *Last Flight from Saigon,* p. 22.

17 Leary, "Last Flights: Air America", p. 5.

18 Brig. Gen. Richard E. Carey and Maj. David A. Quinlan, "Frequent Wind: Part Two, Planning," *Marine Corps Gazette* (March 1976), pp. 35–45.

19 Burns interview, pp. 390–91.

20 Brig. Gen. Richard M. Baughn, USAF, interview by Hugh N. Ahmann, 20–21 March 1979, Oral History Interview K239.0512–1587, USAF Historical Research Center, Maxwell AFB, Alabama, p. 391. Baughn's F-105 missions were flown while on temporary duty to Thailand, from Clark Air Base in the Philippines, as a member of the Pacific Air Forces Standardization Board.

21 Ibid., p. 194.

22 Ibid., pp. 232–33.

23 Ibid. Baughn showed the message to Martin's communications chief, who inexplicably let it go out. Scott Laidig, *Al Gray, Marine: The Early Years, 1950–1970* (Arlington, Va.: Potomac Institute Press, 2013), chap. 14.

24 Laidig, *Al Gray, Marine.*

25 See John F. Guilmartin, Jr., *A Very Short War: The Mayaguez and the Battle of Koh Tang* (College Station: Texas A&M Univ. Press, 1995), p. 19.

26 Cao, *Final Collapse,* pp. 130–33.

27 Carey and Quinlan, "Frequent Wind: Part Two," p. 40. The figures are those that applied for the actual operation. *Midway* took aboard six CH-53s and four HH-53s on the 20th. Two of the HH-53s returned to Thailand on the 22nd, replaced by two CH-53s; author's journal.

28 Brig. Gen. Richard E. Carey and Maj. David A. Quinlan, "Frequent Wind: Part Three, Execution," *Marine Corps Gazette* (April 1976), pp. 35–45.

29 Leary, "Last Flights: Air America", p. 5.

30 Laidig, *Al Gray, Marine.*

31 Lt. Col. William R. Fails, *Marines and Helicopters, 1962–1973* (Washington, D.C.: History and Museums Division, Headquarters U.S. Marine Corps, 1978), appendix, "Standard Aircraft Characteristics," p. 236. The CH-53D carried about two hours of fuel, depending on load and ambient conditions. Air Force CH- and HH-53Cs were fitted with jettisonable external tanks and carried six and four and a half hours of fuel, respectively. The HH-53s could be refueled in the air from HC-130 tankers.

32 See Dunham and Quinlan, *Bitter End,* app. K, pp. 300–301, for the elaborate, thirty-six-step cross-decking plan.

33 Ibid., pp. 181–82.

34 Dunham and Quinlan state (in ibid.) that altitudes of 6,500 feet inbound and 5,500 feet outbound were assigned to get above small-arms fire, avoid artillery fire, and be able to see and thereby avoid SA-2 and SA-7 fire. On the author's strip map, prepared by *Midway*'s intelligence section, both ingress and egress tracks are marked "5,500 feet." Altitudes between 5,500 and 6,500 feet are in the heart of the 37 mm / 57 mm antiaircraft-artillery envelope. FREQUENT WIND helicopter crews were assigned Mark 50 flares to be fired from flare pistols to decoy the SA-7's infrared seeker. They worked when used in time. The only viable defensive maneuver for a helicopter that drew an SA-2 launch was an immediate descent into ground clutter to break radar contact. In the author's view, it is doubtful that the requisite descent could have been accomplished before the missile's arrival, even if the crew received immediate launch warning. Of the helicopters involved in FREQUENT WIND, only the two Air Rescue HH-53Cs were equipped with RHAW (radar homing and warning) receivers to provide launch warning.

35 This is a controversial point and one skirted by published accounts. Air Force helicopter crews aboard *Midway* received a sketchy intelligence briefing, though detailed information on the enemy dispositions was available. (During 21–28 April, the author spent a considerable amount of time with *Midway*'s intelligence section discussing communist capabilities and intentions.) There was only limited face-to-face coordination between Air Force Special Operations personnel and the Marines on board *Blue Ridge,* and junior Air Force officers involved got the impression that the Marines anticipated a permissive environment.

36 Information to the author from the officer identified as the IRON HAND flight lead, mentioned below, at a 1978 tactics conference hosted by the USAF Fighter Weapons School at Nellis AFB, Las Vegas, Nevada.

37 The map is in the author's possession. It was brought out to USS *Midway* on the 29th by an ARVN lieutenant general whom I believe to have been Nguyen Van "Little" Minh. The general gave it to Capt. Verne Sheffield, my wingman in the evacuation, in *Midway*'s informal officers' mess that evening. Sheffield, knowing that I was a historian, passed it on to me.

38 Herrington, *Personal Perspective,* p. 521.

39 Dunham and Quinlan, *Bitter End,* pp. 183–84, 183 note.

40 Leary, "Last Flights: Air America", p. 7.

41 Dunham and Quinlan, *Bitter End.*

42 Herrington, *Personal Perspective,* p. 335.

43 Tobin, Laehr, and Hilgenberger, *Last Flight from Saigon,* p. 90; Butler, *Fall of Saigon,* pp. 390–91.

44 Dunham and Quinlan, *Bitter End,* pp. 178–81.

45 Ibid., pp. 188–89.

46 Leary, "Last Flights: Air America", pp. 10–12.

47 Dunham and Quinlan, *Bitter End,* pp. 181–84; author's journal.

48 Author's recollection. Information to the author from Jay Suggs (see note 36). Scuttlebutt among Air Force crews in Thailand identified Suggs as the flight lead on the strike. Several weeks later, I encountered a young intelligence officer whom I had instructed at the Air Force Academy during 1970–73. He had witnessed Suggs receiving a royal butt-chewing from a general officer on the ramp at Udorn immediately after he landed. This account (save for the butt-chewing) is confirmed in outline by Senior Col. Ho Si Huu et al., *History of the Air Defense Service, Volume III* [Lich Su Quan Chung Phong Khong, Tap III] (Hanoi: People's Army Publishing House, 1994), excerpts trans. Merle L. Pribbenow; Pribbenow e-mail to the author, 1 November 2003.

49 Author's journal. The primary indicator was an instrument the size of an airspeed indicator or instrument landing system indicator. Relative bearing and strength of the radar signal were indicated by the bearing and length of a strobe emanating from the center of the display. The center was surrounded by three concentric rings. A strobe reaching the innermost ring meant an SA-2 out of range; a two-ringer was within range. My scope showed two three-ringers, one bouncing off the rim of the scope.

50 Author's journal. My two "Jolly Greens" checked in and reported our number of evacuees on our first two sorties but were unable to contact the appropriate agencies thereafter, owing to a cacophony of transmissions on the control frequencies.

51 Dunham and Quinlan, *Bitter End,* pp. 195–96.

52 Author's recollection and journal.

53 Burns interview, p. 420. On his final run-in, at about 2130, the author saw a string of six air bursts perhaps five hundred feet above his helicopter, two rounds per second. The Soviet M-1939 37 mm antiaircraft gun fired from a six-round clip at a rate of 120 rounds per minute.

54 Author's journal and recollection. I did not see the exchange and was unaware of it at the time. My window gunner and our wingman's window and door gunners identified the guns as 12.7 mm, on the basis of the size of the tracers and the interval between them, and as on antiaircraft mounts, because they tracked us smoothly. Tracers can be deceptive at night—their size is rarely underestimated—but my gunners, all combat-experienced pararescuemen, had the familiar size of their own 7.62 mm tracers with which to compare them. The descending streams of tracers intersected the rising streams in the gun pits, and the enemy fire ceased.

55 Author's journal.

56 Dunham and Quinlan, *Bitter End,* pp. 200–10.

57 Herrington, *Personal Perspective.*

58 Why Major Kean and his Marines were left behind after the ambassador's departure is unclear and is likely to remain so; cf. Dunham and Quinlan, *Bitter End,* pp. 200–201. I had the pleasure of meeting Jim Kean when we appeared on ABC's *Good Morning America* on 30 April 1985, the tenth anniversary of the fall of Saigon. Addressing the issue, I said, in my usual indirect way, "They forgot you!" Jim adamantly denied it. Which of us was correct I cannot say.

XI *The History of the Twenty-First-Century Chinese Navy*

BERNARD D. COLE

China historically has been a continental rather than a maritime power, despite its more than eleven thousand miles of coastline and more than six thousand islands. It has more often viewed the sea as a potential invasion route for foreign aggressors rather than as a medium for achieving national goals, a tendency that has contributed to the weakness of the Chinese maritime tradition. This attitude had changed by the beginning of the twenty-first century. The remarkable growth of China's economy beginning in the last two decades of the twentieth century, the broadening of Beijing's global political and economic interests, and resolution of almost all border disputes with its many contiguous neighbors have contributed to increased attention to threats to the vital sea lines of communication (SLOCs) on which China increasingly depends.

The historical missions of China's navy—called the People's Liberation Army Navy (PLAN)—were described in 1982 as "resist invasions and defend the homeland," attesting to the service's role as a coastal-defense force in support of the ground forces facing a potential Soviet invasion of China. Deng Xiaoping, however, delineated an "offshore defense" strategy in 1985, while in 1993 the PLAN was directed to "safeguard the sovereignty of China's national territorial land, air, and seas" and to "uphold China's unity and security." This new strategy and direction marked the PLAN's transition to the post–Cold War world.

The four historical missions listed by President Hu Jintao in 2004 were the traditional responsibility of ensuring the military's loyalty to the Chinese Communist Party (CCP); ensuring sovereignty, territorial integrity, and domestic security, to include preventing Taiwanese separatism; and the new responsibilities of safeguarding expanding national interests, including maritime security and "nontraditional security problems," and helping to ensure world peace. The PLAN was being described as "a strategic service" by 2008.[1]

The navy's commander, Adm. Wu Shengli, addressed his service's missions and intentions at its sixtieth-anniversary review, in 2009. He called for strengthened logistics and support facilities "to improve far-sea repair, delivery, rescue and replenishment capacities" while establishing "a maritime defense system . . . to protect

China's maritime security and economic development." These remarks reinforced Wu's 2007 call for creation of a "powerful armed force on the sea" as a "long cherished dream for the Chinese nation."[2]

Imperial China

Despite China's historical dependence on ground forces to guard its national security interests, the PLAN can trace its lineage back through the dynasties. The earliest recorded naval battle in China occurred in 549 BC, during the Spring and Autumn Period, when rival rulers used ships to attack each other.[3] Large-scale naval operations continued to play a role in Chinese warfare through the Han dynasty (206 BC–AD 220). Chinese sea-goers were the first to control their ships with sails and rudders, employ compartmentation, paint vessels' bottoms to inhibit wood rot, and build dry docks. They developed the art of navigation to a high degree, including use of the portable compass as early as 1044.[4] China had established regular commercial sea routes to southwestern Asia and western Africa by the end of the Tang dynasty (AD 907).[5]

The Song Dynasty

The high point of naval developments in imperial China probably occurred during the Song dynasty (AD 960–1279), as part of a five-hundred-year period when China deployed "the world's most powerful and technologically sophisticated navy."[6] During this time, the military organized in times of emergency fleets composed of several hundred warships and supply vessels. One Song fleet in AD 1274 reportedly totaled 13,500 ships.[7] Chinese maritime technology also matured during this age; shipping was an important part of the national economy.

Perhaps most significantly, the Song regime was the first in China to establish a permanent national navy, functioning as an independent service administered by a central government agency. The Imperial Commissioner's Office for the Control and Organization of the Coastal Areas was established in 1132 to supervise a navy of fifty-two thousand men.[8]

The Song experience was based on a rapidly expanding national economy, with a particularly strong maritime sector encompassing commerce, fisheries, and transportation. As the navy expanded, so did port facilities, supply centers, and dockyards; soldiers were trained specifically as marines, and coast-guard squadrons were established. Song navies used both sail and paddle-wheel-driven craft, the latter powered by laborers on treadmills. Doctrine was formalized, and it included the development of formation maneuvers, long-range projectile launchers, and complex tactics.[9]

China remained a sea power during the two succeeding dynasties. In fact, the overthrow of the Song regime by the Yuan (Mongol) dynasty resulted in significant part from the latter's conduct of naval warfare. The Yuan later used large fleets to undertake invasions of Vietnam, Java, and Japan. The 1274 expedition against

Japan, which proved unsuccessful, involved nine hundred ships and 250,000 soldiers; that of 1281 included 4,400 ships.[10] Maritime commerce continued to expand, and cannon made their appearance on board ship.[11]

The Ming Dynasty

During the Ming dynasty (1368–1644) China saw both the pinnacle of its overseas naval deployments and the collapse of its naval power. The crux of the successful Ming struggle to succeed the Yuan was a series of battles on the lakes of the Yangtze River valley. The waterborne forces employed by the Ming and their opponents were not independent navies but rather army units assigned to ships on the local lakes and rivers. Their original mission was to transport men and supplies, but the armies quickly recognized the advantages of using these craft as warships, against both land forces and each other. The Ming ships were manned by about twelve thousand troops and were armed with archers, cannon, and "flame weapons." The "lake campaign" was an effective use of ships and men to take advantage of battlefield topography but did not result in the establishment of a regular Ming navy.

The early-fifteenth-century voyages of Zheng He to the Middle East and Africa also occurred during the Ming dynasty. They demonstrated a standard of Chinese shipbuilding, voyage management, and navigation well beyond European capabilities. Zheng He led large fleets of ships, some displacing over four hundred tons, on seven voyages halfway around the world at a time when Portuguese explorers were still feeling their way down the west coast of Africa in fifty-ton caravels.

After just thirty years, the Ming rulers deliberately ended these voyages for domestic financial, political, and ideological reasons, just at the time when European nations were beginning to use the high seas to achieve economic wealth and to proselytize. Why were these expeditions ended? First, the voyages were expensive, and the Ming pursued a rigid economic policy. Second, the ruling circle was concerned about the growing power of the court eunuchs, who were the voyages' chief sponsors. Third, "Confucian-trained scholar-officials opposed trade and foreign contact on principle."[12]

Perhaps most importantly, however, the threat from Mongols and other Asian aggressors was growing stronger, which both increasingly focused government concerns inland and absorbed a growing portion of the national budget. By 1500, "anti-commercialism and xenophobia [had] won out," and the government thereafter attempted to deal with maritime problems by ignoring them. The navy was allowed to deteriorate; by the end of the sixteenth century the Ming government was unable even to defend its maritime traders against pirates.

During its long period of brilliant maritime scientific progress and dominating power, however, China's national security concerns had focused not at sea but on the north and west—with good reason, since that was where the threat to the regime lay. No dynasty fell as a direct result of maritime invasion or pressure:

usurpers emerged from the Asian interior, and the crucial battles were land fights. The navy was at various times capable and even powerful, but never was it vital to a dynasty's survival, even in the face of the centuries-long threat from Japanese "pirates," as the Chinese habitually called their neighbors.

The Qing Dynasty
Typical of the process of dynastic progression, the Qing (Manchu) dynasty replaced the Ming in 1644 after a long period of land warfare in which naval power played a very small role. The Qing made no concerted effort to rebuild the navy or expand the maritime sector of China's economy following their assumption of power. The Qing regime faced no significant threat from the sea during its first century and a half in power, and there seemed little justification for investing in a modern navy. This was especially true after the most notable Qing maritime campaign, when after several failed attempts it conquered Taiwan in 1683.

Overseas trade grew despite Qing indifference, owing in part to the extensive settlement of "overseas Chinese" throughout Southeast and South Asia that had begun during earlier dynasties. The Qing navy remained powerful enough to prevent coastal piracy from getting out of hand, to maintain order on the canals and rivers, and to perform other coast-guard functions. China had fallen so far behind the global norm in naval power, however, that it was unable to defeat the late-eighteenth- and early-nineteenth-century imperialists—who came by sea.

Failed Modernization
As the Qing reeled from the imperialist onslaught and from the effects of the Taiping Rebellion, which ended in 1864, major "restoration" movements occurred in China. These "self-strengthening" efforts, under the slogan "Chinese learning as the fundamental structure, Western learning for practical use," included building and training a modern navy. This facet of modernization probably resulted from admiration of the technology represented by a modern warship and from the fact that the imperialist powers had used their navies to impose humiliating defeats on China.

An arsenal was established in Shanghai to build steam-powered gunboats, but efforts to modernize China's navy too often fell victim to Confucian traditionalists, who were the rigid ideologues of the day; it was in part a case of ideology defeating professionalism, a problem that has persisted. Nonetheless, by 1884 China had deployed a modern navy, led by the efforts of Li Hongzhang, one of the most prominent of the scholar-bureaucrats who appreciated how far behind the foreign powers China had lagged. Li used three approaches to build the new navy, which he thought should be oriented toward coastal defense: indigenous production, purchases abroad, and the reverse engineering of foreign systems.

Unfortunately, the new navy suffered from high-level governmental corruption and weak administration.[13] It was organized into four fleets that were essentially independent navies. The Beiyang Fleet, organized by Li Hongzhang, was the most modern and powerful; by 1884 it included two 7,500-ton-displacement, German-built battleships. The Fujian Fleet was homeported in Fuzhou; the other two fleets were the Nanyang and Guangdong.

This new navy was well regarded by Western observers but soon became embroiled in battle with two foreign fleets, one of them Western. Disputes with France over its colonization of Vietnam led to the outbreak of hostilities in August 1884; Chinese ground forces did well, but the local French fleet attacked the Chinese Fujian Fleet in Fuzhou Harbor and sank every ship.[14] China's other fleets were not sent to fight the French; Li wanted to conserve and build up remaining naval strength. His efforts were successful on paper, including establishment of a national Navy Office, a better-organized training regimen and shore establishment, and in 1888 standardized naval regulations.[15]

Despite these achievements, China's navy failed to become a coherent national force; its most powerful fleet came to grief attempting to halt Japanese incursions into Korea in the 1890s. The Beiyang Fleet—of two battleships, ten cruisers, and two torpedo boats—lost a sea battle to the Japanese in September 1894 and withdrew to Weihaiwei, a strongly fortified harbor on the northern Shandong coast. In January 1895 the Japanese landed troops who seized the Chinese batteries guarding the harbor and turned their guns on the Chinese ships.[16] The Beiyang Fleet was eviscerated by its losses in ships, in conjunction with the suicides of the fleet commander and other senior officers.[17] Again, the other Chinese fleets failed to join the fight.

These naval conflicts with the French and the Japanese demonstrated that while Beijing had acquired the ships and weapons of a modern navy, it had failed to institute effective central administration, training, logistical and maintenance support, or command and control. Furthermore, operational doctrine was almost completely lacking; the navy's leaders failed to establish interfleet coordination, exercises, or mutual support. Finally, China had failed to provide its new navy with a coherent strategy tied to national security objectives. China's attempt to deploy a modern navy in the late nineteenth century failed miserably as a result of these factors.

The Republic of China (1911–1949)
During the Republican period, Chinese naval forces under Chiang Kai-shek's Nationalists and the Kuomintang Party (KMT) relied almost entirely on ships leftover from the Qing or obtained from foreign nations. No significant efforts were made to rebuild the navy, given China's general political and economic disarray. Individual warlords occasionally made effective use of maritime units, but their ships were employed to augment ground forces, which was how navies had traditionally been employed by Chinese leaders. The low point was probably reached during the height of the warlord period, in the middle to late 1920s, when a Western observer dismissed the Chinese navy as a serious force:

> There has been a steady deterioration in the discipline of the Chinese Navy since the establishment of the Republic, and it has now ceased to exist as a national force, the different units being under the control of various militarists, who treat the vessels as their own private property.... It is impossible today to obtain a complete list of Chinese warships, showing to which party or militarist faction they belong. Vessels have been changing their allegiance . . . with bewildering frequency.[18]

The government did not develop a maritime strategy, since the primary threats to the new regime were on the ground, from the CCP and warlords. Naval actions that did occur took place chiefly on the rivers, especially the Yangtze and the waterways of the Canton delta. Many of the warlords who struggled to gain control of various provinces and districts during the 1916–28 revolutionary period used China's inland waterways for transportation, as military barriers, or as sources of revenue—taxing the dense river and canal traffic. These efforts led to frequent firefights between provincial forces and the imperialist gunboats that patrolled China's rivers and lakes, but most of these episodes were of no significance insofar as coherent maritime thinking or navy building by China was concerned.

There were two notable exceptions. First was a battle at the upper Yangtze River port city of Wanhsien in September 1926. The local warlord, Gen. Yang Sen, had commandeered British-owned steamers to transport his troops; when a British gunboat, HMS *Cockchafer*, attempted to free the steamers it ran into an ambush, very capably managed by Yang, and suffered severe casualties.[19] There was also an October 1929 naval and land engagement on the Heilong (Amur) River between Chinese and Soviet forces, one that foreshadowed the 1969 incident over disputed boundaries.[20]

Sea power was an effective "force multiplier" for the foreign powers present in China, who used sea and river transport to move troops rapidly from crisis area to crisis area.[21] Great Britain, the United States, and Japan were thus able to influence the course of events in revolutionary China with relatively small military forces. Republican China was unable to contest their maritime strength.

China's record as a naval power during the long period of empire and republic shows an understandable focus on the continental rather than maritime arena. Navies were built and employed almost entirely for defensive purposes. Maritime strength was regarded as a secondary element of national power.

The People's Republic of China

The communist victory in 1949 was an army victory; the People's Liberation Army (PLA) was unable to project power across even the narrow Taiwan Strait. The KMT navy continued raiding coastal installations, landing agents, attacking merchant craft and fishing vessels, and threatening to invade the mainland. The government in Beijing of the new People's Republic of China (PRC) sought to defend its coastline and island territories against both the United States and the KMT regime on

Taiwan. Coastal defense was emphasized in January 1950 with the creation of a new East China Military Command, headquartered in Shanghai and deploying more than 450,000 personnel. The East China Navy was formed as part of this force.

The Early Years: 1949–1954

Beijing ordered these troops to defend China's coast against "imperialist aggression from the sea," continue the fight against Chiang's forces, and help with economic reconstruction.[22] This first PRC navy was constituted largely by the defection of the KMT Second Coastal Defense Fleet.[23] The new navy's commander said it was needed "to safeguard China's independence, territorial integrity and sovereignty against imperialist aggression[,] . . . to destroy the sea blockade of liberated China, to support the land and air forces of the People's Liberation Army in defense of Chinese soil and to wipe out all remnants of the reactionary forces."[24] A navy was also required to establish law and order on coastal and riverine waters, help the army capture offshore islands still occupied by the KMT, and prepare for the capture of Taiwan. The CCP Politburo further charged the new navy with "defending both [eastern and southeastern] China coasts and the Yangtze River."[25] Gen. Zhang Aiping was the first commander (and political commissar) of the navy. Among his first acts were the establishment of a naval staff college at Nanjing and organization of a rudimentary maintenance and logistical infrastructure.

The PLAN was officially established in May 1950, under the command of Gen. Xiao Jinguang. The Chinese wanted a defensive force that would be inexpensive to build and could be quickly manned and trained.[26] Zhang and Xiao were typical of the early PLAN leadership—revolutionary officers who had spent their entire careers as ground commanders and had been transferred to the navy for reasons of political reliability and proven combat record rather than for any particular naval experience.

Soviet Assistance. Mao Zedong, as chairman of the CCP's Central Committee, obtained financial assistance during a 1949–50 visit to Moscow; he planned to use half the initial Soviet loan of $300 million to purchase naval equipment. The new PLAN also ordered two new cruisers from Great Britain and attempted to obtain surplus foreign warships through Hong Kong, efforts that were nullified by the outbreak of the Korean War.[27]

China acquired mostly small vessels suitable to combat the coastal threat from Taiwan, initially obtaining four old Soviet submarines, two destroyers, and a large number of patrol boats. The new force also included about ten corvettes, forty ex-U.S. landing craft, and several dozen miscellaneous river gunboats, minesweepers, and yard craft, all seized from the KMT. The Soviets also helped establish a large shore-based infrastructure, including shipyards, naval colleges, and extensive coastal fortifications.[28]

Offshore Islands. Beijing's goal was seizure of the offshore islands still occupied by the KMT; the invasion of Taiwan was scheduled initially for the spring of 1950 but was soon postponed to the summer of 1951. Mao Zedong considered the capture of Taiwan "an inseparable part of his great cause of unifying China."[29] He lacked experience in naval warfare but quickly learned that a successful campaign against Taiwan would require adequate amphibious training, naval transportation, "guaranteed air coverage," and the cooperation of a "fifth column" on the island—requirements that still apply.[30]

China achieved a major victory when in April 1950 the PLA occupied Hainan, after Taiwan the largest island held by the Nationalists. The campaign cost Beijing heavily in personnel losses but captured more than ninety thousand Nationalist troops. This victory resulted from the PLA's careful planning, its ability to neutralize superior Nationalist naval and air forces by use of shore-based artillery to gain effective control of the sea and airspace between Hainan and the mainland, and the characteristically poor performance of Taiwan's senior commanders.

The Korean War began two months later, and China's fear of American aggression was heightened when in June 1950 President Harry Truman ordered the U.S. Seventh Fleet into the Taiwan Strait. This meant America's reentry into the Chinese civil war. Truman claimed that it was intended to prevent either side from attacking the other; however, Beijing understood that the president was committing the United States to the defense of Taiwan—after having refused to do so for many months.[31] Premier Zhou Enlai called Truman's move "violent, predatory action by the U.S. Government [that] constituted armed aggression against the territory of China and total violation of the UN charter."[32] Beijing also understood, as it does today, that the United States possessed complete air and sea superiority in the western Pacific Ocean.

Beijing's concern was reinforced in February 1953, when President Dwight Eisenhower withdrew the U.S. fleet from the Taiwan Strait, thus in theory "unleashing" Nationalist forces on Taiwan to attack China.[33] In December 1953, Mao Zedong assigned the PLAN three priority missions: to eliminate KMT naval interference and ensure safe navigation for China's maritime commerce, prepare to recover Taiwan, and oppose aggression from the sea.[34]

The PRC's young navy faced many problems, including a lack of trained personnel and of amphibious ships, as demonstrated in the very spotty record of assaults on KMT-held coastal islands. Furthermore, in February 1952 Mao diverted the navy's ship-acquisition funds to the purchase of aircraft needed for combat over Korea.[35] Acquisition of equipment from foreign sources also was constrained by Western refusal to sell arms to the PRC and by domestic budgetary limitations.

Furthermore, despite several visits to Moscow by senior PLA leaders, the Soviets continued to insist on immediate payment for their ships, although most of them were obsolete.[36] The PLAN also lacked airpower and was just beginning to establish a capable maintenance and logistical infrastructure.

1955–1959

The Korean War provided China with mixed naval lessons. The amphibious landing at Inchon in September 1950 was a major turning point of the war, while United Nations command of the sea allowed free employment of aircraft carriers and battleships to bombard North Korean and Chinese armies. The UN forces suffered at least one significant maritime defeat, however, when a planned amphibious assault on the east-coast port of Hungnam in October 1950 had to be canceled because the harbor had been mined. Overall, however, Korea was not a maritime conflict, and the PLA ground forces' dominant role there contributed to a continued policy of limiting the navy to coastal defense.

PLAN operations in the mid-1950s continued to focus on KMT attacks against the mainland and on capturing islands still held by Taiwan. The 1954–55 Taiwan Strait crisis included the PLA's capture of the Dachen Islands, an effort that took advantage of superior airpower and a well-coordinated amphibious assault against an outlying island.[37]

The navy's First Aviation School was founded at Qingdao in October 1950, and the navy's air force, referred to as "the People's Liberation Army Navy Air Force," or simply "naval aviation," was formally established in 1952. Its mission was support of antisurface and antisubmarine defensive operations. Its initial inventory was eighty aircraft, including MiG-15 jet fighters, Il-28 jet bombers, and propeller-driven Tu-2 strike aircraft. Naval aviation had grown to about 470 aircraft by 1958.[38]

PLAN operating forces were organized into the North Sea, East Sea, and South Sea Fleets. The decade ended with the PRC in possession of all the disputed islands except Quemoy (Kinmen), Matsu (Mazu), the Pescadores (Penghus), and of course Taiwan. The PLA also had defeated KMT raids on the mainland, as well as attacks on merchant and fishing vessels.[39] The PLAN had been organized, sent to sea, and proven effective as a coastal-defense force within ten years of its founding.

A New Situation: 1960–1976

The 1960s were marked by major foreign and domestic events that further constrained development of a seagoing navy. Most important was the split with the Soviet Union, dramatically manifested in mid-1960 when Soviet advisers (and their plans) were withdrawn from China. The navy suffered, with the rest of the PLA, as military development projects were left in turmoil.

Other significant events in the early 1960s included war with India, the reemerging Vietnam conflict, turmoil in the new African states, and revolutionary movements throughout Southeast Asia. None of these major international events directly involved the PLAN; they did not provide justification for naval modernization, which was accordingly extremely limited. By the end of the 1960s, however, relations with the Soviet Union had deteriorated to the point of armed conflict along the Amur River. The former ally was now the enemy; soon the United States would be China's ally. Beijing viewed the Soviet navy as a major amphibious invasion threat. That navy deployed only weak amphibious forces in its Pacific Fleet, but China was worried by a history of military threats from the north, by Soviet proximity, and by the concentration of economic developments in its own northeast.[40]

Significant naval developments were hampered also by the forced industrialization and collectivization program of 1958–61 known as the "Great Leap Forward," and even more by the Great Proletarian Cultural Revolution, lasting from approximately 1966 to 1976. The PLAN continued to serve as an extension of the army; modernization was limited, since prevailing PLA doctrine, that of "People's War," portrayed technology and weaponry as insignificant compared to the revolutionary fervor of soldiers imbued with Mao's ideology. The Cultural Revolution seriously hampered technological development in general; even the relatively sacrosanct missile, submarine, and nuclear weapons programs were affected.[41] PLAN modernization was retarded by perhaps two decades as a result of program restrictions and personnel losses that occurred during this political maelstrom. Except for the evolution of maritime nuclear power, the PLAN missed or was very late joining developments that were common elsewhere in most warfare areas, including the employment of guided missiles in antiair, antisurface, and antisubmarine warfare; automation and computerization of command and control; expanded use of shipborne helicopters; automation of gunnery and sensor systems; and even the advent of automation and gas turbine technology in ship propulsion.

PLAN modernization was hamstrung in the last years of the Cultural Revolution by the "Gang of Four." Mao's widow, Jiang Qing, led an attack on naval missile development. Another member of the clique, Zhang Chunqiao, expressed its antinavy, "continentalist" view.[42] By 1970, however, despite this attitude and a lack of resources for major conventional force development, the PLAN had moved into the missile age, deploying a Soviet-designed ballistic-missile submarine and ten Soviet-built patrol boats armed with cruise missiles.

Despite the ideological turmoil of the late 1950s and the 1960s, Beijing was in these years investing heavily in developing nuclear-armed missiles and nuclear-powered submarines to launch them. Beijing had relied on Soviet nuclear forces to counter the American nuclear threat during the 1950s. Among the reasons stresses in the alliance with Moscow had become more divisive as the 1960s progressed was that Mao Zedong was determined that China develop its own nuclear forces, proclaiming that "even if it takes 10,000 years, we must make a nuclear submarine."[43] Mao was adamant that China should join the nuclear club. These were national rather than PLAN projects, however, and did not significantly increase the navy's ability to obtain the military resources necessary for modernization.

The budgetary emphasis on nuclear weapons, the economic disruptions resulting from the disastrous Great Leap Forward and the Cultural Revolution, and the continuing belief in Maoist orthodoxy all contributed to the Chinese navy's lack of resources for modernization during the late 1950s and the 1960s.

After the Great Proletarian Cultural Revolution
In May 1975, however, at a meeting of the Central Military Commission (CMC), Mao Zedong reportedly directed the development of a modern navy, probably reacting to both the Soviet threat and the development of a powerful navy by China's ancient adversary Japan. Chinese interests threatened by the Soviet navy in the late 1970s and 1980s included SLOCs vital to Beijing's rapidly increasing merchant marine, as Moscow established a continual naval presence in the Indian Ocean and the northern Arabian Sea. The Soviet Pacific Fleet almost doubled in size during the 1970s and was upgraded by the assignment of Moscow's latest combatants, including nuclear-powered and nuclear-armed surface ships and submarines. Soviet merchant ships and fishing vessels were also omnipresent in Pacific waters historically vital to China's economic interests.

Several factors continued to impede development of a large, modern Chinese navy. The political aftershocks of the Cultural Revolution, as Hua Guofeng and Deng Xiaoping contested for leadership of post-Mao China, limited the resources devoted to military modernization. This struggle was not resolved until 1980, when Deng emerged on top. However, Deng reemphasized the navy's role as a coastal-defense force, a view retained throughout the first half of the succeeding decade. "Our navy," Deng asserted, "should conduct coastal operations. It is a defensive force. Everything in the construction of the navy must accord with this guiding principle."[44]

Naval growth also was limited by the disorder in China's economic and social structures that lasted beyond the end of the Cultural Revolution. This turmoil affected China's military-industrial complex, hindering modernization efforts in the PLA generally. Furthermore, the lesson of the 1979 "punishment" of Vietnam was sobering to the PLA, but this conflict did not involve significant naval efforts. Hence, the PLAN probably benefited only marginally from corrective budgetary measures that resulted.

Finally, the triangular play among China, the Soviet Union, and the United States meant that by 1980 Beijing could rely on the world's largest and most modern navy to counter the Soviet maritime threat. This argued against China's developing a similar force of its own. Furthermore, given the U.S.-Japanese security treaty, Beijing could subsume concern about future Japanese aggression within its strategic relationship with Washington.[45]

Major changes in China's domestic and international situation in the 1980s soon altered Beijing's view of the PLAN, and maritime power became a more important instrument of national security strategy by the end of the decade. Beijing's second maritime priority, after countering the Soviet threat, was securing offshore territorial claims. Taiwan was the most important of these, but the South China Sea was also significant. Although successful action against South Vietnamese naval forces in 1974 resulted in Chinese possession of the disputed Paracel Islands, the fight itself indicated that other claimants to the islands and reefs of the South China Sea would not accede meekly to Beijing's territorial assertions. Furthermore, the Soviet naval base at Cam Ranh Bay was flourishing as the 1970s ended.

These factors contributed to a significant change in the South Sea Fleet's organization: the marine corps, first formed in 1953 but disbanded in 1957, was reestablished in December 1979 as an amphibious assault force and assigned to the southern fleet. The PLAN's slender amphibious assets were concentrated in the South Sea Fleet, which conducted "island seizing" exercises. In 1980, for instance, a major fleet exercise in the South China Sea focused on the seizure and defense of islands in the Paracel Archipelago.[46]

The South Sea Fleet's organization benefited from PLAN force-structure changes that, for the first time, centered on Chinese-built warships. Although still heavily reliant on Soviet designs, the Luda-class guided-missile destroyers, Jianghu-class frigates, and Houjian fast attack missile boats collectively marked a significant increase in China's maritime capability. The submarine force included the first Chinese-built nuclear-powered attack submarines, as well as about sixty conventionally powered boats. A seaborne nuclear deterrent force continued under development, following Mao's earlier declaration that the navy had to be built up "to make it dreadful to the enemy."[47]

Deng Xiaoping's Navy
Naval expansion and modernization were spurred during the 1980s by the coastal concentration of China's burgeoning economy and military facilities. Furthermore, the resources necessary for a modernized PLAN became available as a result of China's dramatic economic development and increasing wealth. Recovery from the Cultural Revolution, well under way by 1985, brought a reinvigorated, if less centralized, military-industrial complex.

Three events contributed prominently to the development of the navy in this decade. The first was Deng's evaluation of the military at an expanded CMC meeting in 1975 as "overstaffed, lazy, arrogant, ill equipped, and ill prepared to conduct modern warfare," an opinion strengthened by the PLA's poor performance during the 1979 conflict with Vietnam.[48] Second was Beijing's 1985 strategic decision that the Soviet Union no longer posed a major threat to China in terms of global nuclear war and that accordingly the PLA would have to be prepared instead for "small wars on the periphery" of the nation.⁴⁹ The emphasis on a "peripheral" (to a significant extent maritime) rather than continental strategic view improved the PLAN's leverage in obtaining resources within the PLA as a whole.

Third was the rise to prominence of Adm. Liu Huaqing. Liu had been schooled in the Soviet Union, had served most of his career in the science and technology arms of the PLA, and was close to Deng Xiaoping.⁵⁰ Liu exerted a strong force on development of the navy as its commander from 1982 to 1987 and vice chairman of the CMC until 1997. He is best known for promulgating a three-stage maritime strategy that provided justification on which PLAN officers and other navalists could base their plans for a larger, more modern navy. More important were his accomplishments in reorganizing the navy, redeveloping the marine corps, upgrading bases and research-and-development facilities, and restructuring the school and training systems.⁵¹

China's widening maritime concerns and increased budget resources in the 1980s favored PLAN modernization, which proceeded along three paths—indigenous construction, foreign purchase, and reverse engineering—much as had Li Hongzhang's "self-strengthening" navy initiative of a hundred years earlier. The 1980s program proceeded at a measured pace, but it created a new navy.

Construction included guided-missile destroyers and frigates, replenishment-at-sea ships, conventionally and nuclear-powered attack submarines, and support craft, including missile-tracking ships and officer-training vessels. Foreign purchases were concentrated in the West, with the United States selling China a small number of modern ship engines and torpedoes and Western European nations selling weapons and sensor systems, including Italian torpedoes, French cruise missiles, and British radars. The PLAN acquired its only Xia-class fleet-ballistic-missile submarine. The successful submerged launch in 1988 of the Ju Lang–1 (JL-1) intermediate-range ballistic missile from this submarine meant that China for the first time could deploy strategic nuclear weapons at sea.⁵²

The PLAN demonstrated its increasing capability in other maritime missions as well during the 1980s. China invested in four large space-surveillance ships to support its growing military and commercial space program; these ships conducted the first long-range PLAN deployments, in support of space launches, in 1980. Task forces supported scientific expeditions to the Arctic and Antarctic. The PLAN's first foreign port visit was conducted in 1985, when two East Sea Fleet ships visited Bangladesh, Sri Lanka, and Pakistan; the officer-training ship *Zheng He* became the first PLAN vessel to visit the United States when it made a 1989 port call in Hawaii.

During the 1990s Beijing continued to expand and modernize the navy it had begun building in the 1970s, but again, at a measured pace. The PLAN engaged in a series of long-range deployments throughout East and South Asia, as well as deploying a three-ship task group to the Western Hemisphere in 1998, visiting the

United States, Mexico, Peru, and Chile. Foreign purchases of improved ships, submarines, and aircraft earned the PLAN headlines as China acquired *Sovremenny*-class guided-missile destroyers, Kilo-class submarines, and Su-27 fighters from Russia, but these constituted only incremental improvements to a large if still limited navy.

Notable Consistencies and Cautionary Messages
The communist regime recognized early on the need to deal with maritime issues, but only after thirty years and a dramatically altered international situation did China apparently acknowledge the necessity of a modernized navy. Beijing currently views "the ocean as its chief strategic defensive direction," since "China's political and economic focus lies on the coastal areas [and] for the present and a fairly long period to come, [its] strategic focus will be in the direction of the sea."[53]

The Chinese navy being built for the twenty-first century owes a good deal to its history, which has been marked by some notable consistencies. First has been recognition of the maritime element in China's national security. Second, Chinese naval efforts have been closely linked to the nation's economic development. Hence, continued naval modernization should be expected, in view of China's continuing economic boom.

Third, Chinese naval development since the eighteenth century has been marked by significant interaction with foreign navies. Qing-dynasty modernization efforts drew on Japanese, German, British, and American naval professionals as advisers, administrators, and engineers. This trend continued under the People's Republic of China, with a sporadic but pervasive reliance on Soviet/Russian advisers, strategy, equipment, technology, and engineers.

Fourth, the Chinese government has not hesitated to employ naval force in pursuit of national security goals. These efforts have not always been successful (witness the failed campaigns in 1884 against France and 1894–95 against Japan) but often they have been, as in 1950, 1954–55, and 1958 in the Taiwan Strait, and in 1974, 1988, and 1998 in the South China Sea. Beijing's willingness to resort to naval force even when significantly outgunned bears a cautionary message for foreign strategists.

Imperial China for the most part ignored the sea except for brief periods and specific campaigns. Republican China was simply too preoccupied with civil war and Japanese invasion to focus on naval development. The communist regime installed in 1949 maintained for almost fifty years a traditional Chinese attitude toward the navy as a secondary instrument of national power.

Mao Zedong recognized in 1950 that deploying a navy to conquer Taiwan required development of expertise in amphibious warfare, seaborne logistics, and maritime airpower, but his plan to organize a strong navy was aborted because of the Korean War and thereafter limited by domestic political events, especially the disastrous Great Leap Forward. Later, naval development was severely impacted during the 1960s by the Sino-Soviet split and the Great Proletarian Cultural Revolution. Only at the end of the 1970s, following the end of the Cultural Revolution and the post-Mao power struggle, was the PLAN in a position to "take off."

That takeoff did not immediately happen, although the PLAN did benefit in the 1980s from a relatively close relationship with the United States, from which China purchased advanced naval systems, including LM2500 gas-turbine engines and Mark 46 antisubmarine torpedoes. The sanctions that followed the June 1989 Tiananmen Square massacre ended U.S. naval assistance, and China has since turned to Europe, Israel, and especially Russia. The following decades have seen a dramatic increase in China's naval capabilities.

Almost all of China's primary sovereignty concerns lie in the maritime arena: Taiwan; territorial and seabed resource disputes with Japan in the East China Sea; similar disputes with Vietnam, the Philippines, Brunei, Indonesia, and Malaysia in the South China Sea; and SLOCs across the Indian Ocean endangered by piracy in the Gulf of Aden. Additionally, the government's authority relies in significant part on continued economic growth, which in turn relies on maritime trade and energy flows.

Finally, Beijing's willingness to resort to force even when significantly outgunned should impart a cautionary message for strategists considering possible Chinese reactions to specific issues, especially Taiwan's efforts to resist reunification. While Beijing will continue to be constrained by American (and perhaps Japanese) naval force, it will not hesitate to employ the PLAN in situations involving sovereignty or other vital national security claims.

NOTES   This chapter appeared as an article in the *Naval War College Review* (Summer 2014), pp. 43–62.

1 This discussion relies on "CMC's Guo Boxiong Urges Improving PLA Capabilities to 'Fulfill Historic Missions,'" Xinhua, 27 September 2005, in Open Source Center CPP20050927320021, and Daniel M. Hartnett, *The PLA's Domestic and Foreign Activities and Orientation*, Testimony before the U.S.-China Economic and Security Review Commission, "China's Military and Security Activities Abroad" hearings, 111th Cong., 1st sess., 4 March 2009, available at www.uscc.gov/. The Central Military Commission (CMC) is the supreme military policy-making commission, issuing directives relating to the People's Liberation Army (PLA), including senior appointments, troop deployments, and arms spending.

CCP senior leaders hold the CMC's most important posts. See *The Central People's Government of the People's Republic of China,* english.gov.cn/, for current CMC membership.

2 Quoted in Cui Xiaohuo and Peng Kuang, "Navy Chief Lists Key Objective," *China Daily,* 16 April 2009, www.chinadaily.com.cn/.

3 Deng Gang's *Chinese Maritime Activities and Socioeconomic Development, c. 2100 BC–900 AD* (Westport, Conn.: Greenwood, 1997) is a well-written history of this topic.

4 Joseph Needham's massive (six-volume) *Science and Civilisation in China* (Cambridge, U.K.: Cambridge Univ. Press, 1954–86) discusses these and related developments.

5 See "China's Sea Route to West Asia Begins in Xuwen," Xinhua, 21 June 2000, in Foreign Broadcast Information System [hereafter FBIS] CPP20000621000077, for an archaeological theory that trading voyages may have departed from Guangdong Province as early as 200 BC, two hundred years before the Silk Road was established; Deng, *Chinese Maritime Activities and Socioeconomic Development,* p. 41.

6 Paul C. Forage, "The Foundations of Chinese Naval Supremacy in the Twelfth Century," in *New Interpretations in Naval History: Selected Papers from the Tenth Naval History Symposium Held at the United States Naval Academy, 11–13 September 1991,* ed. Jack Sweetman (Annapolis, Md.: Naval Institute Press, 1992), p. 3.

7 Ibid., p. 70.

8 Lo Jung-pang, "The Emergence of China as a Sea Power during the Late Song and Early Yuan Periods," *Far Eastern Quarterly* 14, no. 4 (August 1955), p. 491.

9 See Forage, "Foundations of Chinese Naval Supremacy in the Twelfth Century," pp. 6–7, 19–21, for a fascinating account of two battles between Song and Yuan naval forces.

10 John K. Fairbank, "Maritime and Continental in China's History," in *The Cambridge History of China,* vol. 12, *Republican China: 1912–1949,* pt. I, ed. John K. Fairbank and Dennis Twichett (Cambridge, U.K.: Cambridge Univ. Press, 1983), p. 1:15.

11 Forage, "Foundations of Chinese Naval Supremacy in the Twelfth Century," pp. 500–501, provides a brief but interesting description of these early weapons.

12 Quote is from Jin Wu, in Richard Gunde, "The Voyages of Zheng He" (Los Angeles: UCLA Center for Chinese Studies, 20 April 2004), available at www.international.ucla.edu/. The Ming decision also reflected Chinese xenophobia, perhaps best expressed in the response of the Qing emperor Ch'ien-lung to Britain's 1793 attempt to establish relations with Beijing. The emperor told Lord Macartney, "We possess all things. I set no value on objects strange or ingenious, and have no use for your country's manufactures." The best work on Zheng He remains Edward L. Dreyer, *Zheng He: China and the Oceans in the Early Ming Dynasty, 1405–1433* (New York: Longman, 2006). See George Raudzens, "Military Revolution or Maritime Evolution: Military Superiorities or Transportation Advantages as Main Causes of European Colonial Conquests to 1788," *Journal of Military History* 63, no. 3 (July 1999), p. 56, for an interesting but Eurocentric interpretation of the role maritime mobility played in European imperialism.

13 John K. Fairbank, *China: A New History* (Cambridge, Mass.: Belknap Press of Harvard Univ., 1992), p. 220, relates the most famous case of corruption—the diversion of perhaps fifty million dollars in naval construction funds to the building of the empress's Summer Palace in Beijing, complete with a large boat made of marble.

14 Mary Clabaugh Wright, *The Last Stand of Chinese Conservatism: The T'ung-chih Restoration, 1862–1874* (Stanford, Calif.: Stanford Univ. Press, 1957), pp. 59–66, provides the most detailed description of the Sino-French War. The French had eight warships and two torpedo boats. The Chinese had eleven warships and several other craft, but all were made of wood. The French also destroyed the Chinese shore installations.

15 Bruce A. Swanson, *The Eighth Voyage of the Dragon: A History of China's Quest for Seapower* (Annapolis, Md.: Naval Institute Press, 1982), p. 96ff., discusses these developments.

16 Japan's success was simplified by the fact that the forts' guns were designed only to defend against threats from seaward. The British made the same defensive mistake in Singapore in 1941, and Japanese forces took advantage of it.

17 Swanson, *Eighth Voyage of the Dragon,* p. 223. China was only one of several countries building navies at this time: Great Britain, Germany, France, Italy, Russia, Japan, the United States, and even Austria-Hungary were all modernizing their fleets. Those that fell spectacularly short—China, Germany, Austria-Hungary—failed to develop meaningful strategic and operational frameworks for their new navies. William Ferdinand Tyler, *Pulling Strings in China* (London: Constable, 1929), tells some colorful stories about another, more successful maritime force developed in China during the late nineteenth century. British naval officers operated most of the ships of the Revenue Service, established as part of the Customs Service, long supervised by Sir Robert Hart. Tyler, who was on board the Chinese flagship at Weihaiwei in 1895, characterized the navy as "a monstrously disordered epicyclic heterogeneity."

18 "The Chinese Navy," in *Shanghai Defense Force and Volunteers* (Shanghai: North China Daily Herald, 1929[?]), p. 1302.

19 This battle is described in Bernard D. Cole, *Gunboats and Marines: The U.S. Navy in China, 1925–1928* (Wilmington: Univ. of Delaware Press, 1982), pp. 89–90.

20 Swanson, *Eighth Voyage of the Dragon,* p. 157. The "Chinese" naval forces were actually those of Zhang Xueliang, the Manchurian warlord (the "Young Marshal") who had recently sworn allegiance to Chang Kai-shek's Nationalist government. The Chinese account of this battle quoted by Swanson ends with a Soviet victory due to superior firepower,

including air strikes. There was also an October 1929 clash with Soviet forces over disputed boundaries.

21. The United States, for instance, used just two Navy transports and a commercial passenger liner to move a regiment of Marines from the United States to the Far East, and then between the Philippines and China and between northern and southern China, as crises waxed and waned.

22. PLAN vice commander Zhou Xihan, 1957, quoted in David G. Muller, Jr., *China's Emergence as a Maritime Power* (Boulder, Colo.: Westview, 1983), p. 47.

23. Larry M. Wortzel, "The Beiping-Tianjin Campaign of 1948–49: The Strategic and Operational Thinking of the People's Liberation Army" (paper prepared for the U.S. Army War College's Strategic Studies Institute, Carlisle, Pa., n.d.), chart 1, points out that by July 1949 the PLA actually included seventy-seven "naval vessels." Gene Z. Hanrahan, "Report on Red China's New Navy," U.S. Naval Institute *Proceedings* 79, no. 8 (August 1953), p. 847, describes the Nationalist contribution to this force as "twenty-five vessels ranging from LCTs [tank landing craft, about 120 feet long, 260 tons] to destroyers, representing an estimated one-fourth of the total Nationalist naval force."

24. Gen. Zhang Aiping, quoted in Hanrahan, "Report on Red China's New Navy," p. 848. See Bernard D. Cole, *Taiwan's Security: History and Prospects* (London: Routledge, 2006), chap. 2, for an account of KMT activities during this period.

25. Quoted in Shu Guang, *Mao's Military Romanticism: China and the Korean War, 1950–1953* (Lawrence: Univ. Press of Kansas, 1995), p. 51.

26. Hanrahan, "Report on Red China's New Navy," pp. 46–54, provides a useful description of the beginnings of the PLAN. Muller, *China's Emergence as a Maritime Power*, p. 13, estimates that approximately two thousand former Republic of China naval personnel defected to the communist regime in 1949 and formed the core of the nascent PLAN.

27. The Chinese missions to Moscow are discussed, in some cases with verbatim accounts, in "Inside China's Cold War," *Cold War History Project Bulletin*, no. 16 (Fall 2007 / Winter 2008) (edited by Christian Ostermann, at the Woodrow Wilson Center, in Washington, D.C.). Probably the most complete account of PLAN Taiwan Strait operations in this period is He Di, "Last Campaign to Unify China: The CCP's Unmaterialized Plan to Liberate Taiwan, 1949–1950," *Chinese Historians* 5 (Spring 1992), p. 8. Its author worked at the Institute of American Studies of the Chinese Academy of Social Sciences and presumably had good access to PLA archives while researching this paper.

28. Raymond V. B. Blackman, ed., *Jane's Fighting Ships: 1955–56* (London: Jane's Fighting Ships, 1956), p. 151ff., provides these numbers, but they should be treated as estimates. Swanson, *Eighth Voyage of the Dragon*, p. 196, describes such massive projects as a fortified "250-mile, 10-foot-wide communication trench paralleling the southern bank of the Yangtze River from Wusong to Jiujiang up river," noting that a "similar trench was constructed along the coast south of Shanghai for about 200 miles."

29. He, "Last Campaign to Unify China," p. 2, points out that Mao postponed the date for assaulting Taiwan several times as PLA failures against various offshore islands emphasized the additional time required to prepare for a successful large-scale amphibious assault. Muller, *China's Emergence as a Maritime Power*, p. 16, gives August 1951 as the planned invasion month.

30. He, "Last Campaign to Unify China," p. 4. Edward J. Marolda, "U.S. Navy and the Chinese Civil War, 1945–1952" (PhD diss., George Washington University, 1990), p. 139, states that by spring 1950 Beijing "had assembled a motley armada of 5,000 vessels . . . freighters, motorized junks, and sampans" for the invasion of Taiwan; these vessels were to be crewed by "30,000 fishermen and other sailors."

31. See Robert J. Donovan, *Tumultuous Years: The Presidency of Harry S Truman, 1949–1953* (New York: W. W. Norton, 1983), p. 206, for Truman's decision to reposition the Seventh Fleet, and p. 241ff. for a good account of administration (i.e., Truman, Acheson, Bohlen, et al.) thinking about the implementation of NSC-68, which effectively rearmed the United States for the Cold War and potential global war with Soviet-led communist forces: "On the last day of July 1950, Truman and Acheson had a talk about grand strategy. The eyes of the American people were glued to Korea. . . . The president and the secretary of state fixed their gaze on the Rhine and the Elbe." The Chinese reaction is in Mao Zedong, "Speech Delivered at the Eighth Meeting of the Government Council of the People's Republic of China, 28 June 1950," in Jerome Ch'en, *Mao*, ed. Gerald Emanuel Stearn (Englewood Cliffs, N.J.: Prentice Hall, 1969), p. 115. A contrary but very credible view of U.S. intentions is provided by Bruce A. Elleman, *High Seas Buffer: The Taiwan Patrol Force, 1950–1979*, Newport Paper 38 (Newport, R.I.: Naval War College Press, April 2012), esp. chap. 1, available at www.usnwc.edu/press/.

32. Quoted in Marolda, "U.S. Navy and the Chinese Civil War," pp. 119–20.

33. Fred L. Israel, ed., "Dwight D. Eisenhower: First Annual Message," in *The State of the Union Messages of the Presidents, 1790–1966*, vol. 3, *1905–1966* (New York: Chelsea House, 1967), p. 3015. In his 2 February 1953 State of the Union Address to Congress, Eisenhower commented that "since the 'Red Chinese' had intervened in the Korean War, he felt no longer any need to 'protect' them from an invasion by . . . Chiang K'ai-shek."

34. Swanson, *Eighth Voyage of the Dragon*, p. 187.

35. *Dangdai Zhonggun Haijun* (Beijing: China Social Services Publishing House, 1987), translated as *China Today: The People's Navy* [hereafter *People's Navy*] in FBIS, JPRS-CAR-90-014 (16 July 1990), p. 7.

36. Ibid., p. 10, also notes that the Soviet ships were designed for a northern climate and had some difficulty operating in the warmer waters of the East and South China Seas, difficulty that is still a concern with the *Sovremenny*-class guided-missile destroyers purchased by China.

37 Gordon Chang and He Di, "The Absence of War in the U.S.-China Confrontation over Quemoy and Matsu in 1954–1955: Contingency, Luck, Deterrence?," *American Historical Review* (December 1993), p. 1514, describes this action, during which "10,000 PLA troops . . . overwhelmed 1,086 Kuomintang soldiers."

38 *People's Navy*, pp. 36–37. Kenneth W. Allen, Glenn Krumel, and Jonathan D. Pollack, *China's Air Force* (Santa Monica, Calif.: RAND, 1995), p. 205 note 11, also app. E, pp. 221–29, for useful descriptions of PLA aircraft-acquisition programs. Swanson, *Eighth Voyage of the Dragon*, p. 205, estimates 470 aircraft; a reasonable assumption is that the navy's air arm has flown older variants of PLA Air Force aircraft.

39 Other islands remained under Taiwan's control, including the Pratas Islands and Itu Aba in the South China Sea. Taiwan's attacks on the mainland continued into the 1960s. The Taiwan Strait naval campaigns are addressed in Li Xiaobang, "PLA Attacks and Amphibious Operations during the Taiwan Straits Crisis of 1954–58" (paper presented at the Center for Naval Analyses [CNA] Conference on the PLA's Operational History, Alexandria, Virginia, June 1999), and Alexander Huang, "PLA Navy at War, 1949–1999: From Coastal Defense to Distant Operations" (paper presented at the same conference). Thomas Torda, "Struggle for the Taiwan Strait: A 50th Anniversary Perspective on the First Communist-Nationalist Battles for China's Offshore Islands and Their Significance for the Taiwan Strait Crises" (unpublished manuscript, 1999), describes these early battles, which included PLA successes as well as failures. Also see Alexander Huang, "Evolution of the PLA Navy and Its Early Combat Experiences" (paper presented at the CNA Conference on the People's Liberation Army Navy, Washington, D.C., April 2000), p. 3, for a tabular summation of the PLAN's war-fighting efforts during this period. Chang and He, "Absence of War in the U.S.-China Confrontation," pp. 1504, 1510 notes 7–8, documents this.

40 Raymond V. B. Blackman, ed., *Jane's Fighting Ships, 1970–1971* (London: Jane's Yearbooks, 1970), p. 610, credits the Soviet Navy with just four large (four-thousand-ton displacement) and eighty smaller (six hundred to a thousand tons) amphibious ships spread out among all of the Soviet Union's four fleets, from the Pacific to the Baltic.

41 *People's Navy* repeatedly emphasizes the deleterious effects of the Cultural Revolution. John R. O'Donnell, "An Analysis of Major Developmental Influences on the People's Liberation Army-Navy and Their Implication for the Future" (master's thesis, U.S. Army Command and General Staff College, Fort Leavenworth, Kansas, 1995), p. 42, lists the PLAN's political commissar, chief operations officer, the East Sea Fleet commander, two deputy commanders, and two fleet political commissars among the "120 senior naval officers and thousands of lower ranking personnel [who] were purged." Also see John Wilson Lewis and Xue Litai, *China's Strategic Seapower: The Politics of Force Modernization in the Nuclear Age* (Stanford, Calif.: Stanford Univ. Press, 1994), p. 206ff, who note that not even Zhou Enlai was able to protect these programs completely.

42 Quoted in *People's Navy*, p. 13.

43 Cited in Muller, *China's Emergence as a Maritime Power*, p. 154.

44 Lewis and Xue, *China's Strategic Seapower*, p. 223, discusses Hua's decision; Deng is quoted on p. 224.

45 Fred Hiatt, "Marine General: U.S. Troops Must Stay in Japan," *Washington Post*, 27 March 1990, p. A14, quoted Lt. Gen. Henry Stackpole, U.S. Marine Corps, commander of III Marine Expeditionary Force on Okinawa, as describing the United States as "a cap in the [Japanese] bottle," a statement I confirmed in conversation with Lieutenant General Stackpole.

46 Tai Ming Cheung, *Fortifying China: The Struggle to Build a Modern Defense Economy* (Ithaca, N.Y.: Cornell Univ. Press, 2009), p. 28. China's marine corps, disestablished in 1957 as "unnecessary," was reestablished in 1980. The concentration of amphibious forces in the South Sea Fleet continues in 2012, indicating that PLAN amphibious planning is aimed more at the South China Sea than at Taiwan.

47 John E. Moore, ed., *Jane's Fighting Ships: 1976–77* (New York: Franklin Watts, 1977), p. 100ff. The PLAN also included the first Chinese range-instrumentation ships for tracking guided-missile flights and the first Chinese-built amphibious ship. Mao is quoted in Muller, *China's Emergence as a Maritime Power*, p. 171.

48 Deng Xiaoping, "Speech at an Enlarged Meeting of the Military Commission of the Party Central Committee," 14 July 1975, in Joint Publications Research Service *China Reports*, no. 468 (31 October 1983), pp. 14–22 (website now discontinued).

49 Alfred D. Wilhelm, *China and Security in the Asian Pacific Region through 2010*, CRM 95-226 (Alexandria, Va.: CNA, 1996), p. 42.

50 John W. Lewis, *China Builds the Bomb* (Stanford, Calif.: Stanford Univ. Press, 1988), pp. 50–51; Liu had worked for Deng on at least two previous occasions.

51 Liu's accomplishments are summed up in Wilhelm, *China and Security in the Asian Pacific Region through 2010*, p. 43.

52 Lewis and Xue, *China's Strategic Seapower*, provides the best account of the fleet-ballistic-missile and JL-1 programs. A successful launch was made in 1982 from a submerged platform; a 1988 attempt from the submarine probably succeeded. The single Xia itself has been an operational failure, never operating on a regular basis. The boat apparently received an extensive overhaul—probably involving recoring the propulsion plant—that enabled it at least to participate in the April 2009 naval review conducted by China to celebrate the PLAN's sixtieth anniversary.

53 Lt. Gen. Mi Zhenyu, PLA, "A Reflection on Geographic Strategy," *Zhongguo Junshi Kexue* [China Military Science], no. 1 (February 1998), pp. 6–14, in FBIS-CHI-98-208. A brief popular view of China's maritime history was published as "Special Report: China Marks 60th Anniversary of Navy," Xinhua, 24 April 2009, news.xinhuanet.com/.

ABOUT THE AUTHORS

Lori Lyn Bogle is an associate professor of history at the U.S. Naval Academy. She received her PhD from the University of Arkansas–Fayetteville and researches the social and cultural aspects of American military history. Her first book, *The Pentagon's Battle for the American Mind* (2004), investigated the role of the military in establishing the "ideal" national character. She is currently working on a book regarding Theodore Roosevelt's public relations expertise.

Bernard D. Cole is a retired U.S. Navy captain and professor of maritime strategy at the National War College in Washington, D.C., where he concentrates on the Chinese military and Asian energy issues. He served thirty years as a Surface Warfare Officer, all in the Pacific, commanding USS *Rathburne* (FF 1057) and Destroyer Squadron 35 and serving as a naval gunfire liaison officer in Vietnam with the 3rd Marine Division. Dr. Cole has written numerous articles and six books, most recently *Asian Maritime Strategies: Navigating Troubled Waters* (2013) and *The Great Wall at Sea: China's Navy in the Twenty-First Century* (2010). Dr. Cole earned an AB in history from the University of North Carolina, an MPA (National Security Affairs) from the University of Washington, and a PhD in history from Auburn University.

Phyllis Culham, professor of classical history at the U.S. Naval Academy, is the author of "Imperial Rome at War" in *The Oxford Handbook of Warfare in the Classical World* and coeditor of *Classics: A Discipline and Profession in Crisis?,* as well as more than three dozen other academic publications.

John Guilmartin is a professor of history at Ohio State University, where he teaches military history, naval history, and the history of the Vietnam War. Commissioned at the U.S. Air Force Academy in 1962, he received an MA and PhD in history from Princeton University in 1969 and 1971, respectively. Widely published in military and naval history, he is the author most recently of *Gunpowder and Galleys: Changing Technology and Mediterranean Warfare at Sea in the Sixteenth Century* (2nd ed., 2003) and *Galleons and Galleys* (2002). He served as editor of *Air University Review* from 1979 to 1983. A retired Air Force lieutenant colonel and senior pilot, he served two Southeast Asia combat tours, flying rescue helicopters in some 120 missions over Laos and North Vietnam in 1965–66 and in the Saigon evacuation of 1975. He served as Charles A. Lindbergh Visiting Professor of Aerospace History at the National Air and Space Museum, Smithsonian Institution, 2001–2002.

Heiko Herold is a German historian and media scientist. He holds a PhD in history from Düsseldorf University. He has worked as a journalist and as a public relations and media specialist for the military, nongovernmental organizations, and several companies in Germany, the Balkans, and South Asia. He is author or coauthor of several books on German naval and colonial history, military issues, and development cooperation. He currently works as an information specialist at the U.S. consulate general in Hamburg and teaches German history at Elbasan University in Albania.

Marcus Jones is an associate professor of history at the U.S. Naval Academy and the author of *Nazi Steel: The Flick Concern and the Economics of Nazi Expansion in Western Europe, 1940–1944,* as well as of articles and chapters about German naval history and Bismarckian policy. He received his undergraduate degree from Ohio State University and, in 2005, his PhD from Yale University.

Virginia Lunsford is an associate professor of history at the U.S. Naval Academy, specializing in maritime and European history. She holds PhD and MA degrees from Harvard University and is the author of *Piracy and Privateering in the Golden Age Netherlands* (2005). She is currently at work on *Dead Men Tell No Tales: A Cultural History of Piracy in the Modern Age.*

William M. McBride is a professor of history at the U.S. Naval Academy, where he teaches the history of science and technology, the history of engineering, post-1815 military and strategic history, and American naval history. He holds a PhD in the history of science and technology from Johns Hopkins University, an MS in aerospace and ocean engineering from Virginia Tech, and a BS in naval architecture from the Naval Academy. He has taught history at James Madison University and been an Olin Postdoctoral Fellow in strategic history at the International Security Studies Program at Yale University. He was previously a civilian naval architect for the U.S. Navy and later a senior naval architect in private industry, as well as, after graduating from the Naval Academy, a Surface Warfare Officer. He is the author of

Technological Change and the U.S. Navy, 1865–1945 and is currently writing a history of pre-1945 marine engineering within the U.S. Navy.

Andreas Rose is an assistant professor of modern history at Rheinische-Friedrich-Wilhelms-Universität in Bonn. He holds a master's degree from King's College London and the University of Potsdam, Germany, as well as a doctorate from the University of Augsburg. His most recent publications, aside from numerous articles on international, political, naval, military, and cultural history in modern Germany and Great Britain, include *Deutsche Aussenpolitik in der Ära Bismarck, 1862–1890* (2013) and *Die Aussenpolitik des Wilheminischen Kaiserreiches, 1890–1918* (2013). "Readiness or Ruin"? British Military and Naval Journals and the Expectations of War, 1880–1914 is forthcoming in 2014), as is a coedited volume, *Wars before the War 1912/13*.

Angus Ross is a retired Royal Navy commander, currently teaching at the U.S. Naval War College in Newport, Rhode Island. An antisubmarine warfare specialist, he joined the Royal Navy in 1975 and served in Her Majesty's ships until 1996, when he arrived in Newport. He has taught ever since on the Joint Military Operations faculty, earning MAs in national security and strategic studies, from the Naval War College in 1998, and European history, from Providence College in 2005. Upon retirement from active duty in 2000 he settled in the United States and is now pursuing PhD studies in European history, specifically Great Britain's naval transformation in the run-up to the First World War.

Jorit Wintjes earned his doctorate at Julius-Maximilians-Universität Würzburg in 2003 and completed his *habilitation* in 2013. He is senior lecturer for ancient history at the Julius-Maximilians-Universität Würzburg. His main research interests include ancient naval history, women's military history in antiquity, and political rhetoric in the Roman Empire.

NAVAL WAR COLLEGE HISTORICAL MONOGRAPH SERIES

1. *The Writings of Stephen B. Luce,* edited by John D. Hayes and John B. Hattendorf (1975).

3. *Professors of War: The Naval War College and the Development of the Naval Profession,* Ronald Spector (1977).

4. *The Blue Sword: The Naval War College and the American Mission, 1919–1941,* Michael Vlahos (1980).

5. *On His Majesty's Service: Observations of the British Home Fleet from the Diary, Reports, and Letters of Joseph H. Wellings, Assistant U.S. Naval Attaché, London, 1940–41,* edited by John B. Hattendorf (1983).

7. *A Bibliography of the Works of Alfred Thayer Mahan,* compiled by John B. Hattendorf and Lynn C. Hattendorf (1986).

8. *The Fraternity of the Blue Uniform: Admiral Richard G. Colbert, U.S. Navy and Allied Naval Cooperation,* Joel J. Sokolsky (1991).

9. *The Influence of History on Mahan: The Proceedings of a Conference Marking the Centenary of Alfred Thayer Mahan's* The Influence of Sea Power upon History, 1660–1783, edited by John B. Hattendorf (1991).

10. *Mahan Is Not Enough: The Proceedings of a Conference on the Works of Sir Julian Corbett and Admiral Sir Herbert Richmond,* edited by James Goldrick and John B. Hattendorf (1993).

11. *Ubi Sumus? The State of Naval and Maritime History,* edited by John B. Hattendorf (1994).

12. *The Queenstown Patrol, 1917: The Diary of Commander Joseph Knefler Taussig, U.S. Navy,* edited by William N. Still, Jr. (1996).

13. *Doing Naval History: Essays toward Improvement,* edited by John B. Hattendorf (1995).

14. *An Admiral's Yarn,* edited by Mark R. Shulman (1999).
15. *The Memoirs of Admiral H. Kent Hewitt,* edited by Evelyn Cherpak (2004).
16. *Three Splendid Little Wars: The Diary of Joseph K. Taussig, 1898–1901,* edited by Evelyn Cherpak (2009).
17. *Digesting History: The U.S. Naval War College, the Lessons of World War Two, and Future Naval Warfare, 1945–1947,* Hal M. Friedman (2010).
18. *To Train the Fleet for War: The U.S. Navy Fleet Problems, 1923–1940,* Albert A. Nofi (2010).
19. *Talking about Naval History: A Collection of Essays,* John B. Hattendorf (2011).
20. *New Interpretations in Naval History: Selected Papers from the Sixteenth Naval History Symposium Held at the United States Naval Academy 10–11 September 2009,* edited by Craig C. Felker and Marcus O. Jones (2012).
21. *Blue versus Orange: The U.S. Naval War College, Japan, and the Old Enemy in the Pacific, 1945–1946,* Hal M. Friedman (2013).
22. *Major Fleet-versus-Fleet Operations in the Pacific War, 1941–1945,* Milan Vego (2014).